Setting Cornwall on its Feet

Robert Morton Nance 1873–1959

Setting Cornwall on its Feet
Robert Morton Nance 1873–1959

Edited by Peter W. Thomas and Derek R. Williams

Francis
Boutle
Publishers

First published by Francis Boutle Publishers
272 Alexandra Park Road
London N22 7BG
Tel/Fax: (020) 8889 7744
Email: info@francisboutle.co.uk
www.francisboutle.co.uk

ISBN 978 1 903427 34 7

Printed by Biddles Ltd

Oberow y vewnans yu y wyr govath
His life's works are his true memorial

Dhe gof Phoebe Procter (genys Nance), 1912–2007

Contents

List of Illustrations

Above: Decorative drawing by Robert Morton Nance for The Cornish Magazine

Acknowledgments

In addition to their fellow contributors and various members of the Nance family, notably Carola Nance Scupham and Tamsin Donaldson, the editors would like to acknowledge the services rendered by the following in providing information or advice or both: Angela Broome, Librarian, Courtney Library – Royal Institution of Cornwall, Truro; Robert Cook, Photographic Librarian, Royal Institution of Cornwall, Truro; Kim Cooper and colleagues at the Cornish Studies Library, Cornwall Centre, Redruth; Llyfrgell Genedlaethol Cymru/The National Library of Wales; Janet Morris, Cambridge Antiquarian Society; Ron Opie, President, Federation of Old Cornwall Societies; Elizabeth Parkinson; Dr John Pickles, Cambridge Antiquarian Society; Audrey Randle Pool; Dr Laurence Rule; Brian Stevens, St Ives Museum; Peter Winterbottom, Hon Secretary, Society for Nautical Research.

Above: Decorative drawing by Robert Morton Nance for The Cornish Magazine

Foreword

Robert Morton Nance (Mordon) a omjunnyas gans Henry Jenner yn un ledya dasserghyans an Wonysegeth Kernow, ha raghenna yth on ny yn kendon dhodho, dres eghen a'y ober abarth agan yeth. Ef a omry dhe studhya Kernewek dres an brassa ran a'y vewnans hyr, ha dhe servya an Orseth ha'n Cowethasow Kernow Goth. Ny, avel Byrth Gorseth Kernow a dal gothvos gras dhodho.

Gwenenen
Barth Mur, Gorseth Kernow

Robert Morton Nance (*Mordon*) joined Henry Jenner in leading the revival of Cornish Culture, and for that we are in his debt, especially for his work concerning our language. He devoted most of his long life to studying Cornish and in serving the Gorseth and the Old Cornwall Societies. As Bards of Gorseth Kernow we owe him thanks.

Vanessa Beeman
Grand Bard, The Cornish Gorsedd

*Above and cover: Robert Morton Nance, Grand Bard, Gorseth
Kernow (Courtesy of Audrey Randle Pool)*

Preface

Charles Thomas

For this splendid and long-awaited book, the only possible contribution that I can make is more a set of reminiscences than a conventional preface; but it allows me to record what I owe to the life and work of Robert Morton Nance, who was aged fifty-five in the year that I was born.

In autumn 1953 the Cornwall Adult Education Joint Committee, which we all knew as the WEA, put out a circular for a course of twelve lectures on 'The Archaeology of Cornwall up to the Norman Conquest'. The fee for the lot was five shillings. The tutor, who had just finished his two years at the Institute of Archaeology, was Mr Charles Thomas, BA (Oxon), Dip Arch (London). This was in fact the first purely archaeological WEA class ever held in Cornwall. From our Camborne home my parents had packed me off as the resident winter caretaker at 'Cliff Cottage', Carbis Bay, a granite villa just below the railway station, built in the 1880s by my great-grandfather Captain Josiah Thomas. It faces north and can be very chilly. On Thursday 15 October I lit the fire, set up a blackboard, made sure that tea and buns were ready, and waited.

Nine people arrived; all stayed the course. They signed my album and rather later, entering details against the names, I wrote below: 'My first WEA class and, I think, the best.' The roll begins with R. Morton Nance (Bard *Mordon*, Grand Bard of Cornwall, President, Royal Institution of Cornwall), then E.G.R. Hooper (Bard *Talek*, in 1959 third Grand Bard – George, as I knew him, had at the time a sinecure post in Camborne as a head gardener, using a potting-shed to edit Cornish texts), C.C. James from Gwennap (Bard *Penseghnans*, Vice-

President, Royal Geological Society of Cornwall), and Mrs E.M.B. Faull (Bard *Rosmergy*, St Ives). The others, like me members of the West Cornwall Field Club, were all from St Ives; Cecil Coad the photographer, Miss L.M. 'Chips' Larking, who had introduced Australian tree-frogs to her Pelican Hill garden, Mr and Mrs Mason, and my friend Bert Guthrie, the Field Club's Hon Treasurer, who acted as class secretary.

What an array. I was aged twenty-five, knew far less than I supposed, and was about to cover Cornwall's past from the palaeolithic to Launceston Castle. The meetings were cosy and went on for hours. We had a blazing fire, ate dozens of saffron buns, passed around potsherds and stone axes and book illustrations, and discussed interesting finds. *Mordon* had a little box with pieces of grass-marked pottery from the entrance to Trencrom hillfort, still the only known evidence for its post-Roman occupation. C.C. James corrected my notions about early copper-workings, Margaret Mason wrote several poems and 'Chips' Larking produced flints from her Pelican Hill garden (she lived on a Mesolithic site). Most of them came by car, but *Mordon*, of course, simply walked back up the hill to 'Chylason'.

Considerable as the honour of his presence was, Mr Morton Nance was no stranger to me. In the 1930s during our compulsory August visits to 'Cliff Cottage', we would sometimes go to tea at 'Chylason'. While *Mordon* and my father Donald gossiped endlessly about Zennor (both loved the place, both died in 1959 and both are buried there), my brother and I – fed by dear Granny Nance – would stand and gawp in wonder at the magnificent, the truly incredible, models of galleons and frigates and sailing-ships around the dark drawing-room. Sometimes the master would explain bits of the riggings; we never touched anything, hardly dared breathe.

In 1945 when (aged seventeen and a bit) I insisted on leaving school to join the army – three happy years in Northern Ireland, Scotland and Egypt – I had taught myself enough Cornish to get by, had explored almost all of Camborne and Gwithian parishes by bicycle, and was enmeshed in folk-lore, archaeology and place-names. *Mordon*, whom I hadn't seen for some while, took on full meaning because of his published work, which I read, and his enormous range of interests. Both as a young soldier and then, during three years at Oxford pretending to read for a law degree, I wrote to him. His long replies, in which (flatteringly) I now became 'Dear Mr Thomas', spurred me into action. At Oxford in 1949 I wrote an essay on the Glebe lands of Camborne; at his suggestion I submitted this to the Sir Edward Nicholl essay prize competition at the Falmouth Royal Cornwall Polytechnic Society, and won third prize (one pound, plus the first of three bronze medals). In 1950 I published my first pamphlet, *Some Notes on the Folk-Lore of the Camborne District*, at the old Camborne Printing and Stationery Co, which was almost a family concern and in whose clanking works I learnt all about hot-metal printing and editing. *Mordon*, as the champion of local folk-lore, was more than encouraging because, imitating him, I was collecting material orally and not just reproducing what was already in print. The next year, trying to forget my 3rd Class Honours in Jurisprudence, I produced *Studies in Cornish Folk-Lore, No. 1, The Taboo*, which of course did draw heavily on *Mordon*'s work and to which he was kind enough to write a generous foreword. By now I had a little car and could call on him at 'Chylason'. I think that he approved of my decision to move to the University of London and to take a two-year diploma in archaeology. This implied no loss of interest in matters Cornish. In 1951, too, I foisted on him a thick typescript containing all the place-names of Camborne parish compiled from the Tithe Map, early maps and rating lists, Charles Henderson's mss. at Truro and even oral collection. *Mordon* must have spent hours annotating the whole thing in his neat tiny hand, suggesting both meanings and reconstructed forms. It is still among my most treasured possessions.

Back, then, to 1953, a busy year in which I became editor for the West Cornwall Field Club, began serious excavations at Gwithian over Easter and dug elsewhere in Britain. At some event in Hayle that July, another old friend Edwin Chirgwin told me, to my astonishment, that I was about to become a Bard. What bardic name would I choose? I had no idea; Edwin said that he would ask *Mordon*, and back came the answer; it would have to be *Gwas Godhyan*, Servant of Gwithian. On 5 September, according to *The Cornishman*, there was 'the spectacle of the Bards in single file winding through the bracken, a long wavering line of blue'. (We were wavering because this was on the top of Trencrom, uneven and overgrown.) My mother had pressed my robe, which is in the original St Austell pale-blue. In due course three of us – John Casley from Morvah, me, and H.L. (Leslie) Douch from Truro Museum – stumbled forward to be initiated. *Mordon* did the honours, *Talek* (George Hooper) made a speech in Cornish. Later we all had tea at Chy-an-Drea Hotel. A.K. Hamilton Jenkin got me, and *Mordon*, into a corner, droning on about ancient mines in Redruth. I said nothing about the projected WEA class at Carbis Bay because I was now far from certain that I could carry it off, but it was a proud day for a young Camborne enthusiast.

When *Mordon* died in 1959, not long after my father, I was out of Cornwall, having at last got my first job, a lectureship in archaeology at Edinburgh. Peter Pool, who was to become a close and dear friend and with whom I had over-lapped at Oxford, was now *Mordon*'s leading resident disciple. Peter's creation and editorship of the memorial volume *A Glossary of Cornish Sea-Words* (1963), just about the most fitting tribute that anyone could suggest, had been preced-ed by a notice from James L. Palmer, *Bard Palmor Tyr Sans*, the long-time editor of *The Cornishman* (*Old Cornwall*, vol. 5, no. 11 (1960), pp. 450–1). Mr Palmer's prose, if always florid, was also always sincere. Mentioning Jenner and the Gorsedd and then *Mordon*'s long role as 'our patriarch', Palmer thought 'the conclusion remains that Nance's name is more indelibly enshrined [than Jenner's] in Cornish literature and art'. That is true, provided one can define 'literature and art' in appropriate terms. I would add (with Palmer) that *Mordon*'s extraordinary record of getting things down, getting them into print, and prodding others into completion and suitable publication, would suffice to distinguish him in whatever field he might choose to adorn.

Today, there are not many of us who remember *Mordon* or who (like me) have such cause to be grateful for his practical help and encouragement. Would he have been pleased to know that first myself and then Peter Pool were to follow him in the presidential chair of the Royal Institution of Cornwall, and in vari-ous other offices? I say nothing of the current wrangles about the orthography of Middle (and Modern) Cornish – readers can guess where, as the first Professor of Cornish Studies, 1972–1991, I stand on this – and there is insuffi-cient room to describe the legacy of *Mordon*'s voluminous notes or, as the pre-sent book happily does, to applaud all his separate accomplishments in nautical research. All my non-excavational work in Cornwall and Scilly over six decades has been coloured by his initial help and careful advice. Alas, those WEA class-es – and after 1953 I went on conducting them around Cornwall for four years –

no longer exist. In today's sense, they would be the reverse of vocational. But 'Cliff Cottage' on 15 October 1953 remains as vivid as ever. It was a horrible night, cold, windy and rainy. The doorbell rang; I rushed to answer it. Robert Morton Nance from 'Chylason', up the hill, was the first to arrive. For me he will always have been 'the first' in a great many other ways.

'Lambessow', Truro
January 2007

Breton Gorsedd 1938, Robert Morton Nance centre picture
(Courtesy of Gorseth Kernow Archive)

Introduction

Peter W. Thomas and Derek R. Williams

Lachlan MacBean, the Scottish newspaper editor and writer, was in 1920 Convenor of the local Committee of the Celtic Congress which was held in Edinburgh that May. Finding that there was no list of workers in the fields of Celtic literature, music, and culture generally, either in Scotland or in any of the other Celtic countries, he set about producing one and in 1921 *The Celtic Who's Who* was duly published.[1] It is astonishing that only one Cornish name appears among the 360 or so entries – that of Henry Jenner. The optimism engendered by the formation of Cowethas Kelto-Kernuak (the Celtic-Cornish Society) at the beginning of the century and Cornwall's admission into the fold of Celtic nations at Caernarfon in August 1904 had seemingly all but evaporated.

Robert Morton Nance had returned to his Cornish roots in 1906 – three years ahead of Jenner's retirement to his native land. He had begun to learn Cornish, had written the Cornish dialect *Cledry Plays* and was collecting the dialect words that would form the basis of the posthumous *A Glossary of Cornish Sea-Words*. By and large, though, he was more occupied with family and nautical-cum-artistic matters during his first fourteen years in Cornwall than with any overtly Cornish concerns.

And yet, within ten years of the publication of *The Celtic Who's Who*, Cornwall could boast a flourishing network of Old Cornwall societies with their own journal, its own Gorsedd of Bards and the prospect of hosting the first ever meeting of the Celtic Congress on Cornish soil, an earlier attempt having fallen victim to the General Strike of 1926. Although it would be invidious to pin-point one particular event or person as being responsible for initiating such a remarkable turnaround, the co-founding at St Ives of the first Old Cornwall Society by Nance in 1920 was definitely the catalyst that Celtic Cornwall need-ed. As it is hoped that much of the content of the essays in *Setting Cornwall on its Feet* will show, it was also a catalyst for the 'Cornish period' that would domi-nate the remainder of our subject's long life.

Nance built on Jenner's pioneering work during the early years of the twen-tieth century and belonged to the generation that set the Cornish language on its feet, as well as ensuring Cornwall's place among the Celtic nations. Since the 1980s, many have walked away from the form that Nance devised for the lan-guage, and the controversy has tended to overshadow his considerable achieve-ments. *Setting Cornwall on its Feet* sets out to explore the various 'lives' of Robert Morton Nance who, as 'Old Cornwall' founder, Grand Bard, artist, maritime historian, writer, translator, historian, folklorist and 'Celt', helped ensure a role for Cornwall beyond that of mere holiday playground.

While Peter Pool's memorial edition of Nance's *A Glossary of Cornish Sea-Words* (1963) contained some biographical material, notably his own editorial memoir, the various directions that Nance's life took have had to wait nearly another half-century for the spotlight to be turned on them in any detailed and original way. Using to great effect both his knowledge of Celtic literatures and his own pen portrait of this volume's subject for the recently published *Oxford Dictionary of National Biography*, Brian Murdoch pulls together the threads of Nance's life – or lives – and, in doing so, provides a context for the essays that follow his own.

'As long as we still speak and cherish the language which he made his own, and which thanks to him can again be Cornwall's own, *Mordon* will have the only monument which he desired.' This was the late Peter Pool writing in 1963. Despite Cornwall's acceptance as a nation by the Pan-Celtic Congress in 1904, for many years she was regarded as a lesser player in 'Celtia' because of the lan-guage question – a question which, a century later, continues to arouse contro-versy. In the context of Celtic Congress matters, Nance described himself in March 1925 as representing 'a nation <u>heb iaeth</u>' [without language],[2] while just over a year later E.T. John considered the choice of subjects for the projected

Congress at Penzance as 'universally difficult seeing that our main interest, the language question, is so irrelevant to local conditions'.[3] Nance, though, would make the Cornish language central to his concept of Cornishness and in 'Medieval Romantic or Language Visionary?' Rod Lyon, former Grand Bard and fluent Cornish speaker, explores Nance's often tortuous attempts to forge his Unified Cornish, before going on to consider his legacy. In so doing, he draws extensively on unpublished correspondence between Nance, A.S.D. Smith (*Caradar*), E.G. Retallack Hooper (*Talek*) and other users of the language during Nance's lifetime.

In the mid 1920s, the Rev W. Gregory Harris, a Wesleyan Methodist minister, novelist and poet, spent a year as a junior supernumerary in the old Penzance circuit, lodging at Gwithian. There he planned – and possibly wrote – his novel *Trengwith*, for which Professor Charles Thomas has made some tentative identifications of people and places.[4] We can date the action of *Trengwith* [Gwithian] to circa 1925 through Harris's references to the Old Cornwall Society – the nearest, at Hayle, was formed in 1923 – which is described as having 'only been in existence a year or two'.[5] More relevant still, as far as Nance is concerned, is the staging of an 'Old Cornwall Concert' four months after the arrival of the Rev Arthur Willesford in the village. When he asks Frances Tresillian what form the concert will take, she informs him that her father has written to a friend of his at St Ina [St Ives], 'Mr Norton French [Robert Morton Nance], who is an authority on ancient Cornish matters'. 'In addition to being an expert on our old language,' she continues, 'he has been reviving some of the quaint Mummers' Plays which were once so popular in the West of England, and a little company of local actors will perform one of these.'[6] W. Gregory Harris presumably attended a performance of Nance's 'St George', possibly at St Ives, and incorporated a description of that performance, transposed to Gwithian, into *Trengwith*.[7] In 'Some ancientry that lingers', Alan M. Kent focuses on Nance's Cornish language and Cornu-English/Cornish dialect writings which had their genesis in the closing years of the 19th century with Arthur Quiller-Couch's *Cornish Magazine*. He explores in some detail the middle phase of Nance's work in English into which his 'Christmas Play of Saint George and the Turkish Knight' falls, before turning his attention to his Cornish language drama *An Balores* and assessing his legacy as a writer and editor of original

Cornish-language poetry and stories, and as a translator/reinterpreter of many of the major texts from Cornish literature.

The role of Arthur, 'yn corf Palores' [in the guise of a Chough], is, of course, central to the concept of Cornish nationhood and a key component of the Gorsedd ceremony. In 'Robert Morton Nance and Gorseth Kernow', Peter W. Thomas uses the wealth of unpublished source material available in both Cornwall and Wales to tell the behind-the-scenes story of Nance's long association with the Cornish Gorsedd. He reveals an essentially shy man trying to come to terms with being thrust into the spotlight as Grand Bard on Henry Jenner's death in 1934 and agonising over the extent to which the Cornish language should be given pride of place in the Gorsedd ceremony. Particularly illuminating is Thomas's exploration of the address on the Gorsedd Prayer with which Nance opened the Annual Meeting in September 1941, a text which resonates with symbolism.

Nance defined Cornish Culture as 'a continuous tradition of culture that is natively Cornish',[8] an 'essence of Cornishness'[9] upon which all new Cornish art and literature should be based. It was his fervent hope that new generations – a "New Cornwall" – would make good use of the fragments of this culture that the Old Cornwall societies would rescue from oblivion. There are encouraging signs that, despite massive in-migration, in the early years of the 21st century Nance's hope is still being realised. As President of the Federation of Old Cornwall Societies, Brian Coombes is well-placed to tell the story of Nance's role in the formation of the movement, focusing on his sometimes fraught relationship with individual societies over *Old Cornwall*, which he edited or co-edited more or less continuously from 1925 through to his death thirty-four years later.

In his seminal essay on what he saw as the role of the Old Cornwall societies, 'What We Stand For', Nance specified an acknowledgement of 'his kinship with a Breton or a Welshman' as one of the attributes of a typical member. Pressing Cornwall's claim to be viewed as an active Celtic nation was a role that he inherited from Henry Jenner and his correspondence with D. Rhys Phillips, E.T. John and other Welsh activists reveals what an uphill struggle it was. 'Celtic things move very slowly here,' he wrote to Phillips on 24 January 1923, 'and after so long a neglect it can hardly be otherwise…'[10] And exactly two years later he described Celtic things in Cornwall as 'literally grasping for the vital breath that you people in lands more happily placed can bring us'[11] having previously admitted that a Cornish representative at a Celtic Congress – there were three in 1924 – had very, very few friends at home who took the faintest interest in anything Celtic.[12] Despite the rather defensive and retiring approach that Nance seemed to take to such matters in his private correspondence, he and a small team managed to raise Cornwall's profile until Celtic Congresses and other inter-Celtic events were held on Cornish soil. In 'Reawakening Cornwall's Celtic Consciousness', Ann Trevenen Jenkin shows how Nance's dual Welsh and Cornish nationality spurred him on in his endeavours. The author's presence at many of the post-World War Two congresses and festivals ensures that there is a personal perspective in this interesting overview.

Taking his title from the paper that Nance wrote for the Royal Cornwall Polytechnic Society in about 1924, Donald Rawe shows in 'Splinters of a great wreck' how Nance's boyhood interest in folklore developed and was enriched in adulthood by his dialect and Cornish language research. Once again, his correspondence with D. Rhys Phillips throws light on his activities. On 9 August that year he wrote that he had finally decided to attend the Celtic Congress in Quimper and offered 'to fill up any odd corners of the programme ... with something on the extent to which Cornish has survived in tradition ... or a paper on <u>Folklore in the Cornish Language</u> if anything longer is required'.[13] The two exchanged ideas at Quimper and early in 1925 Nance wrote again, describing one of the papers that he was enclosing as breaking new ground, 'no-one with a knowledge of Cornish having previously thought of the language as a source of folklore'.[14] The folklore loss that resulted from the death of Cornish may have been enormous – 'a great wreck, now "scat to scubma"', as Nance put it[15] – but his early research has been built on over the years by a succession of scholars such as Donald Rawe, with the result that the paucity of the remains is arguably not now as great as once appeared to Nance.

For A.K. Hamilton Jenkin, Nance was 'never more at his ease than when walking in Cornwall'[16] and L.R. Moir described how on St Ives Old Cornwall Society pilgrimages 'he would occasionally leap over low hedges and ditches to reach his objective, and outstrip his juniors by yards'.[17] This was in 1954, the very year that Nance was asked to chair a meeting of the West Cornwall

Footpath Preservation Society. The story of his association with it is ably chronicled here by Hugh Miners.

It is interesting to note that the lives of the two most important figures in the early years of the modern Cornish movement, Henry Jenner and Nance himself, followed an outwardly similar course. Both men lived into their mid-eighties and both led full lives in areas with limited apparent connection to the Cornish scene before starting to apply their considerable energies fully to the service of Cornwall during the early twentieth century. Further scrutiny of course reveals a far more complex and integrated picture than this broad summary presents. Having previously performed a similar service for Jenner,[18] Derek Williams, in 'Worshipping 'at the shrine of St Jal" ', explores in detail the first phase of Nance's adult life, when he showed notable talent as an artist, craftsman and authority on early ship design, producing a considerable body of work in these fields (literary as well as artistic). Nance was no dabbler on the arts scene in search of his true vocation but a man intent on making his living as a professional artist. Once settled in Cornwall, however, and having come into contact with Jenner (his senior by nearly twenty-five years), his life took a different turn. There was no outright renunciation of all his artistic impulses, but they came to play a subordinate part in his activities. In some cases, such as his and his wife's design and production of robes and regalia for the Cornish Gorsedd, they fed directly into his work for Cornwall. Thanks to Williams, we now have a thorough account of a previously little known part of Nance's life and a more rounded knowledge of his range of talents.

Notes

1. *The Celtic Who's Who: Names and Addresses of Workers who contribute to Celtic Literature, Music or other Cultural Activities* (1921), Kirkaldy: The Fifeshire Advertiser Limited.
2. Letter ETJ 4352, dated 27 March 1925, in E.T. John Papers (GB 0210 ETJOHN), National Library of Wales.
3. Letter ETJ 4608, dated 19 May 1926, ibid.
4. Charles Thomas (2002), '"Godrevy... Godrevy..."': a postscript', in *An Baner Kernewek*, 107, February, p. 13.
5. W. Gregory Harris (1928), *Trengwith: a chronicle of clerical and social life in West Cornwall*, London: John Lane/The Bodley Head, p. 59.
6. Ibid.
7. Ibid., pp. 62–64.
8. R. Morton Nance (1949), 'Cornish Culture', in *The Cornish Review*, no. 1, April, p. 3.
9. R. Morton Nance (1925), 'What we stand for', in *Old Cornwall*, no. 1, April, p. 3.
10. Letter 3589, dated 24 January 1923, in D. Rhys Phillips 2 Collection, National Library of Wales.

11. Letter 3593, dated 24 March 1925, ibid.
12. Letter 3590, dated 9 August 1924, ibid.
13. Ibid.
14. Letter 3591, dated 22 January 1925, ibid.
15. R. Morton Nance [1925], *Folk-Lore Recorded in the Cornish Language*, Camborne: Royal Cornwall Polytechnic Society/Camborne Printing and Stationery Co., p. 24.
16. A.K. Hamilton Jenkin (1963), 'A Project Fulfilled', in R. Morton Nance, *A Glossary of Cornish Sea-Words*, ed. P.A.S. Pool, Truro/Marazion/St Ives: Federation of Old Cornwall Societies, p. 24.
17. L.R. Moir (1963), 'His Closing Years', ibid., p. 22.
18. Derek R. Williams (2004), 'Henry Jenner FSA', in Derek R. Williams (ed), *Henry and Katharine Jenner*, London: Francis Boutle, pp. 70–110.

An early photograph of Robert Morton Nance (Courtesy of Ann Trevenen Jenkin/Gorseth Kernow Archive)

Robert Morton Nance: A Chronology

1873

10 April   Birth of Robert Morton Nance at 'Clevedon Villa', The Walk, Tredegarville, Cardiff

1874   The family moves to 'Cumberland House', Oakfield Street

1878   They move again, to 'Hawthorn House', Kymin Terrace, Penarth

1891

April   Robert is described as an art student in the census

1892

January   Beatrice Michell joins the Herkomer Art School

October   Annie Maud Cawker joins the Herkomer Art School

1893   Death of Robert's mother, Jane/Jeannie Morton Nance

October   He leaves Cardiff for Bushey, Hertfordshire, where he attends Herkomer's Art School

1895

Summer   Exhibits 3 works at the Royal Academy: 'Portrait of a Woman', 'Old Bowers' and 'Study of a Rustic'. His address at the time is Bourne Hall Road, Bushey

3 December   Marries fellow student Beatrice E. Michell in Watford
They live at 5, Carlton Cottages, Bushey until the summer vacation of 1896

1896   To Penarth for summer holidays, then to St Ives in the late autumn

December   Birth there of Jeniver Morton Nance (1896–1995)

1897   They move to Newton Nottage near Porthcawl

1898–1899	Nance contributes to Quiller-Couch's *Cornish Magazine*
1899	
August	Robert and Beatrice win prizes for oil paintings at the Welsh National Eisteddfod in Cardiff.
October	They exhibit at the 6th Arts & Crafts Exhibition.
1899–1900	Robert has a studio in Central Chambers, Working St, Cardiff
1901	Nance becomes a member of the Arts & Crafts Exhibition Society
31 March	Robert and Beatrice living at Orchard Cottage, Newton Nottage
Last quarter	Death of Beatrice
1902	Spends some months studying art in Paris. Is listed as a member of the South Wales Art Society. Exhibits at the Turin International Exhibition
1903	Exhibits at the 7th Arts & Crafts Exhibition, at the Shipping Exhibition, at the Liverpool Autumn Exhibition and with South Wales Art Society
1904	
April	Provides woodcuts for reprint of Richard Jobson's *The Golden Trade…*
30 April–1 Dec	Exhibits at the Louisiana Purchase Exhibition.
May	Living at 23, Westbourne Road, Penarth, where his father had moved in 1897
1905	Collaborates with E.E. Speight on *Britain's Sea Story* Provides illustrations and maps for an English edition of *Hakluyt's Voyages* and for a selection of *Stories from the Northern Sagas*
July	Naval Portraits & Battle Pieces Exhibition features some of Nance's work
1905–c.1907	Living at 37, Victoria Road, Penarth
1906	Provides illustrations for *The Romance of the Merchant Venturers*, edited by E. E. Speight. Exhibits at the 8th Arts & Crafts Exhibition

27 March	Marries Annie Maud Cawker, former Bushey student. They move to a rented cottage at Nancledra, St Ives, Cornwall
1907	Birth of Robert Trengove (Robin) Nance
1909	Nance writes to Alan Moore suggesting that a society for 'ship lovers' be formed. Listed as a member of the South Wales Art Society
17 October	Birth of Richard William (Dicon) Nance
c. 1909	Writes the Cledry Plays
1910	Exhibits ship models at the Japan-British Exhibition and screens at the 9th Arts & Crafts Exhibition. Listed as a member of the South Wales Art Society
June	Founding of The Society for Nautical Research
1911	
March	Nance's first contribution to *The Mariner's Mirror*
1912	
October	Birth of Phoebe Nance
1914	The Nances leave Nancledra for 'Chylason', Carbis Bay
1916–1918	Nance serves in the 1st Battalion (West) of the Duke of Cornwall's Light Infantry Volunteers
1920	Co-founds the first Old Cornwall Society at St Ives. Exhibits three models at the Royal Cornwall Polytechnic Society Exhibition
1921	
23 May	Lectures to the Cambridge Antiquarian Society
1923	Publication of *A Glossary of Celtic Words in Cornish Dialect*
1924	Nance attends Celtic Congress in Quimper with Charles Henderson and Gilbert Doble. Publication of *Sailing-Ship Models*. Becomes Recorder of the newly formed Federation of Old Cornwall Societies
	Publication of *Folk-lore Recorded in the Cornish Language*
1925	Provides illustrations for Sir Alan Moore's *Last Days of Mast and Sail*
April	First issue of *Old Cornwall*, with Nance as editor

April–June	Visits Brittany
1926	Awarded the Royal Institution of Cornwall's Henwood Medal for his paper on 'Troy Town'
April–July	Acts as contact for the proposed Celtic Congress at Penzance
1927	Attends the unofficial Celtic Congress at Riec in Brittany with D. Rhys Phillips. Contributes 'An den Ha'y Dheu Wreg' to a book of short stories in Cornish. Exhibits model at the Arts & Crafts Exhibition
1928	
7 August	Made a bard of Wales at Treorchy, taking the name 'Mordon' (Sea wave)
21 September	Made Deputy Grand Bard of Gorseth Kernow at Boscawen-Un
1928–1931	Secretary of Gorseth Kernow
1929	Publication of *Cornish for All*
1932	Nance's *An Balores* (The Chough) is performed at the Celtic Congress in Truro. Death of William Edwin Nance
1933	Nance's translations into Cornish of passages from the Book of Common Prayer are used at the revival of church services in Cornish at Towednack
1934	Succeeds Henry Jenner as President of the Federation of Old Cornwall Societies. Publication of Nance's and A. S. D. Smith's *An English-Cornish Dictionary*
April	Contributes to the first issue of Smith's Cornish Language magazine *Kernow*
7 September	Nance installed as Grand Bard of Gorseth Kernow at Padderbury, near Liskeard, a post he holds until his death
1936	Collaborates with Smith on the latter's *An Awayl Herwyth Sen Mark*, the first book of the Bible to be translated into Cornish
1938	Publication of *Gerlyver Noweth Kernewek ha Sawsnek/A New Cornish-English Dictionary*. Represents Cornwall at the Breton Gorsedd

24 Feb	Reads paper to the Royal Institution of South Wales, Swansea
July	Is a member of a party representing Cornwall at a Breton Festival at Châteaulin and at the Breton Gorsedd
July(?)	Delivers a paper on the Cornish Language to the Celtic Congress on the Isle of Man
1939	Publication of *Lyver an Pymp Marthus Seleven*. Represents Cornwall at the Breton Gorsedd
1942	
5 September	Delivers speech in Breton at Cornish-Breton Demonstration at Penzance
1943	Elizabethan warship of Nance's exhibited by the Soldiers', Sailors' & Airmen's Families Association
1948–1959	Nance is Chairman of the Penzance Library
1949	First of the *Extracts from the Cornish Texts*...
April	Nance chairs and, together with his sons, helps judge the craft sections of St Ives Inter-Celtic Festival
1951	Publication of *A Guide to Cornish Place-Names*
July	Extract from *Bewnans Meryasek* performed at Perran Round as an all-Cornish contribution to the Festival of Britain
1952	Publication of a revised *English-Cornish Dictionary*
1953–1955	Nance serves as President of the Royal Institution of Cornwall
1954	Recording issued of Nance reading in Cornish *Jowan Chy an Hor*, Boorde's *Colloquies* and the Lord's Prayer
1955	Publication of a new *Cornish-English Dictionary*. Nance becomes President of the West Cornwall Footpath Preservation Society
1956	Publication of *The Cledry Plays*
1959	
27 May	Death of Robert Morton Nance at St Michael's Hospital, Hayle
3 June	Burial in Zennor churchyard

1961
March   Death of Annie Maud Nance
1963   Publication of *A Glossary of Cornish Sea Words* as a
              memorial volume
April   Memorial erected over Nance's grave in Zennor
              Churchyard

'A Druid or something down in the West Country': the Lives of Robert Morton Nance

Brian Murdoch

The somewhat dismissive-sounding description of Nance that I have chosen as the title for this introduction to his life and works was cited in an obituary appreciation by J.H. Martin in *The West Briton* as coming from someone who knew and indeed appreciated Nance, but only as a notable modeller of ships who did not, moreover, make regular visits to London.[1] It is, however, easy to find comments which might give a better idea of Nance's position and which are certainly not dismissive-sounding. Nance himself might have been surprised to know that, only thirty years after his death, he would be mentioned in the Cornish section of an introduction to the Celtic languages published rather further away even than London, namely in Moscow: 'Drugoi krupnoi figuroi etogo dvizheniya bil R. Morton Nance...' [The other major figure of the movement was R. Morton Nance...], and it is to be hoped that he would have been gratified to find himself included in the *Oxford Dictionary of National Biography*. Nowadays, to be sure, it is also possible to type his name into a search-engine on the World Wide Web, and call up a whole range of pages, including one from an internet encyclopaedia giving a brief biography in Cornish, the language he was instrumental in re-establishing, and another displaying a coloured picture of his installation in 1934 as Grand Bard of the Cornish Gorsedd, an institution which, once again, he was instrumental in establishing.[2]

When Nance died in 1959, the funeral address by the Deputy Grand Bard, the Revd D.R. Evans, stated with some accuracy that Nance's was a life worthy of study, but in the second part of my title I use the plural of 'life' deliberately. Those who knew Nance but not Cornwall knew him as an artist, as a builder of historical sailing-ship models, and as a maritime historian. Even in Cornwall, in the proper context of most of his life, he was not only a scholar and writer on Cornish antiquity and especially on all aspects of the Cornish language, but an organiser, administrator and publicist for Cornish culture. To refer to him, as another website does, as a 'multi-talented Cornish Renaissance man' possibly goes a little too far, even if he can be placed, as we shall see, fairly firmly in the late nineteenth/early twentieth-century arts and crafts tradition. But he was without doubt a man of many parts.[3]

Many details of his life may be gleaned from the obituaries and apprecia- tions that followed his death in May, 1959, even from the brief tribute in the London *Times* on June 1, 1959, in which L.C.J. Orchard noted that Nance wrote letters with a quill pen. Nance's letters were certainly written in a neat and pre- cise round hand until the end of his days, and as a prolific scholar in a pre-com- puter age, he wrote throughout his life a very large number of letters. We are fortunate, too, in having a detailed description of his early life written by his sis- ter, Christine Morton Raymont, and published in 1962. Obituary notices are of necessity usually relatively brief, but her forty-page introduction to Nance's early career gives us a more rounded picture of a child and then young man whose life was in many respects usually happy and comfortingly unremarkable. Nevertheless, there are revealing flashes of what was to come, and pointers to the path that Nance would take. One such pointer, perhaps, is the frontispiece, a photograph of Nance as a little boy (see page 30), in a sailor-suit and hat, in a seaside setting, holding some rope. Other publicly available photographs and portraits of Nance, however, are mainly of him in age, often in bardic costume, gazing into the future.[4]

Robert Morton Nance was the youngest son of William Edwin Nance, who had been born in Padstow, and Jane Morton (also known as Jeannie, according to Christine Raymont), who came from St Ives. Both parents were, therefore, Cornish, although he himself was born in Wales, on 10 April 1873, at Clevedon Villa, The Walk, Tredegarville, Cardiff. However much nationalists of the worst variety might insist on birth as the sole criterion, Nance's life would make quite clear once and for all that this is not the case, and that he earned, as it were, the designation 'a great Cornishman,' used in several of the obituaries. His two older brothers were Ernest and Alwyn, and he himself was apparently known in his early years as Bertie. His sister Christine was a year younger. She reports in her memoir how the family moved in 1878 to Penarth, just outside Cardiff, to a house with a view of the Bristol Channel and the possibility of walks to the docks, where, she tells us, the young Robert was soon drawing ships. She even provides a genetic explanation of Nance's maritime interests, noting that there were sailors and shipbuilders on both sides of his family, including the builder of the first St Ives lifeboat, his great-great-grandfather.[5] Nance spent a lot of time at St Ives, and an interest in Cornish antiquity seems to have been inculcated at a very early stage, largely by his mother; his reading-matter as a child included Cornish tales as well as the late-Victorian staple fare of Ruskin, Kingsley (the *Greek Heroes* as well as the *Water Babies*), and George Macdonald, all of the latter providing a solid underlay for a lifelong romanticism. From his sister's memoir, too, we pick up intriguing smaller details – Nance's dislike of most organised sports, for example – and we see also the activities of an educated late Victorian family, producing *en famille* a *Penarth Magazine*, with illustrations and poems by Nance.[6] From Nance's sister's descriptions, however, we gain little impression of his father, a businessman, a coal agent and colliery manager who died in 1932 in his nineties.

There are more telling insights in Christine Raymont's memoir as Nance became older. His customary adult garb, involving knickerbockers, is mentioned as soon as he graduates from sailor-suits, and the obituaries mention them as well, using the adjective Shavian. Indeed, there are several parallels, and more serious ones than knickerbockers or vegetarian teetotalism, that might be drawn with George Bernard Shaw, only twenty years Nance's senior and very much a part of the artistic liveliness of the eighteen-nineties, the era in which Nance was an impressionable young man.[7] Although Nance learned French at school (and regretted later that he had not learned Welsh from a school-fellow), his bent was clearly artistic, and after spending time (1891–2) at Cardiff Art School he went to the progressive art school in Bushey, Hertfordshire (not far from London, at the North-West end of the Bakerloo

Line), which had been set up in 1883 by (Sir) Hubert (von) Herkomer (1849–1914), with whom Nance's mother, who died in 1893, had corresponded. Herkomer, originally from Germany (where he eventually acquired the nobility-designation 'von') and latterly a citizen of the United Kingdom (where he eventually acquired the knighthood), clearly had considerable influence on Nance. As has been pointed out several times, Herkomer designed the ceremonial robes for the Welsh Gorsedd, but doubtless his meticulous sense of detail and thoroughness as an artist also found a lasting resonance.[8] Christine Raymont's comments about the young Nance arriving at Bushey are of especial interest, even if they were written well over half a century after the events. She heard later, she tells us, that Nance cut rather a dash there, being 'dark and handsome in a romantic style' and somewhat unusually dressed, with hair that was longer than customary – the mark, probably, of every young artist at every period.[9] He was successful at Bushey, and exhibited at the Royal Academy. At Bushey he met, and in 1895 married, his fellow-student, Beatrice Michell (born 1871/2), and on the completion of Nance's course, the couple moved to St Ives, before returning to the family home in Penarth, by now with a daughter, Jeniver. For a while Nance worked for an architect and also had a joint studio with his wife, where they took in some pupils.[10] They exhibited prize paintings at the Eisteddfod in Cardiff in 1899, providing perhaps an initial spark or at least a contributory factor for his later involvement with the Cornish Gorsedd.

Nance and his wife next moved to Newton Nottage, near Porthcawl, but in 1901 Beatrice died. Nance himself studied art in Paris for a short period in 1902, leaving his daughter with the family, and on his return became involved with Walter Crane and the Arts and Crafts Exhibition Society, exhibiting ship designs. The first of his major interests now began to come to the fore, that in maritime history. He made models of early ships, and in 1905 and 1906 collaborated with and illustrated books by E.E. Speight for young people on maritime matters, as well as illustrating Speight's edition of Hakluyt.[11] In 1906 he married another fellow-student from Bushey, who had been a friend of his first wife. (Annie) Maud Cawker (born in 1872) specialised in weaving, and she and Nance moved to Nancledra, a village on the B3313, roughly mid-way between St Ives and Penzance. He was soon settled in Cornwall, where the three children, Robert (known as Robin), Richard (known as Dicon), and Phoebe, were born.

Now begins effectively the next life of R. Morton Nance – and we should now use the name under which he wrote as an adult – namely that of the specialist in Cornish, although this interest still runs parallel for some time with his activities as a maritime artist and historian. He read Henry Jenner's *Handbook of the Cornish Language*, which appeared in 1904, and began to learn Cornish from it.[12] Its influence was to be far-reaching, of course, but for the moment he maintained his interest in local customs and stories by writing Cornish dialect plays, the Cledry (Nancledra) plays, for local production, some of which were published towards the end of his life. The language, then, is English, but the material was often taken from Cornish folktales.

Nance developed a reputation as an expert in aspects of nautical history, illustrated books, and constructed models, examples of which may be found in various museums. Again exhibiting a pattern that would be seen in respect of his later interests, he was concerned not only to acquire, but also to disseminate knowledge, either through the medium of societies or by his own writings. In 1910 he became a founder-member of the Society for Nautical Research, the stated purpose of which is to 'encourage research into matters relating to seafaring and shipbuilding in all ages and among all nations, into the language and customs of the sea, and into other subjects of nautical interest.' The society assisted with the foundation of the National Maritime Museum at Greenwich, which has one of Nance's historical models, as does the Science Museum and The Royal Cornwall Museum, Truro. It also published from 1910 onwards the journal *The Mariner's Mirror*, to which Nance contributed over the years more than forty short articles on subjects such as 'A Fifteenth-Century Trader' (in the first volume), 'Caravels,' 'Some French Carracks,' 'West Cornwall fishing luggers before 1850' and 'The King's College Chapel Window Ship.' In the first decade of the century Nance was painting maritime subjects, including a frieze of Elizabethan ships for the hall of Dartmouth Naval College.[13]

Nance and his family lived at Nancledra (spending time also at Trevail, where he had bought a cottage), trying, according to Christine Raymont, to be as self-sufficient and independent as possible. Vegetarianism seems with him to have been a matter of principle, but his sister links his teetotalism with a wish to live longer and be able to do more for Cornwall; this may, of course, be a *post factum* interpretation, a little hint of incipient legend, but his father and grandfather had also been abstainers, and it fitted well anyway into the philosophy of the simple life. In 1914 the family moved, however, to Carbis Bay, near St Ives, in a house built, we are told, by a Mr Glasson, and to which Nance accordingly gave the Cornish name Chylason, 'house of Glasson,' and he lived there until his death. Reference to 1914 means of course that the family was inevitably affected by the First World War, although Nance, a married man of over forty with four children, would hardly have been drafted. Nevertheless, he joined the Duke of Cornwall's Light Infantry Volunteers, who were based in Bodmin, and although some were sent overseas, others were retained as a reserve in the United Kingdom. After the war he continued his interest in things maritime, and published in 1924 his book on *Sailing Ship Models*, which was revised in 1949. However, he gave up painting, reportedly having decided that the sea itself was pretty visible and better than his paintings of it. He maintained an interest in maritime history, but from the 1920s to the end of his life the main focus must be upon that life of Nance for which he is and will presumably continue to be best known: that of the Cornish language scholar. Of course, he did not switch abruptly from one preoccupation to another, and – to pick up the genetic theme again – two of his children continued different aspects of his life, Richard (Dicon) as the practical artist and sculptor, who carved his father's coffin, and in 1976 made a Herald's wand of office for the Cornish Gorsedd, and Phoebe, who became a Cornish poet and bard with the name *Morwennol*.[14] But it is as a scholar and promulgator of the Cornish language that he is known. Philip Payton's recent work on the historian A.L. Rowse, hardly a man given to gratuitous praise of other scholars (indeed very frequently quite the reverse), cites a 'rare admission' on Rowse's part which is very much to the point on the best-known aspect of Nance's life and works:

> I had always respected Nance's maritime scholarship – he wrote the standard book on Sailing Ship Models, and advised on the collections at Greenwich. But his enthusiasm for the Cornish language – I drew the line at that!
>
> He was right and I was wrong ... Morton Nance did a pile of work on every aspect of Cornish, language, literary remains, folklore, drama, seaterms, place names – and it was all scholarly.[15]

*'Chylason', Carbis Bay (May 2007), the Nance family home
from 1914
(Courtesy of Marion Smith)*

As indicated, Nance had already used the Cornish dialect in his plays at Nancledra and had also begun to collect dialect words associated with the sea, some of which had native Cornish origins, to form a collection which was not published, however, until after his death as a memorial volume. Nance's interest in and promotion of the Cornish dialect of English must not be overlooked in the assessment of his work, however great his interest in the Cornish language would be. But he now made Henry Jenner's acquaintance after the latter retired from his post at the British Museum to Hayle in 1909, and the influence was patent. Nance was able to discuss the Cornish nautical words that he had collected, but they were also able to discuss Cornish antiquities and the Cornish language in general, often meeting in the independent Morrab Library in Penzance.

Nance began to be involved with the Royal Institution of Cornwall and the Royal Cornwall Polytechnic Society, and would publish in their journals over the years, and become, later on, president of the former body. He was in any case an inveterate, enthusiastic and clearly effective organiser, and in 1920 he founded in St Ives an Old Cornwall Society, with Jenner's approval. Eventually such societies spread to other towns and ultimately had to become a Federation of Old Cornwall Societies, of which Jenner was made the president, a position in which Nance would follow him, as indeed he would in other roles, such as that of Grand Bard.[16] The Federation of Old Cornwall Societies soon acquired a journal, *Old Cornwall*, begun in 1925, which over the years printed well over two hundred pieces by Nance, some in Cornish. Independent publications by Nance also appeared under the imprint of the Federation. As Amy Hale has pointed out in her history of the Federation – which was designed 'to educate the public about Cornish heritage' – Nance and the older Jenner were a little different, Jenner being perhaps the more resolutely intellectual, which is not to disparage Nance, who was certainly an intellectual himself. But Nance seems to have had a more grass-roots approach to the preservation and indeed revival of customs and, of course, the language. The revival element was as strong as the more antiquarian aim of the societies as stated in their programmatic motto: *Cuntelleugh an Brewyon us Gesys, Na Vo Kellys Travyth* (Gather up the fragments that are left that nothing be lost), a motto which Nance also took very seriously, and the results of which count very much towards his achievement. Revival is perhaps the key word for this main part of Nance's life, which revolved around Cornish culture in general, and especially the language, and it is appropriate to look at three different aspects of his work. First, at his efforts to revive the language; secondly, at his publications: in the field of Cornish literature in the broadest sense, in his scholarly work on the great medieval texts, his preservation of later fragments, and his original writing in Cornish; and thirdly, at his involvement in the Cornish Gorsedd.

Jenner gave classes in Cornish in St Ives in 1920, but however much the two language scholars and enthusiasts are (rightly) bracketed together, in fact the older man was, as has been noted by Derek Williams and others, far more ambivalent about the revival of the language, whereas Nance clearly was not. Of course Jenner suggested that Cornish be learnt, and he provided a handbook which is an account of the language 'chiefly in its later stages.' His introduction, however, in answering the question of why people should learn Cornish, did consider that to do so was essentially a sentimental act. He modified this by pointing out – quite properly – that there is nothing wrong with sentimentality in this context, but he twice stresses in that introduction that to learn Cornish is not practical: 'There is no money in it, it serves no practical purpose...' and 'The reason ... is ... not in the least practical.' Jenner was even more negative about a possible spoken revival, in fact remarking in the press as late as 1912 that such an idea was 'fantastic and impossible'. To be fair, as Williams has pointed out, Jenner translated 'It's a Long Way to Tipperary' into Cornish in 1916, and hoped to talk to Nance in Cornish.[17] Nance was convinced that Cornish *could* be practical, and that it could be revived as a community language, rather than as a classical one. To this end, he devoted his time and energy to laying down the basis for a language that could be revived in this way, and his essential achievement is that he succeeded, by and large, in doing so, although perhaps not on the scale that he would have liked, nor indeed for as long as he might have hoped. It has been pointed out that he was not Eliezer ben Yehudah, the nineteenth-century proponent of revived Hebrew; but neither, of course, was or is the situation in Cornwall even remotely comparable with that of the State of Israel; the claim, also voiced, that the revival of Cornish is the only true parallel with Hebrew is simply not true.[18] Israel, with incomers speaking a variety of different languages, needed the bonding of a communal language for national identity, but also for survival, and in fact had always had more than one distinctive possibility for such provision, both well attested, widely known, and with important and extensive literatures. At a conference in Czernowitz in 1908, in fact, it was even discussed whether Yiddish, the widely spoken and literary language of Ashkenazic Jews, should be used, but in the event, of course, a revived version of ancient Hebrew won over. Furthermore, Yiddish was a living language, and classical Hebrew was widely known and used in the religious context. Very little of this is at all parallel with Cornish; in Cornwall there was in all honesty (and however much it may be claimed) no real necessity, so that Jenner was in a way right to be hesitant. Be that as it may, Nance encouraged classes in Cornish, and – with another collaborator, A.S.D. Smith (whose bardic name was *Caradar*) – produced over the years a body of well-planned language-learning materials. It is important that the linguistic scholarship behind this long-term work by Nance should not be lost amongst more recent debates about the way Cornish should be revived. Another difference with Jenner, and in the long term a far more significant one, however, was the nature of revived Cornish, of which Nance had a bold and definite vision. Jenner had assumed that Cornish, if revived at all, would continue more or less from where it had left off when it ceased to be a widely spoken community language. It had dwindled gradually, leaving a selection of sometimes not very significant sub-literary fragments for antiquarians to investigate, more or less at the same time as the last day-to-day users of the language were dying. This stage of the language is known as Late Cornish. Alan Kent's attractive dialect short story *Dreaming in Cornish* imagines Edward Lhuyd, the Welsh scholar and antiquary, who was interested in Cornish, visiting the antiquary John Keigwin and encountering a juvenile (and appropriately pert) Dolly Pentreath,[19] and indeed, there was a rising academic interest in Cornish when it was still spoken a little, so that we have an idea of what it was like in its later stages. But this was not the form on which Nance based his revived Cornish. Noting that the actual written material in the later stages of Cornish was relatively limited, Nance opted instead for a (carefully) standardised version of the language used in the medieval literature, most notably in the great mystery plays. In language terms it was a daring move: he had to leapfrog the sound changes that languages make at historical intervals, some of which were clearly visible as features distinguishing Middle Cornish from Late Cornish, and revert to a form of the language that had not in fact been spoken for a considerable time. Thus, by the time Cornish had ceased to be a widely spoken community language, the word for 'head' had become *pedn*. Nance went back to the medieval form *pen*.

There were difficulties, of course, in syntax, semantics and also in lexicon, because there were obscure passages in the medieval texts, and there were also gaps in the vocabulary attested, so that Nance had decisions to make. There has been disagreement with some of his decisions (apart, that is, from his original premise of using the medieval stage of Cornish at all), but he tackled the difficulties and did so with linguistic skill. Much of what he had to do has been summed up most clearly by K.J. George, who cites Nance's approach to the problem of missing words with the nice example of the word 'rat'.[20] Medieval texts do not contain the word for a rat, and we may assume that there was one, so that Nance deduced a Cornish form *rath* from the way in which other Cornish words differ from Welsh and Breton (Breton *razh*, Welsh *rhath*). His solution is entirely plausible, and preferable to that given in the nineteenth-century and earlier dictionaries of *logosan vrâs* 'huge mouse,' although that might well have been understandable. It will be interesting to establish which of the new words attested in the recently discovered late medieval *Bewnans Ke*, 'The Life of St Kea', will match what Nance called 'adventitious forms' in his dictionary.[21] Nance, then, came up with a perfectly reasonable linguistic solution. With concepts that did not exist in the Middle Ages, neologisms were necessary, and Nance created a number, some of which, as George has pointed out, were accepted, while others were not. This is again a normal enough linguistic situation. Words may simply be borrowed as they are – as Middle Cornish took words from Middle English or English absorbed words from French – and adapted to the new language slightly, or new words can be constructed, and these may or may not survive. Those modern languages that avoid foreign loan-words as a matter of policy have a long tradition of making up such words – modern Icelandic can provide parallels to some of Nance's neologisms – but that some of Nance's words were not adopted is hardly a criticism, and more a linguistic fact of life. Sometimes neologisms simply do not last in *any* language; for 'computer', German originally tried *elektronischer Datenverarbeiter*, but even though reduced to an abbreviation (*EDV*) it fairly soon gave way to *der*

Computer (and lest anyone think that 'real' languages are consistent in their make-up, the word is pronounced as an English word, but has a German plural without 's'). Indeed, to continue briefly with a German parallel, Nance was acting much as writers like Philipp von Zesen did when they set up linguistic academies and societies (based in fact on an Italian model) in the seventeenth century and made efforts to standardise, record and purify the German language. Zesen gave the German language words like *Leidenschaft* (meaning passion, literally 'to-undergo-suffering-ness', but more transparent than the French loanword), but of course some words provided by these *Sprachgesellschaften*, such as *Tageleuchter* for window (literally 'day-lighter', against the Romance word Fenster < Latin *fenestra*) did not survive. The linking of Nance and the Federation of Old Cornwall Societies with these seventeenth-century German societies is by no means far-fetched, and German is not the only example that could have been chosen. German (it was at that time not yet possible to speak of 'Germany' as such) was asserting its identity against political and indeed linguistic dominance from outside, and the societies had names like the *Deutschgesinnte Genossenschaft*, 'German-minded Fellowship'.[22]

Nance established a Cornish grammar, standardised spelling and, as a major achievement over a period of many years, compiled and produced a dictionary. All of this is in accord with historico-linguistic traditions, but with two major differences. Firstly, Nance was doing it with the aim of deliberately reinstating a language that had by his day shifted irrevocably from being a community language of everyday intercourse to being effectively a classical language, known but not spoken; and secondly, he made a decision to go backwards and return the language, as it were, to an earlier stage. As we shall see, whether that decision was universally acceptable is still a matter of debate, but it was above all else a pragmatic one. Nance's revised and standardised version of what is technically known as Middle Cornish, a stage of the language with distinctive features spoken from roughly 1200 to about 1550, and which he now in his new version called Unified Cornish, actually worked. Of course there are quite genuine linguistic problems with Nance's Unified Cornish. As George once again makes clear in his paper in *Language Reform* in 1989, the phonology was a major one. Nance wanted to recreate a written and a spoken language, and in necessary default of what linguistics specialists call informants, he based his pronunciation on Later Cornish as described by contemporary scholars such as Edward Lhuyd, on the English dialect in West Penwith, and laid too great an emphasis on modern Welsh (rather than Breton). All of these have run up against criticism. And yet Nance gave a standard form to a language which could be learnt and which was authentic in specific respects: the question of what can be called authenticity in a revived language is always a debatable one. At all events, we have to reiterate the point made by Charles Thomas, Derek Williams and others that the linguistic flaws do not constitute failure: what Nance provided was a platform, and by and large it was a solid one.[23] It was also well supported by written material, in this case by teaching texts – his *Cornish for All*, first published in 1929 and reprinted, and most importantly the dictionary, the first (smaller) volume (English-Cornish) with Smith in the 1930s, and eventually the revised version of 1952 and the *Cornish-English Dictionary* of 1938, revised in 1955, the whole work being reprinted fairly frequently later.[24]

What do we make of all this in terms of Nance's life and achievement, however, in objective terms? It is always difficult to see ourselves as others see us, but it is salutary to step outside Cornwall and Cornish studies for a moment and try to assess the achievement from that point of view. In 1983 Channel 4 produced a series called How to be Celtic, the Cornish portion of which referred to the bringing back of the language 'from its 18th century grave' as a 'harmless and maybe even inspiring necromancy.'[25] Harmless, certainly, and objectively speaking, inspiring too ('necromancy' is a good journalistic eye-catcher, and nothing to worry about), if it inspired the learner, even a casual one, to find out more, whether or not the single-minded desire to revive the language as a community means of communication proved in the long term – and languages do not rise or fall quickly – rather more problematic. It may be that the spoken element of the revival will, again in the long term, prove less successful; claims for spoken Cornish still vary, in spite of discussions in a parliamentary adjournment debate in 1999 on giving some kind of formal recognition (though not, in fact, official language status) to Cornish, and an independent investigation not long thereafter.[26]

The (albeit limited) revival of the spoken Cornish language may be viewed as Nance's major achievement, and possibly was so in his own eyes. What will certainly last, however, is his extensive published scholarly work on the language and literature of Cornwall. P.A.S. Pool's extensive bibliography of Nance's work in *A Glossary of Cornish Sea-Words* (revised for the present book) must speak for itself in terms of volume, but some areas and individual pieces may be highlighted. The injunction used as a motto for the Federation to gather the fragments, and the urge to make them accessible, was clearly a driving force, and Nance published – in *Old Cornwall* in particular but also elsewhere – a great amount of what might be termed linguistic rescue archaeology. There is (following the fairly recent discovery of *Bewnans Ke*) an irony that he could hardly have anticipated in a statement that Nance made in *Old Cornwall* in 1930, but it summarises much of his work in those years. 'The chances are now so greatly against the discovery of any important addition to the Cornish texts already known,' he wrote, 'that the finding of even a word or two in this derelict language is worth noting.' The article – with the telling title 'Two New-Found Cornish Scraps' – investigates an eighteenth-century note by William Gwavas. We may multiply such papers – 'A New-found Traditional Sentence of Cornish' appeared in 1927, for example – but many presented (or published again with commentary) some of the (slightly) more substantial or significant surviving Late Cornish texts – William Bodener's letter, the Pilchard Rhyme, William Rowe's biblical fragments and so on.[27] The interest is often linguistic, but the publications include early songs and poems as well. Under the aegis of the Federation of Old Cornwall Societies, too, Nance published (in 1951) beside his language primer and dictionary, glossaries such as his brief *Guide to Cornish Place-Names*, which is in fact a list of Cornish words appearing in place-names. Bibliographically the little text – a pamphlet of fourteen pages – makes its own point. It is nicely produced, printed in Marazion for the Federation with a cover bearing the emblem of the chough and the motto 'Nynsyu marow Myghtern Arthur' and it sold at two shillings. It would be interesting to find out what the print run actually was and how widely it was distributed; Cornish material was published on a fairly restricted level, because these were largely local publications within Cornwall.[28]

This had not been the case, of course, with the major literary works of medieval Cornish. The major nineteenth-century editors, Edwin Norris and the indefatigable language-scholar Whitley Stokes, published the *Ordinalia*,

Meriasek, Gwreans an Bys and the *Pascon agan Arluth* either with Oxford University Press or with various publishers (or with the Philological Society) in London. Nance, often with the collaboration of Smith, prepared Unified Cornish editions of most of these in their entirety (except *Meriasek*), although they were nearly all published only after his death and mostly still in Cornwall under Len Truran's Dyllansow Truran imprint, in editions by E.G.R. Hooper or Graham Sandercock. He devoted himself to a considerable extent to the great works upon which he based his language revival, and it is obvious, looking at the posthumous printings of the whole texts, that he and Smith were able to correct, emend and clarify many passages in those pioneering nineteenth-century editions, even though some of the medieval texts have been edited again since Nance's work on them. To take a small example, in the Passio Christi section of the *Ordinalia*, Christ addresses to the Virgin from the Cross words translated by Norris as: 'Woman, seest thou thy son?/A thousand times your arms have borne him/ With tenderness.' The Cornish reads (in Norris's text): *benen a welte the flogh/myl wyth dyghtys ages brogh/gans nep mylgy* (lines 2925–7), and we can presume that Norris misunderstood the meaning of *brogh* (badger), reading it instead as *bregh* (arm). In fact he admitted in a note that he had only guessed at what *mylgy* (Welsh *milgi*, 'greyhound') might mean. Nance in a paper published in the 1940s and in his edition clarifies the passage, enabling us to see that Christ is in all probability echoing Psalm 22, 16 (Authorised Version) with a reference to being surrounded by dogs, with the word 'badger' as prey probably dictated by the need for a rhyme on *flogh* 'child.'[29]

Although the whole texts were published after Nance's death, he issued with the Federation of Old Cornwall Societies a whole series of pamphlet 'Extracts from the Cornish Texts in unified spelling with amended translation.' These contained, largely, single episodes or scenes from the plays, and the first in the series (the 1966 second edition tells us) was 'published by and at the expense of Mr E.G.R. Hooper.' Reprints have largely been undertaken by the Cornish Language Board. Nance and Smith chose the episodes on the basis of interest (the first is *St Meriasek in Cornwall*), limited size, and at the same time suitability for the language student wishing to gain greater familiarity with the texts either by reading or by acting. Some of the prefatory judgements give the impression that the medieval plays are more fragmented than they are, and that episodes such as mother and her son in *Beunans Meriasek*, 'The Life of St Meriasek' (from which Nance and Smith also removed what they termed 'extraneous matter') are not really integrated into the cycles. More recent studies have concentrated precisely upon the careful integration of elements in the plays, and Nance's judgement could be awry in this respect. In a paper in *Old Cornwall*, too, he attempted to extract from the Passion play of the *Ordinalia* an originally separate Lamentatio Marie; although he was quite right in noticing the importance of the Virgin's lamentations (which are quite un-biblical) and thus highlighting them, he reconstructs his poem somewhat selectively, and omits part of what the Virgin actually says.[30]

One of the pamphlets – prepared by Nance in 1951 after the death of Smith – is called *An Tyr Marya*, 'The Three Maries', and it was selected, he tells us, because it represented the incident in mystery plays (the *quem quaeritis* passage) that probably served as the starting point for all medieval religious drama, and it is indeed excerpted elsewhere, probably for that reason. In a letter of 19 September 1951 to Peter Gerard Laws, secretary of the Gorsedd, Nance wrote of the Padstow Gorsedd in 1951:

> personally I would much rather have had nothing after the ceremony than the quite inappropriate music that we are usually offered. My Cornish classes were prepared to enact an Tyr Marya, taken from the Resurrection play, in Padstow Church between the musical items, but the parson seems to be a puritan who objects to anything that could be called a "play", or perhaps to words written, in a language unknown to him, before the Reformation. I never heard exactly what the objection was. It was the more a pity as the play had just been printed with the hope of selling copies there, with the English meaning opposite each page of Cornish. We shall do it somewhere else, no doubt, but it seemed specially silly. So many of my own ancestors were at home in that particular church that it was a personal disappointment too.[31]

In his introduction to this little volume, Nance noted that the passage had appeared in *Everyman and Other Interludes*, presumably the original edition of 1909 prepared by Ernest Rhys for Dent's Everyman's Library. That collection of medieval drama was completely revised in 1956 by A.C. Cawley, the medieval drama specialist, and this time included the 'Death of Pilate', a scene from the *Ordinalia* not found in the medieval English cycles. In his preface to the second edition, in May 1957, Cawley recorded his thanks to

> Mr R. Morton Nance for allowing me to consult his unpublished trans-
> lation of the Cornish plays. This translation is based on a new transcript
> of the Cornish text which Mr Nance has made in collaboration with the
> late Mr A.S.D. Smith. Owing to Mr Nance's generous assistance, I have
> been able to revise still further the Norris translation of the Cornish
> *Death of Pilate*...[32]

Nance's own material may have appeared in fairly limited editions in Cornwall, and in full only after his death, but his clearly generous contribution to the Cornish element in a very widely disseminated text is significant.

Richard G. Jenkin ascribes to Nance's personal modesty the fact that he placed the regaining of a traditional literature above creating anything new.[33] Nance did, however, produce material of his own, often either adaptations or translations. Nance's dialect plays written at Nancledra have already been mentioned, and a selection of these appeared in print in 1956. One was even broadcast by the BBC.[34] Concerned to provide material in his Unified Cornish, though, he published a good number of smaller pieces in *Old Cornwall*, as well as a *Lyver an Pymp Marthus Seleven*, based on folktales from St Levan. Some of his verse, too, is included in E.G.R. Hooper's interesting *Kemysk Kernewek*. Better-known than any of these, perhaps, is Nance's play *An Balores*, which takes as a leading symbolic motif the survival of the Cornish chough and was written for performance at the Celtic Congress in Truro in 1932. It ends with a four-verse 'Can Balores', the song of the chough, the last of them celebrating the Cornish language, which has risen up as strongly as has the chough, alive after all. The work ends with the resounding and unfailingly optimistic slogan *Nyns-yu marow Myghtern Arthur*, 'King Arthur is not dead.' The link to a King Arthur, who never really died, but waits to return as the future king, sums up much of Nance's romanticism: it draws its strength from a backward look to a golden age, and invokes a national (though also pan-Celtic) figure who hovers somewhere between history and myth; and it hopes that the age in question will come again.[35]

Most of the works mentioned in the last paragraph do not carry the name R. Morton Nance, but the briefer (and almost as well known) *Mordon*, the bardic name adopted by Nance, echoing Morton and meaning 'sea-wave', and this provides a reminder of the importance that Nance himself attached to the revival of Cornish of the establishing of a Gorsedd in Cornwall, a Gorseth Kernow parallel to the Welsh bardic ceremonies attached to the Eisteddfod. 'A Druid or Something Down in the West Country?' Certainly the best-known pictures of Nance show him in the Cornish bardic robes (based on those designed for Wales by his old teacher, Hubert von Herkomer). It was to be a celebration of the Cornish language.

The origins of the Welsh Gorsedd itself are dubious. The first seems to have been held in (of all places) Primrose Hill in the late eighteenth century, and much of it derives from the imagination and dubious documents of Edward Williams in his guise of Iolo Morganwg. Stuart Piggott's study of the druids gives a brief history of the Welsh Gorsedd that is by no means unfair, and his analysis of the accoutrements worn by various druids in his illustrations are sometimes devastating.[36] And of course, he is quite right – up to a point. Whether or not there is genuine evidence from remote antiquity of bardic gatherings in Cornwall, Wales or anywhere else, is still debatable, but it is also of lesser relevance. The Welsh Gorsedd has by now gathered to itself a couple of hundred years of authenticity, and its offshoots have established themselves as well, the Breton Goursez Vreizh since the end of the nineteenth century and, since 1928, Gorseth Kernow. And if we might feel inclined to comment too adversely on modern folk dressing up in bardic robes, or indeed to endorse too heartily Piggott's 'stage properties of high Victoriana,' it might be worth glancing at a sequence of eight coloured cartoons by Osbert Lancaster produced for the coronation issue of *The Ambassador* in 1953. They comment ironically on the English (one suspects he means British) contempt for foreigners and their fancy national costumes by illustrating the ritual garb of British schools, universities, the military, the Boy Scouts, lord mayors, huntsmen, and indeed both Welsh druids and highland gatherings. The point of the ritual (underscored by the ceremony and costume) is to give unity, and in this case also a sense of antiquity and (however long) of continuity to a formalised situation which becomes a setting for the language.[37]

The build-up towards the establishment of a Gorsedd in Cornwall seems to have been very much – as Brian Coombes (himself a former Grand Bard, *Cummow*) has made clear – in the hands of Nance. Coombes in fact draws a very clear line of development from Nance's Cledry plays as a community activity, to the foundation of the first, and then the Federation of Old Cornwall Societies, and on to the setting-up of Gorseth Kernow. Nance worked together with Dr Rhys Phillips (*Y Beili Glas*) towards the end of the 1920s, in parallel with Jenner's more public hints at the idea, and Coombes also points out two important minor factors: the desire of Nance to avoid any of the perceived outlandishness of druidism; and also the desire (it was later acknowledged by Nance) to establish the Gorsedd whilst Jenner – by now approaching eighty – could still be involved. Early in 1928 officials from the Welsh Gorsedd came to Cornwall, in August of that year the Welsh Archdruid initiated eight Cornish bards, including Nance, and on 27 September the first Gorseth Kernow was held at Boscawen-Un, where Jenner, very much the grand old man of Cornish, was installed as Grand Bard with the name *Gwas Myghal*. Nance was Deputy Grand Bard, and also acted as secretary from 1928 until 1931. Jenner died in 1934, and in the Gorsedd that year *Mordon* was installed as his successor as Grand Bard at Padderbury Top, near Liskeard. The Gorsedd continues as a celebration of Cornish language in public manifestation, and this, of course, is directly due to Nance's interest and vigour. That it now has a website has been mentioned already, as has the fact that the most frequent visual images of Nance show him as *Mordon*, in bardic robes, himself by now very much the grand old man in Jenner's place and clearly offering the post a dignity scarcely implied by the notion of 'a druid or something.'[38]

And yet, despite the success of Unified Cornish, Nance's revived form of the language, as an initial construct, it gave rise to questioning, with a long-term effect on the revival as such, and led to a situation in which Cornish is, it has to be said, no longer unified. A little handbook of the Celtic languages called *Da Mihi Manum*, published in 1994, prints basic phrases and words in six parallel columns: Irish, Manx, Scots Gaelic, Breton, Welsh and Cornish. But the Cornish column contains three separate versions of each, in Unified, Common, and Modern Cornish (Kernewek Unyes, Kernewek Kemmyn and Kernuack), so that for 'a person from the Isle of Man' we have respectively *benen/den Manowek*,

Manoes/Mano, and *dean Ennis Mann*.[39] In spite of the initial success of Nance's Unified Cornish and the basic pragmatism of his establishing what he saw as a working language, it was always liable to radical attack on its medieval basis (especially from language specialists); it was also inevitable that it would be subject, with the passing of time, to emendation and correction. Indeed, Nance himself – although such assumptions cannot but be facile – might well have welcomed the latter, and may have expected the former. The Rawlinson and Bosworth Professor of Anglo-Saxon at Oxford, C.L. Wrenn, made a statement in a lecture in 1958 about Nance's dictionary that has been widely quoted in writings about Cornish (and hence possibly has acquired over the years rather more publicity than the remark merited), to the effect that it 'displays that scarcely scientific revivalist local patriotism which is still so commonly associated with Cornish studies.'[40] Others have been as critical of Nance, referring to his reconstructed language as 'Cornic' or 'Mordonnek'. Glanville Price has commented that 'Unified Cornish was a curious hybrid of authentic medieval and invented modern forms,' but he goes on to say that 'it was near enough to the authentic Cornish of the texts to serve as a useful introduction (and, for those that did not know Welsh, the only serviceable introduction) to the language thereof.'[41] The acknowledgement of Nance's pragmatism is there, of course, and it is interesting that there have been – beside the determination by some to maintain Unified Cornish – first a major revision of it which is named as such, N.J.A. Williams' Unified Cornish Revised, and another revived form, still based on medieval Cornish and close (but not always very close) to Nance's, namely Ken George's Kernewek Kemmyn. There is also, and again it must be said, a persuasive and logical case to be made for Richard Gendall's 'Modern Cornish' or Kernuack, based on the last recorded stage of Cornish. This is the form Jenner might have arrived at, had he continued to develop a revived language, and the divergence of Nance's path at this point is striking. But Kernuack, too, is deficient in lexicon (although the larger lexicon of Middle Cornish can be adapted) and syntax, and there is invariably, as indicated already, some element of artificiality in any revived language. This is true of modern Hebrew in Israel, and although the parallel, as noted, is not very close, the one test of a revived language (or, for that matter, even of a completely artificial one, like Esperanto) is whether it works, whether enough people choose to use it to make it viable. One parallel that does exist, however, is with another European minority language, Rhaeto-Romanic or Romansch, in Switzerland, which was recently reported as losing speakers. Even though a linguistic organisation has tried to establish a standard official version, Romansch Grischun, the insistence of speakers on the use of their own dialects permitted an expert to comment that 'I think it's a terminal position, because they don't agree on pronunciation, they don't agree on vocabulary.'[42] With Cornish, the controversy also continues.

And again: while it is important to consider these developments because they are part of Nance's heritage, the present situation does not, once more, betoken failure on Nance's part. The establishing of a language in a standardised form enabled people to come into contact with it, and that was important of itself. The insights into aspects of written original Cornish – medieval or eighteenth-century – remain valuable. And if it must be reported objectively that the Unified version championed by Nance has not at the moment established itself as 'Cornish,' then it is also, perhaps, appropriate to cite, in terms of loyalty to Nance's memory, P.A.S. Pool's comments in a piece entitled 'Mordon Remembered':

> By those who remember all that Mordon did for Cornwall and Cornish, who tried to continue his work, and brought the revival to the verge of the Promised Land, the outrages now being inflicted on our language will never be accepted, nor their perpetrators forgiven.[43]

Of course, this is a little over-the-top, and 'never' is a very chancy word, especially in a language context; but it does indicate the fact that Nance's revived language came close to success, and that perhaps the famous portrait by Leonard Fuller of the Grand Bard with the visionary look may have undertones of Moses viewing, but not reaching, that Promised Land.

Nance remained busy. Interestingly, P.A.S. Pool also notes that during the Second World War he organised a rally (in 1942) of Breton sailors fighting with the Free French, and after the war was heavily involved again with the Gorsedd (which had been scaled down for the duration), with the Federation, with a number of language projects, especially the revision of the dictionary, and with literary ones on the Middle Cornish texts. His close collaborator, A.S.D. Smith, died in 1950, with the result that he took up much of the work on his own. He served as president of the Royal Institution of Cornwall from 1953–55 and remained actively involved with a variety of other organisations: the Morrab Library in Penzance, the Celtic Congress and – as Pool again emphasises – the West Cornwall Footpath Preservation Society. The breadth of activities speaks for itself.[44]

It may be true, in the words of E.G. Retallack Hooper, that Nance left 'Cornwall more Cornish ... than it was at the turn of the century,'[45] and it certainly seems undeniable that Nance raised the profile of the Cornish language in general terms, and also kept an eye on custom and antiquity in general, whilst accomplishing a good deal of spadework as far as the literature is concerned. Whether or not he felt Unified Cornish to be his main achievement, his gathering and imparting of knowledge about Cornwall and Cornish, and – this is important – not only within Cornwall itself, is highly significant. In many ways, Nance was a man of his time: Charles Thomas (who also commented on Nance's beautiful handwriting) noted that Nance 'led a private life that had in it something of early Fabianism, something of William Morris,' and this is perfectly correct as a summary. (Thomas goes on to refer to Nance's single-mindedness in his pursuit of the Cornish revival.) Nance belonged to a more independent, writing-orientated age – television, he wrote to Peter Laws in 1954, was a novelty to him, as it was for most Britons in the early fifties, and the world of modern media was quite undreamt of. But Nance patiently and carefully gathered the fragments – and some things that were larger than mere fragments – and interpreted and disseminated what he had learned from them with unfailing enthusiasm and clarity.

Still active to the end, Nance died in St Michael's Hospital in Hayle on 27 May 1959 and was buried on 3 June in Zennor churchyard, which is where he had wanted to be buried and which of course is not far from the sea, recalling his roles as artist and as nautical historian. The obituary notices in the Cornish press give an indication of the respect in which he had been held, and his grave (where his wife, who died in March, 1961, is also buried) has an inscription in English and Cornish on a slab erected in 1963. It invokes first the memory of Robert Morton Nance, and then of *Mordon*, Barth Mur Gorseth Kernow, *Mordon* the Grand Bard, with the addition of the sentence *Oberow y vewnans yu y wyr govath*, 'His life's works are his true memorial'. The plural noun *oberow*, 'works', is, again, significant.[46]

Notes

1. J.H. M[artin] (1959) 'Cornish Gorsedd Bereft of its Grand Bard,' in the *West Briton*, 28 May 1959. The (memorable) comment is cited also in the useful introduction to Nance's life, that by Derek Williams (1997) 'Robert Morton Nance' in *An Baner Kernewek/The Cornish Banner*, no. 88, May 1997, pp. 3, 14–18.

2. V.P. Kaligin and A.A. Korolyev (1989) *Vvedeniye v Keltskuyu filologiyu*, Moscow: Nauka, p. 240 ('Introduction to Celtic Philology'). The section on Cornish is by V.P. Kaligin (in fact his dates as given there are slightly incorrect). The entry in the *Oxford Dictionary of National Biography* (2004), Oxford: Oxford University Press, is by the present writer; for the websites concerned, see http://kw.wikipedia.org/wiki/Robert_Morton_Nance and http://www.gorsethkernow.org.uk (as of April 2007). The photograph in question is a hand-coloured one.

3. http://www.chain.org.uk/chain-theme/art_ard27.html. The context is a directory of artists.

4. C. Morton Raymont (1962) *The Early Life of R. Morton Nance*, [Leedstown]: New Cornwall Publications. There is an extract from this, together with a number of other tributes, in Nance's *A Glossary of Cornish Sea-Words*, published posthumously as a tribute and edited with a good biographical introduction by P.A.S. Pool. The picture of Nance as a boy is reproduced in Williams (1997), p. 3.

5. Of the two other major figures in the early Cornish language movement, Henry Jenner, Nance's mentor, although born in Cornwall, left before he was three years old and did not return to live until after his retirement, and A.S.D. Smith, Nance's collaborator, was born in Sussex. See Tim Saunders' extremely pertinent comments on language and identity: ''The Answer is Simple': Henry Jenner and the Cornish Language,' in *Henry and Katharine Jenner*, ed. Derek R. Williams (2004), London: Boutle, pp. 35–48.

6. Raymont (1962), p. 8.

7. Raymont (1962), pp. 18f. cites some of a poem from this family magazine on the Cornish Pasty, which appeared later, in 1898, in Quiller-Couch's *Cornish Magazine*.

8. For a readable and authoritative survey of the period, with special reference to the visual arts, see Holbrook Jackson's much reprinted classic study from 1913, *The Eighteen-Nineties*, reprinted Harmondsworth: Penguin, 1950.

9. Herkomer is himself an interesting figure. For some relevant comments on his techniques, see Peter Conrad (1973) *The Victorian Treasure-House*, London: Collins, pp. 110f. He is cited as having written that 'the desire to take trouble seems to me at the bottom of many good deeds.' On his designs for the Welsh Gorsedd robes (of which the later Cornish ones were an adaptation), see Stuart Piggott (1974) *The Druids*, Harmondsworth: Penguin, p. 144, referring to 'the stage properties of high Victoriana,' and Amy Hale, 'Old Cornwall Societies,' in *Celtic History and Literature* 2, Autumn, 1998, pp. 42–47.

10. Raymont (1962), p. 26.

11. Nance's daughter, Mrs Phoebe Procter, was kind enough to fill in several gaps for me when I was preparing the *ODNB* biography, and I should like to record my gratitude to her (and also to Peter Nance, Nance's great-nephew). Mrs Procter has also clarified for me that they did not actually set up a school as such, as it had been suggested they might, and as my entry in the *ODNB* implies (private letter of 21 April 2001). Most of Nance's own material is held in the Royal Institution of Cornwall's Courtney Library at Truro, to which he bequeathed it in 1959. I am also grateful to several members of Nance's family for their help and support. Mr Toby Procter, Nance's grandson, confirmed that Nance did indeed write with a quill pen, collecting seagull feathers as necessary from Carbis Bay, and another grandson, Professor Damian Nance, supported this with a photograph! I am especially indebted, finally, to Tamsin Donaldson, Nance's

granddaughter, for her interest in this project. Mrs Donaldson is a specialist in Australian Aborginal language, and made clear to me the interesting parallels between Nance's work on Cornish and her own on the Ngiyambaa language as "rescue linguistics". That linguistic controversies can arise very easily in this kind of work is also significant, as is, once again, the genetic link taking scholarship down to another generation. As a small personal aside, Mrs Donaldson also remembered having to count in Cornish to persuade her grandfather to push her on a swing – a pleasant and salutary reminder for us that the subjects of historical biography are human beings.

12. There is a detailed bibliography of Nance's writings in his *Glossary of Cornish Sea-Words*, Pool (1963), pp. 195–204, which is expanded in the present volume. He collaborated with Speight on *Britain's Sea Story*, first published in 1905, with a third edition in 1909, illustrated Speight's edition of Hakluyt in 1905, and his *Romance of the Merchant Venturers* in 1906. Nance later illustrated other works on maritime history.

13. A.S.D. Smith (1947, repr. 1969) *The Story of the Cornish Language*, Camborne: An Lef Kernewek, pp. 13f.

14. See the memoir by Amy W. Baker in *Sea-Words*, ed. Pool (1963), p. 15. That volume contains illustrations of some of Nance's paintings and ship-models. See also A. Sainsbury, 'The Origins of the Society for Nautical Research,' in *The Mariner's Mirror* 80, 1994, pp. 450–458.

15. On Phoebe Nance (later Procter), see P. Berresford Ellis (1974) *The Cornish Language and its Literature*, London: Routledge & Kegan Paul, p. 167 and Alan Kent (1998) *Wives, Mothers and Sisters: Feminism, Literature and Women Writers in Cornwall*, Newmill: Patten Press, p. 28.

16. Philip Payton (2005) *A.L. Rowse and Cornwall*, Exeter: University of Exeter Press, pp. 211–212. Nor, of course, was Rowse much given to admitting that he had been wrong, although his enthusiasm for Cornwall was constant. He considered, too, that Nance was a better scholar than Jenner: Payton (2005), p. 212.

17. See Hale (1998) and Brian Coombes 'Gathering the Fragments': Henry Jenner, the Old Cornwall Societies and Gorseth Kernow,' in *Jenner*, ed. Williams (2004), pp. 161–81.

18. Henry Jenner (1904) *A Handbook of the Cornish Language, Chiefly in its Latest Stages, with Some Account of its History and Literature*, London: Nutt; the preface is reprinted in Jenner, ed. Williams (2004), pp. 49–55. See Saunders (2004) and B. Murdoch (1992) 'Henry Jenner in a Scottish Library,' in *An Baner Kernewek* no. 68, November 1992, pp. 22–23, where I cite Jenner's comments of 1912. The whole matter of his ambivalence is discussed in detail by Derek R. Williams 'Henry Jenner F.S.A.: City Scholar and Local Patriot,' in *Jenner*, ed. Williams (2004), pp. 70–110, esp. pp. 100f. In the nineteenth century, however, the pioneering German philologists occasionally communicated with one another in the languages they were studying, at least in writing, as is shown in a dedicatory letter to Jacob Grimm in Visigothic, a language that by the 1830s really *had* been dead for quite a long time.

19. P. Berresford Ellis (1990) *The Story of the Cornish Language*, 2nd edition, Penryn: Tor Mark Press, p. 29 citing Chaim Rabin. A glance, however, at Chaim Rabin (1973) *A Short History of the Hebrew Language*, [Jerusalem]: Jewish Agency, especially chapters X and XI on the revival, makes very clear that this is an initially seductive, but not in the event remotely close parallel. On the theme of the spoken language, Ellis (1990) refers, p. 23, to R.St.V. Allin-Collins (*Hal Wyn*) as the first 'speaker' of revived Cornish, a nice linguistic point, given that the 'last' speaker of the language has also been seen (rightly or wrongly) as a single named individual (be it Dolly Pentreath or William Bodener or John Davey of Boswednack). The comparison with Eliezer ben Yehudah is made, too, by John J. Parry (1946), 'The Revival of Cornish: an dasserghyans Kernewek,' in *PMLA* 61, pp. 258–268, see p. 261.

20. Alan M. Kent (1998) *Dreaming in Cornish*, Liskeard: Charles Lee Society. On Jenner's use of the last stage of Cornish, see K. J. George (1989) 'The Reforms of Cornish – Revival of a Celtic Language,' in *Language Reform* 4, pp. 355–376, esp. p. 361 and Derek Williams (1996), 'Henry Jenner: the Early Years,' in *An Baner Kernewek* no. 84, May 1996, p. 19.

21. George (1989), pp. 362–366. The article contains portraits of Nance and others involved in the language revival.

22. On the word for 'rat', see Fred W. P. Jago (1887) *An English-Cornish Dictionary*, London: Simpkin Marshall, p. 128, citing various versions from the dictionary of Williams (1865) and the word-lists of Borlase (1769) and Pryce (1790). On *Bewnans Ke*, see Graham Thomas and Nicholas Williams (eds.) (2007), *Bewnans Ke: The life of St Kea*, Exeter: University of Exeter Press and Ken George (ed.) (2006) *Bywnans Ke*, [n.p.]: Kesva an Taves Kernewek. Nance includes, for example, the word *gorthenep*, 'reverse side', in his dictionary, with an asterisk, and the 'new' *Bewnans Ke* text has *gorthenab*.

23. See Karl F. Otto (1972) *Die Sprachgesellschaften des 17. Jahrhunderts*, Stuttgart: Metzler, for a survey and p. 66 on the neologisms. For interesting parallels with the similar standardisation of English from Bishop Peacock down to Dr Johnson's Dictionary, see Ellis (1974), pp. 50f.

24. See Williams (1997), p. 16.

25. See R. Morton Nance (ed.) (1978) *An English-Cornish and Cornish-English Dictionary*, Penzance: Cornish Language Board and (1990) *A New Cornish Dictionary*, Redruth: Dyllansow Truran.

26. *How to be Celtic* (booklet accompanying five programmes made by Pellicula Films of Glasgow for Channel 4, shown in September 1983), produced by Mike Alexander and Douglas Eadie. The pithy formulation is Douglas Eadie's on p. 36.

27. See *Hansard* for 23 February 1999 for the very detailed opening speech by Andrew George, MP for St Ives. I am indebted to Mr George for supplying me with further details at the time. For details of the independent study (in 2000) and of the level of recognition eventually afforded to Cornish (in March 2003) as a regional or minority language in EU terms, see Kenneth MacKinnon (2004) 'As Cornish as Possible' – 'Not an Outcast Anymore': Speakers' and Learner's Opinions on Cornish,' in *Cornish Studies*, 2nd series, 12, pp. 268–287. See also Neil Kennedy (2002) 'Fatel era ny a keel? Revived Cornish: Taking Stock,' in *Cornish Studies*, 2nd series, 10, 283–295. I leave aside the question of what might be termed 'tea-towel Cornish', although even that raises awareness of the existence of the language.

28. The article from which Nance is cited is in *Old Cornwall*, vol. 1, no. 12, Winter 1930, pp. 29–30 (and there is a follow-up to it in vol. 2, no. 1, Summer 1931, pp. 23–24 as 'A Puzzle Solved'.) The new-found sentence, the sorting out of what looked like 'meaningless rigmarole', is an excellent example of Nance's painstaking approach. (Nance read it at the Annual Meeting of the Royal Institution of Cornwall on 14 December 1926 and it was published in its *Journal* 74, 1927, pp. 281–287). See the full bibliography in this volume, of which these are just a few instances.

29. The booklet on place names was printed in 1964 as a third edition, and he published other glossaries of Celtic words.

30. The passage is not entirely clear linguistically, so it is no surprise that both Nance's and Harris's treatments are also a little free. Text in: Edwin Norris (1859, repr. 1968) *The Ancient Cornish Drama*, Oxford: Oxford University Press, repr. London and New York: Blom, and see his note on the meaning of *brogh*, II, 332. Markham Harris (1969), whose text appeared after the death of Nance, also emends the older translation: *The Cornish Ordinalia. A Medieval Dramatic Trilogy*, Washington: Catholic University of America Press, p. 167, with notes on p. 263. R. Morton Nance and A.S.D. Smith, ed. Graham Sandercock (1982) *The Cornish Ordinalia, Second Play, Christ's Passion*, [n.p.]: Cornish Language Board, pp. 192f. See below, note 31, for Nance's comments in a separate paper. I have discussed the passage in detail in a paper 'Mary's Lament, the Gospels, and the Cornish *Ordinalia*,' forthcoming in *Celtic Forum* in Japan. For another example of Nance's very detailed comments on passages in the plays, see his 'New Light on Cornish,' in *Old Cornwall*, vol. 5, no. 2, Summer 1952, pp. 59–60.

31. 'A Cornish Poem Restored,' *Old Cornwall*, vol. 4, no. 10, Winter 1949, pp. 368–371. He notes in this text the *brogh* problem discussed above. I have discussed the lamentation sections in my 'Mary's Lament.' On the question of integration, see Jane A. Bakere (1980) *The Cornish Ordinalia*, Cardiff: University of Wales Press, and Brian Murdoch (1993) *Cornish Literature*, Woodbridge: Boydell and Brewer. I comment on the Meriasek passage in: 'The Holy Hostage: a Religious Motif in the Middle Cornish Drama *Beunans*

Meriasek,' in *Medium Aevum* 58, 1989, pp. 258–273. It appears that what survives of *Bewnans Ke* might, however, genuinely be less well-integrated.

32. *An Tyr Marya*, prepared by R. Morton Nance and A. S. D. Smith (Federation of Old Cornwall Societies 1951), repr. [n.p.]: Cornish Language Board, 1973. The preface is dated May, 1951. I am greatly indebted to Peter Thomas for drawing my attention to and providing me with copies of the correspondence with Laws from the Gorseth Kernow archives. Nance corresponded with Peter Laws for some time, and indeed suggested in May 1949 the bardic name *Crugyow* as a translation of his name, that is 'laws' in the geographical sense, hillocks, rather than the juridical. Nance's comments are interesting for a variety of reasons, including the personal link with Padstow. F.E. Halliday (1955) *The Legend of the Rood*, London: Duckworth, using Nance's text, also separates off the incident.

33. A.C. Cawley (ed.) (1956, 2nd ed. 1957), *Everyman and Medieval Miracle Plays*, London: Dent, p.vi.

34. Richard G. Jenkin (1994), 'Modern Cornish Literature in the 20th Century,' in *The Celtic Pen* 1/3, Spring 1994, pp. 3–5 (esp. p. 3).

35. *The Cledry Plays: Drolls of Old Cornwall for Village Acting and Reading* (1956), Marazion: Federation of Old Cornwall Societies. Special significance has been attached to the play 'Duffy', which was broadcast on 2LO, the first BBC radio station, and other stations, on 4 May 1928, with Nance as Squire Lovell: see the web database on 'The Invisible Play' (early broadcast drama) by Alan Beck of the University of Kent and *The Times*, 4 May 1928. Ellis (1974), p. 175 refers to Nance having made sound recordings of *Jowan Chy an Horth* and other pieces in 1954.

36. *Cledry Plays* (1956); *Lyver an Pymp Marthus Seleven*, St Ives: Lanham, 1939 – these were apparently written in 1923; [E. G. R. Hooper, ed.] (1964 and 1977) *Kemysk Kernewek*, Camborne: An Lef, repr. Penzance: Cornish Language Board, pp. 51 and 63: the Cornish letters of *Caradar* (A.S.D. Smith) refer frequently to Nance on language points; *An Balores*, St Ives: Lanham, [1932] – Cornish and English. See finally by Nance *An den ha'y dheu wreg*, with other short stories by Edith Grenville and Hal Wyn, St Ives: Lanham [1927/1928] for a version of what was originally a Breton folk tale, sometimes discussed in the context of the Tristan stories; and also Nance's *Folk-lore in the Cornish Language*, Camborne, [Royal Cornwall Polytechnic Society], [1925], repr. Penzance: Oakmagic, 2000.

37. Piggott (1974), pp. 142–146 and illustrations.

38. Osbert Lancaster (1978) *Scene Changes*, Ipswich: Gambit, unpaginated.

39. Brian Coombes, in *Jenner*, ed. Williams (2004), pp. 161–181; see pp. 164–171 for a detailed run-down of the various parallel activities. The same volume contains Jenner's comments on 'The Gorsedd of Boscawen-Un' and 'Bards, Druids and the Gorsedd,' pp. 182–196. See on Gorseth Kernow: Hugh Miners (1978) *Gorseth Kernow: the First 50 Years*, Penzance: Gorseth Kernow, and Peter Laws (1982) *Gorseth Byrth Kernow: Bards of the Gorsedd of Cornwall 1928–82*, Penzance: Gorseth Kernow. Derek Williams (1996) 'Henry Jenner: the Early Years' in *An Baner Kernewek* no. 84, May 1996, pp. 17–20 refers to Nance's desire to set up the Gorsedd while Jenner was still able to take part. It is interesting that the Web even has a page for Australian bards.

40. Marion Gunn (1994) *Da Mihi Manum*, Dublin: Everson Gunn, pp. 34f. There are three separate Cornish versions of the foreword. The word was chosen as having been unlikely to have been recorded earlier.

41. The remark is in C.L. Wrenn's Oxford O'Donnell lecture of 1958 (see 'Saxons and Celts in South West Britain,' in *Transactions of the Honourable Society of Cymmrodorion* 1959, pp. 38–75). It is noted by Ellis (1974), pp. 194f., referring to the more modified comments of Charles Thomas (1963), 'An Dasserghyans Kernewek,' in *Old Cornwall* vol. 6, no. 5, Autumn 1963, pp. 196–205 (a lecture given at the Celtic Congress held at Carbis Bay, Nance's home, in 1963). It is cited also by P. A. S. Pool (1975) *The Death of Cornish*, Penzance: Pool, p. 5 and by Philip Payton in his important (and balanced) lecture 'The Ideology of Language Revival in Modern Cornwall,' in Ronald Black, William Gillies, Roibeard Ó Maolalaigh (eds) (1999) *Celtic Connexions. Proceedings of the Tenth International Congress of Celtic Studies I*, East Linton:

Tuckwell, pp. 395–424, see p. 395. The session on Cornish at the Celtic Congress in Edinburgh on 24 July 1995 at which Philip Payton's paper was delivered, following one by Richard Gendall on 'The Rediscovery of Modern Cornish' (and also an entirely non-controversial medieval comparative piece on the *Ordinalia* by the present writer) was the occasion of a sometimes heated debate, which underlines the fragmentation. See also George (1989).

42. Glanville Price (1998) 'Modern Cornish in Context' in *Cornish Studies*, 2nd series, 6, pp. 187–193, cited p. 187 (reviewing Richard Gendall's dictionary of Modern Cornish). See also Glanville Price (1984) *The Languages of Britain*, London: Arnold, pp. 134–145.

43. See Price (1998), especially on Gendall, and the review article that followed it in the same journal, Anthony P. Grant (1998) 'Defending Kernewek Kemmyn,' in *Cornish Studies*, 2nd series, 6, pp. 194–199. The comments on Romansch are from a report in an American newspaper, the *Barre-Montpelier Times Argus* in Vermont, (24 April 2005): I am indebted to Sheila McLachlan, Information Officer at the Scottish Centre for Information in Language Teaching in Stirling, for drawing it to my attention. The parallel with a minority language on the defensive against extinction is of itself a little disheartening, however. Artificial languages (even Esperanto) of course very rarely survive for long. See also the comments above, note 11, on the parallels drawn by Tamsin Donaldson with Australian indigenous languages.

44. P.A.S. Pool (1991) 'Mordon Remembered,' in *An Baner Kernewek* 64, May 1991, pp. 1–11.

45. *Sea-Words*, ed. Pool (1963), pp. 12f.

46. Hooper is cited from *Sea-Words*, ed. Pool (1963), p. 18. The memorial inscription is on p. 8.

Personal Recollections and Reflections

When I recall my earliest memories of the Gorsedd and its leaders, my mind returns to what I regard as a near-perfect venue, the stone circle of the Merry Maidens at St Buryan a half-century ago, with Robert Morton Nance in command as Grand Bard.

Just a short distance from the spot where the first Gorsedd was staged almost 30 years before, the granite 'Maidens' – turned to stone for dancing on the Sabbath – the clear skies, the robes of the bards flowing in the light breeze, made a complete picture. I was a journalist, not then a bard.

Morton Nance stood erect, his eagle-like profile and serious aspect dominating the scene. I saw him occasionally – but never as powerful as this. It was a time when the Cornish language had come to the very forefront with the publication of his Cornish-English Dictionary. He was presented that day with a copy on hand-made paper and bound in leather, surrounded by the Cornish Arms in gold.

It came from the Old Cornwall Societies in token of the dedication of his life and scholarship "to Cornwall, its language and its people".

Many years before he had emphasised the great value of the dialect, but at this Gorsedd, wearing his deep blue robe and the laurel wreath of his office, he declared – and I reported him – before the bardic initiates: "In the past we have had people who have become bards by acquiring a slight knowledge of the Cornish language. Some of them have become bards and done no more with that language since.

That is not the way in which we are going to make the Cornish language revive. That early knowledge is but the first step on the ladder. There are many more rungs ahead, many of them far beyond me, and some perhaps which we shall never reach.

We intend to build up the language so that it can be used as capably as any language in the world."

How prophetic he was. It was a memorable day: one, I believe, when the Gorsedd was establishing itself as a voice of Cornwall. Several language bards, many from within Cornwall for their services, and others from Australia and South Africa, were initiated that day.

Morton Nance, surrounded by the splendour of the annual occasion in this rural setting, as well as many spectators in summer dresses and open-necked shirts on this fine day, pleaded for a greater interest in the study of the language. And this was echoed by bard Revd A. Lane-Davies, Vicar of St Cleer, who said that some standard of proficiency in the Cornish language should be required as one of the conditions of being made a bard if the language was to be properly revived.

Mordon, Grand Bard, would be proud to know of the progress made by the Gorsedd and the language since that glorious summer afternoon.

Douglas Williams, MBE (*Lef ha Pluven*)**, December 2006**

I have been told that I went to my first Gorsedd in 1932 at the Merry Maidens, when Robert Morton Nance was Deputy Grand Bard, and a maternal uncle, Edwin Chirgwin, was made Bard *Map Melyn*.

As I was only 4 at the time, I don't remember it, but I do clearly remember going to the 1935 Gorsedd when it was held in St John's Hall, Penzance, because of bad weather. It was a small gathering on a very wet day, but it was there that I first saw *Mordon* as Grand Bard.

My next recollection is being received by him in September 1939 as an 11 year-old Disciple of the Gorsedd when, because of the outbreak of World War 2, only a few Bards gathered informally in *Mordon*'s garden at 'Chylason', Carbis Bay. It was a warm sunny day and I have tangible proof of whatever ceremony took place, a certificate of admission, in Cornish, signed R. Morton Nance. I am very proud of it as I am now the only survivor of the two Disciples who eventually became Bards.

Gorseth Kernow, St John's Hall, Penzance, 1935. Morton Nance, Grand Bard centre picture (Courtesy of the Western Morning News/Gorseth Kernow Archive

From 1939 to 1956 I attended no Gorsethow because there were no proper ceremonies during the war years and I served in the Royal and Merchant Navies for a number of years thereafter. However, I do remember *Mordon* well during his final years when he conducted Gorsethow in resonant Cornish: a tall, very impressive figure on the Men Omborth, wearing his crown of laurel leaves and looking like all the pictures I had ever seen of Roman emperors.

I don't recall ever speaking to him except at my 1939 admission, but I remember that he was always spoken of with great respect and, indeed, reverence, two things very noticeable at his funeral at Zennor in 1959, which I was privileged to attend.

John Jenkin (*Carrek an Jawl*), **12 November 2005**

A brief tribute to Mr R. Morton Nance or 'Mordon' of the Cornish Gorsedd, is fitting from one whose faltering footsteps to begin the study of the Cornish language were guided by him over 20 years ago. A largely self-taught scholar, the position he occupied in the field of the Cornish language and antiquities was unique. He was always ready to give friendly guidance and it was an additional pleasure to see the penmanship of his letters, written with a quill. He was himself an "old master".

Letter from L.C.J. Orchard to *The Times,* **1 June 1959**

Mordon had a wry sense of humour ... a sort of mock modesty, but could always hold his own if someone stepped out of line ... You did not take liberties with him ... He had dignity – and was wise, an unusual attribute ... In [the] 1930s ... I imagine *Mordon* bore the brunt of the first Arthurian Conference and the Celtic Congress held in the R.I.C. He seems to have done it kindly and unstintingly ... [I]t was Nance with his tireless working and tenacity for the language, his love for Cornwall and the Cornish language that has <u>given Cornwall back its language</u>. He spent endless time unifying the language, composing the Dictionary and working on the ancient texts ... It was through him that we have Language Bards... Henry Jenner produced his Handbook but very little was then done about the language. When he and Kitty returned to Cornwall, they gave classes, but it was finally Morton Nance who took the cause up. I am sure [that] if he had not done so, the Cornish language would now be extinct and just a memory.

Audrey Randle Pool (*Keltya*)**, 2004–2006**

Family Notes

William Edwin Nance [1837–1932]

The writer of this is William Edwin Nance born in Padstow Cornwall 19th July 1837 eldest son of Henry Nance at that time a schoolmaster (of a private school) in that town. Henry Nance was one of 16 children (8 sons) a son of Richard Nance who was Postmaster (and mail carrier under Bodmin) in Padstow for many years. Retiring he went first to Cardiff and then to Cheltenham with some of his family and then died while I was quite young. I have been told that he learned the woolcombing business in Padstow, which place was then a centre of that business and the shipping place for the wool gathered in the district. His father was William Nance of Padstow. I only know of him that he lost his first wife (my grandfather's mother) and took another wife and had a second family, the consequence to Richard Nance being that he lived in the same place with his father's brother Richard Nance who lived in the house near the Quay called the Ship Inn, having ground at the back with various buildings and conveniences upon it many years later when in my boyhood I knew the Champions who then lived there and with them as boys rambled over it. I have often thought of a painted board I saw there against some outbuildings painted with the name and date Richard Nance 1777. This was when I was 12 or 13 years old I think, for I was brought from Cardiff to Padstow with the rest of the family in 1848 and there remained till I returned to Cardiff in 1855 and commenced to work in the export coal trade under my first employer (David Jones) who emigrated to America after I had been with him about 7 years. Subsequently I found other employment and continued in the same class of business for

Nance's father, William Edwin Nance
(1837–1932),
(Courtesy of Carola Nance Scupham/Gorseth Kernow Archive)

myself and for others until in 1912 I gave up active business. Most of my time was spent at Cardiff Docks which in my time had vastly grown in extent and importance.

★ ★ ★ ★

These notes by Robert Morton Nance's father are dated January 7th 1922 and are to be found in an envelope labeled 'Miscellaneous papers, including Family Notes by Nance's father' in Nance Papers Additional. They are reproduced with the permission of The Royal Institution of Cornwall, Courtney Library (Nance Collection).

Medieval Romantic or Language Visionary?: Robert Morton Nance and the Cornish Language

R.T. Lyon

The name of Robert Morton Nance is synonymous with the Cornish language, but how was he viewed historically and how is he viewed today, with respect to his work on behalf of the language? In the eyes of some, Nance's contribution has been outstanding. Without his input, say his supporters, the language would not have advanced beyond the basic revised standard introduced in Henry Jenner's *A Handbook of the Cornish Language*, published in 1904. His opponents, however, say that the work carried out by Nance was greatly flawed, and that much of what he did should be ignored. There are arguments in support of both opinions, and these will be examined as this chapter progresses.

Firstly, the question must be asked, 'Why did Nance take the Cornish language to heart?' He himself states in *Old Cornwall*:

> My own interest in Cornish came, I expect, from my father's comparison of Cornish names with Welsh ... I first learnt any Cornish that I knew from two books – Borlase's *Antiquities*, with its Cornish Vocabulary full of strangely spelt words ... and Sandys' *Specimens of Cornish Provincial Dialect*, which gave me, as well as the dialect, two specimens of Cornish – the conversation from Andrew Borde's *Introduction to Knowledge* and William Bodener's Cornish letter, both of which I soon had by heart, misprints and all ... It was actually my interest in nautical research

which, after I had come to live in Cornwall, led me to go more deeply into Cornish studies.'[1]

Nance came to Cornwall with his second wife Annie Maud (née Cawker) in 1906, and settled at Nancledra, between St Ives and Penzance. By this time, he had been studying Jenner's *Handbook*, and although he stated in the same article in *Old Cornwall* that '[f]rom about 1885 to 1904, when Jenner's *Handbook* came out, I may have picked up a very little more here and there, but even the *Handbook* did not get me to the stage of attempting to write or speak the language', he goes on to say appreciatively of Jenner, 'I first met Mr Jenner, and then began a friendship during which he literally told me all that he knew of Cornish, and set me finding out more for myself'. This initial meeting between the two was recorded by Nance in more detail exactly twenty years earlier:

> At that time I was very interested in Cornish dialect words, of which I found many that had never been recorded … Many of these words were not to be explained by English, neither was Williams' *Cornish Dictionary* very often helpful, and it was when I was puzzling over them with such help as I could get from Breton and Welsh dictionaries in the Penzance [Morrab] Library that I first made acquaintance with Mr Jenner. He was at once interested in what I was doing…[2]

And, according to P.A.S. Pool: 'At this time Nance's main interest was the study of the dialect words used by Cornish fishermen for such things as parts of boats, pieces of equipment, fish and birds, and he enlisted the help of Jenner in working out the meaning of those words which were of Cornish origin'.[3]

Both Nance and Jenner worked together on the revival of Cornish over the coming years, but it was Nance who eventually took over the reins. His vision for the future of the language was different from that of Jenner, who could see no prospects for the language in real terms: 'The reason,' he wrote, 'why a Cornishman should learn Cornish, the outward and audible sign of his separate nationality, is sentimental, and not in the least practical...'[4] Although Nance 'always had his head in medieval clouds',[5] he did consider the possibility and express the hope that Cornish might gain some *official* recognition. Writing in his paper 'Cornish in 1951' concerning the next hundred years, he predicts:

By that time, although no-one wants compulsory Cornish, in school or out, we may find that those who are capable of teaching it may be given some sort of official recognition, and that to know Cornish may bring with it some advantage beyond the simple pleasure of having knowledge.[6]

Also, when he wrote 'The Revival of Cornish', he had obviously been think-ing about the future of Cornish as a viable language, but his visions or hopes were still very much shrouded in pessimism: 'If to "revive" Cornish,' he wrote, 'would be to make it live again as the vernacular of Cornwall, or as the official speech of the County Council [sic], and nothing less would do, then there has [not] been, and as far as one can see there never will be, a "revival" of Cornish. The word "revival" may be used, however, of the bringing into a limited vogue by a limited number of people of a thing that has gone out of fashion...'[7] Towards the end of his life he appeared a little more confident about the future, writing, 'One generation has set Cornish on its feet; it is now for another to make it walk'.[8]

In the 1920s, Nance was running the first Cornish classes at St Ives, using Jenner's *Handbook* as a starting point. Jenner had done his best to 'pick up Cornish where it left off', but this was far from successful, according to Nance, because 'the available material for reconstructing the whole language as it exist-ed in 1700 was far too scanty'. Furthermore,

Lhuyd could not always be found trustworthy, and contemporary Cornish spelling was chaotic, so in the end he [Jenner] had to go back to 15th-Century Middle Cornish for most of the grammar and syntax, re-spelling it all after a phonetic system that was based on Lhuyd's, but unlike any that had ever been used before. This artificial Cornish had the drawback that it was no longer much like the Late Cornish that it had set out to be, while it still fell far short of the language in its finest form; and it did not greatly help its learners to read the old texts which form the best examples of how Cornish should be written, for to do this they had to learn different spellings of almost every word, and to accus-tom themselves to other ways of saying things.[9]

At the time that Nance was starting to get to grips with Cornish and finding from his St Ives classes that Jenner's *Handbook* fell short of what was required, he was obviously considering taking steps to bring Cornish into line with his way of thinking – returning to the texts of the medieval period and basing his version of the revived language on them. In 1923 he prepared a short manuscript entitled 'Gwary Abram hag Ysak',[10] which was taken from *Gwreans an Bês* and which, as the manuscript indicates, was written in two forms, Old and New. Underneath he wrote four years later: 'Gwell yu an vaner goth, herwyth ow thybyans-vy' [*The old way is better, according to my thinking*]. This preferred form was not yet 'Unified' as it is recognised today, and Nance does not say exactly what form it is. It appears to be loosely based on his vision of a 'standardised' medieval spelling. However, some seven years later, alongside each line he added a version using a form of 'unified' spelling. But this is still not his recognised 'Unified' system, as he uses *dhemmo* instead of *dhymmo*, *len* instead of *lun*, and *dheso* instead of *dhyso*. Nevertheless, the seed was now sown for Nance to embark upon his first grammar book, making use of his own 'Unified' spelling system.

How was this shift of Nance towards his 'Unified' system of spelling and a return to medieval Cornish taken by Jenner? In a letter to Francis Cargeeg, Nance wrote:

> All this is of course a fulfilment of what Henry Jenner hoped for, and worked for. In a way, "unified" Cornish upsets his own, but he was large-minded enough to see that a restored Middle Cornish was the only form of the language that could bring back the use of Cornish idioms, and that the old spelling unified was the only spelling that all could be got to accept as the best possible, and we have always been not only on friendly but on affectionate terms in all our work together.[11]

Nance was probably encouraged in his pioneering work originally by Richard Hall, one of the more fluent Cornish speakers of the time, who, in a letter dated 7 September 1922, says, 'I was glad to learn of your interest in our dear old tongue and of your taking steps to preserve its traditions'.[12] It is interesting to note that in this letter Hall advocates the use of the spelling *dh* to represent the sound of voiced 'th', as distinct from the unvoiced sound, to be spelt *th*.

Then, in a further letter some five weeks later, he says that he has had to use 'makeshifts' in spelling Cornish and that we ought to have a proper phonetic alphabet. 'Taking all the circumstances into consideration,' he writes, 'so as to preserve the identity of Cornish it might be advisable to keep to the old ways of spelling in the ancient manuscripts.'[13] With these encouraging and supportive letters from Hall, Nance now pressed ahead with work on his first grammar book, initially entitled 'Notes on Cornish Grammar, Spelling and Pronuncia-tion',[14] but eventually cut down to form his *Cornish for All*, which was to be pub-lished in 1929. As an introduction to the 'Notes', Nance stated that 'this grammar should be a help and not a hindrance to the study of our language at its prime … [A] spelling has been adopted that is near the average of spelling of the Ordinalia…' He goes on to say that he has adopted Lhuyd's spelling *dh* for the soft sound of 'th', in preference to the *z* used sometimes in Middle Cornish, chiefly because the latter had also been used for *th*, *y* and *z*. He avers that the use of *dh* 'as a final is lost in Cornish; following a general tendency to sharpen final consonants it became hard *th*. Lhuyd either failed to observe this or looked upon it as a corruption…' Referring to the consonants *f* and *s*, he says that the letter *f* 'as a final, is lightly sounded, tending to disappear (this especially in Meryasek) or to become a *v*. In the MSS, it is often written for *v* even as initial, but this is not followed.' With respect to *s*, he says, 'Cornish, like Breton, has a mutation of *s* to *z*, but this is not written…'

Having been disappointed generally with Jenner's *Handbook*, which did not allow him or his students to read the medieval texts, Nance definitely turned away from anything connected with Late Cornish – or anything much after the *Ordinalia*, come to that – unless he was searching for a Cornish word which he could not find elsewhere. This avoidance of any later developments in the lan-guage, which Nance generally referred to as 'corruption', is exemplified in his 'Notes'. He says, '[T]he verb *gothvos* has many contracted forms' and goes on to give the following examples: *go'vos* (infinitive), *gu'sta* (for *godhes-ta*), *goffo* (for *godhfo*), *guffan* (for *godhfen*), and even *wydhen*, *w'ya* for *wodhyen*, *wodhya* as mutations of *godhyen* and *godhya*. Although these were customary contractions at the time, Nance refused to include them, as they were, in his opinion, 'cor-rupt'. Likewise in dealing with the third person preterite ending *-ys*, he says that the later development *-as* should not be adopted. However, the truncated

CORNISH FOR ALL.

A BOOK with the above title, prepared for the Federation of Old Cornwall Societies by Mr. R. Morton Nance, is now ready for the press. In it several practical difficulties that have hindered any general revival of Cornish have been removed, and by various teaching devices the language has been made as easy to learn as any other, easier, in fact, than most.

CORNISH FOR ALL contains an *Introduction* to the text ; a *Précis of Cornish Grammar* (which is not a mere abridgement of existing works, but contains much new information, and, is arranged in clear and compact form for ready reference) ; an *Old Cornish Folk-tale*, "John of Chyanhorth," written C. 1670 ; *100 Sentences of Colloquial Cornish*, all from old and trustworthy sources, but printed, like the tale, in *Unified Spelling* and with full *Translations*. Directions for *Pronounciation* form part of the Grammar, and a *Vocabulary* of every word in the text is included. The whole gives a solid grounding in the National Language of Cornwall which makes the rest little more than the acquirement of a larger vocabulary.

Those whose ambition does not yet go beyond the learning of a few chosen Cornish sentences will find themselves catered for in this book as well as the most advanced and enthusiastic of Cornish students. The latter are of course as yet too few to pay by themselves the cost of its publication; but even in the English transalation, "John of Chyanhorth" is a story that should be known to all Cornish people, and it is hoped that every supporter of *OLD CORNWALL* will make a point of ordering a copy. If adequate support is forthcoming the price of *CORNISH FOR ALL* to *subscribers before publication* will be 2/-, a price which will be raised immediately on publication to 3/- or more.

All Secretaries or Journal Secretaries of Old Cornwall Societies who will obtain the names of as many subscribers as possible amongst their own members and send them before June 1st, to the Hon. Journal Secretary of the Federation : Mrs. A. Pool, "Woodside," St. Ives, will thereby render not only valuable but indispensable service towards the publication of

CORNISH FOR ALL.

Prospectus for Cornish for All

version of his 'Notes on Cornish Grammar, Spelling and Pronunciation' which became *Cornish for All* was published in 1929 by the Federation of Old Cornwall Societies, priced 2/6d (12½p), and became the standard textbook for students of Cornish. Its subtitle boldly states that it is 'a First Book, containing a Précis of Cornish Grammar; the Tale of John of Chyanhorth or the Three Maxims, and One Hundred Cornish Colloquies, in Unified Spelling, with Translations and Vocabulary', and the October issue of *Old Cornwall* announced its arrival on the market.[15] Nance's 'unified' spelling system was now being introduced for all to use, although, as was noted above, its structure was seemingly not yet finalised. 'Uniformity of spelling,' wrote the author, 'is no more found in such 15th-century Cornish than it is in English of the same period, but it is usually possible, if never very easy, to select one spelling of a word as being most worth perpetuating in the "unified" system of spelling which all our Cornish-writers have now agreed to adopt. [How this agreement was reached is not recorded!]. The publication of a dictionary, when this becomes possible, will be the most effective means of fixing the spelling for all words; meanwhile Williams' Dictionary serves, as far as it is complete, by giving most of the various spellings, including usually the "unified" form or something very near it.'[16] *Cornish for All* did at the time appear to be a panacea for all the previous problems associated with Jenner's *Handbook*, but in spite of a congratulatory letter from Roparz Hemon,[17] the famed Breton philologist, the book was strewn with errors, there being no less than thirty-four noted in the *Old Cornwall* announcement. Further proof that 'Unified' spelling was not yet perfected came in the form of a short article by Nance himself in the following issue of *Old Cornwall*, where he wrote of suggested 'improvements on the spelling and other details hitherto accepted for "unified Cornish" '.[18] Then again, in the Summer 1933 number, Nance introduced further amendments and suggestions for improving his system and his revised form of Cornish generally.[19] But in spite of these original errors and amendments, Nance had reached his first milestone. He had studied the medieval texts (rightly or wrongly bypassing later writings), pulled together the Cornish of that earlier period from various sources and, filling in any missing gaps in the paradigms of verbs, had produced his *Cornish for All*, which would be the foundation stone for Cornish students for some years to come. Now it was time for Nance to embark on his next venture, and that was to produce a dictionary which could be used alongside *Cornish for All*. But in this venture he was not to work alone.

In 1933 Arthur Saxon Dennett Smith (*Caradar*), who was to do so much in reviving Cornish, came to live in Cornwall. Before his retirement Smith was a teacher at Blundell's School, where he taught Cornish to the boys as an extra subject. Although he remained in Cornwall for only three years before returning to Sussex to look after his invalid mother, he became heavily involved with the language, striking up a life-long working association with Nance, which produced a wealth of Cornish material. It was this partnership which in 1934 resulted in the publication by the Federation of Old Cornwall Societies of the first English-Cornish dictionary in a 'standardised' spelling system. This dictionary, which was dedicated to Henry Jenner, consisted of approximately 12,000 headwords – a vast step forward in the revived language. However, in spite of amendments and improvements to his system – he even referred to it as 'unified' – Nance had still not arrived at his final 'Unified' system. In this dictionary, for example, he is still using a long *u* which he unfortunately decided later to replace with a similarly accented *o*, thus losing the distinction between two quite different sounds. Typical words affected were *lus* (grey), *rus* (net) and *bus* (food), which later became *los*, *ros* and *bos* respectively. *Dout* (doubt, fear) and *fout* (fault, lack) became *dowt* and *fowt*, just as *keges* (hemlock), *egery* (to open) and *gorghery* (to cover), became *kegys*, *ygery* and *gorhery*. (All these changes appeared in his *Cornish-English Dictionary* of 1938). *The English-Cornish Dictionary* of 1934 was not reviewed in *Old Cornwall*, although there was a brief notice in the Summer 1934 issue, as well as a half-page advertisement stating that it was now ready and that '[c]ontaining the Cornish of nearly 12,000 English words, in pocket size, it will put the study of Cornish on a new footing, the lack of such a work having been hitherto a stumbling-block to those who wished to use the language in writing or speech'.[20] Then in the Winter 1935 number of the journal, it was announced that '[e]arly in the New Year it is hoped that the *Cornish-English Dictionary* will be in the press, helping to make everything written in Cornish more easily understood'.[21] This, unfortunately, did not materialise at that time, it being another two years before the famed dictionary of 1938 hit the market.

What was the reason for the delay? Well, according to Smith it was lucky that

the printing ever got off the starting blocks. It would seem that in the preparation of his 'life's work', Nance had not taken Smith into his confidence, as he
had done with the 1934 *English-Cornish Dictionary*, and this led to some acrimonious and damning correspondence between Smith and Francis Cargeeg. The
first record we have of dissatisfaction in the Smith camp appeared in his letter
of 17 March 1937, when he wrote:

> I am disgusted by the delay for three reasons: it provides a ready excuse
> for slackers to do nothing: a year ago I unexpectedly met R.M.N. at
> Lanham's, and he then told me he had just handed over the MSS to the
> printers: so it seems that it is only his fussiness over the accuracy of a few
> unimportant details that has induced him to take all this time to revise
> what was apparently ready for the printers a year ago: and lastly I am
> sorry because about five years ago I was going to issue a working vocab-
> ulary, Cor.-Eng., containing most of the main words, so that the move-
> ment might work more smoothly, when R.M.N. begged me not to do so
> on the grounds that he had been preparing a more serious dictionary for
> years past – his life's work, he called it – and my issue would spoil any
> chance he might have of selling his book. His dictionary was ready five
> years ago, except that it needed revision before proceeding to the print-
> ers. It is just five months ago that R.M.N. wrote saying that he was start-
> ing a final revisal![22]

Perhaps Smith's comments were to a certain extent justified in view of the
time that Nance took to make his revision, but on the other hand were they
made because Smith's own Cornish-English vocabulary had not been produced? Perhaps also a factor in any breakdown in communication was the fact
that Smith had returned to Sussex and so was working 'apart' from Nance in
many respects. Smith had not cooled down very much by the following July,
when he again wrote to Cargeeg:

> [N]yns-yu Mordon mes corsen ow-crenna y'n gwyns. Gwan yu y gnas –
> kepar ha benen goth kens es den – na ny-yller byth fydhya ynno, mar po
> whans a <u>wul</u> neppyth![23]

[Mordon is no more than a reed trembling in the wind. His nature is weak –

more like an old woman than a man – nor can he ever be relied upon, if one
wishes to do anything!]

Smith was obviously not very happy! Later in the same letter he castigated
Nance for his approach to a keen Cornish student: '[A]n kensa lyther a-scryfas
dhedhy ef a-n-scryfas yn Sawsnek!' [*The first letter he wrote to her he wrote in*
English.] Smith also criticised Nance on a number of other aspects of his work,
condemning the use of diacritics, especially as they had been used by Edwin
Chirgwin (*Map Melyn*) in his booklet *Say it in Cornish*. In the same paragraph
Smith wrote: 'Mes an pyth a-worras own y'm colon o an samplow a-welys a jan-
jyans yn lytherenyeth re a'n geryow kemyn es usyes genen pup deth, drefen bos
an re-na hep dout an formow a-wra mos y'n Gerlyver noweth'. [*But what put fear*
in my heart was the examples I saw of change in the spelling of too many of the common
words that we use every day, because those will be the forms that will doubtless go into
the new Dictionary.] Smith himself switched to English later in this letter, and
although initially praising Nance – 'I hold Mordon to be the greatest Cornish
scholar now living in so far as a knowledge of the old Texts is concerned' – he
soon became critical:

> And if he were content to give us a safe and sound dictionary reflecting
> the language as it actually was shown to be, I should not complain. But
> he is going far beyond that. He is attempting what is possible only to a
> trained philologist, namely a reconstruction. Unfortunately Mordon is
> no linguist and has had no training in philology. The result is that some
> of his reconstructions are simply childish. I have not been allowed to see
> many, but quite enough to raise grave doubts in my own mind. When I
> cooperated with him four years ago in preparing the Eng.-Cor. part, I
> took it for granted that his spellings were traditional. But I have since
> found that this is not the case.

Smith then gives examples of words which do not exist in Nance's spellings,
concluding, 'If he would only give the traditional Cornish forms, without trying
to be clever, he would be conferring a boon'. Another issue on which Smith
attacks Nance is proofreading. 'Also long ago,' writes Smith, 'I offered to read
through his proof-sheets: a task for which M. is the least fitted of any man I

know: he simply cannot detect errors! but he was not very keen, so I let it drop. *Mordon* is not an easy man to offer to help: he has been the sole authority on Cornish in Cornwall since Jenner's death, and in fact for some time previous, so that he may be pardoned for thinking that if he cannot solve a problem, then no-one else can!' Further on in the same paragraph he continues, '[C]an you tell me why he chooses to shut me out of every problem in connection with his dictionary? It is beyond my comprehension'. Finally, after berating Nance about the Gorsedd, Smith signs off by writing: 'But that Dictionary! I dread the many changes at the whim of one man: they are enough to kill all interest in Cornish: whatever one writes becomes obsolete as soon as printed!' This letter alone would be enough to show that Smith was the most outspoken of Nance's critics (in private at least), though, as seen above, even he was unstinting in his praise of Nance's work in particular areas.

Despite Smith's attack on Nance over the preparation of the new dictionary – whether Nance ever got to hear of or see Smith's letters is not known – it appeared in 1938, in time for the Summer issue of *Old Cornwall* to say that it was 'now ready'.[24] There was a short piece about it in the same issue,[25] though, like the 1934 *English-Cornish Dictionary*, it did not get a review as such, despite the fact that Nance generally received a great deal of approbation from the Federation of Old Cornwall Societies. Smith, though, had still not finished! On 30 October 1938 he wrote to E.G. Retallack Hooper (*Talek*).[26] From what he says in this letter, it appears that Nance might have had a change of heart, because he was proposing a supplement of additional words etc. to accompany the dictionary and had asked for help so that the list could be as complete as possible. Smith agreed to help and spent several weeks checking the word lists submitted, attaching additional words of his own and sending them back to Nance. 'Yth-hevel nag-yu Mordon pes da a'n pyth a-ve gwres genef' [*It seems that Mordon isn't pleased with what I did*], wrote Smith in his letter. He had submitted 160 words which were not included in the main dictionary, and it would appear that these were ignored by Nance. Smith goes on to criticise further some of Nance's decisions, and by the end of the letter was obviously near to exploding:

Yth-hevel bos Mordon pes da a'n gologhas a-n-jeva dyworth ysyly
Unyans C.K.G. Bytegens nyns-us kemmys hag onen anedha yn pup cans

a-wor Kernewek da lour rak gweles an foutow y'n Gerlyver. Dhe'm tybyans-vy, ef yu yn-teffry an gwetha gerlyver re-welys yn ow dedhyow: ha my re-welas nyver bras lour anedha, Dew a-wor.

[*It seems that Mordon is well pleased with the praise he has had from members of the Federation of Old Cornwall Societies. However there isn't as many as one in a hundred of them who understands Cornish well enough to see the mistakes in the Dictionary. To my thinking, it's truly the worst dictionary that I have seen in my life: and I have seen a large enough number of them, God knows.*]

In spite of this and further attacks by Smith on Nance's work generally in his letters to Hooper, the 1938 *Dictionary* became the standard work for future students until the arrival of the 1952 (English-Cornish) and 1955 (Cornish-English) dictionaries, and even then it was still a valued source of reference, as it gave many derivations and examples of Late Cornish developments and alternatives. The distinct impression left by Smith's comments in letters to Cargeeg and Hooper is that he was consistently over-critical of Nance and would seem to have had some private axe to grind. Although it is not the intention in this chapter to delve into Smith's character traits, it would appear that he could at times be a difficult man to get on with, particularly with respect to matters relating to the Cornish language. In one of his fault-finding letters to Hooper he did, however, find another good word to say about Nance, when in January 1940 he conceded:

Bytegens, ny-res dhyn-ny mos re bell ha dyspresya gerlyver Mordon hep ken. Yma ynno cansow a daclow yn-kever an tavas na-gefyr yn nep le aral, ha henna drefen bos Mordon ow-cothvos moy es denvyth bew a'n hynwyn tylleryow yn Kernow. Yma yn y erlyver mur a skyans usy grondyes warnedha.[27]

[*However, we mustn't go too far and decry Mordon's dictionary without cause. There are hundreds of things in it about the language that are not found anywhere else, and that's because Mordon knows more than anyone living about the place-names in Cornwall. There is a good deal of knowledge in his dictionary which is founded on them.*]

But he still had to get in a dig at the end of the paragraph, writing: '... ha nyns-us dowt y'n bys bos an ober mur y les dhyn-ny, kyn nag-yu, martesen, an gwella ober a-alsa bos gwres, mara pya y scryfer paryssa dhe omgusulya ha kesobery gans tus erel a-gar Kernewek' [... *and there isn't a doubt in the world that the work is of great interest to us, although it isn't, perhaps, the best work that could have been done, if its writer had been more ready to consult and co-operate with other people who love Cornish*]. Perhaps another piece of unwarranted criticism from Smith, though it does appear from earlier correspondence that Nance did tend to work on his own, without conferring with those 'other people who love Cornish'.

Following the publication of the 1938 dictionary, Nance's work in the field of the language was to a certain extent curtailed by events of World War II. He still wrote many articles – both in Cornish and about Cornish – in *Old Cornwall*, which continued apace when peace returned in 1945. Perhaps his next major linguistic preoccupation (one that, again, eventually involved Smith) came about through the Rev John Mackechnie of Glasgow, a well-known Celtic scholar who knew Cornish as well as Gaelic. In 1949 he was proposing to edit a hitherto unpublished Cornish manuscript and wanted Nance's co-operation in the project. Apparently, Mackechnie was the only scholar who had noticed the manuscript catalogued in a recent report of the Historical Manuscripts Commission. It had been found amongst papers preserved by the Puleston family of Emral and Worthenbury in Flintshire, and had been in the care of the British Museum since 1947. The manuscript was of course *The Tregear Homilies*, written around 1555. On receiving the manuscript, Nance studied it and noted that its discovery was a valuable find, the text being a prose piece of considerable length, and over a century older than any other surviving Cornish that was not written as verse. He does however bemoan the fact that the subject matter was not more pleasing, writing: 'If we could have had our choice of a subject for so long a run of the language it might have pleased us to find in it Arthurian romances, a local account of the Cornish risings or traditions of the Cornish saints, or we might have welcomed something about Cornish industries and trade. We are not choosers, however, but must take what time has spared us'.[28] He is critical of the Cornish written, at times justifiably so, and elaborates on the over-use of English words in places where the Cornish equivalents would have been known to John Tregear, who, however, was probably writing with a particular readership or audience in mind, for whom English loan words might well have been better understood, particularly in those parts of Cornwall where the language was in the steepest decline. Smith wrote to Nance actually agreeing with him, saying that 'the subject-matter is deadly dull, but the language redeems it and makes it a worthy study'.[29] Despite his reservations, Nance gave a paper on the subject to the Royal Institution of Cornwall[30] and wrote two articles for *Old Cornwall*. The first appeared in the Summer 1950 issue, introducing the manuscript and including a version of part of one of the Homilies and a vocabulary.[31] He followed this up in the Summer 1951 number, in which he goes into more detail regarding the language used by Tregear. He is somewhat critical of Tregear's translation of Bishop Edmund Bonner's original, mainly because of the unnecessary retention of English words within it. 'Even here we meet with some disappointment', he writes, and he goes on to suggest that Tregear left some English words untranslated 'partly perhaps because he feared to tamper with the exact sense of the English, partly perhaps as falling in with the view of his congregation that high subjects needed loftier and less understandable language than popular Cornish, but chiefly I am afraid out of sheer slackness'.[32] He admits, however, that the *Homilies* had enabled additions and adjustments to be made to current knowledge of Cornish vocabulary and grammar, going on to write in support of Tregear's work: '...and besides giving us a most welcome specimen of the language of their times it helps us to add several words to the dictionary and to remove a qualifying asterisk from some others which hitherto could only be presumed as likely Cornish because they exist in both Welsh and Breton. Besides this he has given us the means of correcting some makeshift plurals, genders and infinitive endings for which there had been no Cornish authority.'[33] In spite of his criticisms, Nance was pleased at having seen the document, not only because it gave him an insight into the language as it had developed by 1555 but, more importantly perhaps, because it proved him correct in some of his 'reconstruction' work and supported some of the assumptions which had been a bone of contention amongst his peers, not least A.S.D. Smith.

With the excitement of the discovery of *The Tregear Homilies* behind him, Nance would now look forward to the publication of his next dictionary, an

English-Cornish volume that doubtless came about as a result of the new words, confirmations and corrections derived from the Tregear manuscript. This new dictionary was an update of the *English-Cornish Dictionary* of 1934, but now with the benefit of his final 'Unified' spelling system; and, of course, it included new headwords, from both Tregear and further Welsh and Breton borrowings. This new dictionary was published in 1952, two years after the death of Nance's biggest critic, A.S.D. Smith, and included this dedication to him: 'Dhe gof CARADAR, ow hesoberor skentyl ha dywysyk dres lyes bledhen ow-whylas dry golow a-berth yn tylleryow tewl an Yeth Kernow' [*To the memory of CARADAR, my learned and zealous co-worker over many years in seeking to bring light into the dark places of the Language of Cornwall*].[34] Even though Smith had died prior to the publication of this latest dictionary, criticism still flowed in from Celtic linguists, in particular J.E. Caerwyn Williams, whose assessment appeared in the press on 1 July 1953. The main criticism, in this instance, related to the inclusion of 'borrowed' words from Welsh and Breton, some of which had been acknowledged as borrowings in the 1934 dictionary but were not specified as such in this revision. Caerwyn Williams sums up by saying, 'The Celtic scholar will use it with the utmost caution or not at all, and it is my belief that he would gladly do without it to have a standard Cornish-English Dictionary, the sole purpose of which would be the inclusion of all Cornish words recorded in manuscript or printed text'.[35] Nance has written in the margin of his copy of the review, 'This is rather what we would expect from this type of Welsh critic. He is not at all interested in what this dictionary was trying to do'. Again one has to stand up in defence of Nance. Caerwyn Williams was obviously expecting the dictionary to be of a truly historical nature, produced solely for philologists and other academic students, whereas Nance was thinking otherwise, as his marginal note makes clear. He was not concerned so much about any historical aspect of Cornish, but wished to provide a working dictionary to enable twentieth-century students to get to grips with the language as a modern and viable means of communication.

Although Nance was now in his 80th year, he had still not finished his work, and there was another dictionary to come. This was to be an updated Cornish-English edition, really a 'reversal' of the *English-Cornish Dictionary* of 1952, but without the source references, Late Cornish examples, paradigms of verbs etc.

and the very useful section on prefixes and suffixes which had been included in the 1938 version. This dictionary – Nance's last – came out in 1955, just four years before his death. Unlike the first two dictionaries, which had at least some coverage in *Old Cornwall*, this latter pair, apart from the critical comments by Caerwyn Williams relating to the 1952 volume, almost slipped out unnoticed. Nance's output, though much reduced during the last decade of his life, continued right up until the end, with publications such as his *Guide to Cornish Place-Names* (1951) and articles for *Old Cornwall*. It must be said here that, although A.S.D. Smith gave Nance a very rough ride with respect to many aspects of the language – in particular the latter's approach to the 'reconstructing' of Cornish – they did work together in producing extracts from the Cornish texts, such as *An Tyr Marya, St Meryasek in Cornwall, Abram hag Ysak, Sylvester ha'n Dhragon* etc. These were published mainly through the Federation of Old Cornwall Societies, and reprinted in part during the 1970s by the Cornish Language Board.

So far this has been a broadly chronological account of the major works undertaken by Nance in Cornish, from his first involvement with the language through to the publication of his last dictionary in 1955. But what about the man himself? There is no doubt that Nance was a stalwart where the language revival movement was concerned. From the time that his interest in Cornish was aroused by his study of Jenner's *Handbook of the Cornish Language* and his meeting with the author himself in the Morrab Library, through to his dying day, the amount of research which he carried out and the quantity of Cornish material which he wrote and published were prodigious. For *Old Cornwall* alone he wrote no fewer than sixty articles in Cornish and over forty on his findings concerning Cornish, in addition to all the other material relating to Cornish customs, pastimes, habits etc. All this was in addition to the work involved in preparing his *Cornish for All* and the four dictionaries. It must be remembered, too, that the preparation of these dictionaries for publication was not the relatively simple process it is today, when alphabetical arrangement can be achieved by the touch of a key on the computer. In Nance's time each word had to be sorted manually into alphabetical order, either by means of a card-index or by painstakingly numbering all the entries in the order in which they were to be set up by the printer. It was not all plain sailing for Nance, and there were

times when his spirits seemed to be low; and, of course, he received a lot of criticism – privately and publicly – for his ideas and work in promoting his
'Unified' Cornish. He had already shown signs of despondency or disappointment about the small number of those wishing to study Cornish (even among
the membership of the Old Cornwall Societies), when he wrote to Cargeeg
towards the end of 1936: 'As you know, most readers of O.C. [*Old Cornwall*] have
no use at all for the Cornish pages, and some of them refuse to buy it at all if it
seems "full of Cornish"'.[36] The following year, a letter to Smith quotes Nance as
writing that 'the Service in Cornish has not led to a single fresh Cornish student, while one hears of it annoying people who hate "foreign" languages in
Church.'[37] Later, in 1941, Nance was also quite disaffected by the Royal
Institution of Cornwall, as a pencil note on his manuscript 'Notes on Cornish
Miracle-Play Manuscripts' shows: 'Since Doble there has been no-one on the
Council of the R. Inst. Cor. who takes any interest at all in Cornish, though
there are a few of the ordinary members who do'.[38] And following the Gorsedd
at Trethevy, St Cleer, in 1952, a very down-hearted Nance said to G. Pawley
White (*Gunwyn*), who was a junior marshal at the time, that he did not see any
future for Cornish at all, because people were not speaking it.[39] Those moments
of despondency must have been short-lived, however, because it seems that he
never stopped working on the language.

His main aim in life with respect to the language was to introduce and gain
acceptance for his 'unified reconstructed Cornish'. As noted above, in trying to
utilise Jenner's *Handbook* to read and teach from the medieval manuscripts,
Nance became so frustrated that he very soon decided that the only way forward
for the language was to go back to these earlier manuscripts and 'reconstruct'
Cornish for present-day use. This meant not only standardising the spelling,
but also advancing his ideas on the 'reconstruction' of the language itself, something which led to considerable criticism. Possibly because Nance was so disen-
chanted with Jenner's *Handbook*, he would appear to have become quite averse
to the use of any Cornish written after the date of the last of these medieval
manuscripts. In his studies of the writings of Tonkin, Jenkins and other writers
of Late Cornish, they were always 'wrong' or 'miscopied'. He also referred to the
later development in Cornish of inserting (under certain circumstances) a *d* and
b respectively before *n* and *m* as constituting 'alterations due to the wear and

tear of time, or corruptions'.[40] And in a letter to a Mr King of the Oxford Cornish Society he states, 'In the late texts one has to deal with a language artificially made to serve a literary purpose, but lacking all but the barest colloquial forms'.[41] In looking for 'new' Cornish words for his 'reconstruction work', Nance was also very selective, writing in one essay: 'I have now cut out words from English that were in use in Cornish, some even since the time of the Cottonian MS. vocabulary, words from English or French that are used in Welsh and Breton also, and all words that seem to have gone out of use before 1800'.[42] Similarly, he commented on sixty or so words in Lhuyd's vocabularies 'which I have found to be new', altering the original spelling to suit his 'unified' spelling and thus losing some of the original pronunciation noted down from speakers. Admittedly, this was done to bring these words into line with Middle Cornish, but he chose to ignore the later development of the language and the way in which words were actually pronounced in the 18th century. Smith frequently castigated Nance's ideal of a pseudo-perfect Cornish based on the medieval works because of his refusal to accept anything that, in his judgment, ought not to have appeared in Cornish writing at that early period. Referring to Nance's work on *The Creation of the World*, Smith wrote: 'I think the original version should be reproduced exactly as it stands, only in unified spelling ... Another question is whether to preserve certain characteristics peculiar to a late text like CW or to bring its Cornish completely into line with that of the *Ordinalia*. You tend towards the latter, but I can't help thinking you go too far'. '*[D]eth, be, cows, na fell*, changed to *duth, bu, kews, nep pell*,' he continues, 'seems to me to be putting the clock back too far. Likewise, *mara cos'ta, woffya, woffes, kyn na'm boma, y vosa*, etc., these are all good colloquial forms warranted from the oldest texts, and are a feature of CW. I have shown in my notes that there is nothing wrong with them.'[43] (In fact, these notes by Smith run to thirty-eight pages in all!) It should be said in Nance's defence that although he did not favour any late forms of Cornish, he had already stated in a letter to Cargeeg, 'Dygheth yu Caradar dhe vos hep godhvos a Gernewek Dewedhes'[44] [*It is a pity that Caradar lacks a knowledge of Late Cornish*]. Paradoxically, Smith made a similar comment about Nance: 'I believe his knowledge of Cornish was restricted to Classical Cornish, as some words in later Cornish he did not seem to be able to understand'.[45] This is a most unfair statement, as Nance was unparalleled in unravelling place-names and a host of apparently jumbled scraps of Late Cornish. Smith was, indeed, very much a medievalist himself, but he did appreciate the fact that one cannot change a language just to suit one's own ideals. Such criticism of Nance is further exemplified by his 'Celtic Bird-Names of Cornwall'.[46] Here there is considerable evidence of traditionally used names being twisted to comply with Middle Cornish/Unified spellings and words. For example, the traditional *mola* (blackbird) is written *molgh*, and the word *kelligrew* (chough) is disregarded, being substituted by *palores*. In addition, some bird names included in the dictionary were 'devised' by Nance, following comparison with Welsh and Breton. He notes that there are some which seem peculiar to Cornwall, but as they do not seem to be 'Celtic' they are not included in his vocabularies or dictionaries!

Many of the problems with Nance's working practices were perhaps caused by his tendency to stubbornness and his consequent alienation of those who were prepared to help and advise him. It is easy to receive the impression that Smith was continually finding things to criticise in Nance, but after all, as he told Cargeeg, 'I have this advantage over him that I know several languages fluently, including Welsh, and have had a fairly good training in philology, seeing that I took a first in classics at Cambridge.'[47] Perhaps a more flexible attitude to Smith's input might have been the better option for the language. Former Grand Bard Hugh Miners was of much the same opinion as Smith, saying: 'Nance was domineering and always wanted things to go his way...'[48] These criticisms of Nance of course stand out boldly when quoted in isolation, but one must ask the question, 'Where would Cornish be today without him?' There are many who learnt Cornish up to at least the 1960s who would probably never have bothered without his direct or indirect help, resulting in far fewer speakers than there currently are. Although it has been stated on a number of occasions that Nance refused to acknowledge the use of Late Cornish, sometimes, strangely, he is quite appreciative of this stage in the development of the language and those who spoke it. In support of the Cornish used by Dolly Pentreath and William Bodener, he states that the language 'remained very little corrupted by admixture with English, and ... the grotesque changes in some Cornish words as used in the dialect are not due to decay in the language itself, but simply to their long use by people who did not speak it'.[49] Although not condemning Late Cornish *per se*, in the same paper he bemoans lost opportunities:

> It maddens one to think of these learned, laborious Cornishmen, mis-
> printing earlier collectors, misreading ancient manuscripts, jumbling
> their own few Celtic, or West Country English, words with an indis-
> criminate hurling together of Cornish, Welsh, Breton, and Irish from
> Lhuyd's *Archaeologia Britannica*, compiling dictionaries, in fact, before
> learning the language and making cryptograms for Cornish students
> that take ten times as long to unravel as they did to write, while all the
> time the language itself was being spoken by the poor old "backjowster"
> bringing fish round to the back-door, or even by the bent old gardener,
> mowing the grass in front of the library window, from whom – alas! – it
> would be *infra dig.* to learn.[50]

So, on reflection, it would appear that Nance's disregard for Late Cornish
was really based on the fact that the Cornish handed down and to which he had
access was not the true Cornish of the time, but a form corrupted by those who
were not indigenous speakers of the language and who had cobbled together
something from what little they knew of it, bolstered up with extraneous bits
and pieces. However, this should not have led him to disregard truly idiomatic
Cornish in such writings as *The Creation of the World*. Another facet of Nance's
'Unified' Cornish which drew criticism (particularly from Smith) has not yet
been mentioned – his over-use of hyphens. Smith wrote to Hooper of the
amount of work he had to do 'in getting Mordon to see my points, e.g. to omit
hyphens (except to join up enclitics, e.g. ny allaf-vy, etc)';[51] and in a later letter,
he refers to 'seeing Cornish uglified by a superabundance of hyphens.'[52] It is
unfortunate that Nance received so much criticism, but then in any pioneering
work criticism does come thick and fast.

What else can be said about Nance? That he worked assiduously for the language cannot be denied, but what were his aspirations? Undoubtedly to see
Cornish succeed – who would not, having put so much time and effort into it? –
but, it has to be conceded, mainly as a concise medieval written medium. He
did mention at times the conversational use of Cornish, but from what has been
said by others, he did not himself speak it a lot. Smith says in a letter that while
robing in St John's Hall, Penzance, prior to attending the Gorsedd at the Merry

Maidens in 1932, 'Mordon a-wruk pysy warnan na-wrellyn kewsel Kernewek y'n Orseth, ha henna rak own an ruth a dus dhe sevel ha gul tros'[53] [*Mordon begged us not to speak Cornish at the Gorsedd, just in case a crowd of people should stand up and make a fuss*]. In another letter Smith wrote: 'Cows Kernewek yu moy y vern ages cows adro dhe'n Kernewek, del wra Mordon'[54] [*Talking Cornish is more important than talking about Cornish, as Mordon does*]. G. Pawley White also noted that when Nance stated at the 1952 Gorsedd that he was downhearted because he did not see any future in Cornish when nobody was speaking it, he said it in English.[55] But, of course, Nance did not always receive criticism – there was also praise. It has already been noted, for example, that Roparz Hemon congratulated Nance on *Cornish for All*. He also earned praise from Richard Hall for tackling the complexities of Cornish spelling in the 1920s, and in a footnote to a letter from Smith, Hooper wrote: 'Nyns oma sur ny dhe wul justys lowr dhe Vordon rak an ober bras a wrug-e gul. Gwyr yu bos cansow a fowtow y'n gerlyver, bytegens yma ynno cansow a eryow da re be cuntellys gans Mordon y honen' [*I am not sure that we do Mordon sufficient justice for the great work he did. It's true that there are hundreds of mistakes in the dictionary; however, there are hundreds of good words in it which Mordon collected himself*]. These words and thoughts have been echoed in more recent times, when it has been said that without Nance there would be a far smaller number of fluent speakers today.[56] As previously noted, even Smith had good words to say about him, writing on one occasion: 'Mordon a-wor moy a Gernow ha Kernewek ages dyscajoryon Kembry oll warbarth: nyns-yns mes fleghes orto-ef'[57] [*Mordon knows more of Cornwall and Cornish than all Welsh teachers put together: they are mere children compared to him*]. And again, in a letter to Cargeeg he wrote: 'He is the only man alive who is capable of grasping problems which have arisen in connection with the language, and I should certainly not know as much as I do now but for the fact that there was one man who had the time and inclination to go thoroughly into these matters, especially problems connected with the Texts'.[58] Praise indeed from a man who over the years had been so critical.

So that was Robert Morton Nance. There is so much more one could say about him. There are those who rate him highly, there are those who decry his work. He has been condemned for living with his head in medieval clouds, severely criticised for his 'reconstruction' work and castigated for his 'Unified' spelling system. But whatever is said about him, it cannot be denied that he contributed a huge amount to the knowledge and spread of Cornish. If he had not been with us, where would the Cornish language be today? Would it have died away into insignificance, even perhaps into oblivion, or would the torch have been carried by someone else – perhaps W.C.D. Watson (*Tirvab*) or R. St Vincent Allin-Collins (*Hal Wyn*) – and been carried down a much different path? Who knows?

Notes

1. R. Morton Nance (1958) 'Cornish Beginnings' in *Old Cornwall*, vol. 5, no. 9, 1958, p. 369.
2. R. Morton Nance (1938) 'Wales & the Cornish Language & Gorsedd' (paper read to the Royal Institution of South Wales, Swansea, 24 February 1938), Nance Collection, Courtney Library, Royal Institution of Cornwall, Truro.
3. P.A.S. Pool (1967) 'The Cornish Language' in *The Cornish Review*, no. 4, New Year 1967, pp. 9–10.
4. Henry Jenner (1904) *A Handbook of the Cornish Language*, London: David Nutt, p. xii.
5. Statement by R.R.M. Gendall in a personal conversation with the author.
6. R. Morton Nance 'Cornish in 1951', Nance Collection, Courtney Library.
7. R. Morton Nance 'The Revival of Cornish', Nance Collection, Courtney Library.
8. Cited in Pool (1967), p. 12. In his *Cornish for Beginners* (3rd revised edition, 1970), Pool dates this quotation to 1955.
9. Nance (1938).
10. R. Morton Nance 'Gwary Abram hag Ysak', Nance Collection, Courtney Library.
11. R. Morton Nance, Letter to F.B. Cargeeg, 8 May 1934 (private hands).
12. R. Hall, Letter to R. Morton Nance, 7 September 1922, Nance Collection, Courtney Library.
13. R. Hall, Letter to R. Morton Nance, 14 October 1922, ibid.
14. Nance Collection, Courtney Library.
15. R. Morton Nance (1929) 'Cornish for All' in *Old Cornwall*, vol. 1, no. 10, October 1929, pp. 36–38.
16. Ibid., p. 37.
17. Roparz Hemon, Letter to R. Morton Nance, 9 November 1929, Nance Collection, Courtney Library.
18. R. Morton Nance (1930) 'Cornish for All' in *Old Cornwall*, vol. 1, no.11, Summer 1930, p. 19.
19. R. Morton Nance (1933) 'Cornish for All' in *Old Cornwall*, vol. 2, no. 5, Summer 1933, pp. 27–28.
20. *Old Cornwall*, vol. 2, no. 7, Summer 1934, p. 35 & inside front cover.
21. 'Cornish Language' in *Old Cornwall*, vol. 2, no. 10, Winter 1935, p. 43.
22. A.S.D. Smith, Letter to F.B. Cargeeg, 17 March 1937 (private hands).
23. A.S.D. Smith, Letter to F.B. Cargeeg, 4 July 1937 (private hands).
24. *Old Cornwall*, vol. 3, no. 3, Summer 1938, following p. 132.
25. 'New Cornish Dictionary', ibid., p. 116.
26. A.S.D. Smith, Letter to E.G.R. Hooper, 30 October 1938, Talek Papers, Cornish Gorsedd Archives.
27. A.S.D. Smith, Letter to E.G.R. Hooper, 22 January 1940, Talek Papers, Cornish Gorsedd Archives.
28. R. Morton Nance, Notes on the Tregear Manuscript, Nance Collection, Courtney Library.
29. A.S.D. Smith, Letter to R. Morton Nance, 1 March 1950, Nance Collection, Courtney Library.
30. The paper was delivered on 20 December 1949, and the text appeared as 'Something new in Cornish' in Journal of the Royal Institution of Cornwall, New series, vol. 1, part 2, 1952, pp. 119–121.

31. R. Morton Nance (1950) 'The Tregear Manuscript' in *Old Cornwall*, vol. 4, no. 11, Summer 1950, pp. 429–434.
32. R. Morton Nance (1951) 'More about the Tregear Manuscript' in *Old Cornwall*, vol. 5, no. 1, Summer 1951, p. 23.
33. Ibid., p. 24.
34. R. Morton Nance (1952) *An English-Cornish Dictionary*: Marazion: Federation of Old Cornwall Societies, p. [v].
35. Cutting in Nance Collection, Courtney Library.
36. R. Morton Nance, Letter to F.B. Cargeeg, 12 December 1936 (private hands).
37. Charles Taylor (?), Letter to A.S.D. Smith, 12 July 1937, Talek Papers, Cornish Gorsedd Archives.
38. R. Morton Nance 'Notes on Cornish Miracle-Play Manuscripts', Nance Collection, Courtney Library.
39. *Interview with Gunwyn… 26th July 2000 [by W.E. Chapman]*, Falmouth: Tower Films.
40. Nance (1938).
41. R. Morton Nance, Letter to Mr King, 29 January 1931, Nance Collection, Courtney Library.
42. R. Morton Nance (1922) 'Celtic Words in Cornish Dialect. II' in *The eighty-eighth Annual Report of the Royal Cornwall Polytechnic Society*, New series, vol. 4, part 4, 1921–1922, p. 71.
43. A.S.D. Smith, Letter to R. Morton Nance, 10 February 1941, Cornish Gorsedd Archives.
44. R. Morton Nance, Letter to F.B. Cargeeg, 18 June 1934 (private hands).
45. Note, Nance Collection, Courtney Library.
46. R. Morton Nance 'The Celtic Bird-Names of Cornwall', Nance Collection, Courtney Library.
47. A.S.D. Smith, Letter to F.B. Cargeeg, 4 July 1937 (private hands).
48. Personal conversation with the author, Penzance, 1 March 2006.
49. Nance (1922), p. 78.
50. Ibid., p. 72.
51. A.S.D. Smith, Letter to E.G.R. Hooper, 12 October 1949, Talek Papers, Cornish Gorsedd Archives.
52. A.S.D. Smith, Letter to E.G.R. Hooper, 6 May 1950, ibid.
53. A.S.D. Smith, Letter, probably to E.G.R. Hooper, 1939 or 1944, ibid. (photocopy of p. 2 only).
54. A.S.D. Smith, Letter to E.G.R. Hooper, 29 December 1945, ibid.
55. *Interview with Gunwyn… 26th July 2000*.
56. Personal conversations between the author and, in particular, P.A.S. Pool, Audrey Randle Pool and Ann Trevenen Jenkin.
57. A.S.D. Smith, Letter to E.G.R. Hooper, 14 January 1940, Talek Papers, Cornish Gorsedd Archives.
58. A.S.D. Smith, Letter to F.B. Cargeeg, 25 December 1947 (private hands).

Two Poems by Robert Morton Nance

Can Kernow Dyvres [1]

Pup ur-oll down y'm colon-vy, galow
   Pur gref son y lef dhym a-gry:
Dres an nor, tyr ha mor, dus dhe'm hallow, ha salow
   Y'm gwryth ty a-vyth, pur dhefry.

Yn cres nos dre hunros, Kernow gerys,
   A-bell my a-th-whel pur dhyblans,
Hag a-vyr dres forth hyr, degemerys ow spyrys,
   Dre hyreth orth tyreth a'm whans.

Kynth hevelly dhys pell dha vos neghys,
   Ankevys genef byth nyns-os;
Scullyes yns gans an gwyns, delyow seghys, dha fleghes,
   Dhe'th pren mar ny-lenens pur glos.

Kyn fyf kellys mar bell lyes bledhen,
   Ow holon a-wolsow dhe'th lef;
Nyns-of delen dywelen, na gwedhen dywredhen,
   Ow gwryth prest y'm tythy a-sef.

[Song of a Cornish Exile

Always, deep in my heart, a call, the healing charm of its voice crying most urgently to me: over the earth, land and sea, come to my moors, and my roots will keep you truly safe.

In the middle of the night, as I dream, beloved Cornwall, I see you very clearly from afar, and, over a long road, my spirit accepted, through longing I look at the land of my desire.

Though it seemed to you for a long time that you were disavowed, I never forget you; your children, dried leaves, are scattered by the wind unless they cling very closely to your tree.

Though I have been lost so far away for many years, my heart hears your voice; I am not a leaf without a stem, nor a rootless tree, my roots stand firm always in the place where I belong.]

Lost Gwyn[2]

Ha Lost Gwyn an conyn ow kerdhes un jeth,
Y teth erbyn gwas ganso gwarak ha seth:
"Na den orthyf," dhodho y pysys, "dremas;
Whek yu dhym ow bewnans ow quary y'n pras."

Yn meth an gwas, "Awos dha gows my a den,
Rag dhym yma ethom a'th kyk hag a'th ken:
Dha gyk a vyth kynyow dhym, denty ha tom
Ha'th ken a vyth cappa, ow fen na vo lom."

Yn meth Lost Gwyn, "Ankevy, sur, ty a wra,
A'm kyk ha'm ken dhym, ynweth, ethom yma."
Y tennas an gwas; mes y seth eth dhe goll,
Rag Lost Gwyn o scusys dhe woles y doll!

[*White-Tail*

As White-Tail the rabbit was walking one day, he came upon a man with a bow and arrow: "Don't shoot at me, there's a kind chap," he pleaded. "Life is sweet for me, playing in the meadow."

The man said, "I will shoot despite what you say, for I need your flesh and your skin: your flesh will make dinner for me, tender and hot, and your skin will be a cap, to keep me from going bareheaded."

White-Tail said, "Surely you forget that I too need my flesh and my skin." The man shot; but his arrow was wasted, for White-Tail had scurried to the bottom of his hole!]

Notes

1. First printed in *Old Cornwall*, vol. 3, no. 9, Summer 1941, pp. 360–361, with A.L. Mata's music. English translation by Peter W. Thomas.

2. First printed ibid., vol. 10, no. 2, Spring 1986, p. 101. English translation by Peter W. Thomas. There is a photocopy of a manuscript version of this (not in Nance's hand) among the Talek Papers, Cornish Gorsedd Archives. The only difference in wording between the two is that the manuscript has 'Y tuth' at the beginning of the second line. Underneath the handwritten version is written 'Mordon typed Caradar 20/9/1941', with a note that it was sent to *Old Cornwall* in October 1985. Though Nance was not a poet of Charles Causley's stature, this poem seems to stem from similar impulses to those which led Causley to write the much more powerful *I Saw a Jolly Hunter*.

Acknowledgement

These poems are reprinted by kind permission of the Federation of Old Cornwall Societies.

'Some ancientry that lingers': Dissent, Difference and Dialect in the Cornish and Cornu-English Literature of Robert Morton Nance

Alan M. Kent

Collision and Conflation in 'Mordon'

In recent years, no figure has perhaps been more celebrated or vilified in Cornish culture than the subject of this volume: Robert Morton Nance. Celebrated not only for acting as the true ignition point of the twentieth-century Cornish language revival and the invention of the Cornish Gorsedd,[1] but also for rediscovering and recording much 'lost' folklore of western Britain,[2] Nance has also been fiercely attacked for his apparently 'synthetic' construction of Unified Cornish[3] (untouched and ignored for many years by the mainstream Celtic academic establishment)[4] and his 'reconstructionist' approach to culture, merging the 'found' and newly-created, so that they became fused. To his supporters, Nance offers a productive example of textual nationalism in the collision of past and present. To his detractors, his conflation is an unhistoric 'invention'.

While Nance has been ardently championed by some observers, such as Smith, Pool and Weatherhill,[5] and ignored until now by Celtic Studies, his influence (waning in the 1980s, when Unified Cornish was under its most severe scrutiny and deconstruction)[6] has been undeniable. In the twenty-first century, some observers began a new appreciation of his work, arguing that given the important textual and manuscript discoveries of recent years (such as *The Tregear Homilies* and *Beunans Ke*),[7] his 'Unified' Cornish project was not as problematical as was first feared. Since 1995, a reformed version of Unified Cornish has been promoted by some speakers and writers as still the best direction for Cornish.[8] Alongside a wider appreciation of earlier Cornish activists (such as L.C. R. Duncombe Jewell, Henry Jenner and Katharine Lee Jenner)[9] and a seriousness about Cornwall's relationship to Celtic Studies (neglected for much of the late nineteenth and twentieth centuries),[10] Nance now appears to be one of the most interesting cultural-revivalist figures of modern times.

This essay seeks to re-evaluate Nance's often undervalued literary work in English as well as Cornish. As I hope it will demonstrate, Nance's work provides an interesting touchstone of dissent, both within British-Celtic literature of the period and wider devolutionary political debate. Nance was seemingly a less confident author in Cornish than in Cornu-English, itself an issue that resonates with all kinds of controversy, particularly with those aligned to the Cornish Gorsedd and Celtic activists in Cornwall who see the Cornish language as the foremost demarcation of Cornish claims to nationhood and Celticity.

The Cornu-English Poetry: Passels of Pasties and Press Gangs

The earliest and most neglected phase of Nance's literary career is his Cornu-English poetry. The reasons for this neglect are not difficult to understand. Most of the surviving literature was written when Nance was still a young man in his mid-twenties, and when his fame lay chiefly in his work as an artist and artisan rather than scholar and writer. Secondly, at first glance, the material may appear rather trifling when compared to the nation-defining work of his later life; and perhaps thirdly, like his Cornu-English drama, being written in English guaranteed that this work would be relatively easily marginalised. No doubt Nance had been developing his literary talent since his teens, but it did not come to full realisation until he was twenty-five, when the scholar of English literature and Anglo-Cornish poet and novelist, Arthur Quiller-Couch,[11] offered him the opportunity to contribute to his new publication *The Cornish Magazine*.

Quiller-Couch's purpose with the magazine was to gather Cornish talent to provide articles, fiction and poetry, but also to encourage, in its 'Opinions of Eminent Cornishmen and Others' section, debate and discussion over the future direction of Cornwall in the wake of industrial decline. A certain kind of article came to personify the identity of *The Cornish Magazine*. Aimed at Cornish exiles, as well as those at home, the theme of the series was celebratory and historical, typical articles being on 'Truro Cathedral', 'Madame Fanny Moody at Home: A Talk with the Cornish Nightingale' and 'The Duchy's Harvest'.[12] Nance had been asked by Quiller-Couch to contribute artwork for the magazine – notably a motif made for the 'Opinions' page, comprising five fish and a scrolled banner bearing the motto 'One and All' in Celtic script.[13] Other smaller folkloric motifs (such as piskies) and symbols also feature in later issues.

At the same time he must have submitted the idea of larger illustrations coupled with Cornish poetry. Nance was in good company in the magazine; other core contributors included James Dryden Hosken, Eden Phillpotts, H.D. Lowry and S. Baring-Gould. To the first issue of the magazine Nance contributes 'The Merry Ballad of the Cornish Pasty'. Apparently written to the 'tune of The Leather Bottel', the poem is accompanied by three classic Nance illustrations. The first is a young woman rolling out pastry to make a pasty; the second – a full page illustration – is of a 'merry' party cavorting in the streets; the third is of an old man on a boat. The second is the most interesting and also the strangest of the three, as the party is made up of characters from the 1660s rather than the 1860s, and features bombard-like instruments. It is an imagining of festive Cornish-speaking Cornwall, with a notable Breton 'gaze'. The poem itself consists of seven verses of four couplets and celebrates the pasty as a staple in working communities (mining, fishing and farming) and later as a bond between couples. For the rhythm to work, Nance liberally doses the text with anachronisms (o'er, hath, victuals) while the overall rhyme is written in dactylic metre:

> When the Tinner to Bal takes a touchpipe for crowse
> He cannot have Hot-meat sent from his house:
> Yet hath no stomach for victuals cold,

Decorative drawing by Robert Morton Nance for The Cornish Magazine

> So a Pasty he takes in a Napkin rolled:
> And though he leave it for half the day,
> Within his Hogan Bag warm 'twill stay.
> So I wish him joy whoever he be
> That first found out the Cornish Pastie.[14]

In exploring folklore through the imagery of food, the poem reminds us of Charles Causley, with the same game-playing with language employed by the twentieth-century Launceston poet.[15] And while there are echoes of nineteenth-century Anglo-Cornish poetry, notably in the vocabulary of mining,[16] the poem does not achieve the quality of his later Cornu-English work, and compared to the work of other dialect poets of the period,[17] it relies heavily on Standard English. Nevertheless, this is a charming poem, and perhaps no more than an amusing look at Cornwall's most famous food:

> When of dancing the Maidens have had their fill:
> Although their swains would be dancing still:
> Is not Nick's Pasty the sweeter yet
> For being shared with his sweetheart Bet?
> And does not Jan's the better taste,

For that his Jenifer made the paste?
So I wish him joy whoever he be
That first found out the Cornish Pastie.[18]

Nance was to become the foremost folklorist of Cornwall in the early half of the twentieth century, distorting perceptions of his earlier writing and accentuating its cultural relevance. In other circumstances the poem might have become better known, perhaps featuring on postcards and other tourist products,[19] though to be fair, it is the lead poem in Stephen Hall's study of the history of the Cornish pasty, published in 2001.[20] It is difficult to deduce the impact of Nance's poem in 1898, although it is curious that for what seems to have been his next poetic endeavour, he published anonymously. With his version of 'The Press-Gang'[21] we begin to discern the hallmarks of Nance's later literary activity. 'The Press-Gang' has many of the features of the former poem – narrative, with long stanzas and end rhymes, here formed into double quatrains – but there is also the earliest play with dialect and an attempt to imitate the real Cornu-English voice (jist, vather, passel, wrastling, 'un, 'ee).

It is here, however, that the reconstructionist position of Nance first emerges. He rightly labels the poem an 'Old Ballad'. As Ralph Dunstan, quoting an unidentified source, tells us, the 'ditty was sung not only from the Tamar to the Land's End, but from Barnstaple Bay to the Rame Head'.[22] Dunstan was writing a good deal later than Nance, in 1932, but notes that Christopher Childs of Liskeard had succeeded in piecing the song together 'from fragments scattered over Cornwall'[23] and a version was also printed by R.N. Worth in his *West Country Garland* of 1875.[24] The version printed by Worth is very similar to Nance's retelling, but Nance's version is more infused with Cornu-English. Dunstan himself notes that '[t]here is a fund of rich vernacular in this old song'[25] – which presumably Nance wished to exploit further. In accentuating the Cornu-English of the piece, Nance would appear to be trying to convince the reader of its 'ancientness' in a new attempt to define and progress Cornish identity.

As in the 'The Merry Ballad of the Cornish Pasty', the illustrations do not to my mind have much bearing on the text. The illustrated title depicts an old couple accompanied by a younger woman, the middle full-page illustration of the press-gang itself looks more like a chaotic rural scene with vague mariner figures, while the end illustration is of a smiling man, possibly a Frenchman, to whom Nance alludes in the ballad. This promulgation of 'ancientness' is not a technique that we see only in the work of Nance. Indeed, it is a feature of a number of Celtic activists and writers,[26] as well as those from elsewhere in Europe at this time,[27] ironically those very writers who were quick to dismiss Cornwall and Nance's genuine 'Celtic' credentials.

While it is easy to knock this invention, it is actually a long-standing method of operation for cultures aiming for recognition. To borrow Eric Hobsbawm and Terence Ranger's famous conceptualisation, this is Nance 'inventing tradition'.[28] It was a technique that formed the basis of his literary work – both in drama and in poetry and song lyrics. 'The Press-Gang' is more dated than 'The Merry Ballad of the Cornish Pasty' because it deals with preconceived folkloric ideas about press-gangs and their impact and is set against the background of years of conflict with France. There are some wonderful touches of the different attitudes between Cornwall and England, and a description of Plymouth – the first English city that most Cornish people encounter:

> When I went up to Plymouth town,
> There to a inn a hostling,
> I went over to Maker Green
> To ha' a scat to wrastling.
> A pair o' leatheren breeches was the prize,
> A little the wuss for wear;
> Jan Jordan and I drawed two valls a-piece,
> And Dick Simmons comed in for a share.[29]

Nance's poem contains the observation that English crews pick upon Cornishmen to 'press' into service, while Cornish lads usually know how to outwit the rigours of service in the Navy, but can also do justice to fighting the French. As in the fiction of Joseph Hocking, this is Cornish internationalism at its very best, with other nations having respect for Cornish bravery, ingenuity and technical skill. The ballad is both comic and action-filled, its Standard English cleverly mixed with Cornu-English:

> Then this here French ship up she come,
>   And a whole broadside let she;
> The sulphur did vly so cruel high,
>   I could neither hear nor see.
> One got his head a nackèd off
>   By means o' a cannon ball;
> My Lor! ses I, if it's honour to die,
>   I don't like sich honour at all.[30]

The final stanza may also be problematical for Cornish activists. While the central characters of the poem threaten a good dose of Cornu-English 'what vor' if the French ever raid Cornwall, the plea is to maintain 'Old England's right'. Nance may have reached a point of cultural enlightenment in his understanding of the history of Cornwall in its relations with the rest of Britain, but he was not about to subvert the tradition that far. As we shall see, it was a concept that was to be repeated in his interest in Christmas folk drama. The reconstructionist project is also present in 'Cawsand Bay'[31] described as an 'Old Ditty'. The reality suggests that although the narrative may have been about an earlier period in history, the 'Old Ditty' was composed in 1898. Like 'The Press-Gang', this poem has a nautical theme, reflecting Nance's lifelong interest in the subject.[32] His accompanying illustrations fit their purpose well here. The theme of this poem is sailor Henry Grady's courting of a young lady. A captain is jealous of the sailor and argues that he is not good enough for her, yet she knows Henry to be a good man. The poem is another project showing the Cornish working classes making good, despite prejudice:

> Then she got a shore tailor for to rig up her sailor
>   In white nankeen trowsers and long blue-tailed coat;
> And he looked like a squi-er, for all to admi-er,
>   With a dimity handkercher tied round his throat.[33]

In 1899, the second year of *The Cornish Magazine*, Nance's poetry became less prolific, though he did illustrate a comic poem of Quiller-Couch's about the Duke of Cornwall's Light Infantry, entitled 'The Big Review'.[34] The song 'Sweet

Nightingale' was also illustrated by Nance,[35] the lyric being described as another 'old ditty' commonly sung in Cornwall, and he illustrated another poem, 'Parson Hogg', as well (with a wheel-headed cross),[36] but whether the poem is a Nance composition is not known. Certainly the chorus pattern is strongly Nance, but the organisation of the text is somewhat different. While there is a fine record of Nance's dialect and language studies in the Nance Collection in the Courtney Library of the Royal Institution of Cornwall, there is only minimal further evidence of his Cornu-English poetry. There is an unpublished later skit titled 'The Terrors of the Deep: An Off-Fish-ial Guide to Cornwall'. The poem is a comedic exploration of the Cornish names for fish, beginning with:

> I'd always loved the finny tribe
>   That dwells in the deep blue sea –
> Studies icthyological [sic], that some folk "stodgy" call,
>   Never seemed dry to me.[37]

It contains a conversation with a 'grey old man'[38] at Mousehole, who offers in English and Cornish a dizzying, half-rhyming and other-worldly litany of local sea creatures:

> The guckows; pezaks; wrahs and wreaks;
>   The crogans and gweeans; the zarts;
> Calcars; cōblas; and conks; guzzalezzas and monks,
>   And keligans of those parts...[39]

Cornish and Cornu-English are here thoroughly mingled. Marine vocabulary, of course, would be a core theme of Nance's study of the Cornish language.[40] Though such verse cannot, in any sense of the word, be labelled great, we have a tantalising glimpse of a man who might even have become a major Cornish poet writing in English. Nance's route as a writer, however, would not be that simple.

In the end, Quiller-Couch's project lasted only a couple of years, but the magazine remains a useful portrait of Cornwall at the end of the 1890s. As successive scholars have commented, Quiller-Couch was passionate about Cornwall, but more cynical over the aims of the wider Cornish Revival,[41] not least the revival of Cornish, and also in new performances of medieval Cornish drama, where he argued that the audience would have to be acting harder than the actors.[42] However, Nance and Quiller-Couch remained friends, and Quiller-Couch was made a bard at the first Cornish Gorsedd in 1928.[43] Nance's earliest steps into poetry were, indeed, tenuous and a little laboured, but there is much evidence of his talent, even if it is couched in innocent subject-matter. That said, at times there are indications of a radicalised future literature and activism. By the end of 1899, his alignment with the literary establishment of Cornwall was clear, while at the same time, his first interest – in Cornu-English as both marker of difference and as mechanism of entry into Cornish itself – had been established.

The Cornu-English Drama

The middle phase of Nance's writing in English is dominated by his interest in mummers' plays and Christmas and folk dramas. Although there is no record of how he came to be aware of the Cornish dimension of this tradition, it is perhaps through his interest in Cornish language drama that he first encountered the existing mummers' plays of Cornwall, as well as those documented but now lost. Mummers' plays, as R.J.E. Tiddy and E.K. Chambers argue in their classic studies *The Mummers' Play* (1923) and *The English Folk Play* (1933),[44] have been performed for hundreds of years. They are usually folk dramas based on the legend of St George and the Seven Champions of Christendom, the principal characters being St George (sometimes Sir George, King George, Prince George), Captain Slasher, the Turkish Knight, the King of Egypt, a Doctor and several men-at-arms. Minor characters bear a great variety of names, normally locally determined. After a brief prologue, the characters introduce themselves, or are introduced, in basic rhymes. A duel or several duels follow, and one or other of the combatants is killed. The Doctor then enters and demonstrates his skills by resuscitating the dead knight. Supernumerary grotesque characters are then presented, and a collection is made.

Performed usually at Christmas or at the end of the year, the plays are connected with a celebration of the death of the year and its resurrection in the spring, and as Hutton demonstrated in his ground-breaking 1994 study *The Rise and Fall of Merry England*, a crucial theatrical component of the 'ritual year' in England.[45] All the characters were played by men who kept the same part for many years. Eventually dialogue was added, and was passed on by word of mouth through generations of performers. A useful and celebrated depiction of mumming is to be found in Book 2, Chapters 4–6 of Thomas Hardy's *The Return of the Native* (1878) in which the heroine Eustacia Vye disguises herself as the Turkish Knight, in the place of the young lad Charley, in order to engineer a meeting with Clym Yeobright.[46] Hardy also incorporated elements of mumming and folk drama into his singular 1923 play *The Famous Tragedy of the Queen of Cornwall at Tintagel in Lyonesse*, based on the pan-European narrative of Tristan and Iseult.[47] Indeed, the text is subtitled 'A new version of an old story arranged as a play for mummers'.

The scholar in Nance had already been drawn to the surviving medieval plays outside of Cornwall, but his rediscovery of texts such as 'The Truro Mummers' Play', 'The Truro Cordwainers' Play' and 'The Mylor Christmas Play'[48] supported his developing notion that Cornwall had a complex and sustained folk drama tradition of its own. The acceptance of a separate English-language tradition of drama within Cornwall inevitably led Nance to make a connection between the populace (who he imagined spoke Cornu-English) and the drama which most suited them. His project, therefore, was to encourage interest in Cornu-English, leading performers and their audience into a re-engagement with Cornish itself, a view which Jenner (Nance's mentor) had expressed earlier, but which was broadly rejected later on in the Revivalist movement. Cornu-English was most often sidelined, and – as we have learnt here – considered second best. Nance's fascination with Cornu-English did not sit well with a Revivalist culture seemingly hell-bent on a Cornish language future, resistant to all things English. Looking back, it is easy to see how this happened, but also how naive the view was. The subject of St George is not restricted to English culture alone, and despite several recent attempts to 'erase' perceived English material, St George and his narrative always formed a crucial part of the pictorial and lyrical backdrop. Nance knew that the legend has been integrated into Cornish folk culture and was therefore unafraid of addressing and reworking the material. In very many ways, it was a brave move.

Historical interest in St George paradoxically features in two of Cornwall's most 'Cornish' festivals – the Helston 'Furry' or 'Flora Day' and Padstow May Day.[49] Quite early on in his folkloric studies of Cornwall, Nance identified the importance of these days in the Cornish ritual year and became intensely interested in their origins and development. Both had elements of mumming within their festivals. As Deane and Shaw note, 'The Furry' is 'perhaps derived from the Cornish *fer*, meaning 'fair' or 'feast-day''[50] and was originally held to celebrate the Feast Day of St Michael on 8 May. Nance's major interest in the May celebrations at Helston, however, was in the so-called 'Hal-an-tow'. The ceremony of the 'Hal-an-tow' was revived by Helston Old Cornwall Society in 1930, with much input from Nance,[51] so that it has become associated with 'The Furry'. However, the ceremony and song of 'Hal-an-tow' seem a good deal older, with their roots in May ritual and mumming. The characters are standard mumming characters; Robin Hood was a popular character, as was St George. Spanish references in the ceremony may be linked to the attacks made on Mousehole and Paul in 1595. This version is recorded by the nineteenth-century writer William Sandys:

> Robin Hood and Little John,
>   They both are gone to Fair, O,
> And we will go to the merry green wood
>   To see what they do there, O
> And for to chase, O,
> To chase the buck and doe,
>   With Halantow,
>   Rumbelow!

> For we were up as soon as any day, O,
>   And for to fetch the Summer home.
> The Summer, and the May, O,
>   For Summer is a-come, O,
>   And Winter is a-gone, O!

Where are those Spaniards,
   That make so great a boast, O?
They shall eat the grey goose feather,
   And we will eat the roast, O;
In every land, O,
The land, where'er we go.
         With Halantow, etc.

As for St George, O,
   Saint George, he was a Knight, O!
Of all the Knights in Christendom,
  Saint Georgy is the right, O!
In every land, O,
The land where'er we go.
         With Halantow, etc.

God bless Aunt Mary Moses,
   And all her powers and might, O,
And send us peace in merry England,
   Both day and night, O,
And send us peace in merry England,
Both now and evermore, O!
         With Halantow, etc.[52]

'Hal-an-tow' offers all kinds of problematical issues, with mention of 'merry England' the tip of a cultural-imperialist iceberg. For all its possible pagan origins, the piece is fundamentally Christian, reflecting a transitional phase in Cornwall's history when it was being incorporated into England geographically, as well as politically. Yet the piece remains resolutely Cornish, Deane and Shaw offering an interesting definition of the language of its chorus:

> The chorus of the Hal-an-Tow song has been dismissed as a corruption of 'heel-and-toe' but this seems dubious. In the mid-seventeenth century the custom was referred to as the 'haille-an-taw': *hal*, or *hayl*, is a Cornish

word meaning 'moorland', while *tyow* means 'houses'. Surely, then, hal-an-tow could represent 'in the moorland (country) and the town'; 'rum-blelow' is a word denoting jollity and movement, so the full line would translate as 'in the country and the town there will be merrymaking'.[53]

This is not fully convincing, however, as the etymology is somewhat con-trived. According to Murdoch, there is a more likely translation to be found in modern Dutch:[54] 'haal an touw', meaning 'haul on the rope'. The obscurity of its origins has not stopped some wanting to 'Cornishise' the song. Sowena, a con-temporary Cornish folk-group, recently recorded a version of the song which substitutes St Piran for St George.[55] St George makes further appearances in Cornish folk dramas, notably in a now discarded version of the Day Song at Padstow:

> Awake, St George, our English knight O,
> For summer is acome O and winter is a-go,
> And every day God give us his grace,
> By day and night O.
>
> Where is St George, where is he O,
> He is out in his long-boat all on the salt sea O,
> And in every land O, the land that ere we go.
>
> And for to fetch the summer home, the summer and the May O,
> For summer is acome O, and winter is a-go.[56]

Nance has legitimacy in using St George for cultural revivalist purposes in Cornwall. If Helston and Padstow could use it in May, then there was good rea-son for him to use it at Christmas. This he did in one of Cornwall's finest sur-viving modern mumming plays 'The Christmas Play of Saint George and the Turkish Knight'. Among the Nance Collection at the Courtney Library, Royal Institution of Cornwall, there are numerous drafts of the play. I have selected the 'prompt copy' for accuracy, not least for the additional marks made on the stage directions, but also for the additional lines (added in Nance's hand). The interested reader can seek out the minor variations of the texts. This would appear to be the version of the play that was successfully produced at a Christmas meeting of St Ives Old Cornwall Society. The Nance Collection also contains much correspondence on mumming traditions elsewhere in Britain, as well as notes, articles and theories on the same subject. Here, the characters broadly resemble those found elsewhere: Saint George (played originally by Nance), The Turkish Knight (played by A.K. Hamilton Jenkin), The King of Egypt and The Doctor (Bernard Leach). However, Nance also adds Father Christmas (R.J. Noall), Princess Sabra (Phoebe Nance), Slasha and The Dragon. Michael Cardew also performed in the original version, but it is unclear which part he played. The parts appear to have been in draft for some time, in a continuous state of evolution. Indeed, there is a shorter draft from 1911, which appears to have been acted in Nancledra in that year, a good deal earlier than traditional scholarship of the Revival suggests.

The play begins with a two-part Prologue, written in rhyming couplets. Speaking as if he is a member of the audience, one of the players asks 'Who comes here, this time of night,/Neither by day nor by candle-light?' and in response, enters Father Christmas, who pleads for 'room' for the actors who follow.[57] The stage directions inform us that 'no scenery is required',[58] making the performance characteristically mobile. Father Christmas is, of course, a useful seasonal touch, but also acts as narrator for the start of the main action – the entrance of the King of Egypt and his daughter Princess Sabra, whose speech ends in a rhyming couplet. The Turkish Knight salaams (makes a low bow in the Islamic fashion, with his right palm on his forehead) as he arrives to inform them that '[a] dragon vile/Has left the waters of the Nile'[59] and has been terrorising the locality. The King demands that the Knight should provide food for the dragon, but the audience soon learns that the creature wants younger meat. Lots are drawn and it is Sabra who is to be fed to the dragon; yet the Knight is too cowardly to fight for her. The Princess describes the pathetic nature of the Turkish Knight, with Nance using the language of mining and metallurgy to hammer home the point in controlled and powerful couplets.[60]

Act II begins with an image of Sabra in chains. Nance's touches are both apt and amusing. The stage directions say that 'her chain may be made of twisted paper or cardboard. Links painted gold'.[61] This suits the seasonal popularity of such home-made decorations. At the same time, Sabra's triplet plea carries the real sense of horror she faces:

> I hear his horrid jaws go snap;
> I hear his leathern pinions flap;
> I hear his claws that beat the ground – [62]

At this point St George enters 'on Hobby Horse'[63] to a flourish of trumpets. Nance, being an artist, cleverly imagined exactly how he wanted the Hobby Horse to work in the production, and within the Courtney Library's Nance Collection are several detailed drawings of the costume design. He obviously had in mind the Padstow Obby Oss, though the eventual design owes perhaps more to children's toys than the ritualised dance from North Cornwall. The St George imagined here is identical to that of the Hal-an-tow of Helston and the Day Song of Padstow. Nance gives him 'corny' lines, but they are essential to the character, if the overall mumming is to work. St George is a kind of Everyman, and if he does not speak in Cornu-English, he is at least straight-talking and honest.[64] The conflict with the dragon is comic. As we might expect, there are touches of the Mechanicals performing 'Pyramus and Thisbe' in Shakespeare's *A Midsummer Night's Dream*. Nance also designed the dragon's costume in some detail, allowing it to be mobile and to be chased by St George. The dragon has melodramatic rhyming couplets, filled with 'bad' rhymes ('Ho! Ho! Here's something like a dinner!/I'll snap her nose off, to begin her!')[65] which enhance the deliberate amateurishness of the production. However, there is a complexity in the direction, with later diagrams showing the exact moves St George and the Turkish Knight are to make in their choreography. The effect, then, is to make the piece seem 'amateur' while being highly stylised and non-naturalistic.[66] Once defeated, the dragon is carted off to market, with Sabra riding pillion on St George's hobby horse. Symbolically, she carries with her a lamb. It is only before the King of Egypt that St George kills the dragon. This is completed cleverly by the use of 'red flannel tatters' which 'hang from the severed neck',[67] an image strikingly medieval in nature, and perhaps used in earlier Cornish-language drama. When possible, Nance will always revert to 'folk-drama' techniques to enhance the 'ancientness'. It is both artful and sophisticated.

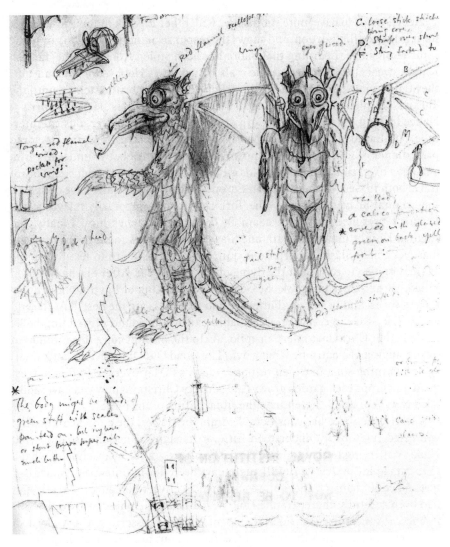

Nance's sketches for costumes for the Dragon in the St George Mummers' play
(Courtesy of the Royal Institution of Cornwall)

Act III tends to have more similarities with other English mumming dramas, for it is the conflict section, and shows the response of the 'Quack' Doctor to the injuries on stage. Learning that Sabra has been stolen from him, the Turkish Knight swears to kill St George. He is also fitted into a Hobby Horse. Comically, they fight or joust at each other with 'artichoke or other brittle stems'[68] until the Turkish Knight falls. At the Knight's death, the music is 'Helston Furry' – Nance linking the two texts of Cornish literature. It is a clever musical interlude, familiar to many in the audience. Father Christmas calls for the Doctor (a practitioner of folk medicine), who arrives with 'a huge bottle under his arm, and has a blacksmith's pincers in his girdle'.[69] The Doctor's speech is a litany of travel both in west Cornwall and in Europe.[70] This would clearly have delighted the original St Ives audience. The Turkish Knight temporarily revives at the Doctor's presence, but once again St George dispatches him. Finally, the English Knight must deal with one Slasha, who arrives to be 'avenged of my master's son'.[71] Slasha's purpose is quite clear. He is there to test St George again, but also to represent the dying of the ritual year. After Slasha has been killed, Father Christmas asks St George and the King of Egypt to 'Lay down those swords, and be at rest,/For peace and quietness are the best'.[72] At the end of Act III, St George and Princess Sabra exit to the sound of wedding-bells, while Father Christmas offers an epilogue. In the prompt copy, this is followed by the singing of a patriotic 'Trelawny', 'The Good Old Duke of York' and, finally, a mumming song in which responses such as 'May every field fine harvest yield, full crops each garden grow!/And a Merry Christmas may you have, and a good New Year also!'[73] accentuate the ritual nature of the piece.

Clearly, the piece has considerable dramatic power; the audience who first witnessed it probably understood little of its significance in terms of what Nance was trying to achieve with Cornish culture – a reconstruction of what a mumming play in west Cornwall might have been like in times past. Nance had researched his subject, and while each 'rustic' delivery had an air of realism, it had been carefully choreographed and developed to demonstrate Cornish difference. It was a piece of Yuletide dissent, aimed at asserting a very Cornish New Year. Constructed this way, St George did not need to be an imperialist symbol. He was purely a character, who happened to talk 'broad'.

The success of the Christmas play inspired Nance to continue writing drama

Nance's sketches for costumes for the St George Mummers' play
(Courtesy of the Royal Institution of Cornwall)

during the late 1920s and the early 1930s. A number of plays were drafted, but not all of the pieces have been published and these (alongside drafts of the published texts) remain in the Nance Collection. In 1956, however, three plays were selected by Nance, and published by the Federation of Old Cornwall Societies in a volume titled *The Cledry Plays: Drolls of Old Cornwall for Village Acting and Home Reading*.[74] The title of the collection was derived from Nance's fondness for the west Cornwall village of Nancledra,[75] known locally by the familiar name of Cledry, and also, according to Henry Jenner,[76] from the word 'Daralla' (Cornish: a tale) from which comes the Cornu-English term 'Droll'. Using the word 'Droll' was, of course, an act of homage to older tellers, while the 'Village Acting' and 'Home Reading' referred jointly to the folk-play heritage of Cornwall,[77] alongside the pre-radio and pre-television age of early twentieth-century home entertainment. Nance suggests in his preface to the collection that the plays were first conceived for children. I have found no evidence of drafts intended purely for children (though this is, of course, not to say they did not exist). They may have originally been conceived in this way, but perhaps even the most literate child of the 1920s would have struggled with the sheer detail of the language. In the Preface, Nance explains their assembly and development, from the perspective of the late 1950s:

> Written first nearly fifty years ago for acting by the children of a village school, these plays aimed at carrying on the West-Penwith tradition of turning local folk-tales into plays for Christmas acting. What they took over from these guise-dance drolls, as they were called, was their love of the local speech and their readiness to break here and there into rhyme or song; what they left was what in them seemed to stress the farcical at the expense of the tale to be told. From their native village they were taken round to many others as Christmas or feastentide entertainment.[78]

The evidence for the touring of these dramas in Cornwall is scarce,[79] though Nance may be referring to oral recollection. He is correct, however, with the Cornish tradition of breaking into song or poetry in the middle of a droll. Many of the tales in Bottrell and Hunt incorporate this technique,[80] very often used to accentuate the mood or emotions of a particular scene, and this method continues in all of the *Cledry Plays* and in the remaining unpublished plays. Clearly the plays went though several drafts, as can be seen in the contents of Boxes 4 and 9, and it seems likely that in urban environments and for larger occasions, minor changes in both staging and dialogue were made. Nance reflects upon this and the crucial performance of 'Duffy' which helped create the first Old Cornwall Society:[81]

> Later, grown to their present form and interpreted by mature actors, they found their town audiences too. It was a performance of "Duffy" at St Ives that led to the formation there in 1920 of the first Old Cornwall Society – and so in time to the Federation of Old Cornwall Societies and to the Cornish Gorsedd. Apart from public performances there have been many readings of these plays to small audiences of lovers of dialect.[82]

Nance is also keen to accentuate the primitive nature of the dramas, in a way Thomas Hardy might have approved. The audiences were never large, but Nance realised early on the impact of such productions: what Kershaw has termed 'a theory of performance as ideological transaction, culture intervention and community action ... used to illuminate the potential social and political effects of radical performance practice'.[83] Put another way, Nance knew that his reconfiguration of folk drama in Cornwall could actually influence socio-political history and this radicalised 'mumming' could help prevent incorporation into the status quo of early twentieth-century England. The fact that the text was written in extreme or even 'hardcore' Cornu-English was only one part of this act of cultural intervention: a process which has present-day echoes, perhaps, in the Cornu-centric work of Kneehigh Theatre and in new configurations of *Ordinalia*.[84] There were other strands to Nance's drama: the clever and sustained incorporation of phrases in Cornish, the fact that there was a 'punk' ethos of home-produced, low-tech entertainment, and the view that local people were certainly good enough to perform the pieces. As Nance comments:

> The simple airs do not ask for accompaniment or for trained voices to do them justice. They are only a slight extension of the music that West-

Penwith voices will put into the dialogue. The plays have few characters and very little change of scene; the furniture and properties should be carefully chosen, however, and the costumes and accessories convincing, if they are to have the right effect.[85]

This is an interesting statement. 'Trained voices' suggests that by now Nance rejected the imposition of Standard English and was fully committed to a linguistically-devolved drama that did not require a perceived English sophistication. Likewise, the statement was committed to the transformation of the working-class Cornish as an ideological experiment.

Three plays made up this collection: 'Duffy: A Tale of Trove', 'Sally's Shiners: A Droll of Smuggling Days' and 'The Kite in the Castle: A Legend of Lamorna'. It is hard to say why these three were published while other texts were not. Possibly, they were Nance's favourites, although there seems little difference in quality from the unpublished texts considered below. However, 'Duffy' and 'The Kite in the Castle' have character linkages (in the form of Duffy herself and Squire Lovel), so the latter at least makes for an interesting continuation of the first play. Remarkably, these texts have been more or less ignored by Cornish Studies for many years now.[86] I would like to suggest that they are the finest depiction of Cornu-English in print. Although the plays are filled with archaisms (as elsewhere in Nance's writing) in their sustained ideology, language and characterisation, there has been little to touch them in terms of their achievement. Criticism might be levelled at the texts because Cornu-English itself has altered remarkably,[87] with the result that many terms and concepts have dropped from usage, while, as I have argued elsewhere, others have been adopted.[88] What is more, in their published form the scripts remain almost unperformable by any modern actor, even one familiar with Cornu-English delivery.[89] There are not many examples of Cornu-English plays, or even fragments, surviving,[90] and those that do exist do not support what Nance was thinking; for the most part, they were written in Standard English. By the time Nance was writing, many of the old dialect writers of the nineteenth century, such as John Tabois Tregellas, William Sandys and William Bentinck Forfar, had been forgotten.[91]

As a folk tale, what is broadly called 'Duffy and the Devil', is an interesting narrative, but its reception and popularity appear to have waned during the twentieth century in favour of more fashionable folklore, such as Madgy Figgy and her Pig, Tom and the Giant, and the Mermaid of Zennor.[92] In the late twentieth century the truncated tale is contained in Eileen Molony's *Folk Tales of the West* (1971)[93] but not in Donald R. Rawe's influential *Traditional Cornish Stories and Rhymes* (1972).[94] It was briefly revived, however, for Eric Quayle and Michael Foreman's *The Magic Ointment and Other Cornish Legends* (1986)[95] and Shirley Climo and Anthony Bacon Venti's *Magic and Mischief: Tales from Cornwall* (1999),[96] yet always occurs as a lesser tale. Often considered to be the Cornish variant of the international 'Rumpelstiltskin'[97] (and with similarities to St Agnes' 'Skillywhidden'), the tale was clearly more popular and better known in the nineteenth century. Indeed, it is the lead tale in William Bottrell's Second Series of *Traditions and Hearthside Stories of West Cornwall*,[98] first published in 1873, and in that collection is nearly double the length of the rest of the narratives. It also features in the First Series of Robert Hunt's *Popular Romances of the West of England* (1865),[99] though here it is somewhat shorter than Bottrell's version. It must have been Bottrell's subtitle of his 'Duffy and the Devil' that most interested Nance, as he calls it 'An Old Christmas Play'[100] and this would have made him reconsider and scrutinise the tale very closely.

The Cledry Plays are prefaced with a single Nance poem, titled 'Little Cledry' which sets the cultural-geographic context for the dramas which follow. Written in five verses, each composed of sixteen lines, alternating between broadly eight and six syllabic lines, the poem harks back to an earlier phase of Nance's writing for *The Cornish Magazine*, although the rhyming and rhythm appear more sophisticated and controlled. The poem is not a lament, but rather a Betjemanesque tribute to an area of Britain which remains undisturbed, peaceful and, therefore, culturally genuine ('It's quiet down in Cledry, /We're out of all the fuss./Winds roar right over Cledry/And never trouble us').[101] Isolation and a lack of modern conveniences are, according to Nance, both desirable and fitting for the world of the drama about to unfold: 'We've got no trains, no gas, no drains,/No telegraph, nor 'phone', though in some ways this is contradicted by an earlier line referring to '[t]he stamps that's working still',[102] ('stamps' being ore-crushing machinery), technology resolutely Cornish, reflecting the fact that such industry was filled with Cornu-English discourse.

'Duffy: A Tale of Trove' establishes the textual layout for the rest of the volume. On the verso of the final page of the poem is Nance's illustration of Duffy at her spinning wheel, watched by Squire Lovel.[103] The picture is in a similar style to those contained in *The Cornish Magazine*. Opposite there is a list of characters, usually no more than four to each play, which suited both small-scale performance and home-reading. This also makes for equal stage-time for each of the four actors. Here they are described in considerable detail. For example, of 'Squire Lovel, an old-fashioned sportsman', we are told that:

> He wears a red, skirted coat; flowered waistcoat, and stockings drawn up over the knee, grey or brown with darns of divers colours in the first act; in the second, white with green clocks; in the third act his legs are bare and mudstained, and his shoes muddy.[104]

Similar detail is given to Terrytop ('a deluding imp'), Duffy ('a giddy giglet, later Lady Duffy'), and Joan ('housekeeper to Squire Lovel'). This is very typical of Nance's Cornu-English drama – he often indicates the dramatic function of the character, so that the actors clearly know their purpose, a technique found in most other folk drama. Nance also appears to prefer the tripartite model of folk drama, retaining Acts I, II and III as exposition, expansion and conclusion, a pattern in which 'Sally's Shiners' is the one exception, having just two acts. In 'modernist' drama of the early twentieth century, prologues were falling out of fashion and seen as unnecessary hindrances to the opening of the play, but the prologue here is of interest, since it is explicitly concerned with linguistic shift and, crucially, Nance's fascination with 'some ancientry that lingers':

> Old Cornwall, too, is changing,
> As surely if as slowly –
> New words and ways estranging
> With time transform us wholly –
> The tongue our forebears cherished
> Is lost from living speeches;
> Yet, as of vessels perished

> The boards drift up on beaches,
> So here and there, time still may spare
> Some anciantry that lingers –
> Let's, as each goes, its eyelids close
> At least with loving fingers.[105]

This rather beautiful verse has never quite been equalled as an English-language lament for the loss of Cornish, as well as a more positive exploration of the Cornish language entering Cornu-English.[106] It is after this that the drama proper begins at Trove Manor House, with the thoughts of Joan the housekeeper who, seventy-seven and near-blind, is having difficulty knitting as she used to. Joan is the physical manifestation of this lament. She is like Dolly Pentreath in Nance's representation, but also highly practical, and shows understanding for the Cornish underclass in the period the tale is set (the late eighteenth century). In William Bottrell's version of 'Duffy and the Devil' Joan (there 'Jone'[107]) is a minor character, but Nance cleverly enhances her role by making her critical of Duffy and Lovel, narrator and comic interest. The multi-functional role is important, and as in the other plays, Nance allows Joan to enter in a burst of language, seemingly pulling out every 'dialect trick in the book' in one speech that lasts for nearly two pages, a small sample of which is given here:

> Aw! 'Tes a wisht poor ould piliack I've comed to be, sure 'nough – what weth the wan eye clain gone, and t'other jist upon, my woorkin' days es most awver! – Why, I caen't sa mooch as knitty like I da belong – this'll maake the fower times, now…[108]

This is powerful Cornu-English drama. Not only is the Cornu-English very developed and therefore difficult for most modern readers both inside and outside of Cornwall, but the grammar is also vastly different from Standard English and acutely manipulated for effect. Few scholars have sought to understand the grammar of Cornu-English,[109] but on the strength of Joan's speech here, Nance had considerable understanding of the major trends as well as the tiny nuances of difference. There is not the space here to enter into a full discussion, but the word 'she' is used to good effect here: 'But, law! that'd be too swait for *she*, I reckon; for nothin' edn' to her mind, seemin', but what da look ill and smill woorse!' as is the adverb 'some' to indicate degree: 'Well, some proud I'll be ef he don't breng me back a click-handed edjack'.[110] The finest contemporary essay on Cornu-English grammar is by K.C. Phillipps,[111] and several of the features that he mentions are to be found in Joan's opening speech. Another strand is also present. A number of the words are explicitly drawn from Cornish, to demonstrate the linkages and the sound systems in operation, so there would seem to be a secondary strand within the plays – to educate and expose the audience to Cornish and, in a way, to counteract the sentiments of lamentation in the prologue. In the Nance Collection, one parcel has an early list of 'Keltic [*sic*] Words' entering Cornu-English, and this is expanded in the Glossary at the end of *The Cledry Plays*.[112] An example comes early on when Joan mentions 'pajerpaws' [English: newts] and 'grammersows' [English: woodlice] in this statement: 'And now, time she da come to saay as a pultice o' pounded-up pajerpaws and grinded-up grammersows es like to be the theng.'[113]

Despite the compromises which all writers of dialect have to face, the Cornu-English of this opening play is as striking and as 'exotic' as that of any writers of any British dialect in the twentieth century[114] and a wholly recognisable (to the working classes, at least) depiction of Cornish difference – a requirement that has gained momentum among scholars, writers and activists in the twenty-first century.[115] The burning question is perhaps how accurate Nance's depiction of the dialect is. It is a question which is impossible to answer fully in this essay. Rather than attempting to reproduce the living Cornu-English of Nancledra and West Cornwall during the late 1920s and early 1930s, the evidence points to Nance inventing an historic setting for the play – a world in which the Cornish language is almost palpable, reachable and, indeed, recoverable.

Nance does not see Cornu-English as one-dimensional and associated with lower-class or humorous characters. Lovel speaks 'posh' Cornu-English ('But as for who she es, I don't know, no more than thee; for I niver thoft to ax it'),[116] so that class is delineated in the text. This is rarely achieved by other Cornu-English dialect writers and novelists of the nineteenth century. Usually a straightforward black and white division of English for upper-class characters and Cornu-English for lower-class characters is employed, but there is a degree of sophistication here which demonstrates class differences in the use of Cornu-

English. Although Nance does not explicitly mention his awareness in any of the plays or in his notes, seemingly he was careful not to apply simple linguistic rules to dialect studies (be they creative or academic), a view that has found growing support in late twentieth-century studies of dialect, from scholars such as Penhallurick and Mufwene who have moved away from a modernist, empirical view to a more sympathetic understanding of just how dialects affect the identity of people.[117] Nance's 'reconstruction' becomes less problematical in the light of Kershaw's argument on the politicality of theatre, Penhallurick's alignment of deconstruction with dialectology and Nance's own desire to preserve and nourish what Mufwene terms the 'ecology' of language systems, which are almost always complex.

All of these issues come to the fore in 'Duffy: A Tale of Trove', and although it is important to emphasise Nance's linguistic achievement with the play, we should not forget his narrative skill either. His main accomplishment was to reduce the rather circuitous telling offered by Bottrell, and to concentrate on the core components of the folk tale's narrative. Bottrell shifts his telling between narrative and drama, apparently filling in with narrative the parts of the story that were unrecorded or unclear. He uses the Christmas framework explicitly throughout, but Nance really only offers this at the end, and in the epilogue in particular, when Squire Lovel and Duffy are married ('But 'tis good to have things righted/With a husband and his bride –/And, if not when troth is plighted,/Next best time is Christmastide').[118] At the same time, there is much correlation between the two versions, which may in itself be worthy of separate study in the future. In short, the narrative is concerned with the arrival of Duffy at Trove, in part-replacement for the elderly Joan. Duffy is to work for Squire Lovel, but he clearly has his eye on her for marriage. She is pretty, but idle, and when challenged to spin and knit, she makes a bargain with Terrytop the imp, who will magically provide both the spinning and knitting. Such a deal comes with a price, and although she can wish for whatever she wants, Terrytop explains the rules of the game:

> Your spinning all I'll do, Duffy,
> And all your knitting too, Duffy,
> I give my promise true, Duffy;

A lady you shall be.

Three years I'll play your game, Duffy –
Three years – and all I claim, Duffy,
Is that you guess my name, Duffy;
Or then come off with me![119]

Although Duffy is keen to accept his services, she responds by thinking his words are 'a g'eat yafful o' yarn'.[120] Nance, however, never makes Terrytop innately evil; he is more an 'imp at work' completing his daily business to survive in the harsh landscape of west Cornwall. At the same time, though, Terrytop is a grotesquely imagined character – always hunched, limping with 'elbows jauntily crooked'[121] – melodramatic and goblin-like, with personality and morality linked to appearance in the manner of fiction and European constructions of fairy creatures from the nineteenth century.[122] Act I of the drama concludes with Duffy accepting Terrytop's offer, thinking that nothing will come of the threat. Meanwhile, Squire Lovel decides that Duffy is a miracle and, despite Joan having the measure of her idleness, she proves herself to be 'the best spinner in the parish'.

Another reason why 'Duffy: A Tale of Trove' may be viewed as a typical Nance drama is because of the musical interludes. These are not operatic, nor even similar to songs in a musical, but rather more reflective, monologue sequences, where the audience gains insight into the character's motivation, as well as a cultural-materialist reflection on class, marriage and opportunity for women in the early twentieth century. Lovel's song at the start of Act II is a reflection on the benefit of spinning and knitting clothing, but comes to reflect on Duffy herself.[123] There is a darker and perhaps even salacious and materialist edge to the narrative here, with Lovel asking Duffy '[A]ren't 'ee *finely* set up?',[124] before asking her if she will marry him. There are benefits, Squire Lovel argues, to marrying the more mature man. When she accepts, understanding the 'betterment' of her class, it is Joan who offers the Cornu-English rebuke to the time they are spending together: 'What are 'ee tellin' of, 'en, che'l'-vean? Kaipin' comp'ny? Thee and Squire?'[125] It is interesting that at this crucial point in the narrative, Nance reverts to Cornish [*vean*, meaning 'little'].

A second visit by Terrytop allows him to taunt Duffy, but now that she has risen through the classes and is about to become Lady Lovel, she confidently ignores his threat. In Act III, returning home late from hunting, one of Squire Lovel's hounds happens to go down a *fugo*[126] and he follows the dog into the dark, finding a gathering of 'buccas'[127] led by Terrytop. When Duffy realises it is the bucca who has been helping her, and who is about to take her away, she quickly questions Lovel about his name. When Terrytop returns on Christmas Eve to take her away, he is filled with confidence: 'Have you finished your packing, Duffy?'[128] On her third guess, however, she names him correctly. With Terrytop now revealed, he is devastated and leaves dejected, carol singers arriving to demonstrate it is Christmas Day, with evil and greed defeated. Here, the drama works as a morality play, exposing sins which the audience should not indulge in. Duffy herself has been lucky, like other characters in Cornish folklore who make bargains with ne'er-do-wells and 'devils', but still come out on top. In this sense, Duffy's beating of sex, class and materialism (in the form of the greedy bucca) makes her a potent symbol of Cornish feminism, which Nance recognises and celebrates in the drama. Interestingly, an innovative radio version of the drama of 'Duffy' was broadcast on the BBC on Friday 4 May 1928, with Kathleen Frazier voicing Duffy, Mrs Stanley James playing Joan, A.K. Hamilton Jenkin as Terrytop and Nance himself as Squire Lovel. The piece was recorded in Plymouth, but broadcast across the whole of the United Kingdom, the setting being 'a room at Trove Manor house in ancient times'.[129]

Sequentially, the next drama in *The Cledry Plays* is 'Sally's Shiners: A Droll of Smuggling Days', but perhaps it is more logical to deconstruct the final play 'The Kite in the Castle: A Legend of Lamorna', since in several ways it is a direct sequel to 'Duffy', and forms the second part of the narrative in Bottrell's version. Duffy is a background character in the play, which is set soon after she has married Squire Lovel. It examines the fortunes of one Ezekiel Lanine, a poor cobbler, whose family lost the mansion of Trove and who is now forced to live in poverty. He discovers this through his meeting with a strange gentleman customer – the Demon Mason – who arrives at Lanine's cobbler's shop to have a pair of shoes made. The Demon Mason has one hoof, so Lanine's task will be difficult. If, however, he makes the shoes so they are comfortable, the cobbler will be placed in a mansion (built by the Mason) with all the riches he requires.

The comedy in the early part of this play is clever. Lanine understands the Demon Mason as 'exotic other' and is trying to banter with him, aiming to find out where he is from. Confusion reigns as Lanine believes he might be a Frenchman, which allows Nance to make a Breton-Cornish connection ('I mind my gran'f'er tellin' o' much about the saame thing, time he were in the smooglin' sarvice, gooin' awver to Roscoff and they Frinch plaaces. Thoft as how he were spaikin' the ould Carnish to em, he ded'[130]), but we have already been alerted to the Demon Mason's origins: 'You see, with us, it's all *down* – down, down, down, down, down – and never a bottom'.[131] There is also an intriguing reference to Lanine thinking that the Demon Mason is a Saracen, which has parallels with the Tudor Cornish drama *Beunans Meriasek* and the Turkish Knight of Nance's *Christmas Play*.

Lanine's speeches are fascinating pieces of Cornu-English, which would be enormously difficult for a contemporary actor to deliver, not least because of their length, but also because of the complexity of their ideas, and as noted above, their grammar. One of Nance's methods of working up the speeches was clearly to incorporate core dialect phrases or sayings into them, so that this phrase might then form the subject-matter. A good example is to be found early on in Act II, when the saying '[T]hey as caen't *schemey* … ha' got to *louster*'[132] allows him to explain his family history. This comes with considerable irony, of course, as Duffy has already proved that she can indeed 'schemey'. In their conversation about Lanine's heritage, he draws on the heraldic symbols of a 'kite in a castle' to explain how it has been stolen from him:

> Why, there's a *market-town* awver to Fraance to we, by rights. Et da goo by aour name, yit, Lanine; and, to prove et, that very saame coat-an-arms, theer, es cut upon the market-house. My gran'f'er seed'n to one time, when he were awver 'pon the smugglin' – *a Kite in a Caastle*![133]

The relationship between Lanine and the Demon Mason is one of Nance's greatest dramatic achievements, filled with deft linguistic touches and puns. When the Demon Mason returns to remind Lanine of his promises, Lanine neatly calls him 'Cap'm'![134] The Demon Mason chillingly asks for 'the best sole you have to give me'.[135] The Demon's hoof is labelled a 'trifling malformation'[136] while Lanine advises him that he could get a blacksmith's iron for him ('That would do for you-party, fine!').[137] However, the castle awarded to Lanine makes him miserly, and when he is visited by Polly, his grand-niece, he will not lend her any money. Importantly, she is told to visit him by 'a straange, ugly-lookin' man'[138] who is the Demon Mason. Not only this, but Lanine refuses to repair the Demon's shoes, and in the end, he loses everything. Again, the play has a moral, which argues that the audience should be happy with their lot and that Lanine should certainly never have 'sawld [his] sawl for a house'.[139] The Demon Mason as devil in disguise has the same function as Terrytop, but here the bargain made is more serious, and unlike Duffy, who comes up roses, Lanine's future is bleak. This is emphasised in the epilogue:

> Grasping yet empty, he,
> She, giving, rich in love,
> Lanine a kite would be,
> While Polly stayed a dove.
> Despite our curtain's fall,
> Perhaps, some later day,
> The moral you'll recall,
> Though you forget the play.[140]

This is not the whole of Nance's work in Cornu-English. There remain other important unpublished works. There is, in the Nance Collection, an undated draft of another Christmas-themed play titled 'Change-about is Fair Play: A Christmas Droll', concerning the characters of Squire Roseveor (an old-fash-ioned country squire), Jeremy Bawze (a bellows maker), an Astrologer, Lady Bezantia Roseveor, Tamsin the Housekeeper[141] and Moll, the bellows maker's wife. A longer drama than the published works, the play is concerned with Lady Bezantia's cynicism over Christmas: Tamsin describes her as '[a] kill-joy – tha's what she es – weth her high-fancical notions'.[142] Characteristically, in a Nance drama, the lead character, Jeremy, sings two songs, which are summarised in one line of the second song, 'I must work that others may play'.[143] Eventually, it is Tamsin and Jeremy who convince Bezantia to enjoy the season. Nance's

Cornu-English in this text is as vibrant as in the published pieces, and although it is interesting, it seems unlikely that it will ever reach publication. The same might be said for 'The Tragedy of Chronohotonthologos: being the most Tragical Tragedy that ever was Tragediz'd by any Company of Tragedians'.[144] Written by Henry Carey, under the pseudonym Benjamin Bounce, and first published and performed in 1734, the work is a learned, cryptic, Latinate satire on early eighteenth-century drama, the stage business full of archaisms, billowing rhetoric and over-inflated acting. It remains a curious reminder of Nance's knowledge of this genre and period, something perhaps to share with educated friends.

A more accessible and congenial unpublished play is 'Tom and the Giant: A Christmas Play' – a retelling of this folktale. The characters are Tom of Boujyheer, Giant Blunderbore, Jack the Tinkard, and Joan, the giant's wife. This is a more complete draft than 'Change-about is Fair Play: A Christmas Droll', but it is much shorter, consisting of only five pages. It takes a similar mumming approach to the other Christmas dramas, as can be seen from Tom's opening lines:

> Here comes I, Tom – Long Tom of Boujyheer,
> From Market-jew bound for Saint Ives, with beer.[145]

The story develops in much the same way as in other published versions. Joan and Tom outwit the Giant Blunderbore, although the Giant's death speech is more interesting as it incorporates a traditional Cornish language motto:

> Fortune <u>must</u> favour such a pious pair! –
> Farewell! – Write on my tomb, "He could play fair."
> Though all my life false-play has been my plague,
> I've learn't now, <u>GWARY WHÊG YU GWARY TÊG</u>.[146]

As Nance progressed, his Cornu-English plays became more ambitious. 'John Knill' (n.d.) is a more epic and ambitious prose drama, which merits much further study.[147] The subject is a life of Knill, the one-time mayor of St Ives, who was greatly admired by the people of the town, and who is said to have also been a smuggler. Knill decreed that every fifth year on St James' Day (25 July), the town should honour him by a parade of ten local girls all dressed in white, who would dance through the town up to his pyramid-shaped monument on Worvas Hill. At the monument, the girls would dance around it, and be met by the town's mayor and two widows. People watching would sing the 'Old Hundredth'. The topic for the play is inspired, prefiguring the subject matter of later twentieth- and twenty-first century Anglo-Cornish drama and, once again, it is a curious marshalling of folklore and drama, filled with historical allusions. Part of the play survives within the Nance Collection. It is one Nance play that really deserves to be much better known, and possibly revived.

Drama in Cornish
The 1920s had been a busy decade for Nance. Not only had he developed a body of work in Cornu-English that would stand unrivalled for the rest of the twentieth century, but he had also founded the first Old Cornwall Society in 1920 at St Ives, igniting other Societies in other Cornish towns to grow into a Federation. The unique development and structure of the Old Cornwall Societies has been the subject of considerable academic energy. The same may also be said for the establishment of the Gorsedd of the Bards of Cornwall, which is given coverage in many scholars' works, ranging from Ellis and Miles, to Carr-Gomm and Val Baker.[148] The inauguration ceremony, conducted by *Pedrog*, Archdruid of Wales, took place at Boscawen-Un on 21 September 1928. Nance's writing was, of course, to have considerable influence on the invented ritual of the Gorsedd and will be examined in the context of his Cornish language work below. In the following year, Nance published his influential textbook *Cornish for All*.[149]

Henry Jenner, and other activists such as L.C.R. Duncombe Jewell, had long been working towards Cornwall being accepted into the Celtic Congress. As Ellis details, Cornwall had been consistently rejected by the Celtic Congress in the opening years of the twentieth century, failing because of the 'linguistic criterion'.[150] In particular, when the Congress first met in Dublin in 1900, other Celtic territories appeared to pull Celtic weight on the smaller and university-less Cornwall. However, after a convincing address by Jenner on 31 August 1904,[151] Cornwall was admitted, although it took almost thrity years for the Celtic Congress to be held in Truro for the first time in 1932. According to

Smith, 'eight among those present delivered short addresses in Cornish'.[152] The timing, however, was perfect for showcasing Nance's work, though he now exchanged Cornu-English for Cornish in his dramas. The reasons behind this are twofold. First of all, Nance's own Cornish had, over the past decade, become highly sophisticated, and he wanted to create a literature worthy of the earlier writings in Cornish. Secondly, with the eyes of the contemporary Celtic world watching, he had the opportunity to display the viability of his Unified project and to demonstrate that the language was alive and kicking – not least in that most potent symbol of Cornish identity and the title of the allegorical play – *An Balores* [The Chough].[153] It was a meditation on nationalism that was to awaken hope in Cornwall.

One of the most important strands of Cornish identity, as Nance perceived it, was King Arthur and the ongoing imagination of his presence in the form of a chough.[154] If Arthur and choughs might one day return and lead a reconstructed Cornwall, then there was at least hope for a Cornwall in industrial, economic and cultural turmoil. In the drama, Nance promotes a vision of a Cornish-speaking Arthur – something rarely conceived of outside Cornwall – while the play's structure appears to incorporate elements of mumming as well as Cornish liturgical and medieval drama. The drama is comparatively short, having on the cover 'owth-aswonvos gweres Syr Thomas More' – a short acknowledgement of the judge and writer Sir Thomas More (1477–1535),[155] the central character of Nance's drama being also 'The Justice' – and clearly Nance had in mind the story of More's imprisonment for treason by Henry VIII. There also appear to be veiled references to other dramas on More.

The first stage direction tells us that 'An bobel, peswar den ha dyw venen, a-sef adro dhe un vasken vyghan, warnedhy palores varow, yn-dan elerlen [*The folk, four men and two women, stand round a little bier with a dead chough on it under a pall*]'.[156] The two male characters, who we later learn are called Peter Grief (Peder Dughan) and Bartholomew Battler (Bertyl Breseler) (a naming technique already established in Nance's Cornu-English drama), debate the reasons behind the death of the chough – or rather allegorically, the Cornish language. Battler believes it to be the Saxons who drove his forefathers out of their country [Britain] and into the peninsula of Cornwall, though Grief believes it to be the Cornish themselves:

My a-bref bos henna gow – Ny agan-honen yu dhe vlamya! Ny, an dus Kernow, yu, re-s-ladhas! Hy res-ombrederas, "Pandr' a-dal dhem bewa, ynnof ow-quytha yn-few spyrys Myghtern Arthur, aban na-vyn tus Kernow kewsel Kernewek na-moy? – Pandr' a-dal bos Arthur bew, marow mar pe y davas?" Ena, hep mar, hy a-wrowedhas a-hes, ha dascor an spyrys-na, ha merwel, terrys hy holon-hy!

[*I will prove that to be false. We ourselves are to blame! We, the people of Cornwall, it is, who have killed it! It thought within itself, "What good is it for me to live, keeping the spirit of King Arthur alive in me, since the folk of Cornwall won't speak Cornish any more? What is the use of Arthur being alive, if his tongue is dead?" Then, doubtless, it lay down and gave up this spirit, and died, broken-hearted!*][157]

Further debate is caused by the discussions of Jack Smart (Jowan Connek), Tom Hardhead (Tubby Pencales) and Aunt Molly Thickhead (Mally Pentew). The Justice, meanwhile, tries to find out the truth of the matter. The true status of each of the characters is tested in the play, generally through further absurd allegories of hens, eggs and clothes. Aunt Molly Thickhead believes that, just as 'an old woman and a monstrous wise one' of her acquaintance could locate such items if they were stolen, so she could tell who killed the chough. She is also called a gypsy – reminding us of Egypt and of the King in the 'Christmas Play'. The Justice says that there would be no point in going after this wise old woman who has left for Egypt, whereupon the dead chough comes to life. In this construction Nance invokes one of the most powerful symbols of 'revivalism' in Cornwall in the twentieth century, inspiring countless other poets to continue to use the chough as an icon.[158] The short, stichomythic lines near the end of the piece offer a vigorous new energy to the language (a movement later termed *Dasserghyans* [Resurgence]), newly 'flying' above Cornwall:

An Kensa Den:	Otomma marthus! Ass-yu hemma da!
An Nessa Den:	Hy a-agor hy deulagas!
An Kensa Benen:	Yma-hy ow-lesa hy dywaskel!
An Tressa Den :	Hy a-nyj!
An Peswara Den :	Hy a-vew!

An Nessa Benen:	Nyns-yu marow an balores!

[1st Man:	*Here's a miracle! How good this is!*
2nd Man:	*It opens its eyes!*
1st Woman:	*It's spreading its wings!*
3rd man:	*It flies!*
4th Man:	*It's alive! Hurrah!*
2nd Woman:	*The chough's not dead!]*[159]

In the rampant stupidity of the comic characters, there are traces of Nance's mumming folk drama, but in the Justice figure, we see echoes of the arrest of Jesus from *Passio Christi* and the Emperor's Doctors from *Beunans Meriasek*. While the Cornish of the play is comparatively basic (the prose tends to stumble rather than flow), *An Balores* is still something of an achievement. What the piece loses in dramatic complexity, it gains in radicalised theatre. There are relatively few other pieces of drama in Cornish during this phase, and Nance's imagining was to have a lasting effect. The culmination of the drama is a song – epilogue-like in its structure – which celebrates Arthur's spirit within the chough, as well as a new phase for the Cornish language.[160] Arthur, therefore, is neatly and ideologically connected with the language:

> Yeth Kernow, re-be hyrneth
> A'y groweth yn enewores,
> Ena a-dhassergh ynweth
> Maga few avel palores.

> Nyns-yu marow Myghtern Arthur!

> *[So again our Cornish tongue,*
> *That has lain so long a-dying,*
> *Shall rise up as strong and young*
> *As is e'er a chough that's flying.*

> *King Arthur is not dead!]*[161]

King Arthur and the Chough would become major themes in Cornish literature It was in all likelihood Nance who added, possibly in stages, these lines to
what was in 1930 and is now Part XIII of the Gorsedd ceremony – Cledha
Myghtern Arthur [*The Sword of King Arthur*], a powerful experiment in dramatic ritual, based on call and response, with many similarities to *An Balores*:

Cannas Barth Mur:	An als whath Arthur a wyth, Yn corf Palores yn few: Y Wlas whath Arthur a bew, Myghtern a ve hag a vyth.
An Vyrth Oll:	Nyns yu marow Myghtern Arthur!
Barth Mur:	Otomma Cledha us yn le Calespulgh, Cledha Myghtern Arthur, a dhuth dyworth an Logh, ha dhe'n Logh eth arta. A vynnough-why ty warnodho bynytha bos lel dhe Gernow, agan Mamvro?
An Vyrth Oll:	Ny a'n te!
[*Deputy Grand Bard:*	*Still Arthur watches our shore* *In guise of a Chough there flown;* *His Kingdom he keeps his own,* *Once King, to be King once more.*
All the Bards:	*King Arthur is not dead!*
Grand Bard:	*Behold a Sword which represents Excalibur, the Sword of King Arthur, which came from the Lake, and went to the Lake again. Will you swear upon it to be ever loyal to Cornwall, our Motherland?*
All the Bards:	*We swear it!*][162]

Not only was Nance sanctifying the chough, he was reactivating it as myth. Here, ritual, reconstruction, poetry and patriotism merge. Not only was *An Balores* indicative of Nance's achievement, it was also to be the launch-pad for the final phases of his literary career. There was a large amount of ceremony and ritual about Nance's theatre, reflected in his conceptualisation of a Cornish Gorsedd. It was, like the Gorsedd, a place of enchantment, with Nance as a glorious assimilator.

Doleful dirges? The Cornish-language Poetry and Stories
The assimilation would continue in Nance's other Cornish-language writings. His Unified Cornish project would see him incorporate sometimes disparate strands of Cornish grammar and vocabulary into a modern vision of the language, not to mention elements of Welsh and Breton. That said, the project was necessary at this point in the development of Cornish. Nance did not have the linguistic infrastructure of modern scholarship at his fingertips, and the revival of Cornish was given short shrift by supposedly superior academics in universities in England and in the other Celtic territories.[163] Unsupported in this way, Nance's work was a lonely occupation. The surviving poetry from Nance is not vast, and most of it has already been compiled in Tim Saunders' ground-breaking anthology *The Wheel*.[164] Composed originally in a period from the late 1920s to the late 1930s, Nance's verse forms are generally short, broadly conservative and mostly ballad-like, the subject being either Arthuriana, Breton-Cornish unity or studies of animals. He is not as sophisticated a poet as his contemporaries, L.R. Moir and Edwin Chirgwin,[165] and it would be another generation before more progressive work in Cornish began to flourish with poets like Richard Gendall, J.A.N. Snell and N.J.A. Williams leading the way.[166] Saunders cites 'Nyns-yu marow Maghtern Arthur!/King Arthur is Not Dead!' as Nance's first important poetic achievement in Cornish, alongside a piece entitled 'Arta Ef A-Dhe/He Shall Come Again', which was first published in the Gorsedd programme of 1930. Its subject matter is predictable enough, although it does contain some beautiful imagery:

War scoren noth pren derow py kefer del yn gwaf?
Whath arta mylvyl delen las a-dyf pan dheffo haf!

[*Where are leaves found on the bare branch of an oak tree in winter?*
Yet a million green leaves will grow again when the summer comes!][167]

In 'Dynergh dhe Dus a Vreten Vyghan/Welcome to Men from Brittany',[168] Nance offers a poem obviously written to celebrate a visit of a Breton group – in all probability the wrestlers who performed at the tournament held in conjunction with the Gorsedd at Carn Brea – and takes pleasure in celebrating their joint Brythonic heritage. To an extent, the piece is a heavily romanticised vision, filled with exclamation and declaration ('Brython a-gar Brython bys gorfen bys!/Briton will love Briton till the end of the world!'),[169] as well as a Yeatsian desire to shape human consciousness,[170] hoping to fire a specifically Brythonic imagination. At first glance, this may seem naive and irrational, though actually Nance's purpose here is not dissimilar to that of another important twentieth-century writer, J.R.R. Tolkien, who was attempting, within his own 'Northern European' mythological work, to create Middle Earth from existing strands of Anglo-Saxon, Norse and Celtic.[171] Like Tolkien, Nance perceived the lasting presence of Brythonic culture, and simply made it concrete. In terms of his verse, this mythology is rendered in his successful translations of Breton pieces for a Cornish readership, as in 'Honna dres oll a-Garaf/She Whom I Love the Dearest':

> Honna dres oll a-garaf yu avel un steren,
> Aberth-yn nef ow bewnans a-dhewyn bys vyken.
>
> Honna dres oll a-garaf yu gwyn avel an lor,
> Tewolgow a-wra fetha, ha golowy an nor.
>
> Honna dres oll a-garaf avel an howl a-splan;
> Na-ve hyhy, a dekter y'n bys ny-welen man.
>
> [*She whom I love the dearest to me is like a star,*
> *That in my life-sky sparkles though she be near or far.*
>
> *She whom I love the dearest to me is like the moon,*

That drives away the darkness till midnight seems as noon.

She whom I love the dearest to me is like the sun;
Were she not there, of beauty on earth I could see none.][172]

For Nance, this was a mechanism for showing readers how 'great' Cornish could be. It legitimised his work and drew the right kind of connections between the two cultures, one of which had seemingly lost its way. There were other ways of legitimising Cornish for the populace as well. In 'Yeghes Da dhe'n Myghtern!'/'Good Health to the King!' Nance offers a praise-poem to George V,[173] demonstrating that Cornish could be used for any purpose. It is not great poetry, but perhaps for Nance, that was not the point. In essence, by this stage, the project of Cornish reconstruction was more important. This is not to say, however, that some of Nance's poems were without ambition. 'An Margh Coth'/ 'The Old Horse' was originally written as a Cornish action song for the girls of St Ives Council School. Described humorously as 'a doleful dirge', quite why it was conceived as an action song is obscure. The poem is a combination of the kind of dialogue found in the earlier folk dramas, with the moralising effects of the prose work described below. Perhaps it is the rhythmical effect of the song which Nance was alluding to, for it does work as the kind of song heard on a chain gang. The rhyme and rhythm push this work into a different league of creativity. Nance was also expanding the length of his work, this poem running to twelve verses:

> Whel cref a-borthas war an tyr,
> > *Eghan! Govy!*
> Ow cones lyes bledhen hyr,
> > *Eghan! Govy!*
> Sconya nep eghen whel ny-wruk,
> Pup saw dh'y allos ef a-n-duk.
> > *Ogh tru, dun kynyn oll warbarth, eghan, govy!*
>
> [*It did hard work on the land,*
> > Alas! Woe is me!

serving for many a long year,
                 Alas! Woe is me!
without refusing any kind of work,
and carrying every load it could.
                 O pity, let us come and all sing together, alas, woe is me!]^{174}

The animal theme comes to the fore with another poem – 'An Edhen Huder'
/'The Magical Bird'. This is perhaps Nance's greatest poetic work: a magical
realist consideration of a man hearing birdsong. The birdsong takes him on a
journey in a dream, and, like the laughter of a girl, enables him to forget everything. There is a Christian overtone to the poem, yet the subject matter remains
astutely 'magical and Celtic'. There are touches here of how impressive Nance's
verse could be. Again, there seems to have been a Yeatsian influence on the
piece, which is perhaps not surprising, considering how Yeats had shaped much
Celtic poetry around the turn of the twentieth century. Eventually, in the allit-
erative final lines, we learn that the bird has stolen his very being.[175]

Other works of this phase follow a similar format. 'An Vowes Doth'/'The
Wise Girl' has the feel of Edward Chirgwin's reworking of the late seventeenth
century song, 'Pelea era why moaz, moes fettow teag?'/'Where are you going,
pretty fair maid?' – commonly known as 'Strawberry Leaves'.[176] Nance seems to
suggest that virginity is the best state for the wise girl, when her suitor offers
money ('Byth na-rof' yn-meth hy,/'Bay rag arghans:/Rag travyth gwraf y ry/Pan
y-m-be whans.' [*I shall never give,' said she, 'a kiss for money: I shall give it for noth-*
ing, when I want to.']).[177] Several poems double as songs. 'An Dullores'/'The
Deceitful Girl' is a piece in which Nance confesses jealousy towards a man who
is with the girl he loves. The piece concludes with him bitterly observing
'Namoy nyns-us gesys dhymmo,/War nep torn tam kerensa y'n bys!' [*There is*
not a single bit of love left me in the world any more!']^{178} Nance worked with the
musician Arthur L. Mata to put the poem to music, retaining the 'magical
Celtic' feel alluded to above. As he observes:

The words of this [and the other song] have been fitted to "fairy" music
– not consciously composed but heard in dreams. Mr Mata, struck by
their air of coming from a far Celtic past, has taken pleasure in giving to

these three melodies the harmony which brings out their antique flavour, however unorthodox it may sound in modern ears.[179]

Two other pieces were worked upon in this way: the romantic 'An Vugh hy Holon Trogh [The Broken-hearted Cow]' and the more modern 'Can Kernow Dyvres [Song of an Exiled Cornishman]'.[180] During the mid-1930s there were also shorter prose and poetic contributions, as well as translations, in A.S.D. Smith's ground-breaking Cornish-language magazine *Kernow*.[181] These were often short and academic, but one piece – 'Kan Nadelik [Christmas Song]'[182] – is a pristine evocation of the season.

As can be seen from the above, Nance's work was unorthodox in the very best sense of the word, and although his poetic output dwindled in later years, he had offered up both the subject-matter and the linguistic tools to the next generation of writers. Nance's real skill in Cornish came in prose, and again his work here is very neglected. While he was editor of *Old Cornwall* in the magazine's infant years, Nance initially created the Cornel Kernuak as a vehicle to reinvent the Cornish folk continuum. This section of *Old Cornwall* created a trend which has continued in late twentieth-century and early twenty-first-century Cornish-language magazines,[183] for the Cornel Kernuak's pieces were, in essence, learning mediums, where the small, but growing group of Cornish speakers could read (and occasionally write) new texts. As the form developed, Nance abandoned the Cornel Kernuak device and simply used his bardic name, *Mordon*, for most of his pieces. Initially, the contributions were fairly short, but later on they became more ambitious. There was both a sense of linkage to previous narratives, names and concepts in the Cornish literary canon, and a conscious 'borrowing' of narrative form from the folk-tale canon, as collected by Bottrell and Hunt. We have seen how this worked before with his folk dramas, but here the intention was to recraft the narrative into Cornish. Typical of this phase in the early 1930s is 'Nyns-yu dhe ladra nep na-n-jeves man/There is no robbing one who has nothing'.[184] The story begins with the description of the central character – a poor Cornishman. We note the archaic formality of both the Cornish and the literal English translation:

Yth-esa kens, ny-won yn-fas leverel py tyller, un den esa gyllys mar ysel

yn ponvotter ha boghosogneth ma na-n-jeva na creven a vara dhe dhe-
bry, na quethow vyth rag omgudha gansa, na nyns-o gesys a'y gorf lemen
eskern ha croghen.

Noswyth, hag ef ow-crowedha y-honen-oll war wely-usyon noth yn y
growjy gwak, ha gortos y dremena a'n bys dre ewn yender ha nown, y-
clewas lader dhe entra aberth y'n chy.

*[There was formerly, I can't exactly tell where, a certain man who was gone so
low in misery and poverty that he had neither a crust of bread to eat nor any
clothes to cover himself withal, and of his body there was left only bones and
skin.*

*In the night, as he lay all alone on a bare pallet of husks in his empty cot-
house, awaiting his passing from the world through very cold and hunger, he
heard a robber to enter within the house.]*[185]

There are strong echoes here of 'John of Chyanhor'[186] (indeed this remains
Nance's core model for Cornish narrative), whilst retaining the fable element.
All of these narratives work like the folk drama, as morality tales – didactic in
their approach to how one should lead one's life. Here, a thief tries to rob the
man because he thinks the old man is dead. The only thing the thief can find in
the house is an earthenware pot filled with flour, which the old man didn't know
was there. When the man awakens and says, 'Drop it, thou thief!' the thief not
only drops the flour, but also his warm cloak. The man then makes bread and
uses the thief's cloak to keep himself warm. The tale ends with an *englyn* or
triplet, a form of verse which Nance had identified as part of the Cornish continuum:

> Nyns-yu dhe dhry dhe'n dor an pren na-saf yn-ban;
> Nyns-yu dhe denna dour ha'n pyth deseghys glan;
> Na whath nyns-yu dhe ladra nep na-n-jeves man.

> *[The tree that stands not up, to ground can not be brought;*
> *A draught from a dry well as vainly will be sought;*
> *Nor can a man be robbed when he possesses nought.]*[187]

In fact, many of the Cornel Kernuak stories end with triplets similar to this.

Another early tale in Cornish is 'Jowan hag Arluth an Maner'/'John and the Lord of the Manor'. The tale is set in the age of Arthur and involves John the lad's witty reply to the Lord of the Manor's question concerning the number of commandments in the Bible. John says there are nine and accuses the Lord of stealing the parts of his father's milch cow. Fortunately, the Lord sees the boy's wit, and realises he is bright. His wit is keen enough. Again, we note the formality of the telling and that, interestingly, Nance does not revert to Cornu-English in the translation – it remains markedly formal:

> Yn dedhyow mas Myghtern Arthur, yth-esa ow-pewa yn Kernow, pur oges dhe Ben an Wlas, map un tyak boghosek, ha Jowan a'y hanow, esa brusys bos maw lym y skyans dres oll y gentrevogyon.
>
> War un prys, hag ef y'n ur-na devedhys dhe nep seyth bloth a'y os, y das a-n-goras y'n park rag gwytha y warthek, hag ef pan y-n-gwelas ena, Arluth an Maner a-dheth dres an keth park-na yn-un-marghogeth ha dalleth govyn orto nep maner govyn, rag y assaya, esa mar lym a'y skyans es del lavara anodho an dus-oll po nag-esa.

> [*In the good days of King Arthur, there was living in Cornwall, very near to the Land's End, the son of a poor farmer, John by name, who was reputed to be a lad keen-witted beyond all his neighbours.*
>
> *Upon a time, when he had then come to some seven years of his age, his father set him in the field to keep his cattle, and when the Lord of the Manor saw him there, he came riding across that same field and started to question him somehow, to test him, whether he was as keen-witted as everybody said of him or no.*][188]

This is Nance's translation. The early pieces were in Cornish only, but from issue 11 onwards translations were provided, presumably to help learners. Nance reverted to the Cornish-only practice later. Tales in Volume 2 included 'An Lorgan y'n Dour' ['The Moonlight in the Water'] and 'An Oy-yar ha'n Velyn-wyns' ['The Hen's Egg and the Windmill'],[189] while Volume 3 contained the following narratives: 'An Varf' ['The Beard'], 'An Try Lavar' ['The Three Sayings']', 'An Besont Tarosvanus' ['The Illusory Bezant'], 'Jowan Bras ha

Jowan Byghan' ['Big John and Little John'], 'Skyans us Pernys yu an Gwella Skyans oll' ['Bought Knowledge is the Best Knowledge of all'], 'Sa, Sa! Gas hy dhe Wandra!' ['Stop, stop! Let her roam!'] and 'Hycca ha Davy' ['Richard and David'].[190] More ambitious pieces include 'An Marner Du' ['The Black Sailor'], 'Omdowl Bras Coryn ha Goemagot' ['The Great Wrestling of Corineus and Gogmagog'], 'Benen Worth hep Nam' ['A Downright Contrary Woman'] and 'Cas ha Caradewder' ['Hatred and Graciousness'].[191] The Second World War years appear to have had little impact on Nance's production, although it does seem that his narratives here take a darker direction. Core stories include 'Bewnans Sen Florent' ['The Life of St Florentius'], 'Synt Galdwyn ha'n Trethoryon' ['Saint Galdwyn and the Ferrymen'], 'Melyn-dreth' ['Mill on the Beach'], 'An Pysk Ryal' ['The Royal Fish'], 'An Canjeon' ['The Changling'], 'An Managh a-Synsys dhe'n Gwyryoneth' ['The Monk who held to the Truth'] and 'Sagh Dom Jowan' ['Dom John's Bag'].[192]

There had, however, been an interesting precedent for this kind of narrative. In 1939, Nance had published a small work titled *Lyver an Pymp Marthus Seleven: Warlergh an Dus Coth Cuntellys ha Scryfys* [The Book of the Five Miracles of St Levan: Collected and Written in the manner of the Old People].[193] Taking for his starting point the stone in St Levan churchyard, purportedly struck by the saint's fist and split in two, Nance seeks to recreate the narrative of the saint recorded in other printed sources.[194] Linguistically the project remains as before – an attempt to reconstruct the original form (what philologists usually term the 'starred form'). The piece is divided into five sections:

> An Kensa Marthus, hen yu, Marthus an Men Seleven.
> An Nessa Marthus, hen yu, Marthus Hens Seleven.
> An tressa Marthus, hen yu, Marthus an Dheu Sew.
> An Peswera Marthus, hen yu, Marthus an Lowarth.
> An Pympes Marthus, hen yu, Marthus Cravas Satan.

> [*The First Miracle, namely the Miracle of St Levan's stone.*
> *The Second Miracle, namely the Miracle of St Levan's path.*
> *The Third Miracle, namely the Miracle of the Two Bream.*

The Fourth Miracle, namely the Miracle of the Garden.
The Fifth Miracle, namely the Miracle of the Clawing of Satan.][195]

Many of the later stories which appeared in *Old Cornwall* had a similar moralistic feel to these miracles of St Levan. As well as reconstructing the philology, Nance also seems to indicate that St Levan would have made good subject matter for a localised miracle play. This concept and others like it were crucial to him during the years of the Second World War. By 1951, however, he appears to be consciously handing over the reigns of *Old Cornwall* to new contributors. He still found time to contribute the following stories, while at the same time evolving his spelling of Unified Cornish: 'An Kenyas ha'n Lugh' ['The Singer and the Calf'], 'An Tregher a-dorras y Benys' ['The Tailor who broke his Fast'], 'Skentoleth Prenys' ['Bought Wisdom'], 'An Den y'n Lor' ['The Man in the Moon,], 'Dres an Glaw a-berth y'n Chy' ['Rain Brought Indoors'], and 'Gwythyas an Dremenysy' ['The Guardian of the Travellers'].[196] Continuing earlier concerns, Nance also 'Cornishises' a Welsh poem – 'Gwytha 'n Gwaneth Gwyn' ['Guarding the White Wheat'].[197] Perhaps the most interesting text of this late phase of folkloric interest is his story 'An Aval Ruth' ['The Red Apple'], a retelling of the internationally-known 'The Juniper Tree'.[198] These narratives have never been collated. There does exist an undated volume entitled *An den ha'y dheu wreg ... and some short stories in the Cornish language...*[199] but this contains only one piece by Nance, the title story 'The man and his two wives'; the rest consists of a longer story by R.St.V. Allin-Collins and his translations into Cornish of pieces by Edith Grenville.

While Nance was completing these stories, he had also been at work translating and exploring the major canonical texts within Cornish literature. In the summer of 1931 he completed what he terms '[a] "unified" rendering' of "If Cornish folk would but hearken" ',[200] and in 'A Cornish Poem Restored' reflected on the possible insertion into the *Ordinalia* play 'Passio Christi', at different points, of verses from another poem.[201] He and A.S.D. Smith (1883–1950) had worked on both *Ordinalia* and *Beunans Meriasek*, making core sections of the plays available in Unified Cornish for the first time ('Extracts from the Cornish Texts in unified spelling with amended translation'). These were published as a series of pamphlets by the Federation of Old Cornwall Societies and the

Cornish Language Board.[202] The culmination of this work came much later, however, after the deaths of Nance and Smith. The Cornish Language Board published Nance's and Smith's edition and translation of *Christ's Passion* and *Resurrection* in 1982 and 1984 respectively.[203] *Origo Mundi* [The Beginning of the World] remained available in manuscript form only until 2001, when, almost twenty years after the first titles, it was published by Agan Tavas.[204] This, in itself, had been a huge project for Nance and Smith to complete, and in very many ways was the culmination of their lives' work.

Far from being a 'doleful dirge', Nance and Smith had put the status of Cornish literature back on the European cultural map. Nance himself had drawn imaginatively on the Brythonic tradition, in much the same way as other activists such as Tolkien and Yeats had respectively with Anglo-Saxon and Gaelic culture. His poetic legacy in Cornish, though not large, contained pointers towards the future development of poetry in Cornish, and at the same time his interest in the 'magical Celtic' prefigured the concerns of many interested observers, from groups as diverse as neo-pagans to minority language enthusiasts.[205] His prose work and translations, of course, remain more important – the prose because, in Nance, we see for the first time someone activating a new culture of Cornish; the translations, because Nance was to allow a new generation of readers and performers access to dramas crucial in understanding the theatrical history of these islands.

Conclusion: Understanding Mordon's 'Conjectural Description'

As Nance knew well, culture can take bizarre twists and turns. On 23 December 2004, this writer attended the celebrations at Mousehole in west Cornwall commemorating the famous mission of Tom Bawcock to end the famine in the village. Now known as 'Tom Bawcock's Eve', the event has not only developed Mousehole's own tradition of Starry Gazy Pie and Christmas lights, but has integrated 'exterior' texts such as one of the most lasting children's picture books of recent years – *The Mousehole Cat* by Antonia Barber and Nicola Bayley.[206] As a torchlight procession (complete with bombards and drums) headed through the streets of the village, adorned with willow and paper recreations of starry gazy pies and Bawcock's boat, the children of the village sang a song, not too different from that which follows:

> *A merry plaace, you may believe,*
> *Was Mouzel 'pon Tom Bawcock's Eve.*
> *To be there then who wudn' wesh,*
> *To sup o' sibm soorts o' fesh.*

> When morgy brath
> Had cleared the path,
>   Comed lances for a fry,
> And then us had
> A bit o' scad,
>   An' starry-gazy pie![207]

Nance 'reconstructed' this song early on, in the Cornu-English phase of his poetic career. In the April 1927 number of *Old Cornwall* he describes how he found this 'little verse ... written years ago, that I have turned out of a drawer'. He also comments:

> At Mousehole this is the eve before Christmas Eve, which was formerly kept as a feast among the fisher-folk there. Its particular feature was the eating ... of seven different sorts of fish ... with [if possible] plenty of "moonshine" to wash them down.[208]

In the eyes of Nance, the above song was a 'conjectural description' of what might have been sung at this feast in former times.[209] That conjectural description, like much of Nance's work, is now fully embedded in Cornish culture. The children of Mousehole seem unlikely to stop singing it. This one small song is perhaps symbolic of Nance's literary achievement in Cornwall. Although his methodology may now seem questionable, its result has been increased 'Cornishness'. That mantra exudes from all his work. When Nance died on 27 May 1959, aged 86, an observer of the time commented:

> Realistically, not metaphorically, Nance saw the Cornish language of our ancestors permanently revived and produced meticulously in volume form. Thus today the Cornish language and dictionaries remain

safely with global literature, often prized in the libraries of universities and in the loving care of scholars.[210]

The same might be said for his achievements in Cornu-English and folklore. Nance's grave in Zennor churchyard is still visited by admirers and pilgrims, who understand his need for 'conjectural description'. There are, therefore, many descriptions of Nance we might apply with regard to his literature, above and beyond 'some ancientry that lingers'. He was an arch-reconstructionist, yet so were J.R.R. Tolkien and W.B. Yeats; his work prefigures and predates the work of respected folklorists such as Georgina Boyes and Ronald Hutton;[211] his assimilation of Breton and Welsh vocabulary may be a borrowing too far;[212] his work in English was filled with archaisms of language; his dramatic interpretation of the folk play in Cornwall may itself be labelled 'conjectural' at best, and invented at its worst. However, as this chapter has demonstrated, given his 'moment of production', and in response to his detractors, Nance actually copes supremely well with the promise and problems of literary revival in Cornwall. Nance was a harbinger of a new kind of Cornish writer – one who was practical, pragmatic and politically active and who would make Cornwall culturally respectable again. His linguistic dissent, his realisation of Cornish difference, and his interest in the twin 'dialects' of Cornish and English (as well as their interaction) confirm his core position in modern Cornwall.

Notes

1. See Den Toll (Hugh Miners) (1978) *Gorseth Kernow: The First 50 Years*, Penzance: Gorseth Kernow, pp.7–34; Dillwyn Miles (1992) *The Secret of the Bards of the Isle of Britain*, Llandybie: Gwasg Dinefwr, pp.226–231.
2. Tony Deane and Tony Shaw (2003) *Folklore of Cornwall*, Stroud: Tempus. See also R. Morton Nance 'What we stand for' in *Old Cornwall* (1925), April pp.3–6, (1973); *When was Cornish Last Spoken Traditionally?* Truro: Royal Institution of Cornwall.
3. See Tim Saunders, 'Cornish – Symbol and Substance' in Cathal Ó Luain (ed.) (1983) *For a Celtic Future: A tribute to Alan Heusaff*, Dublin: The Celtic League, pp.253–9; Piotr Stalmaszczyk (2005) *Celtic Presence: Studies in Celtic Languages and Literatures – Irish, Scottish Gaelic and Cornish*, Lódz: Lódz University Press, pp.126–31. Nance was also satirised in the progressive and comic Cornish language magazine *Eythen*, which ran between 1976–80. Nance's main principles are outlined in R. Morton Nance (1958 [1929]) *Cornish for All: A Guide to Unified Cornish*, Cornwall: Federation of Old Cornwall Societies.
4. A representative example includes J.E. Caerwyn Williams (ed.) (1971) *Literature in Celtic Countries*, Cardiff: University of Wales Press; Victor Edward Durkacz (1983) *The Decline of the Celtic Languages*, Edinburgh: John Donald Publishers Ltd; Paul Russell (1995) *An Introduction to the Celtic Languages*, Harlow: Longman. There are many others.

5. A.S.D. Smith (1947) *The Story of the Cornish Language: Its Extinction and Revival*, Camborne: Camborne Printing and Stationery; P.A.S. Pool (1995) *The Second Death of Cornish*, Redruth: Dyllansow Truran; Craig Weatherhill (1995) *Cornish Place Names and Language*, Wilmslow: Sigma Leisure, pp.163–165.

6. See Pool (1995), ibid.; Ken George (1986) *The Pronunciation and Spelling of Revived Cornish*, Cornwall: The Cornish Language Board.

7. Ray Edwards (ed.) (1994) *The Tregear Homilies*, Sutton Coldfield: Kernewek dre Lyther. The Homilies were discovered as late as 1949. *Beunans Ke* is another recent discovery. See Graham C.G. Thomas (2002) 'The Middle Cornish Plays: A Note' in *The National Library of Wales Journal*, 32.

8. See N.J.A. Williams (1995) *Cornish Today: An Examination of the Revived Language*, Sutton Coldfield: Kernewek dre Lyther, (1997) *Clappya Kernowek: An Introduction to Unified Cornish Revised*, Portreath: Agan Tavas.

9. Sharon Lowena, "Noscitur A Sociis': Jenner, Duncombe Jewell and their Milieu' in Philip Payton (ed.) (2004) *Cornish Studies: Twelve*, Exeter: University of Exeter Press, pp.63–87. Cornish Studies has dealt with the Cornish Revival in considerable depth.

10. For this, see contributors to David C. Harvey, Rhys Jones, Neil McInroy and Christine Milligan (eds.) (2002) *Celtic Geographies: Old Culture, New Times*, New York and London: Routledge, and those to Philip Payton (ed.) (1993–2006) *Cornish Studies [Second Series]* 1–14, Exeter: University of Exeter Press. The long-standing exception is the work of Peter Berresford Ellis. See, for example, Peter Berresford Ellis (1985) *The Celtic Revolution: A Study in Anti-Imperialism*, Talybont: Y Lolfa.

11. For Quiller-Couch's contribution to literature in Cornwall and in England, see Alan M. Kent (2000a) *The Literature of Cornwall: Continuity, Identity, Difference 1000–2000*, Bristol: Redcliffe, pp.164–168. Quiller-Couch was enormously influential in the careers of Daphne du Maurier and A.L. Rowse.

12. A. T. Quiller-Couch (ed.) (1898) *The Cornish Magazine*, Vol. I, Truro: Joseph Pollard.

13. Ibid., p.70.

14. Ibid., p.48. Nance wrote material for the family-produced newspaper when still a boy. An earlier version of this poem appeared in this newspaper. Cf. Morgan Anthony 'The Taaty-Paasty' in *Old Cornwall* (1926) no. 3, April, pp.31–32.

15. For a comparison, see Charles Causley (1996) *Collected Poems for Children*, London: Macmillan.

16. Compare with the extract from 'The St Agnes Bear Hunt' by John Tabois Tregellas, in Alan M. Kent (ed.) (2000b) *Voices from West Barbary: An Anthology of Anglo-Cornish Poetry 1549–1928*, London: Francis Boutle, pp.85–86.

17. See William Sandys and William Bentinck Forfar, in ibid., pp.90–94 and pp.121–124.

18. Quiller-Couch (ed.) (1898) op.cit., p.50.

19. Compare this with Ernest Morton Nance's words about Cornish tartan.

20. See Stephen Hall (2001) *The Cornish Pasty*, Bridport: Agre Books, p.7.

21. Quiller-Couch (ed.) (1898), op. cit., pp.261–265. Only the illustration is actually credited to Nance.

22. Ralph Dunstan (ed.) (1932) *Cornish Dialect and Folk Songs*, Truro: Jordan's Bookshop, p.38.

23. Ibid.

24. R.N. Worth (ed.) (1875) *The West Country Garland: Selected from the Writings of the Poets of Devon and Cornwall, from the Fifteenth to the Nineteenth Century, with Folk Songs and Traditional Verses*, London: Houlston and Sons, pp.169–174.

25. Dunstan (1932), op. cit.

26. See A. Norman Jeffares (ed.) (1990) *W.B. Yeats: Selected Poetry*, London: Pan; James Macpherson, Howard Gaskill and Fiona Stafford (eds.) (1996) *The Poems of Ossian*, Edinburgh: Edinburgh University Press.

27. A good example is the *Kalevala*, or 'Land of Heroes', the national epic poem of Finland, transmitted orally until 1835, when a substantial portion was published by Elias Lönnrot. The myths are purportedly derived from the time when Finns and Hungarians were the same people. Modern Greece is largely an invention of

the Enlightenment, just as Pan-Slavism derives from a period in the mid-eighteenth century.

28. Eric Hobsbawm and Terence Ranger (eds.) (1992) *The Invention of Tradition*, Cambridge: Canto.

29. Quiller-Couch (ed.) (1898), op. cit., p.261.

30. Ibid., p.264.

31. Ibid., pp.127–129. Once again, Nance is credited with the illustrations alone.

32. See, for example, R. Morton Nance (1963) *A Glossary of Cornish Sea-Words*, Marazion: The Federation of Old Cornwall Societies.

33. Quiller-Couch (ed.) (1898) op.cit., p.129.

34. A. T. Quiller-Couch (ed.) (1899) *The Cornish Magazine*, Vol. II, Truro: Joseph Pollard, pp.54–56.

35. Ibid., pp.126–128.

36. Ibid., pp.228–230.

37. See 'The Terrors of the Deep: An Off-Fish-ial Guide to Cornwall' in the Nance Collection, Courtney Library, Royal Institution of Cornwall, Truro, p.1.

38. Ibid., p.2.

39. Ibid., p.3. Guckows [wrasse], pezaks [decayed pilchard], wrahs [wrasse], wreaks [smooth dog], crogans [limpet shells], gweeans [periwinkles], zarts [sea-urchin], calcars [weever], coblas [snake pipe-fish], conks [conch or whelk shells], guzzalezzas [octopus], monks [monk-fish], keligans [razor fish]. These definitions are taken from Nance's manuscript 'A Guide to the Guide' which he appends to the poem.

40. See Nance (1963), op. cit.

41. See Kent (2000a), op. cit.; Philip Payton [c. 1992] *The Making of Modern Cornwall: Historical Experience and the Persistence of "Difference"*, Redruth: Dyllansow Truran, pp.127–128.

42. See Arthur Quiller-Couch cited in Alan M. Kent and Tim Saunders (eds.) (2000) *Looking at the Mermaid: A Reader in Cornish Literature 900–1900*, London: Francis Boutle, p.338.

43. Den Toll (1978), op. cit., p.55.

44. R.J.E. Tiddy (1923) *The Mummers' Play*, Oxford: Clarendon Press; E.K. Chambers (1969 [1933]) *The English Folk Play*, Oxford: Oxford University Press. For a Cornish perspective, see Tom Miners 'The Mummers' Play in West Cornwall' in *Old Cornwall* (1928), no. 8, October, pp.4–16.

45. Ronald Hutton (1994) *The Rise and Fall of Merry England: The Ritual Year 1400–1700*, Oxford: Oxford University Press, pp.8–9.

46. Thomas Hardy (1994 [1878]) *The Return of the Native*, Harmondsworth: Penguin, pp.141–172.

47. Thomas Hardy (1923) 'The Famous Tragedy of the Queen of Cornwall at Tintagel in Lyonesse', in Amy Hale, Alan M. Kent and Tim Saunders (eds.) (2000) *Inside Merlin's Cave: A Cornish Arthurian Reader 1000–2000*, London: Francis Boutle, pp.144–172.

48. For modern scholarly views on these texts, see Peter Millington (2003) 'The Truro Cordwainers' Play: A "New" Eighteenth-Century Christmas Play' in *Folklore*, 114, 1, pp.53–73; Tom Pettit (2003) 'From Stage to Folk: A Note on the Passages from Addison's Rosamond in the "Truro" Mummers' Play' in *Folklore*, 114, 2, pp.262–270. In the Nance Collection there is a version of 'The Mylor Play' in Nance's hand, alongside a copy of 'The Tenby Christmas Play'. There is also a paper titled 'Folk-Plays of Cornwall' which was read to the Village Drama Society, Exeter in 1921, and to the Cambridge Antiquarian Society in November 1929. See also 'A Redruth Christmas Play' in *Old Cornwall* (1925), no. 1, April, pp. 29–31. This was communicated by Miss L. Eddy to Mr A.K. Hamilton Jenkin, a witness of its performance. The characters are King George, Jack, Doctor Brown and Jacky Sweep. This drama seems to have been originally written in the light of Nelson's victory at Trafalgar. See in addition, 'A Guise-Dance play, St Keverne' in ibid., pp.31–32. This was communicated by Capt F.J. Roskruge, R.N. and written after Mr William Mitchell's memory of a performance over seventy years before (c.1850). The characters were Father Christmas, Turkish Knight, King George (St George), Doctor and Little Man Jack.

49. For pictorial representation, see Douglas Williams (1987) *Festivals of Cornwall*, St Teath: Bossiney Books.

50. Deane and Shaw (2003), op. cit., p.156.

51. Ibid., p.158. Nance apparently added another verse: 'But to a greater than St George our Helston has a right-O, / St Michael with his wings outspread; the Archangel so bright-O,/Who fought the fiend-O, of all mankind the foe'. Deane and Shaw rightly argue this 'totally misses the point of its original meaning'.

52. William Sandys [Uncle Jan Trenoodle] (1846) *Specimens of Cornish Provincial Dialect*, London: John Russell Smith, pp.60–61. Since 1998, Andrew George, the Member of Parliament for St Ives, has played the part of St George.

53. Deane and Shaw (2003), op. cit., p.158. This has a curious echo in the following title: Raymond Williams (1973) *The Country and the City*, St Albans: Paladin.

54. Correspondence with Brian Murdoch, dated 1 November 2005. Murdoch also notes that modern German has the word Tau [rope].

55. Sowena (1999) *A Month of Sundays*, St Agnes: Sowena.

56. Cited in Donald R. Rawe (1990 [1971]) *Padstow's Obby Oss and May Day Festivities*, Padstow: Lodenek Press, p.7. There are noticeable similarities here to the Helston Hal-an-Tow song. Nance makes comprehensive notes on Padstow's folkloric heritage, and these are contained in the Nance Collection. For contemporary scholarship on this, see Jason Semmens, 'Guising, ritual and revival' in *Old Cornwall*, vol. 13, no.5 (2005), pp.39–46. For a consideration of the St George motif, see Bob Steward (1988) *Where is St George?: Pagan Imagery in English Folk Song*, London: Blandford.

57. 'The Christmas Play of Saint George & the Turkish Knight' in Nance Collection, p.1 (Nance Collection).

58. Ibid.

59. Ibid., p.2.

60. Ibid., p.4. These quotations may be found in the version of the play included in the present volume.

61. Ibid. p. 5

62. Ibid.

63. Ibid.

64. Ibid., p.6.

65. Ibid., p.7.

66. Ibid., p.8. Nance is very specific about the musical motifs used in the production.

67. Ibid., p.10.

68. Ibid., p.12.

69. Ibid.

70. Ibid., p.13.

71. Ibid., p.16.

72. Ibid., p.17.

73. Ibid., p.19.

74. R. Morton Nance (1956) *The Cledry Plays: Drolls of Old Cornwall for Village Acting and Home Reading*, Marazion and Penzance: The Federation of Old Cornwall Societies. After Nance's name comes the phrase: Dun yn-rak gans an gwary! [*Let's get on with the play!*]. Cornish phrases introduce all three plays.

75. See O.J. Padel (1986) *A Popular Dictionary of Cornish Place-Names*, Penzance: Alison Hodge, p.127. Padel indicates that this was once 'valley of Clodri'. The local pronunciation is Nancledry or Cledry.

76. Henry Jenner 'Some Possible Arthurian Place-Names in West Penwith' in *Journal of the Royal Institution of Cornwall* (1912), p.87.

77. This is given considerable discussion in Rosalind Conklin Hays, C.E. McGee, Sally L Joyce and Evelyn S. Newlyn (eds.) (1999) *Records of Early English Drama: Dorset and Cornwall*, Toronto: University of Toronto Press and Brepols, pp.397–438.

78. Nance (1956) op.cit., p.3. Nance collected fragments of folk-play scholarship from all over Britain. See, in particular, Arthur Beckett (ed.) (1927) *The Sussex County Magazine*, Brighton: T.P. Beckett, pp.545–552; and

'The Plough Boy's Play: A Version Recorded' in the *Yorkshire Post*, January 11 (1937). See also the bundle marked 'Mumming Plays'. Various events are mentioned including the Stithians Play, a St Keverne Guise Dance and other fragments.

79. Joyce and Newlyn indicate some limited touring activity, but only to the next village. Jane A. Bakere (1980) *The Cornish Ordinalia: A Critical Study*, Cardiff: University of Wales Press, p.17 offers that sometimes players did move to alternate venues in medieval Cornwall. Touring medieval folk-theatre is given an interesting fictional treatment in Barry Unsworth (1995) *Morality Play*, London: Hamish Hamilton, where Cornwall is mentioned. In later centuries, there is actually less evidence of the kind of mobile drama Nance alludes to.

80. See William Bottrell (ed.) (1870) *Traditions and Hearthside Stories of West Cornwall: First Series*, Penzance: W. Cornish, (ed.) (1873) *Traditions and Hearthside Stories of West Cornwall: Second Series*, Penzance: Beare and Son, (ed.) (1880) *Traditions and Hearthside Stories of West Cornwall: Third Series*, Penzance: F. Rodda; Robert Hunt (ed.) (1865) *Popular Romances of the West of England: The Drolls, Traditions, and Superstitions of Old Cornwall – First and Second Series*, London: John Camden Hotton.

81. For a useful introduction to this, see Philip Payton (1996) *Cornwall*, Fowey: Alexander Associates, p.268. See also Derek Williams (1997) 'Robert Morton Nance' in *An Baner Kernewek/The Cornish Banner*, no. 88, pp.14–18.

82. Nance (1956) op.cit., p.3. It appears that 'Duffy' was in draft for several years. *The Times* (1919) 23 June has an intriguing reference to a Cornish play by Nance being performed in the Pavilion Theatre. This was part of the centenary celebrations of the Penzance subscription library. The likely candidate is *Duffy*.

83. Baz Kershaw (1992) *The Politics of Performance: Radical Theatre as Cultural Intervention*, London and New York: Routledge, p.1. See also Sandy Craig (ed.) (1980) *Dreams and Reconstructions: Alternative Theatre in Britain*, Ambersgate: Amber Lane Press.

84. See Kneehigh Theatre (2005) *Tristan & Yseult*, London: Oberon Books; Alan M. Kent (2005) *Ordinalia – The Cornish Mystery Play Cycle: A Verse Translation*, London: Francis Boutle.

85. Nance (1956) op.cit., p.3.

86. Exceptions are Williams (1997), op. cit. and Alan M. Kent (2000a), op. cit., p.158 and p.173.

87. Compare two recent 'dialect' glossaries: K.C. Phillipps (1993) *A Glossary of Cornish Dialect*, Padstow: Tabb House, Les Merton (2003) *Oall Rite Me Ansum! A Salute to Cornish Dialect*, Newbury: Countryside Books, with earlier glossaries such as Nance (1956), op. cit., pp.103–109 and even W.F. Ivey (ed.) (1976) *A Dictionary of Cornish Dialect Words*, Helston: Helston Printers. The difference is greater still with F.W.P. Jago (ed.) (1882) *The Ancient Language, and the Dialect of Cornwall, with an enlarged Glossary of Cornish Provincial Words*, Truro: Netherton and Worth. The bundle in the Nance Collection marked 'Cornish Dialect' is an excellent collection and merits further study.

88. Alan M. Kent, '"Bringin' the Dunkey Down from the Carn": Cornu-English in Context 1549–2004 – A Provisional Analysis' in Hildegard L.C. Tristram (ed.) (2006) *The Celtic Englishes IV*, Vienna: Benjamin.

89. Such an actor might be David Shaw of Penzance, famed for a recent interpretation of William Bottrell.

90. See Joyce and Newlyn (1999), op. cit.

91. See Alan M. Kent (ed.) (2000b), pp.85–89, pp.90–92 and pp.121–124.

92. For the former, see Will Coleman (2005) *Madgy Figgy's Pig*, Cornwall: Brave Tales; (2005) *Tom and the Giant*, Cornwall: Brave Tales. For the latter, see Charles Causley and Michael Foreman (1999) *The Merrymaid of Zennor*, London: Orchard Books.

93. Eileen Molony (1971) *Folk Tales of the West*, London: Kaye and Ward.

94. Donald R. Rawe (1972) *Traditional Cornish Stories and Rhymes*, Padstow: Lodenek Press.

95. Eric Quayle and Michael Foreman (1986) *The Magic Ointment and Other Cornish Legends*, London: Andersen Press.

96. Shirley Climo and Anthony Bacon Venti (1999) *Magic and Mischief: Tales from Cornwall*, New York: Clarion Books.

97. See Jacob Grimm, Wilhelm Grimm, Carol Ann Duffy and Marketa Prachaticka (1999) *Rumpelstiltskin and other Grimm Tales*, London: Faber and Faber.

98. Bottrell (1873), op. cit., pp.1–26.

99. Hunt (1865), op. cit., *First Series*, pp.239–247.

100. Bottrell (1873), op. cit., p.1.

101. Nance (1956), op. cit., p.4.

102. Ibid.

103. Ibid., p.6.

104. Ibid., p.7. ['Clocks' are ornaments on the sides of stockings. Eds.]

105. Ibid., p.8.

106. Similar sentiment in Cornish is offered in the rhyme given to Edward Lhuyd in 1700 by the parish clerk of St Just-in-Penwith, and later recorded by William Pryce: 'An Lavor gôth ewe laver gwîr, / Ne vedn nevera doas vâs a tavaz re hîr;/Bes dên heb tavaz a gollas e dîr' [*The old saying is a true saying, No good will be counted to come from too long a tongue; But a man without a tongue lost his land*]. Nance knew this triplet well. See Kent and Saunders (eds.) (2000), op.cit., pp.246–247. In a letter to Jenner, dated 29 May 1918, Nance refers in passing to 'my salvage work on the flotsam and jetsam of Old Cornish' (meaning the words of the Cornish language still to be found in Cornu-English). See the Nance Collection.

107. Bottrell (1873), op. cit., p.4.

108. Nance (1956), op. cit., p.9.

109. The exception is Phillipps (1993), op. cit., pp.9–13.

110. Nance (1956) op.cit.

111. Phillipps (1993), op.cit.

112. Nance (1956), op. cit., pp.103–109.

113. Ibid., p.9.

114. See, for example, James Kelman (1994) *How Late it Was, How Late*, London: Secker and Warburg.

115. See Kent, (2000a), op. cit., pp.269–271, (2005) *Proper Job, Charlie Curnow!* Tiverton: Halsgrove; K.C. Phillipps (ed.) (1995) *The Cornish Journals of Charles Lee*, Padstow: Tabb House; Payton (1996), op. cit., pp.252–253; Nick Darke (1999) *The Riot*, London: Methuen; N.R. Phillips (2005) *Apocalypse Dreckly*, Tiverton: Halsgrove.

116. Nance (1956), op. cit., p.11.

117. See Robert Penhallurick (ed.) (2000) *Debating Dialect: Essays on the Philosophy of Dialect Study*, Cardiff: University of Wales Press, (2003) *Studying the English Language*, Basingstoke: Palgrave Macmillan, pp. 143–155; Salikoko S. Mufwene (2001) *The Ecology of Language Evolution*, Cambridge: Cambridge University Press.

118. Nance (1956), op. cit., p.35.

119. Ibid., p.14.

120. Ibid.

121. Ibid., p.13.

122. See Christina Rossetti (1830–1894) 'Goblin Market' cited in Liz Goodman (ed.) (1996) *Literature and Gender*, London: Routledge, pp.272–276.

123. Nance (1956), op. cit., p.17.

124. Ibid., p.18.

125. Ibid., p.20.

126. *Fugo* derives from a Cornish word for a cave. The modern term fogou is generally applied to the stone-lined and roofed passages found west of the Fal estuary in Cornwall. Their function is still unclear.

127. *Bucca* is the Cornish word for a mischievous sprite or goblin.

128. Nance (1956), op. cit., p.33.

129. See *BBC Drama 1922–1928* at www.kent.ac.uk/sffva/invisible. This web database created by Alan Beck, is highly useful. *The Times* 4 May (1928) says 'This symphony concert will be preceded by a performance of 'Duffy' in three acts by Mr Morton Nance, with Miss Katharine Frazier, Mrs Stanley Jones, Mr Robert Morton Nance and Mr A.K. Hamilton Jenkin in the cast.' The performance was scheduled for broadcasting at 9.35pm on 2LO, the first BBC radio station, and on other stations.

130. Nance (1956), op. cit., p.79.

131. Ibid.

132. Ibid., p.86. To lowster means to perform hard, labouring work.

133. Ibid., p.87.

134. Ibid., p.90.

135. Ibid.

136. Ibid., p.89.

137. Ibid.

138. Ibid., p.90.

139. Ibid., p.91.

140. Ibid., p.100.

141. 'Change-about is Fair Play: A Christmas Droll' in Nance Collection. The character was originally called Becky. [Nance's handwriting is less clear than usual, but 'Tamsin Housekeeper' seems a likely interpretation, given that the character is the Squire's old nurse and makes a show of doing housework. Eds.]

142. Ibid., p.2.

143. Ibid., p.14.

144. 'The Tragedy of Chrononhotonthologos: being the most Tragical Tragedy that ever was Tragediz'd by any Company of Tragedians' in Nance Collection. [There is a microcard copy in Exeter University Library (Microforms Section) 'Three Centuries of Drama', Box 11, card 90. It seems likely that Nance transcribed the play. His wording for its provenance is 'Written by Benjamin Bounce, Esq., [Henry Carey, 1734]'. Eds.] Nance was clearly following a tradition: there is a seventeenth-century German play by Gryphius, titled *Horribilicribrifax*, which features a character called Daradiridatumtarides.

145. 'Tom and the Giant: A Christmas Play', ibid. All of these dramas, and several drafts of the published plays, are hand-written. For the most part, Nance is chaotic in his scholarship. Notes and ideas are recorded on scraps of paper, undated and unreferenced.

146. Ibid. This means 'Fair play is good play'.

147. See 'John Knill', ibid. There is also, among other things, a drama titled 'Honest Folk' concerning exploits of the Rosevear family, but this is not in Nance's hand, and appears to be a later composition.

148. Peter Berresford Ellis (1974) *The Cornish Language and its Literature*, London and New York: Routledge and Kegan Paul; Miles (1992) op. cit.; Philip Carr-Gomm (ed.) (2003) *The Rebirth of Druidry: Ancient Wisdom for Today*, London: Harper Collins; Denys Val Baker (1980) *The Spirit of Cornwall*, London: W.H. Allen.

149. See Nance (1958 [1929]), op. cit.

150. Peter Berresford Ellis (1993) *The Celtic Dawn: A History of Pan-Celticism*, London: Constable, p.78.

151. See Henry Jenner, 'Cornwall: A Celtic Nation' in Derek R. Williams (ed.) (2004) *Henry and Katharine Jenner: A Celebration of Cornwall's Culture, Language and Identity*, London: Francis Boutle, pp.56–69. This paper was originally read before the Pan-Celtic Congress in Caernarfon in August 1904 and orginally published in the *Celtic Review* in January 1905. See also Derek Williams (1996) 'Henry Jenner: The Years of Fulfilment' in *An Baner Kernewek/The Cornish Banner*, no.85, pp.15–18.

152. Smith (1947), op. cit., p.16.

153. R. Morton Nance [1932] *An Balores*, St Ives: James Lanham. There are some parallels in *An Balores* to an earlier skit by Nance involving a jury. See R. Morton Nance (1926) *The Cornish Jury: A Dialect Dialogue for XII Characters*, St Ives: St Ives Old Cornwall Society. The twelve are Foreman, Trebilcock, Angwin,

Chegwidden, Mennear, Trenerry, Spargo, Pengelly, Quinterell, Polglaze, Trevaskis and Bosence, and the play investigates the guilt of an old woman. [Interestingly, E. G. Retallack Hooper's papers in the archives of Gorseth Kernow contain annotated copies of the published text of *An Balores*, one of which has a cast-list at the back, with Nance as Justice. Eds.]

154. The link is made explicit in numerous sources, but one of the most famous is in Cervantes' *The Ingenious Hidalgo Don Quixote de la Mancha* (1604–5 and 1625). The translation reads: "'Have you not read,' cried Don Quixote, "the Annals and History of Britain, where are recorded the famous deeds of King Arthur who according to an ancient tradition in that Kingdom never died but was turned into a crow (chough) by enchantment and shall one day resume his former shape and recover his Kingdom again? For which reason, since that time the people of Great Britain dare not kill a crow. In this good king's time the most noble order of the Knights of the Round Table was first instituted.'" Cited in Jas. L. Palmer (n.d.) *The Cornish Chough Through the Ages*, Cornwall: The Federation of Old Cornwall Societies, p.4.

155. For a life, see Peter Ackroyd (1998) *The Life of Thomas More*, London: Chatto and Windus.

156. Nance [1932], op. cit., pp.2–3. The translation is Nance's own.

157. Ibid.

158. The iconography and imagery is continued in the Richard Jenkin-edited magazine *Delyow Derow* (1989–96). There is a contemporary publishing house called Palores Publications. See also the concerns of the poets in Tim Saunders (ed.) (1999), *The Wheel: An Anthology of Modern Poetry in Cornish 1850–1980*, London: Francis Boutle.

159. Nance [1932], op. cit., pp.8–9.

160. No doubt the early twentieth-century poets would be genuinely impressed with the real chough's return to Cornish cliffs, as well as with the official status now afforded to Cornish.

161. Nance [1932], op. cit., pp.10–11.

162. *Ceremonies of the Gorsedd of the Bards of Cornwall* (n.d.), pp.12–13. For a useful perspective on the imagining of a past 'Celtic world' see contributors to Gerard Carruthers and Alan Rawes (eds.) (2003) *English Romanticism and the Celtic World*, Cambridge: Cambridge University Press.

163. The agenda was set by Magnus Maclean (1902) *The Literature of the Celts*, London: Blackie and Son.

164. See Saunders (ed.) (1999), op. cit.

165. Ibid., pp.88–95 and pp.98–103.

166. Ibid., pp.146–163, pp.184–197 and pp.198–209.

167. Ibid., pp.52–53. Translation slightly revised by Peter Thomas, 2006.

168. Ibid., pp.52–55. [The poem is printed in the 1929 Gorsedd programme, with a rhymed English translation. Eds.]

169. Ibid., pp.54–55.

170. See Robert Welch (ed.) (1993) *W.B. Yeats: Writings on Irish Folklore, Legend and Myth*, London: Penguin.

171. See J.R.R. Tolkien (1977) *The Silmarillion*, London: Unwin; Brian Bates (2002) *The Real Middle Earth: Magic and Mystery in the Dark Ages*, London: Sidgwick and Jackson.

172. *Old Cornwall* (1935) vol. 2, no. 9, p.6 and p.10. Another Breton song titled 'Can an Yar [The Song of the Hen]' was given similar treatment later on. The English version is Nance's own.

173. Saunders (ed.) (1999), op. cit., pp.54–57. This was first published in 1929.

174. Old Cornwall (1932), vol. 2, no. 4, pp.31–32. This writer's translation.

175. Cited in Saunders (ed.) (1999), op. cit., pp.60–63. Several copies of the poem are to be found in the Nance Collection.

176. R. M[orton] N[ance] (1947), 'Edward Chirgwin's Cornish Song' in *Old Cornwall*, vol. 4, no. 6, Summer, pp. 210–213; H. W. L[loyd] (1883), 'A Cornish Song ("Kân Kerniw")' in *Y Cymmrodor*, vol. 6, pp. 88–97; Kenneth Hurlstone Jackson (ed.) (1951) *A Celtic Miscellany*, Harmondsworth: Penguin, pp.221–222.

177. Saunders (ed.) (1999), op. cit., pp.64–65.

178. Ibid., pp.62–63.

179. *Old Cornwall* (1940) vol. 3, no. 8, p.337.

180. Ibid., no. 7, p.299 and (1941), vol. 3, no. 9, pp.360–361.

181. See, for example, 'An Vowes Doth' in Kernow (1934) no.7, p.1, 'Nicholas Boson' in *Kernow* (1935), no. 12, p.7. Phoebe Nance supplies a poem entitled 'Pyu a-Wor?' [Who Knows?] in *Kernow* (1935), no. 12, p.9. The contribution of A.S.D. Smith needs a separate study.

182. See *Kernow*, (1935), no.8, pp.3–4. The song begins 'En pedn an vledhan, pan gwav o gwyn,/Be gennes Map Dew a Varya wyn,/Rag sawya dhort pehas an bys-ma,/Ha bownans rag dry dh'an poble da. [At the end of the year, when winter was white,/The Son of God was born of blessed Mary, / To save this world from sin,/And to bring life to the good people].

183. See *An Gannas*.

184. *Old Cornwall* (1932) vol. 2, no. 3, pp.23–26.

185. Ibid., p.23.

186. For a version of this famous narrative, see Kent and Saunders (2000), op. cit., pp.212–218.

187. *Old Cornwall* (1932) op.cit., p.24 and p. 26.

188. Ibid., (1933), vol. 2, no. 5, pp.25–27.

189. Ibid., (1935), vol. 2, no. 9, pp. 25–27; no. 10, pp.19–24.

190. Ibid., (1937), vol. 3, no. 1, pp. 22–25; (1938), no. 3, pp. 111–116, no. 4, pp. 142–147; (1939), no. 5, pp. 200–204, no. 6, pp. 240–244; (1940), no. 7, pp. 300–301, no. 8, pp. 343–346.

191. Ibid., (1941), no. 9, pp. 388–391, no. 10, pp. 422–425; (1942), no. 11, pp. 464–465, no. 12, pp. 518–520.

192. Ibid., (1943), vol. 4, no. 1, pp.25–27, no. 2, pp.72–74; (1945), no. 4, pp.119–121; (1946), no. 5, pp.152–155; (1947), no. 6, pp.182–184; (1948), no. 8, pp.288–289; (1949), no. 9, pp.332–336.

193. R. Morton Nance (1939) *Lyver Pymp Marthus Seleven: Warlergh an Dus Coth Cuntellys ha Scryfys*, St Ives: Lanham.

194. Hunt (1865) Second Series, op. cit., pp.265–268.

195. Nance (1939), op. cit., pp.5–15.

196. *Old Cornwall* (1951), vol. 5, no. 1, p.37; (1952), no. 2, pp.65–67; (1953), no. 4, pp.152–153; (1954), no. 5, pp.214–215; (1958), no. 9, p.380; (1959), no. 10, pp. 426–429.

197. Ibid., (1953), no. 3, p.134.

198. Ibid., (1956), no. 7, pp.321–324.

199. R. Morton Nance, Edith Grenville and Hal Wyn (R. St V. Allin-Collins) (n.d.) *An den ha'y dhen wreg ... and some short stories in the Cornish Language*, St Ives: James Lanham.

200. *Old Cornwall* (1931), vol. 2, no. 1, pp.24–25.

201. Ibid., (1949), vol. 4, no. 10, pp.368–371.

202. Nance and Smith edited and translated into Unified Cornish for the Federation of Old Cornwall Societies the following extracts: No. 1: Bewnans Meryasek (1949 and, as St Meriasek in Cornwall, 1966), No. 2: An tyr Marya [c. 1951], No. 3: Sylvester ha'n Dhragon [c. 1952], No. 4: Abram hag Ysak [c. 1954–55], No. 5: Adam ha Seth [c. 1955], No. 6: Davyd hag Urry [c. 1955]. The Cornish Language Board published No. 7: An Venen ha'y Map in 1969 and subsequently reprinted the others.

203. Graham Sandercock (ed.) (1982) *R. Morton Nance and A.S.D. Smith: The Cornish Ordinalia, second play: Christ's Passion*, Cornwall: Cornish Language Board, (ed.) (1984) *R. Morton Nance and A.S.D. Smith: The Cornish Ordinalia, third play: Resurrection*, Cornwall: Cornish Language Board. See also R. Morton Nance (1935) 'The Plen an Gwary or Cornish Playing-Place' in *Journal of the Royal Institution of Cornwall*, 24.

204. Ray Chubb, Richard Jenkin and Graham Sandercock (eds.) (2001) *R. Morton Nance and A.S.D. Smith: The Cornish Ordinalia, first play: Origo Mundi*, Redruth: Agan Tavas.

205. See Carr-Gomm (ed.) (2003) op.cit.; Nigel Pennick (1996) *Celtic Sacred Landscapes*, London: Thames and Hudson; Mark Abley (2003) *Spoken Here: Travels Among Threatened Languages*, London: William

Heinemann; Marcus Tanner (2004) *The Last of the Celts*, New Haven and London: Yale University Press.

206. Antonia Barber and Nicola Bayley (1990) *The Mousehole Cat*, London: Walker Books.

207. 'Tom Bawcock's Eve' in *Old Cornwall* (1927), no. 5, April, pp.20–22.

208. Ibid.

209. Ibid. See also Ralph Dunstan (ed.) (1932) *Cornish Dialect and Folk Songs*, Truro: Jordan's Bookshop, p.7. A separate study is needed of Nance's song-lyrics and his contribution to the musical heritage of Cornwall.

210. J. L. Palmer (1960), 'Nyns-yu marow Mordon' in *Old Cornwall*, vol. 5, no. 11, pp.450–451.

211. See Georgina Boyes (1993) *The Imagined Village: Culture, Ideology and the English Folk Revival*, Manchester: Manchester University Press; Hutton (1994) and (1996), op.cit.

212. R. Morton Nance (ed.) (1990 [1934 and 1938]) *Gerlyver Noweth Kernewek-Sawsnek ha Sawsnek-Kernewek [A New Cornish-English and English-Cornish Dictionary]*, Redruth: Dyllansow Truran.

Acknowledgements

I am grateful to the following people in the preparation of this chapter: Professor Charles Thomas, Professor Brian Murdoch, Tim Saunders, Derek Williams, Mick Paynter, Audrey Pool, Angela Broome and the Royal Institution of Cornwall, Kim Cooper, Joanne Hillman and the staff of the Cornwall Centre, Redruth, and Annabelle Read of the Morrab Library, Penzance.

The Christmas Play of Saint George & the Turkish Knight[1] (including parts of the traditional play)

R. Morton Nance

Dramatis Personae
1. Saint George.
2. The Turkish Knight.
3. Father Christmas.
4. The King of Egypt.
5. The Dragon.
6. The Doctor.
7. The Princess Sabra.
8. Slasha.
[*Courtiers may be added at discretion to attend the King of Egypt and, on her first and last appearances, the Princess Sabra.*]

Prologue

[*Spoken by one of the players outside.*]
Open your doors, and let us in;
We hope your favours all to win.
Whether we rise, or whether we fall,
We'll do our best to please you all.

Nance's illlustration for the Christmas Play

[*Spoken as from the house.*]
Who comes here, this time of night,
Neither by day nor by candle-light?

[*Curtain rises.*]

ACT I

[*No scenery is required. A cleared floor makes an excellent stage.*]

[*Enter Father Christmas.*]

F. Christmas   Here come I, Old Father Christmas,
                           Welcome or welcome not.
                  I hope Old Father Christmas
                           Will never be forgot.
          Room, a room, brave gallants, room! and give us room to enter,
          We here resort to show some sport, to while away the winter!
          Room, a room, brave gallants, room! and give us room to ride,
          And we'll display our Christmas Play, all in the Christmas Tide!
          Room, a room, brave gallants, room! and let our actors come
[*Trumpet. Drum.*]   To the <u>sound</u> of the trumpet, and the <u>beat</u> of the drum!
                  All in this room there shall be shown
                  The dreadfullest battles that ever were known!
                  The like was never on this stage,
                  In this or any other age –
                  If you can't credit what I say,
                  Come in, thou King of Egypt – clear the way!

[*Enter King of Egypt and Princess Sabra, to a flourish of trumpets and a roll of drums. Exit Father Christmas.*]

King   I am the King of Egypt,
                  As plainly doth appear;

And here is Princess Sabra,
     My only daughter dear;
The apple of my aged eye,
     My hope, my joy, my pride.
Great Egypt's throne shall come to him
     Who gains her for his bride.
Step forth, then, O my daughter,
     And act thy part with me:
Come show thy lovely features
     Unto this company!

[*Princess comes forward.*]

Princess   I am the Princess Sabra:
        My beauty here behold –
I have two eyes; a nose; a mouth;
        A little crown of gold.
From far and near, still suitors crowd
        To seek me as a bride;
But he who'd wed me must be shown
        A knight of courage tried –
Who seeks my golden crown and heart to win
Must his own mettle prove nor lead nor tin!

[*Trumpet. Enter Turkish Knight. On foot here.*]

King   Here comes just such a man of might –
Come forth and speak, thou Turkish Knight!
With silvern tongue to us unfold
The treasures of thy heart of gold.

T. Knight [*salaams*]
     Sad news your Majesty I bring –
     I dread to tell it to my King.

King   Say on!

T. Knight   O King! A dragon vile
               Has left the waters of the Nile.
               He first, in hunger ate a lamb;
               Next tried a ewe and then a ram.
               He soon had gobbled all the sheep;
               Then chased the boy that watch did keep.
               Our soldiers fought him – but in vain,
               And now they've all run home again.
               So venom'd is this Dragon's breath,
               To cross his path is instant death.
               And now, outside the city gates,
               This hungry monster lies and waits.

Princess   Oh! What a nasty, greedy thing!

King   Go, feed the brute!

T. Knight   O! Mighty King!
               Our live-stock all he's had, to eat,
               And all our store of butcher's meat:
               We've cleared the market – stripped the hooks –
               There's not a chop left for the cooks.
               And yet the ravening monster calls
               For more outside the city walls.
               We've fed him all the food we can;
               And now, there's nothing left but – man!

King   Alas, my people! Pick him out
               The toughest that you see about –
               Old bachelors, that none could miss,
               Old maids, that never knew a kiss.

[*Exit Turkish Knight.*]

> This sacrifice we gladly make
> For our unhappy people's sake.

[*Re-enter Turkish Knight.*]

T. Knight   O! King! The Dragon's in a rage;
                  He won't touch food of such an age.

King   Unhappier people! Then the young
                  And tender to him must be flung.
                  Our crown shall hold their names; then draw
                  To see which next shall fill his maw.

[*Gives crown, inside which is a red cap.*]

T. Knight   It shall be done!

[*Exit with crown.*]

King [*aside*]   If truth be told,
                  I'm glad he will not eat the old!
                  When young food fails, should there be need
                  That I against this pest should lead
                  An expedition, punitive,
                  To come back from it I may live;
                  So boldly I, should matters worsen,
                  May lead this army forth in person.

[*Re-enter Turkish Knight with crown.*]

T. Knight [*bows to King*]
                  Sad news, your Majesty! The lot

Has fallen on a tender spot –
The Princess Sabra, [*bows to Princess*] by your law,
Must go. We first her name did draw!

[*Shows slip of paper.*]

King   The Princess? Sirrah, you mistake!
                  That law for her We did not make!

[*Then puts on crown and looks majestic.*]

T. Knight   O, mighty King! Such is her lot.
                  The law, once fixed, can alter not.
                  The Princess must a victim be;
                  Made dragon's-meat by thy decree.

Princess   Ah! Say it not, thou naughty Knight!
                  Speak father, speak! and ease my fright!

King   Alas, my child, I fear he's right –
                  [*aside*] What a disastrous oversight!

Princess   Is there no remedy; and must I go?

T. Knight   I see no remedy; it must be so.

King   Alas, no remedy, my daughter dear!
                  Without some worthy champion should appear,
                  To slay the dreadful Dragon that's outside
                  And win my lovely Sabra for his bride –
                  My Sabra, if thou love, thou Turkish Knight,
                  Get thee to horse, and straight the Dragon fight!

T. Knight   I'm brave! – I love her! – Yet to fight I'm loath.

Who knows? – the Dragon might devour us both!

Princess   Where's now thy heart of gold, base-metalled suitor? –
Thy silver-seeming tongue turns out but pewter.
Whose tinkling tin with lumpish lead alloyed
Thy paltry heart proves pinchbeck, false and void –
A tinselled spangle glittering in thy breast,
That turns to dross when put beneath the test!
Farewell for ever, coward! Quit my sight!
Rather I'd die than wed <u>thee</u>, Turkish Knight.

[End of the First Act.]

ACT II

[The Princess is seen chained – her chain may be made of twisted paper or cardboard. Links painted gold – it should have a large ring of the same at its end. She leads a woolly toy lamb on a leash of blue ribbons; with her is the King of Egypt.]

Princess   Alas! In all the country round,
No champion bold enough is found,
With spear in hand to spur his nag on,
And ride to rid me of the Dragon –
I, like my lamb, have no defence
Against his claws, save innocence!

King   Sabra, farewell! Here must thou wait,
And like a princess meet thy fate.
I could not bear thy end to see –
Worse than ten deaths 'twould seem to me!

[He wipes his weeping eyes.]

Princess   Farewell, then, Father! *[sound of hoofs off]* Haste away!

I hear the Dragon seek his prey:

[*Exit King of Egypt hurriedly.*]

> I hear his horrid jaws go snap;
> I hear his leathern pinions flap;
> I hear his claws that beat the ground –
> Nay! – Yonder horseman makes the sound!
> How bold his mien! How fine his steed,
> As o'er the plain he spurs at speed.

[*Enter S. George on Hobby Horse with red-cross shield and cross-hilted sword. –*
Trumpets.]

S. George   O, Princess, lovely without peer,
Why art thou left alone out here,
Within this waste of sand and stones,
Where nothing human rests but bones?
No chaperon! No aged nurse!
It seem most careless, if not worse.

Princess   O, go thy ways, thou goodly Knight.
We'll both be gobbled at one bite!
I'll stay here, as I'm bound to do;
But what keeps me need not keep you!

S. George   Fair maid, I cannot leave thee so –
Alone, alarmed, and full of woe –
I've vowed a vow, O fair Princess,
To aid all damsels in distress!
I prithee then make known thy grief –
This sword is sworn to thy relief!

Princess   Thou canst not help me, noble Knight.

Spare then thine eyes a shocking sight –
Here must I die to save this land!
O, fly! The Dragon is at hand!

S. George   The Dragon? Tell me! Hast thou seen
That scaly beast with hide of green?
I've sought him long, both high and low –
I am Saint George, his mortal foe,
Who drinks no water, eats no bread,
Till from its trunk I've hewn his head!

Princess   Saint George? – I thought mine hour had struck,
But yet there's hope of life and luck!

[*She clasps her hands in joy.*]

S. George   Ay, more than hope! A moment wait,
Chained there to make a charming bait;
Then, though his jaws were ten times stronger
I'll have him caught – like any conger.

[*Exit S. George. Drums.*]

Princess   How brave! How handsome! – Hush!! He comes again –
[*shrieks*] Ah, no! – The Dragon! – Now all hope is vain!

[*Enter the Dragon.*]

Dragon [*capering round the Princess Sabra and her little lamb*]
Ho! Ho! Here's something like a dinner!
I'll snap her nose off, to begin her!

[*Princess Sabra cowers and shrieks.*]

Or no, at pudding-time I'll eat her,
And start upon this woolly bleater!

[*He is about to devour the lamb, but Princess Sabra snatches it in her arms, shrieking more loudly still. Re-enter S. George. Drums. As he declaims, he rides up and down, beating his sword on his shield.*]

S. George   Here come I, Saint George,
From England did I spring!
I'll fight this Dragon bold,
My wonders to begin –
I'll clip his wings, that he shan't fly:
I'll cut him down, or else I die!

Dragon   Who's this that seeks the Dragon's blood,
And calls so angry and so loud?
Who is this rogue of manners rude,
That comes betwixt me and my food?
Who's this that comes
With sound of drums
The Dragon to defy?
His back I'll strip,
His coat I'll rip,
If he to fight should try.
I'll cut his doublet full of holes
And make his buttons fly!

S. George   I am Saint George, Old England's pride,
That man of mighty name!
With sword and buckler by my side,
I hope to win the game!

Dragon   Low shalt thou lie, thou English clown –
With my strong claws I'll cut thee down!

With my long teeth and scurvy jaw
I'll seize thee up within my maw –
Of such I'd break up half a score,
To stay my stomach, till I'd more!

[*They fight up and down stage, to 'Brian Boru's Lament'. The Dragon falls. All the fights in this play are done to music, each movement being arranged and rehearsed. S. George then frees Princess Sabra from her chain, which he throws over the Dragon's back with 'strong man' actions. Trumpets as S. George bows before her and she curtsies.*]

Princess   Well fought, thou noble Knight!
                      Low now the monster lies;
                      But still I faint with fright –
                      Ah! See him roll his eyes!

[*She points with horror at the Dragon.*]

                      Pray clip those wings and pare those claws;
                      Uproot those fangs that line his jaws,
                      Ere on me yet he flies!

S. George   His venom's spent; his wings are weak;
                      And harmless are his claws and beak;
                      He cannot scratch, nor even peck –
                      Come, put thy girdle round his neck!

[*Princess Sabra takes off her girdle and puts it about the Dragon's neck as a leash.*]

                      He and thy lamb will make a pair
                      So meek he'll be, and debonair –
                      So! – Lead him at a gentle pace;
                      He'll follow to the market-place.

[*They proceed around the stage; S. George in front, Sabra bearing her lamb and leading the Dragon, who shambles behind. If Hobby Horse is of suitable shape Sabra may ride 'pillion' on it, towing Dragon astern, but with her feet actually on the ground.*]

Princess   Remorse my conscience sore doth bite,
                  Now that the battle's done,
                  That ere for me I let thee fight,
                  I did not warn thee, gallant Knight,
                  I, also, should be won:
                  [*coyly, with averted face*]
                  The King, my father, vowed that he
                  Should wed me, who should set me free.
                  [*She is here more bashful.*]

S. George [*with great enthusiasm*]
                  Who set thee free? – That's me!! – Oh joy!!!

[*The procession halts. S. George and Princess Sabra stand facing one another across Dragon, who lies humbly between them. He is about to embrace her, but she puts up a restraining hand.*]

Princess   Hush, here's the market, foolish boy!
                  You would not bring me to disgrace
                  With love made in the market-place!

S. George   'Twere as discreet to hug thee here
                  As in the desert vast and drear;
                  The town is void! – No living thing
                  Is seen! – Yet stay! Here comes the King!

[*He assumes 'correct attitude' – Re-enter King of Egypt. Trumpets – drums.*]

King   Victorious Knight, my people hide:
                  The Dragon scares them, though he's tied.

At sight of him they, helter-skelter,
Up chimneys, under beds, took shelter.
If broken necks bring not their death,
They'll suffocate for want of breath.
The cellars are stuffed full of people;
Like flies they cling to spire and steeple.
I prithee, then, to ease their dread,
Cut off this hungry monster's head.

[*S. George with a mighty blow severs the Dragon's head from his body, with his left hand raising it high, at which trumpets sound the 'Mort'. As the head is cut off, the actor of Dragon should, tortoise-like, withdraw his own head within the skin of the beast. Red flannel tatters hang from the severed neck of the Dragon's head.*]

S. George   He's killed! He's dead!
              I've cut off his head!
                   So here is the end of the Dragon!
              [*Throws down Dragon's head*]

              Come, drag away
              His head on a dray,
                   And trail off his trunk on a wagon!

              Come all ye people,
              Leave cellar and steeple;
                   Away once this carcase is carried,

              The Dragon's beheading
              Shall end with a wedding,
                   And I to fair Sabra be married!

[*S. George and Princess Sabra take hands; the King of Egypt joining the pair, and afterwards raising his hands in benediction over them as they kneel on either side of the Dragon's carcase.*]

[End of the Second Act.]

ACT III

[Turkish Knight rides up and down stage, mounted upon a Hobby Horse, and armed with oval shield, scimitar and spear. He declaims loudly, turning about and knocking his spear on the floor at the end of each line.]

T. Knight *[parades]* Here come I, the Turkish Knight,
      Come from the Turkish Land to fight.
      And if Saint George do meet me here,
      I'll try his courage without fear.
      He stole from me the bride I sought.
      Therefore I'll kill him, as I ought.
      The King has said, once he is dead,
      If I should take his life,
      That I should wed, all in his stead,
      Fair Sabra as my wife.

[He ends in corner facing S. George's entrance. Enter S. George mounted on his Hobby Horse, with red-cross shield, sword and spear, to the sound of the trumpets and drums. He rants in the same way as the Turkish Knight.]

S. George *[parades]* Here come I, Saint George,
      That worthy champion bold.
      In fight I won my bride,
      With her little crown of gold.
      I fought the Dragon, I,
      And brought him to the slaughter:
      'Twas thus I gained fair Sabra,
      The King of Egypt's daughter!
      What man shall dare dispute my right,
      Or with the Dragon-slayer fight?
      What man that's mortal shall dare stand

Before me with my spear in hand?
I'll slash and hash him small as flies,
And sell him at Christmas to make mince-pies!
I'll pound his very bones to dust,
And sell them too, to make the crust.

[*He ends at his entrance-place.*]

T. Knight   Be bold, Saint George; but not too bold!
                 Thy blood so hot shall soon run cold.
                 To kill a beast is nought to brag on;
                 Come, fight a man, now, not a Dragon!

S. George   Thou Turkish Knight, I pray forbear;
                 I'll make thee dread my sword and spear![2]

[*They fight with spears to music, 'Lillibullero', riding half round the stage and tilting at one another from opposite corners of it and breaking spears (of artichoke or other brittle stems) upon one another. Turkish Knight falls and kneels.*]

T. Knight   O pardon me, Saint George! O pardon me, I crave!
                 O spare me but my life, and I will be thy slave!

S. George   I keep no slaves, nor black, nor white!
                 I'll never pardon a Turkish Knight!
                 While either of us stands, we fight;
                 Therefore, arise and try thy might!

[*They fight again, this time with swords only, to 'Helston Furry': Turkish Knight falls and dies. (If Hobby Horses are of the broom-handled pattern, these are abandoned for this fight. If not, S. George and Turkish Knight remain on Horseback all through.) –Enter Father Christmas.*]

F. Christmas   Ladies and gentlemen, you see what he's done –

He's cut the Turk down like the evening sun! [*weeps*]
Is e'er a Doctor to be found,
To cure his deep and deadly wownd?

[*Enter Doctor, in long gown, and seamed cap of antique pattern; he carries a huge bottle under his arm, and has a blacksmith's pincers in his girdle. On his nose are large spectacles.*]

Doctor Here is a Doctor to be found,
To cure his deep and deadly wownd!

F. Christmas Doctor, Doctor, let us know
Where for training didst thou go?
To gain that light that can unravel
Life's mysteries, where didst thou travel?

Doctor I've travelled far that Light to gain –
In Italy, Sicily, France and Spain;
Three times round the world and back again.
I've climbed the mountain tops of Cripple's Ease,
Crossed from Lelant to Hayle, the raging seas;
And tramped, mid bleaching bones, on desert sands,
In parching thirst, o'er Gwithian's barren lands!
Till with these eyes I've caught the glorious sight,
The far-flung radiance, of Godrevy Light!
And still undaunted kept on – only think!
Till Hell's Mouth yawned, and I, upon its brink. [*yawns*]

F. Christmas Doctor!! Doctor! Hast thou cures
For all ills that man endures?

Doctor I cure all diseases,
Whatever thee pleases,
The toothache, the stitch, or the gout;

Whenever a fly
Flutters into your eye,
My tweezers shall twiddle it out! [*shows pincers*]

            I cure all disorders
            Until further orders.
            No secret is hidden from me!
            At thy face let me look,
            And, like print in a book,
            I can read – thou hadst jam with thy tea!
            [*glares at Father Christmas through his spectacles*]

F. Christmas   'Tis plain, Doctor, jam thou'st a very good eye for;
                 But, tell me now, Doctor, how far can 'ee cipher?

Doctor   Think'st thou the learned cipher paltry sums,
                 Or add up on their fingers and their thumbs?
                 Ask what you will, I'll tell the answer straight –
                 No need have I to scribble on a slate.

F. Christmas   Doctor! Doctor! Canst thou tell
                 What will make this dead man well,
                 And cause him for to rise?
                 Come, speedy let thine answer be;
                 The sight of him doth trouble me,
                 To see how dead he lies!

Doctor   I have a little bottle here – just twenty drops remain –
                 An electuary hydrate of the liquorice of Spain.
                 An elegant elixir, emollient to the brain;
                 Empiric; homeopathic; which I warrant to contain
                 Ipecac and opodeldoc, and in short I may explain,
                 Squills, rhubarb and podophyllin – nomenclature's in vain –
                 The entire pharmácopoeia, which includes elécampane.[3]

'Twould make the very dead to rise to fight – and die again.

F. Christmas Doctor! Doctor! What is thy fee?
Let's know if he's worth it, before we agree!

[*He and S. George confer silently.*]

Doctor Fifteen pound it is my fee, the money to lay down,
But since 'tis such a rogue as he, I'll cure him for ten pound.

[*Father Christmas and S. George agree in dumbshow.*]

[*to Turkish Knight*] Here's my little bottle of elegant elecampane!
Take a drop of my flip-flop,
Pour it down thy tip-top,
Merrily, merrily drip-drop,
Down the long red lane,
Drink and drain the bottle.
Throw it down thy throttle.
Rise up! Rise up, dead man! Rise up and fight again!

[*He doses Turkish Knight from his great bottle labelled 'Poison'. Turkish Knight sits up.*]

T. Knight My back is wownded, my heart confounded,
I'm struck from seven senses into four-score.
My head is battered, my sword-arm shattered;
If I get over this, I shall fight no more.

S. George Rise up, rise up, thou Turkish Knight.
Go home to thy own land,
And tell them there what champions bold
In England yet do stand!

[*Turkish Knight pretending to be almost dead, suddenly rises and attacks S. George, who fights and kills him.*]

S. George   Come, Father, carry off this traitor slain:
                    He's fairly killed by me – or el'campane.

Doctor   Let's see if he be dead; these Turks are tough –
                    Ah, yes; if not quite dead, he's dead enough!

S. George   Then hasten, Father, bear the slain away.
                    If not quite killed, he's fairly killed, I say.
                    The Turkish Knight is dead! – I've won the day!

F. Christmas   I can no more lift him than shift the hills:
                    I say – let him bear off his slain that kills!

[*Exit.*]

S. George   Then Doctor, bear him off, thou man of pills:
                    He's dead twice over who thy potion swills.

[*Doctor begins to drag off Turkish Knight. – Enter King of Egypt.*]

King   As I stepped forth from out my bed,
                    I heard the Turkish Knight was dead.
                    O, cruel Christian, what hast thou done?
                    Thou'st ruined me, killing my only son!
                    O had this battle but gone right
                    And he slain thee, thou Christian Knight.
                    Hereafter he my heir had been,
                    To rule, with Sabra as his Queen.
                    Thou'rt but a Knight of lowly rank,
                    While he had <u>millions</u> in the bank!

S. George   I did him kill, I did him slay, my honour to maintain,

And had you been set in my place, you must have done the same.
   He gave me first the challenge. – How could I then deny?
   But see how I have brought him low, for all he talked so high.
   I've slain him, like the Dragon, and brought him to the slaughter,
   And so will slay each man that stands between me and your
                    daughter.

[Helps Doctor to carry off Turkish Knight.]

King   I'll seek the boldest champion in the realm,
        This Christian in his blood to overwhelm.
        O Slasha, Slasha, help me with speed,
        For never stood I in greater need!

[Enter Slasha.]

Slasha   In come I, the Valiant Soldier.
         Bold Slasha is my name.
        To be avenged of my master's son
         Unto this place I came.

[Re-enter S. George.]

S. George Stand off, stand off, Bold Slasha,
         And let no more be said;
        For if I draw my sword on thee,
         I'll surely break thy head!

Slasha   My head is made of iron,
        My body made of steel,
        My feet and hands are knucklebone.
        No man can make me feel!

King   Thy words are wind when all is said:

Have done, and give us deeds instead!
Do not stand there with sword in hand,
But come and fight at my command!

Slasha   Yes, yes, my liege, your order I'll obey,
               And with my sword I hope to gain the day.
                    If that be he who standeth there
                    That slew my master's son and heir,
                    Though he were sprung from royal blood
                    I'll make it flow like ocean's flood.

S. George   Bold Slasha, do not be too bold,
               Nor talk nor think so great;
               Thy master's heir lies dead and cold
               That soon shall be thy state.
               O, villain, as I live, this very night
               Thou shalt lie dead beside the Turkish Knight.
               Battle to battle, on thee I call,
               To see which on the ground shall fall!

Slasha   Battle to battle, on thee I cry,
               To see which on the ground shall lie!

[*They fight to 'Dargesson'. Slasha is killed.*]

King   Is there no doctor to be found,
                    Or to be had this night,
               Can heal this dead man's ghastly wownd,
                    And make him stand upright?

[*Re-enter Doctor.*]

Doctor   Here is a doctor to be found,
                    And to be had this night,

Can heal this dead man's ghastly wownd,
                 And make him stand upright.
If any man has a scolding wife,
                 My balsam will her cure,
Let her take one drop, upon my life,
                 She'll never scold him more.
I have it in my little bottle here; its name is elecampane.
Now drink, live once more, dead man; but do not fight again!

[*Doctor doses Slasha, who rises.*]

Slasha   That blow by thee was struck that pierced my master's heart,
                 The very same I'll do to thee before we two shall part.

[*Threatens S. George.*]

S. George   Bold Slasha, set thy rage aside,
                 For I shall tame thee of thy pride.

[*They fight again, to 'Sir Roger'; Slasha is killed again and dragged off by Doctor.
The King of Egypt takes up Slasha's sword to attack S. George, who defends himself.
Re-enter Father Christmas, who parts them.*]

F. Christmas   Lay down those swords, and be at rest,
                 For peace and quietness are the best.

S. George   Then shake we hands, and swear to fight no more.

King   Let's live in friendship as we did before.

[*They shake hands.*]

S. George
[*parading*]   The Dragon first I routed,

>   And then struck off his head.
> The Turkish Knight and Slasha
>   Lie doctored, double-dead.
> My right to Princess Sabra
>   None lives now to dispute –
> Come forth then, noble lady,
>   And stay no longer mute.

[Enter Princess.]

Princess   Here stand I, Princess Sabra,
>   And gladly shall I speak,
> My love to show to him whose blow
>   Is dealt to shield the weak.
> My crown of gold is his to hold,

[Offers S. George her crown. He takes it.]

>   For 'tis my chief delight,
> My joy and pride, to be the bride
>   Of this brave English Knight.

[S. George kneels and kisses her hand, giving back the crown, which she wears again. Father Christmas stands behind them, holding his hands in blessing over their heads.]

F. Christmas   Lo here's a sight to do a man's heart good,
> To see a Dragon-slayer thus subdued.
> Before him Turk and Paynim dead may fall;
> Yet here he kneels and says, "LOVE CONQUERS ALL".

[S. George and Princess Sabra march off to the sound of wedding-bells, followed by the King of Egypt and Father Christmas.]

[End of the Third Act.]

Epilogue

[*Spoken by Father Christmas, the other characters being in line to right and left behind him.*]

Ladies and gentlemen,
Our Christmas Play is done,
And now, that you may see
Our fights were all in fun,
Our slain appear alive,
To quiet all alarm,
And prove, at least to them,
That we have done no harm.
We all have done our best,
Though our best may be but poor.
We all have done our best,
And the best can do no more.
The best can do no more than do
The best that they are able:
Some do their best upon the stage,
And others at the table.
Should you think right, us to invite
To taste your Christmas Fare,
You need but send, you may depend
We'll all do better there.

[*All march off, after circling the stage three times, led by Father Christmas, and Dragon last, and singing 'Trelawny', 'The Good Old Duke of York', etc.*]

All O, a-mumming we will go, will go, and a-mumming we will go!
(1) With a bright cockade in all our hats, we'll make a gallant show!
(2) May every field fine harvest yield, full crops each garden grow!
(3) And a Merry Christmas may you have, and a good New Year also!

[*Repeat until the last exit. Dragon makes his bow as curtain falls.*]

[*Finis.*]

Notes

1. There are several versions of the play among the Nance Papers in the Courtney Library, Royal Institution of Cornwall, Truro. The version selected is the 'prompt copy' (typescript, with additions in Nance's hand).
2. At the top of the page of the script on which the following action is described, Nance has drawn diagrams to show the course of the three turns involved in the actors' movements.
3. Nance has accented the two syllables which need to be stressed unnaturally in order to give the line its correct rhythm.

Acknowledgement

This transcript of Nance's play is reproduced by permission of the Royal Institution of Cornwall, Courtney Library (Nance Collection).

Robert Morton Nance and Gorseth Kernow

Peter W. Thomas

Introduction

In Cornwall, the name of Robert Morton Nance is probably best known in connection with his role as Grand Bard of the Cornish Gorsedd (Gorseth Kernow). To many, perhaps even to some bards, the Gorsedd means little more than an annual gathering in which men and women in blue robes enact a ceremony in Cornish, but for Nance, the founding father of the Gorsedd, its establishment was a major step towards realising his visionary goal of a Cornwall which would reconnect with its Celtic soul and fulfil its true potential. This chapter is an attempt to trace the story of his long association with the Cornish Gorsedd, particularly in its early years, and to outline the significance it held for him.[1]

Before the first Cornish Gorsedd of 1928

By Nance's own account, the idea of instituting a Cornish Gorsedd to stand alongside the Welsh Gorsedd of the Bards of the Isle of Britain and the Breton Gorsedd had been in the air well before he himself became enthused by the idea. The re-establishment of a Gorsedd was one of the main aims of the short-lived Cowethas Kelto-Kernuak (Celtic-Cornish Society), founded by L.C.R. Duncombe Jewell in 1901,[2] but the Society's demise left Henry Jenner[3] almost alone to keep the Gorsedd idea alive. He became a Breton bard in 1903, and a handful of Cornish people, including his wife Kitty Lee and Jewell himself,

were initiated into the Welsh Gorsedd around the turn of the 19th/20th centuries. Jenner translated the important parts of the Gorsedd ritual into Cornish
in 1907, in case it might one day be used.[4]

While it is true that Nance's active interest did not begin till somewhat later,
a seed was sown as early as the end of the 19th century, thanks to 'the intense
love of country'[5] which he saw in the Welsh people. With his first wife Beatrice
he had come back from St Ives to live in Wales, and they both won prizes at the
1899 Eisteddfod in Cardiff:

> I learnt that to be a bard of the Gorsedd could be looked on as a sacred
> trust, and that as a rallying-point for the national sentiment of Wales the
> Gorsedd was a great institution ... but Cornwall as a Celtic nation was
> not represented at all, and it was impossible to help feeling that it ought
> to be, and that it might yet be possible to find Cornishmen of the same
> opinion who would be ready to join hands with other Celts in keeping
> themselves Celtic in spite of an age that tends to wipe out all distinctions
> and bring everyone to the level of some great majority. Perhaps it was
> then and there that my own wishes for a Cornish Revival took form,
> though it was not with any idea that I should take any part in bringing it
> about.[6]

Key themes for Nance were already emerging: the value of (particularly
Cornish and Celtic) identity, individuality and cultural distinctiveness, of
Cornish patriotic fellowship and of solidarity with other Celts. He also saw that
the Gorsedd would help to promote these interrelated ideals, and indeed revive
them where they had become dormant. Time and again he returns to them,
regarding them as a means of saving Cornwall from losing its essential character, and the many and varied activities he engaged in on behalf of the Cornish
Gorsedd were intended to serve them. They were underlined by the symbolism
of the Gorsedd, and the conferring of bardship honoured those whose achievements honoured Cornwall. One further fundamental element would be added
to the role Nance came to envisage for the institution: the promotion of the
Cornish language, the centrality of which he was to emphasise increasingly as
it became more firmly established within the Gorsedd.

For the next five years or so, however, Nance had personal difficulties to surmount. Beatrice died in 1901, and it was only after he moved back to Cornwall with his second wife Maud in 1906 that Cornish issues started to occupy his attention more and more. He has left us a sketch of the beginning of his active engagement with the idea of a Cornish Gorsedd, which was brought about through discussing Cornish issues with Jenner in the Morrab Library, Penzance, where they first met:

> I had formed a friendship with Mr Jenner ... soon after he retired [May 1909] ... I think there can be nothing that he knew about Cornish that he had not passed on to me. It is not surprising, then, that what I could do to fulfil his hopes of a Cornish Gorsedd, I did most readily and glad-ly, especially as it was ... very helpful to my own beloved "Old Cornwall" movement towards the same end of rousing the Celtic spirit of Cornwall from its long sleep.[7]

Nance was always very clear about the crucial part played by Jenner, 'whose prestige and whose venerable appearance were so helpful to [the Gorsedd's] beginnings'.[8]

The two men's determination and enthusiasm for their vision of Cornish resurgence proved strong enough to survive the trauma of the First World War.[9] At the 1918 Eisteddfod in Neath, Jenner had been strengthened in his idea of 'reviving the old project of a Cornish Gorsedd',[10] and with his backing Nance formed the first Old Cornwall Society at St Ives in 1920, followed by the Federation of Old Cornwall Societies in 1924. He credited the realisation of the dream of a Cornish Gorsedd, after earlier attempts had failed, to this ground-work.[11] Also in 1924, he was one of the Cornish delegation to the Celtic Congress at Quimper.

The possibility of a Gorsedd for Cornwall was discussed with the flamboyant Welsh Gorsedd representative David Rhys Phillips (*Beili Glas*), who proved to be Nance's most valuable and enthusiastic ally in Wales. There was an extensive correspondence between the two between 1926 and 1943 on all aspects of Gorsedd procedure and practical arrangements.[12] In 1926, Nance was suggest-ing to Phillips the desirability of a special gathering of the Welsh Gorsedd at Boscawen-Un stone circle near St Buryan,[13] regarded as the most appropriate site because it was considered to be the 'Beisgawen yn Nyfnwal' [Boscawen in

Dumnonia] of a Welsh triad naming the 'Tair Priforsedd' [Three Principal Gorseddau (session-places)] of the Bards of the Isle of Britain.[14] If so, the last Gorsedd held there would have been some 1,000 years earlier. In 1927 Nance attended the Celtic Congress at Riec, where informal conversations with Welsh bardic officials brought the actualisation of the dream that much closer. Nance wrote of the proposed Gorsedd:

> Mr Rhys Phillips ... is showing the greatest interest in this ceremony, not only as a Welsh one, but as a step to future ceremonies to be held by a Cornish Gorsedd. A few Cornish people personally known to him as good Celts will, if this is approved, be sponsored by him for admission to Bardic orders at the Welsh National Eisteddfod at Treorchy... in August [1928], and these, with Mr Henry Jenner as their Grand Druid, but owing fealty to the Archdruid, would have the authority to include all suitable persons in a Cornish Gorsedd.[15]

From the start, then, the Cornish Gorsedd acknowledged the Welsh college of bards as the parent body, and in September 1927 Nance asked Phillips for the words of the Welsh Gorsedd ceremony for translation into Cornish.[16] At the same time, while closely following Welsh precedent, the Cornish branch asserted its right to introduce its own individual features to 'suit the needs and prejudices of Cornwall'. In particular, feeling that Cornwall should dispense with the degrees of Druid and Ovate, Nance had come to favour the

> initiation of all members on equal terms as Bards only, so as to follow our watchword of "One and All," and incidentally avoid the accusations of "paganism" or "bogus antiquity" that might be stirred against us by any suggestions of reviving Druidism.[17]

Jenner would therefore be designated 'Grand Bard' ('Barth Mur'), a title which Nance says was invented for the Cornish Gorsedd.[18] The quotation provides an instance of the fact that Nance (like Jenner[19] and Phillips[20]) was perfectly clear-sighted regarding the strictly limited degree to which ancient authenticity could be ascribed to Gorsedd ceremonial, which in any case is not static, having changed in various particulars during Nance's time and since.

(He was later to defend the historicity of aspects of the Gorsedd, while indicating that its real justification was the assemblage of those working for Cornwall's cultural advancement.)[21]

Accusations such as those mentioned by Nance had already been levelled at the proposed Gorsedd. As early as 1923, the mere idea of holding such a ceremony had aroused fears of pagan rites. Nance pointed out that the business of the Gorsedd was 'promoting education and encouraging literary ability' rather than reviving druidism, the actual nature of which was in any case virtually unknown. Recent Welsh Archdruids had almost all been Christian ministers, and aside from mere decoration, the point of the 'druidic' elements was to foster a link with the Celtic past:

> It will no doubt be misunderstood by the Anglicized majority in Cornwall, but it should appeal to the little remnant of real Cornish, who have still the sentiment of being Celts, and a strong desire for such a means of saving the Cornishness of Cornwall from destruction as an eisteddfod ought to be.[22]

As this quotation indicates, Nance (and others, including Jenner,[23] Charles Henderson[24] and the Federation of Old Cornwall Societies[25]) wanted to establish a Gorsedd not merely for its own sake, but as the core of a future Cornish Eisteddfod. He wrote in 1923:

> To seek the co-operation of all the existing societies of Cornwall in making one big festival week would, perhaps, be enough to give us at once something outwardly resembling the Royal National Eisteddfod of Wales, but ... the life and soul of the Welsh festival is the "gorsedd," which makes claim to be founded upon the bardic court of the Ancient Britons, and, if the Cornish "esedhvos" is to have a Celtic standing, we shall need to have something in Cornwall that may at least be recognized in Wales and Brittany as the best that Cornwall can do towards forming such a court. The Cornish language will have to be satisfied, at first at all events, with a very small, if greatly venerated, part in the proceedings, but we are still just sufficiently Celtic in Cornwall to prevent our aspirations towards such a recognition from being absurd ... Once established, such an annual festival might well be the means of producing a great revival of interest in all the things of Celtic Cornwall, includ-

ing the old language; but, in any event, it could not fail to stimulate the independent self-respect that used always to be characteristic of the Cornish branch of that old British race that has given its name to the Empire, and the mere possibility of it must appeal to the imagination of every true Cornishman.[26]

Nance was a pragmatist as well as a visionary and romantic, and with the benefit of hindsight it could be argued that at this point in the prehistory of the Gorsedd he was too ambitious in some respects and not ambitious enough in others. (He was certainly to become much less tentative about the importance of Cornish to the institution.) Some three weeks later, he played down the relative status of the Gorsedd:

> The Cornish Gorsedd, I should take it, will be little more than a formal fulfilment of the minimum conditions for its acceptance, as a kindred body, by the Gorseddau of Wales and Brittany; the eisteddfod would be the first object.[27]

The idea of holding this larger festival was never altogether lost – indeed Nance spoke of his hope for its fulfilment just before his installation as Grand Bard[28] – but the realisation of his 'first object' in the form of the inaugural national[29] Eisteddfod (Esethvos Kernow) did not in fact take place till 1983. In the Grand Bard's address at that time, Hugh Miners celebrated the fulfilment of the vision which Nance and the other 'Cornish zealots' had expounded sixty years before.[30]

Phillips suggested that the Federation of Old Cornwall Societies should address an invitation to the Welsh Gorsedd, requesting that a group of Cornish people should be initiated as bards at Treorchy in readiness for a ceremony to be held in Cornwall in September 1928. Nance, Recorder of the FOCS, assisted in drawing up this invitation, in Cornish and English.[31] Eight Cornish people were duly initiated as Welsh bards[32] on 7 August 1928, with Nance probably the first[33] to receive his bardic name – that of *Mordon* (Seawave) – from Archdruid *Pedrog* (Revd J.O. Williams), thus setting a precedent for the many Cornish bards who would make punning use of part of their conventional name in their bardic name. (He was later to recommend avoidance of 'those hackneyed "Son of", "Lover of", etc., which so many bards want'.)[34] He had prepared an official speech for the occasion if there were time,[35] but in the event he and others stood down in favour of W.C.D. Watson (*Tirvab*), who spoke in both Cornish and Welsh.[36] Earlier, discussing the difficulty of restricting the number of suitable Cornish candidates at Treorchy, Nance had told Phillips that he would be happy to step down and be initiated later.[37] He consistently expressed reluctance to stand in the Gorsedd limelight, though that was where he was to stand for the rest of his life.

A meeting of the Cornish group, chaired by Nance, was held at Cox's Café, Cardiff in the evening of 7 August.[38] Among the resolutions passed were: that the Council of the Cornish Gorsedd should consist of the eight and the Jenners; (on Nance's proposal) that Jenner be Grand Bard; and that Nance be Deputy Grand Bard ('pro tem.' according to a pencilled note). In a letter to Phillips in April 1928 Nance made it clear that there was already an intention to settle the office of Deputy on him but, he said, 'I am looking for someone else for that position: for I would far rather remain a simple bard or ovate myself'.[39] He apparently did not consider that it gave him any status within the college of bards.[40]

Nance as Deputy Grand Bard (1928–1934)

The group of ten had thus been established as the nucleus of a Cornish Gorsedd. On 25 August 1928, at 'the first meeting in Cornwall of those who had been accepted as members of the Breton and Welsh gorseddau',[41] twelve further names were agreed upon as suitable candidates for bardship at the forthcoming inaugural Cornish ceremony. There was close liaison between Jenner and Nance regarding such matters as bardic names, the wording of the ceremony and the proposed initiates.[42]

'With the object of making its meaning clear to the "man in the street" ', on the day before the Gorsedd the *Western Morning News* printed a long interview with Nance:[43]

> "When we talk of establishing a Cornish Gorsedd, we mean establishing a College of the Cornish Bards."

"And what exactly is a Bard?"

"The title Bard is an honorary one, given in recognition of some unusual manifestation of the Celtic spirit."

Nance goes on to talk of the history and nature of the Welsh and Breton gorseddau and of the background to the establishment of the Cornish Gorsedd. He describes the forthcoming ceremony in some detail, then makes his main point:

"The impression I want to leave ... is that our object is to restore in Cornwall the idea that it is a Celtic country. The Gorsedd is not political or anti-English, but we want to foster the self-respect of Cornish people by making them regard themselves as one of the Celtic nations."

Then, on 21 September 1928, at Boscawen-Un, *Pedrog* 'instituted the first Gorsedd in Cornwall by the special dispensation of the parent Gorsedd of Wales'.[44] Though Phillips's hope that Breton bards might also take part in the ceremony[45] could not be realised, it proved possible to have the first verse of *Bro Goth agan Tasow* [Old Land of our Fathers ('the inter-Brythonic National Anthem')] sung in Breton as well as in Cornish and Welsh, because Nance enlisted the help of a young Breton he knew, Louis Seite, who was then living in Penzance.[46]

It would have been unthinkable for anyone other than Jenner, the patriarch of the Cornish Revival, to have been the first Grand Bard, but he was 80 years old at his installation, and from the first Nance took a major role in Gorsedd affairs. According to Amy Hale, 'it could be argued that Jenner was more of a figurehead for the emerging movement, not one of its primary strategists' and 'it was really Nance who secured the Cornish Gorseth and suggested Jenner as its head'.[47] Jenner thanked him at the time of the first Gorsedd 'for looking after the music and recitations behind the scenes ... and incidentally for singing us a song of his own composing. Of course, he did a lot of other things too, which would be a long story'.[48] As is still the case today, Nance's *Arta ef a-dhe* [He (i.e. King Arthur) shall come again] was also sung.[49] (Other songs of his were later to be performed at individual Gorseddau.)

Prior to the ceremony itself there had been a trip to Paul Church, the Merry Maidens and Land's End, during which Nance and Jenner talked to the rest of the group on topics such as the history and current state of Cornish. Following the Gorsedd, there was a mayoral reception in Penzance, at which Nance was a speaker,[50] and a business meeting held in the Mayor's Parlour, chaired by Jenner (now Grand Bard *Gwas Myghal*), at which an executive committee was appointed for one year in order to carry out the aims and objects of the Gorsedd. (Nance was of course an *ex officio* member.)[51] 'What pleases me most in thinking of the day', he wrote, 'was the absolute dignity of the whole proceedings and the excellent spirit of the crowd of about 2000 people, the great majority of whom were obviously in sympathy with our ideals'.[52] The first executive meeting of the Gorsedd took place at Murdoch House, Redruth, on 28 November 1928, when Nance was appointed temporary secretary, a post which he held till 1931, throughout his first term as Deputy Grand Bard.[53] (He was re-elected for a second three-year term as Deputy in September 1931.)[54]

Looking back on their aspirations for the Gorsedd at this period, Nance wrote, in one of his many letters to F.B. Cargeeg:

> I can't remember that anyone had any hope that the Cornish people could be induced as a whole to take to the Gorsedd as something that belonged to them all; not at all events within say fifty years – with luck. I think the most that we hoped was that all the Old Cornwall members would do so, and that all Cornish people who had any sense of romance or continuity with the past would take it as meant for them. Such people are rarer in Cornwall than in most places, apparently, but there are not many of them who hold aloof.[55]

Nance had worked on Ralph Dunstan's *Cornish Song Book* (*Lyver Canow Kernewek*). (Two of his contributions to it – *Arta ef a-dhe* (as already mentioned) and *Kernow agan Mamvro* ['Cornwall our Motherland' – designated 'A Cornish National Anthem'] – still feature in Gorsedd ceremonies, and his words to a third are still used as the Cornish grace at the Gorsedd Tea). At the Gorsedd Council meeting of 20 April 1929 he and Jenner explained the Gorsedd patronage of the book, and Nance asked whether he might claim a similar status for his *Cornish for All*. 'On Mr Jenner's assurance that the book was good this was agreed to'.[56] (Both books were published in 1929.)

At the second modern Cornish Gorsedd (the 'first independent ceremony')[57] Nance was a banner bearer and his wife was made a bard.[58] Phillips again attended, but on this occasion the Breton contingent, led by Grand Druid *Taldir* (F.-J.-C. Jaffrenou),[59] was prominent. Nance had described it as 'a combined Breton and Cornish Gorsedd' since he had helped to organise a Cornwall versus Cornouaille wrestling competition as a parallel attraction.[60] He hoped indeed that with the help of the Federation of Old Cornwall Societies more than one day of events would be staged, including musical performances and, ideally, hurling.[61] Nance's song *Dynergh dhe Dus a Vreten Vyghan* was composed in honour of the occasion and printed in the Gorsedd programme with an English translation ('Welcome to the Bretons'). At the evening concert his *Morvah Fair* was sung.[62]

The most convenient source for an 'official' explanation of the nature and purpose of the Cornish Gorsedd is the summary which was first printed in the 1929 programme and which is still found in the booklet used at the annual open ceremony:

> It exists to maintain the National Celtic Spirit of Cornwall and to give expression to such spirit; to encourage the study of Cornish History and the Cornish Language; to foster Cornish Literature, Art and Music; to link Cornwall with other Celtic countries, and to promote a spirit of peace and co-operation among those who work for the honour of Cornwall.[63]

Nance's thinking went a good deal beyond the printed summary, and for him the annual ceremony was merely the outward symbol of a deep commitment, a point which he often expressed in evangelical, indeed revivalist, terms:

> [T]he Cornish Bards ... meet less to form a pageant than to put an idea before the Cornish people: that for very long they have been asleep, to their own detriment, and that they should now wake to the fact of their nationality, and take an interest in their own history and their own language.[64]

There is perhaps a general impression that the Gorsedd ceremony happens every year as a matter of course, but even as early as 1929 the whole enterprise reached a crisis point and could easily have foundered. It was by no means certain that the second Gorsedd would take place that year, as Nance indicated:

> There is a complete lack of enthusiasm and support, which I am afraid will bring the Cornish Gorsedd to an early end. Without a language nothing can be done.[65]

> There will evidently be great disappointment if no Gorsedd should be held ... [T]he Gorsedd itself as constituted seems far from ideal as a business committee. We shall probably shake down in time, and a triennial or biennial Gorsedd will probably be found to solve some of our difficulties.[66]

As it was, the fact that many of the arrangements for the event were made at the last minute 'went very near to wrecking the whole thing', and Nance found the ceremony disappointing in many ways, albeit a salutary lesson for the future.[67]

The Gorsedd was already establishing itself as a cultural event nonetheless, and the following ceremony was timed to take place during the course of the Arthurian Congress in Cornwall, in which however Nance involved himself to only a limited extent.[68] Having made the effort to show a commitment to the belief that the Gorsedd should represent the whole of Cornwall by holding it in the east (at the Hurlers), Nance also admitted that the present Council was at a disadvantage, being 'a scratch committee got together after the Boscawen Gorsedd' which was 'decidedly and parochially West Cornwall'.[69] After this third ceremony, Nance was called upon to defend the Gorsedd as a working institution. His reply to a claim that arrangements were not sufficiently public and that bards were elected arbitrarily gives some idea of his perception of the stage which the Gorsedd had reached at that time:

> In the present state of Cornish studies it was held that it was too much to ask initiates to submit themselves to even an elementary examination in the Cornish language and literature ... though ability to write an appli-

cation for membership addressed to the Grand Bard in grammatical Cornish would probably lead to an invitation as a matter of course. Failing examinations, the readiest test of "Celtic Spirit" is the amount of work done for the cause of Cornwall as a Celtic nation by those who have furthered the Old Cornwall movement from which the Cornish Gorsedd sprang; but from the first, membership of the Gorsedd has been open to "all intelligent Cornish[70] men and women, irrespective of sect or status," who have shown themselves to possess the necessary qualification ... To the onlooker the choice made must often appear arbitrary, for it honours work that is done very quietly ... It must be remembered, however, that many prominent Cornish people have no Celtic sympathies whatever.[71]

Nance no doubt saw part of his role as responding to such criticism. He was able to dismiss the flurry of agitation after the 1930 ceremony as superficial,[72] but the fact remains that throughout his time the Gorsedd was subject to attacks, constructive and destructive, from within its own ranks and from outside. External criticism was usually directed at the institution alone and, though more widely disseminated and sometimes virulent,[73] was often less substantial than internal criticism. It was not quite invariably ill-informed, though a greater understanding of the concept of symbolism might have helped some of the detractors. Editorially, the local press was generally very supportive, but not entirely so. 'Cornishman' of the *Western Morning News* was a trenchant though not always destructive critic.[74] Internal criticism was usually less public and tended to be motivated by concern for the welfare of the Gorsedd. It was also sometimes directed at Nance personally. Such criticism often focused on his leadership style and the direction (or perceived lack of it) in which he was taking the Gorsedd, as in this note written by 'insider' G.H. Doble, expressing concern about the viability of the Gorsedd as early as 1931:

> I quite agree with you about the need of more business-like methods being introduced into the Gorsedd, also that there should be a general meeting of the order, & things done with the knowledge and consent of members. But I can do nothing myself. Nance is a dear, but he is so temperamental, & so liable to fits of despondency, that it is difficult to get life into the movement.[75]

There was no doubt some truth in these comments, though Nance was concerned that the movement should be democratic, and meetings for all bards were held throughout his time as Grand Bard, and indeed before it. His own initiative, and the innovations made by him or under his leadership, were to a large extent responsible for keeping the movement going throughout the difficult early years, the Second World War, and beyond. As to his personality, in retrospect a more generous interpretation might be that his zeal for the Gorsedd overcame his melancholic tendencies sufficiently to enable him to work consistently and tenaciously for its welfare for over 30 years, despite the setbacks and difficulties he encountered.

It was Nance who outlined, at a Council meeting in January 1932, what arrangements would need to be made for the Celtic Congress to be held in Truro later in the year.[76] (He also took a leading role in implementing them, was a speaker at the Congress and was one of the actors in his own short play in Cornish, *An Balores* [The Chough].)[77] The position of the Gorsedd with respect to Cornish had moved on since his letter of September 1930, since at the same meeting he agreed that the time had arrived when candidates for bardship could be admitted by examination in Cornish language and literature. In fact, at the Council meeting on 23 July Jenner announced that essays in Cornish had been called for in *Old Cornwall*, with a view to accepting successful entrants as bards, and that one of the two already received was written by Nance's daughter Phoebe, who as a child had been taught Cornish by her father. (Nance himself was appointed one of the judges.)[78] He was happy to give generously of his time and knowledge to many individual students in the Cornish movement, and there are numerous instances of his informally encouraging potential candidates for bardship by examination. To cite just one example, in a letter to Cargeeg he wrote:

Why a prest yn-un-wellhe, ha raghenna ny-m-bus dout vyth a'gas scryfa neppyth a-vo dygemerys yn prof agas bos gwyw dhe vos barth an Orseth.

[*You continue to improve, and so I have no doubt at all as to your writing something which will be accepted as proof that you are worthy to be a bard of the Gorsedd.*][79]

In another letter, though, he again shows his pragmatic standpoint on what in his opinion should realistically be required of potential 'language bards' at that time in order to gain their qualification, stating explicitly that to become a language bard it was necessary only to write Cornish properly, not necessarily to speak it.[80] People will have differing views on this approach, which in general terms was still followed long after Nance's time (though the examinations became much more exacting), but at this relatively early stage in the resurgence of Cornish Nance was anxious not to alienate potential learners of the language, and potential bards, who might later embark on more advanced studies.[81] There is no doubt that Nance considered the Cornish language to have a central place in the Cornish Revival – a point which he emphasised more and more strongly as time went on – but he was deeply anxious about the continued viability of the Gorsedd and the possibility of all his and others' pioneering work coming to nothing:

> Here at home people "can't see the wood for the trees", but the exiles have a better view of things, and they are not only keener on Cornish nationality themselves, but are a bit inclined to think that nobody in Cornwall cares anything for it, which is fortunately not quite literally true, though near it. In time, if it goes on, the Gorsedd may form a bond of union for all these variants of the Cornish movement.[82]

Language bards were duly initiated for the first time at the 1932 Gorsedd, including Phoebe Nance, A.S.D. Smith (*Caradar*) and E.G.R. Hooper (*Talek*), who was eventually to be Nance's successor as Grand Bard. According to Smith, it was while robing for this ceremony that Nance asked him and others not to speak Cornish at the Gorsedd for fear of causing unrest. Smith saw himself as virtually a lone voice advocating the wider use of (particularly spoken) Cornish, as opposed to Nance's view, as Smith saw it, that Cornish was no more than a language to be studied.[83] An alternative emphasis was expressed by Herbert Thomas, also in 1932, in an article in which he stated that Nance's opinion was that only the study and use of the language would save the movement from swift decay and extinction.[84]

The first modern church service in Cornish, Anglican evening prayer in Nance's translation, was held at Towednack on 27 August 1933 (the day before that year's Gorsedd).[85] This was the start of the continuing tradition of Cornish services being held at the time of the ceremony. The service, like the other pre-war services, was arranged by the Cornish youth movement Tyr ha Tavas [Land and Language], who also held a summer camp at Trevail, where Nance had a house. (Nance worked on the Cornish of these services[86] and attended them, but not being a churchgoer, he did not want to play a part in them.)[87] Jenner also attended the 1933 service, though his health was failing seriously at this stage. Arrangements were made for Nance to stand in if the Grand Bard had to miss the Gorsedd for the first time, but in the event he was able to be present at Roche Rock, Nance assisting him throughout.[88] On the same day, the Annual Meeting (open to all bards) was chaired by Nance owing to Jenner's fatigue following the ceremony.[89] He explained to his fellow bards how candidates for bardship were selected and indicated that they could make suggestions to the Council, wishing no doubt to make them feel that the organisation was run transparently and that they had a stake in its composition.

Henry Jenner died on 8 May 1934, and on 8 June Nance wrote to Phillips:

> As Deputy Grand Bard it would fall to me to carry on this year if no election takes place, and that of course I should be proud to do, but I feel diffident about accepting the nomination of the small Council as Grand Bard, which they are likely to offer me, though unfortunately there is no-one with the prestige of Mr Jenner to whom it could be offered.[90]

(On a later occasion he stated that Sir Arthur Quiller-Couch 'should have been Grand Bard if he had been willing'.)[91] At the start of the Council meeting on 13 June Nance, as Chairman, spoke of the irreparable loss to the Gorsedd in the death of Jenner. Later in the meeting he was indeed nominated for the office of second Grand Bard of Cornwall and unanimously approved (as was J. Hambley Rowe[92] as his Deputy), but it was felt that an expression of opinion should also be obtained from the absent members.[93]

A major question to be settled before the 1934 Gorsedd was the form of the ceremony for Nance's installation, and at his request[94] Phillips provided a suitable formula, based largely on the ceremony for the installation of Archdruid *Gwili* (Revd Professor J.G. Jenkins) in 1932. He had revised it to suit the case

*Robert Morton Nance's initiation as Grand Bard by J. Hambley Rowe (Tolzethan),
Padderbury, near Liskeard, 7 September 1934*

and expected the Cornish to make further revisions.[95] He and Nance swapped ideas on the event, based largely on practicalities and the particular situation in Cornwall rather than the application of rigid regulations or historical precedent.[96] It was, however, necessary to conform to Gorsedd rules by creating a wreath or crown to distinguish the Grand Bard (to Nance's regret) from the hooded rank and file of bards. (Jenner had not followed the rule himself, wearing his Breton bardic costume with a wreath over the hood.)[97] Another matter which Nance discussed with Phillips, before and after the 1934 Gorsedd,[98] was the newly conceived idea of making the person who was adjudged the best writer in Cornish the Gorsedd 'laureate' for the year, reflecting Welsh Eisteddfod practice. At the same time, Nance can be seen feeling his way, with Phillips's help, towards a tactful solution of the potential problem of avoiding a schism in the Gorsedd between the Cornish speakers and the rest.[99]

At the Gorsedd Council meeting of 4 July 1934, it was reported that the nominations of Nance and Rowe had been unanimously ratified, and they were therefore elected to the two highest positions in the Cornish Gorsedd.[100]

'Grandest of Grand Bards' (1934–1959)

(i) The pre-War Period (1934–1939)

Shortly before being installed as Grand Bard, Nance outlined to Cargeeg some of his current thinking on the Gorsedd:

> [W]hile the work of oldsters on non-Celtic lines is still recognized as from the first, no young person who is indifferent to Cornish is likely to be admitted. At the same time I don't think we must be too sweeping in saying that the Gorsedd <u>alone</u> stands for Celtic things. The Fed. O.C.S. has always been supposed to do this, and ... it still provides the backbone of the Gorsedd as far as work is concerned. In Brittany they have set themselves to cultivate an <u>élite</u>. If we can find a satisfactory substitute for that word in Eng. it would describe what the Bards should be. I like everything you say except the one word "exclusive". I don't think the Gorsedd will ever want to be that.[101]

As to the ceremony itself, Phillips had stated that the new Grand Bard

should strictly be installed by *Gwili* as Archdruid, the second choice being
Elfed (Revd H.E. Lewis), the only ex-Archdruid then living, and the third a
'Chief Bard <u>pro tem</u>'.[102] In the event, neither *Gwili* nor *Elfed* were able to attend,
and the 1934 Gorsedd was the first at which no representatives of other Celtic
countries were present. There was no installation ceremony for Rowe, who
himself installed Nance.[103] ('You had better carry out your scheme as best you
can', Phillips had concluded.)[104] The installation of *Mordon* as Grand Bard of
Cornwall duly took place at the Gorsedd at Padderbury Top, near Liskeard, on
7 September 1934, where, having undertaken 'to protect the Rights and maintain the Dignity of the Cornish Gorsedd', he was 'confirmed in his office by
voice of the Bards, and invested with its symbol, conventionally representing a
Gorsedd Circle'.[105] (He had himself designed this badge of office and includes a
sketch of it in a letter to Phillips.)[106]

The local press was very supportive, even effusive, at this crucial time:

> The new Grand Bard of the Cornish Gorsedd entered upon his high
> responsibilities … with the hearty good wishes of the whole Cornish
> nation. In every respect Morton Nance is the proper successor of the
> patriarchal Henry Jenner. By ripe scholarship and yeoman service to
> everything Cornish, Mordon has captured the hearts of one and all, and
> enchained their devotion … Early fruits of the Gorseth Kernow already
> are beginning to ripen … Under the guidance of Mordon it is as certain
> as tomorrow's dawn that the dignity and erudition of the Gorsedd will
> be strenuously maintained, and … the immediate future of the Cornish
> movement is, like the new oak boughs, rich in promise.[107]

Looking back on this period, J.H. Martin was equally certain that Jenner's
successor had been rightly chosen, adding intriguingly:

> In the Gorsedd, as in other human conclaves, all were not of the same
> mind. There were some who thought that the qualities which admirably
> suited the conception of a Grand Bard were, by a paradox, unlikely to
> foster the Gorsedd spirit in the rude and noisy modern world. However
> that may be, the Gorsedd survived.[108]

Following the installation, Nance himself took over conduct of the proceed-

ings. He called on the other bards to help him in his work and voiced his deep-
est interests and concerns, including the need to keep in contact with the other
Celtic peoples and gorseddau. After paying his own public tribute to Jenner, he
put forward his vision of Gorseth Kernow as a bastion against the would-be
destroyers of the true Cornwall:

> Cornwall, today, to the outside world is a holiday playground. The place
> has been made known in recent years to such an extent that in the small-
> er places its features are being wiped out. That is what Cornwall is
> becoming if it is left to itself. We represent another Cornwall – the
> Cornwall that has always been the Celtic land, the land where dreams
> come true.[109]

In earlier comments to the press, Nance had minimised his own role and
anticipated an improvement in the ceremony:

> As Mr Morton Nance said ... he can scarcely hope to look the venerable
> Grand Bard that Mr Jenner was ... It is [his] hope that the Gorsedd
> Kernow [sic] will grow in importance ... [T]he Gorsedd is not a mere
> revival of ancient druidical ceremony even if its ritual is immemorial; it
> is a genuine attempt to express in the symbolism of ritual the continuity
> of the Celtic life of Cornwall. If that is so (and that is the purpose of the
> Gorsedd) it should be possible to make the celebrations more impressive
> than they are at present.[110]

Despite his self-deprecation, Nance was described at his installation, and
frequently thereafter, in terms similar to those used of Jenner:

> At [the Cornish bards'] rear walked a tall man with a striking profile,
> whose chaplet of gleaming copper leaves gave him the appearance of a
> Roman Emperor... It must have been one of the proudest days of Mr
> Nance's life. Not only was he installed as Grand Bard, but his wife, his
> daughter, and his nephew were standing round him, all wearing the blue
> robes of bards.[111]

(Phoebe Nance was one of those who spoke in Cornish at the Gorsedd.[112]
Nance's nephew was E.E. Morton Nance, one of the 1934 initiates – 'not a fla-

grant case of nepotism', as Nance was at pains to point out.)[113] The impressive-ness of Nance's bearing as Grand Bard was frequently commented upon. On other occasions his appearance was compared to that of a high priest and of Dante.[114]

An interesting document held in the Courtney Library is Nance's own copy of the 1933 Gorsedd programme,[115] heavily annotated and amended by him, not just with the addition of details of the installation ceremony but with many other alterations for the new era in both the Cornish and English wording. The 1934 programme incorporates versions of his new wording, and the Cornish installation ceremony appears in print for the first time. (The advice and sug-gestions of both Phillips and Rowe as to the installation were taken on board by Nance in arriving at the final form of the ceremony.)[116] Alterations continued to be made to Gorsedd ceremonial in later years. Indeed, in Nance's retrospective view the 1934 proceedings, which lasted about two hours, were an hour too long – 'we have decided on rather drastic cutting-down in future'.[117]

During his long tenure as Grand Bard Nance was involved in every aspect of Gorsedd activity, practical as well as cerebral, including matters of ceremonial, costume and regalia, examinations and competitions, prizes and certificates. He took personal charge of many arrangements and events as well as making and supporting innovations (not all of which survived). In addition he used his authority to promote Cornish culture in such areas as music, literature, educa-tion and scholarship, flying the flag, sporting activities, Cornish publications and preserving and recording dialect and customs. He regarded outreach to Cornish organisations, and particularly to the Cornish diaspora and other Celtic countries and gorseddau, as of great importance, and he worked consis-tently to maintain and promote these contacts. On top of this he pursued his own scholarly research and other work for Cornwall outside the Gorsedd.

Other Council members and bards in general were of course deeply commit-ted to the well-being of the Gorsedd, made their voices heard and played an important part in various kinds of work for the institution. As befitted his bardic name, *Tan Dyvarow* [Undying Fire], Cargeeg was a passionate advocate of bringing Cornwall back to the true Celtic path and wanted to use the Gorsedd to help achieve this. In November 1934, in reply to a letter from him, Nance set out his own position, likewise passionate but more pragmatic:

Mur a lowena a-m-be ow-redya an pyth-oll es leverys genough yn kever "Gwlascor Kernow" ha'n Orseth. An gwyr yu genough, y-whon lowr, ha why ow-predery bos aberth-y'gan colon agan-honen an wlascor-ma, ha mar pyth kefys ajy dhe nebes bledhynnow kemmys ha dek y'gan mesk a-gresso kepar ha why hag a-vo ervyrys gansa gul neppyth dhe wora an gryjyans-na yn ober, ny-vyth gwres yn-ufer Gorseth Kernow.[118]

[*I was very glad to read all you say about the "Kingdom of Cornwall" and the Gorsedd. I know well enough that you are right in thinking that this kingdom is within our own hearts, and if within a few years as many as ten are found among us who believe as you do and are determined to do something to put that belief into practice, the Cornish Gorsedd will not have been created in vain.*]

He goes on to say that Cargeeg's wish to create a 'Revival Army' ('Lu an Dasserghyans') would be better served by the creation of an additional Gorsedd for bards only, a development of the function of the Annual Meeting but distinct from it. He took this concept forward in a letter of January 1935, and it was later realised in the Closed Gorsedd:

Yma nep gwaytyans dhem y-fyth sysnsys Gorseth cudhys genen kens es dos haf, may hyllyn keskewsel a'n fordhow dredha a-yller gwellhe an Orseth hy-honen, hag ynweth may hyllyn gwell omaswon yntredhon ... Ny a-alsa dysky an Kernewek a-res y leverel dhe'n Orseth hag assaya an kescana, may halsa bos enor dhyn yn le meth, mes dres pup-oll ny a-alsa godhvos an pyth es yn brus agan tus.[119]

[*I have some hope that we will hold a hidden Gorsedd before the summer, so that we can discuss the ways in which the Gorsedd itself can be improved and also get to know each other better ... We would be able to learn the Cornish which must be spoken at the Gorsedd and practise the communal singing, so that it might bring us honour rather than shame, but above all we could know the opinions of our people.*]

Nance has been seen as one who found it difficult when his opinions were questioned, who was reluctant to consult others, and whose leadership style as Grand Bard was not conducive to progress in the Gorsedd. In part, this may be

merely a reflection of the fact that people have different views as to what constitutes progress and how it might be achieved, but in any event this letter is
just one indicator that these facets of his personality went along with more col-
legiate instincts. He certainly felt that the college of bards should be democratic and the Council representative.[120] The term 'Closed Gorsedd' (after brief use
of 'Secret', 'Hidden' or 'Private Gorsedd') was soon settled on for the new meeting, at which bards might confer, air their views on relevant issues, hear papers
and debate them. It was first suggested by Nance to Council on 20 March 1935,
and the first such meeting was held on 15 June that year at the Royal
Institution, Truro.[121] (The morning session for Cornish speakers was first held
in 1951.)[122]

There was a degree of drama at the Annual Meeting before the Gorsedd on
30 August 1935. A paper was presented by Herbert Thomas, asking for a
rethink on the criteria for bardship:

> The Grand Bard took it that Barth Colonnek's remarks showed a want
> of confidence in himself & the Council & vacated the Chair. Barth
> Colonnek explained that this was the last thing he had in his mind & ...
> a vote of confidence ... was carried unanimously.[123]

Nance's conviction that the Gorsedd should now aim to be a completely
Cornish ceremony was leading to progress on the ground. In the context of the
1935 Gorsedd, it was noted that the Cornish speakers 'were not voices in the
wilderness', in contrast to earlier years. Nance expressed satisfaction at the
increase in the number of bards who could follow the Cornish and hoped that
there would be more language bards the following year.[124] As previously noted,
his desire to give Cornish pride of place was to some extent in conflict with his
wish that potential workers for the Cornish movement should not be put off,
which led to his attracting criticism, notably from A.S.D. Smith, for not making enough use of Cornish,[125] while at the same time 'the increasing use, under
Mordon, of Cornish alone, was bound to put a strain on those who could not
understand it'.[126]

Nance also mentioned another vision which had his strong support. Having
initiated by proxy two Cornishmen from overseas,

Gorseth Kernow, Boscawen Un, 14 August 1937. Robert Morton Nance, Grand Bard, with raised hand (Courtesy Carola Nance Scupham/Gorseth Kernow Archive)

he reminded the Gorsedd of Sir Arthur Quiller-Couch's scheme for a Cornish home-coming. He asked them all to use their utmost endeavours to make the scheme a success, because of its enormous possibilities. The Cornish people were naturally scattered all over the world, and if they kept Cornwall as their home in focus it would be possible to keep the race together.[127]

This idea of a 'Cornish Fortnight' was also discussed at the Council meeting of 4 October 1935.[128] Though actively supported by Nance, it came to nothing during his lifetime, but it finally took shape in the Dehwelans, first held in 2002.

In 1936 the annual church service in Cornish was held in Truro Cathedral two days after the Gorsedd. There was enthusiasm in the press following these events, and after the service Nance himself 'remarked that it had been a great day for him, because he had been trying for years to get it into the heads of Cornish people that the Cornish language was a thing they could not afford to lose.'[129] As always, for Nance the Gorsedd and the language were intimately linked. Not all views on the service were so positive, however, and Nance himself was still very concerned about the future of the Cornish movement. Referring to the fact that there was only one new language bard that year, he said that he 'wanted people, bards included, to … see if they could not keep the Cornish language going. If they could not get more people to learn it, it would fade out after they had restored it. That would be a shame to Cornwall.'[130] Nance's appeal for more teaching of Cornish to schoolchildren was no doubt connected to the need he felt to reply to attacks claiming that there was agitation for the compulsory teaching of Cornish in schools and 'rabid nationalism' in the Cornish movement.[131]

Disquiet within the college of bards was again evident at the Closed Gorsedd on 5 June 1937, when Trelawny Roberts raised fundamental issues, such as the need for the Gorsedd to have a definite objective and be more than mere pageantry in order to avoid decline and ridicule, and (like Herbert Thomas in 1935) for a more rigid formulation of the qualifications needed for bardship.[132] Cargeeg wrote to Smith about this meeting, and in his reply (in which he writes in both Cornish and English) Smith criticises Nance in extremely harsh terms, as he often did in private letters:

> [B]yth ny-wra agan Mevyans sowyny erna vo genen hembrynkyas creffa. Pyth a-dal dysquedhes dhe Vordon an fordhow – hag yma lyes anedha – may haller gwellhe an Orseth? Ufer yu, ha scull termyn! [*Our Movement will never succeed until we have a stronger leader. What's the use of showing Mordon the ways – and there are many of them – in which the Gorsedd might be improved? It's in vain, and a waste of time!*] … With regard to the Gorseth: long ago I tackled M. about an annual subscription [to *Kernow*], and he promised to see what could be done. Nothing at all has been done … Also I have more than once urged that official notices be first written in Cor. with Eng. translation. Nothing doing … Really, the way the Gorseth is managed is childish, and I feel certain it will never be any better as long as M. is Grand Bard. He has no feeling for organisa-

tion. As an instance I might cite the opportunity missed of taking those essay-children under the wing of the Gorseth, and letting them feel ... that they were a promising leaven of a Celtic Cornwall. But no! Morton Nance could not rise to this height ... [W]hat a lot the Gorseth could do under proper leadership![133]

Despite these remarks, in the same letter Smith has unqualified praise for Nance's accomplishments in other areas, such as his profound knowledge of the Cornish texts, and while Smith was not the only bard to voice criticisms, his very negative view of features of Nance's work and character does not represent a consensus.

On 24 February 1938 Nance read his important paper *Wales & the Cornish Language & Gorsedd*[134] to the Royal Institution of South Wales, Swansea, in which he gives a cautiously optimistic view of the current state of the Cornish Gorsedd. He also reaffirms his conviction of the centrality of the Cornish language to the Gorsedd, his assessment of the current position of the language and perhaps an over-optimistic aspiration for the future:

[T]o ask for literature of great merit from [students of Cornish] would hardly be fair, but this recognition of their ability to write passable Cornish by making them "Bards by Examination" is much appreciated, and in time it will also mean that the great majority of the bards will be capable of writing and speaking Cornish, as of course they should be.

He also indicates his pleasure at the inclusion of Cornish exiles within the college of bards and, at some length, his enthusiasm for the 'great occasion' of the annual church service as an all-Cornish event associated with the Gorsedd, which has 'certainly led some ... to take up Cornish studies'. (This sits uneasily with what LV [*Lorgh Vras*? (Charles Taylor)] wrote to Smith in 1937: 'Mordon writes:– the Service in Cornish has not led to a single fresh Cornish student, while one hears of it annoying people who hate "foreign" languages in Church'.)[135] Regarding more deep-seated criticism, he saw the situation in 1938 in these terms:

[W]e in Cornwall, whose only substitute for a popular backing is the support of Old Cornwall members, can only expect to find more such critics [than in Wales], for the very idea of Cornwall being Celtic or standing in any relationship to Wales and Brittany is almost a novelty to Cornish people outside the Old Cornwall Societies and as distasteful to them as any other novelty. To many, however, the Gorsedd already conveys the message of peace and friendliness that it was intended to bring.

Nance was able to tell the assembled bards at the Annual Meeting in 1938 that the Celtic Congress was to be held in Cornwall the following year and that it would be desirable to stage the 1939 Gorsedd to tie in with it.[136] This ceremony was to be 'one of the most important ever staged, attended, it is hoped, by Welsh and Breton representatives, and representatives of the Gorsedd of the Gauls'.[137] There was also an intention to hold the Cornish service in Truro Cathedral again,[138] but in the event wider issues brought all these plans to nothing. A few weeks before the Annual Meeting Nance had attended the Breton Gorsedd as head of the first official Cornish delegation to take part in the event, where he delivered a speech in Cornish in the name of the bards.[139]

At the Council Meeting in April 1939, Nance introduced the idea of creating Gorsedd Disciples, under-18s who had shown their commitment to the Cornish cause and who could take part in the Gorsedd and later, if they proved their eligibility, be admitted as bards.[140] The scheme was implemented for a time but petered out after the Second World War. The Council meeting on 22 July 1939 was the last meeting recorded in the Gorsedd Minute Book before the outbreak of war, though Nance and Phillips attended the Breton Gorsedd at Vannes a week later. This occasion strengthened Nance's belief that it was a mistake to include any speeches in English at the Gorsedd and that the ideal to aim for was a simple one-hour ceremony all in Cornish, with a bare minimum of speeches. ('I never make speeches myself beyond the word or two that is necessary at times'.)[141] Just days before the war he shows that he was still on tenterhooks because of the possibility that one false step might undo the work done to nurture the delicate flower of Gorseth Kernow:

> Here … it is a "foreign" innovation, very much on its trial, and with only the support of a <u>proportion</u> of the members of Old Cornwall Societies. We have not reached the stage of contact with the crowd when eloquence

or humour can do anything for us. As far as the crowd is concerned ... all we can hope is that the suggestion of continuity with the past that is given by the use of Cornish in the ceremonies may reach them and impress them with the idea that if they don't understand why we do these things, we at least seem to understand it ourselves. In this way we are gradually getting more sympathy, I think, at all events the ridicule and opposition of a few is not, so far, taken up by the crowd. It is often touch-and-go, however, and even last year, when ... we had the best Gorsedd we have ever held, one long English speech nearly did for us. We had produced an atmosphere that was hard to recover when this had dispelled it. An English Gorsedd (unrobed) might make a popular appeal which ours does not, but this would have to abandon all sugges-tion of continuity with Celtic Cornwall, which is what we put first, as something to build on.[142]

It was to be another seven years before an open Cornish Gorsedd was staged again.

(ii) The War Years (1939–1945)

Quite apart from Nance's fears for the future of the Gorsedd, it might be thought that such a relatively new organisation of minority interest would be in particular danger of going under following the outbreak of the Second World War in September 1939. This was indeed the fate of Tyr ha Tavas, due partly no doubt to the fact that it was an organisation of young people, those most direct-ly involved in the war effort. From the beginning of the war, however, Nance was determined to do all he could to maintain momentum by continuing to hold as many meetings as possible and by Gorsedd encouragement of Cornish studies in all practicable ways:

> P'ur fyth dhyn arta Cres may hyllyn lowen omguntell yn Gorseth Ygerys
> ny-wor den-vyth: dhe sul a-vynno entra dhe'n Orseth dre apposyans,
> bytegens, y-fynnyr ygery forth lan pynag a-wharfo. Neb a-vyn yndella
> bos degemerys, rag henna, gwrens danvon y scryfa, pymp-cans ger a'y
> hes, dhe'n Scryvynyas ... ow-cortos gwell dedhyow.[143]

[When we shall again have Peace so that we can assemble gladly at an Open

Gorsedd no-one knows: it is desired, however, that whatever happens a clear means be provided for anyone who wishes to join the Gorsedd by examination. Whoever wishes to be accepted in this way, therefore, should send his script, 500 words in length, to the Secretary ... awaiting better days.]

At the beginning of the war Nance and the Gorsedd Secretary, W.H. Eva, sent a notice to bards, explaining that the Open Gorsedd and Annual Meeting could not be held on 16 September. 'It is proposed to hold instead, with such members as <u>can easily</u> reach "Chylason," Carbis Bay ... on that afternoon, an emergency Annual Meeting ... and a curtailed Gorsedd to admit, by proxy or otherwise, those accepted as Bards or approved as Disciples. No Rule seems to forbid this and your silence will be taken as consent.' So it was that, having sought advice from Phillips and *Crwys* (Revd W. *Crwys* Williams), Archdruid of Wales, and been assured by them of the propriety of the meeting,[144] the 1939 bardic assembly was held in Nance's house and garden. He wrote a simple but effective 'Solempnyta an Orseth yn Termyn Bresel' [War-Time Gorsedd Ceremony], in which the Gorseth Prayer – the only part retained from the standard ceremony – remained central, and the Grand Bard's part includes the following (Cornish followed by Nance's own translation):

Yn Hanow Dew.

Aban nag-us Cres, agan deth a lowena yu trelyes yn deth a voreth.

... Aban nag-us Cres, cot-treghys vyth agan Gorseth hedhyu.

Bytegens, y-tegoth dhyn moy es kens pysy Dew rag y weres tryflek, Nerth, Gothvos, Kerensa, ow-perthy cof bos an brassa a'n re-ma ynweth Kerensa; rag hep Kerensa, nefra ny-yl bos Cres a-bys.

... Y'n bys a-dro kyn nag-us Cres, re-bo Cres omma yntredhon-ny yn Kernow: re-bo kelmys warbarth yn agan brys ha'gan colon pup ur-oll – Kernow, Cres, Kerensa.

Ha'n Tas Truethek mabden roy bos Cres y'n norvys yntredhon-ny, y fleghes-oll, kens es nep-pell.

Yndella re-bo.

[*In God's Name.*

Since Peace is not, our day of rejoicing is become a day of sorrow.

… Since Peace is not, our Gorseth will be cut short to-day.

Yet, it behoves us more than ever to pray to God for His threefold help, Strength, Wisdom and Love, remembering that the greatest of these also, is Love; for without Love, never can there be a lasting Peace.

… Though in the world around there is not Peace, may there be Peace here amongst us in Cornwall: may there always be bound together in our minds and hearts – Cornwall, Peace and Love.

And may the merciful Father of mankind grant that there be Peace in the world among all of us, his children, ere long.

So be it.][145]

The echoes in the Gorsedd Prayer of 1 Corinthians 13 are reinforced here, and the symbolism is explored in detail by Nance in the address he delivered in 1941 (discussed below). Nance had also consulted his Deputy, Trelawny Roberts, about the amended ceremony. He agreed with the outline proposal but, since he was one of those who believed that a Gorsedd could be held only in peacetime, did not regard the event as a true Gorsedd.[146] Be that as it may, initiates were awarded their diplomas, Disciples their certificates, and competition prizes and certificates were sent, in an attempt to maintain normality as far as possible.[147] At the Closed Gorsedd in 1940 Nance reported that *Crwys* and he had agreed that the war did not prevent the holding of a Gorsedd because the peace called for in the ceremony referred to peace within the college of bards. At this stage Nance was against holding an open Gorsedd and favoured the same abbreviated Annual Meeting and ceremony as in 1939,[148] and indeed the next six gatherings (1940–1945) were conducted along those lines (all at the Royal Institution of Cornwall, Truro), though after the 1942 ceremony he expressed regret that it had been curtailed.[149]

E.A. Rees gave the Council the startling news, at their meeting on 19 July 1941, that he could find no record in the Minute Book of either of the two occasions on which Nance should have been re-elected as Grand Bard since 1934. Recollections of Council members varied, but the proposal that he should be deemed to have been so re-elected was carried unanimously.[150]

Nance appreciated the resonances of symbolism, and a key text for understanding his thoughts on the deeper significance of the Gorsedd is his address on the Gorsedd Prayer, with which he opened the ceremony in September 1941, the wartime setting no doubt adding to the poignancy of the occasion. The fullest version of the address is that found among the Nance Collection at the Royal Institution, Truro, where it is renamed *The Symbolism of the Gorsedd*.[151] He prefaced it 'with the remark that he did not attend church and did nothing to support forms of religion, yet anyone who was acquainted with him knew he had some religious feeling, which was centred in the Gorsedd.'[152] He said that he 'had been accused of being a humbug and other things, but he did not claim to be better than any other bard.'[153] Though a non-religious festival designed to foster the Celtic spirit of Cornwall, the Gorsedd had as its most vital part the Gorsedd Prayer:

> It has been generally agreed that its petitions sum up the needs of mankind so well that all men of goodwill, whatever their creeds, can join in it sincerely, and in basing our brotherhood of bards upon it we accept an ideal which if followed would help all human beings to live together in peace and happiness. Kernow, Cres ha Kerensa, "Cornwall, Peace and Love," the watchword of the Cornish Gorsedd, is only an application of its hopes to ourselves.

The Celtic world can thus bring a message of hope to the world at large. Nance goes on to discuss the Welsh provenance of the Prayer (including the possible part played by Iolo Morganwg) and analyses the complex links and associations of its threefold petition. He continues:

> But if <u>Power</u>, <u>Wisdom</u> and <u>Love</u> – <u>Nerth</u>, <u>Skyans</u> and <u>Kerensa</u> or <u>Dader</u> – are the basis of the Gorsedd Prayer, it is because this triad is the central idea of the Gorsedd itself ... These three attributes of "the Spirit of God, which is not the spirit of fear", are symbolised further in the mystic sign of the Gorsedd, the three descending and diverging rays.

He links the origin of this bardic symbolism, and the inspiration for the Gorsedd Prayer, with Christianity rather than druidism, particularly with the Holy Trinity and the Lord's Prayer, and he cites passages from the medieval Cornish texts which echo the same concepts as well as drawing on allusions from many other sources, including *Hymns Ancient and Modern* and the Thirty-Nine Articles. He also discusses 'the deathless Arthur who shall come again, who symbolises for us the Celtic spirit of Cornwall' and the use of Arthur's Sword in the Gorsedd. Alluding to the individual attributes symbolised by the three orders of Druid, Bard and Ovate, and by the colours of their robes, he makes an interesting observation:

> When the Cornish Gorsedd was formed, none of those who decided that for Cornwall it would be fitting to avoid the three Orders ... had any idea of the symbolism involved ... but purely by accident we seem in our Gorsedd to have laid all the stress on the Spirit of <u>Love</u>, and in this we did much better than we knew, for we have been drawn together not as people having or wanting <u>Power</u>, or as specially conspicuous for <u>Wisdom</u>, but because in common we have a great <u>Love</u> of Cornwall, and having it are pledged to look for the best in one another ... and so as closely as we can to approach the great ideal of the Love of what is Just, the Love of all that exists, of God and all Goodness ... If by chance we have sacrificed some part of the symbolic meaning of the Gorsedd, as long as we keep this, we still have what matters most, though we may have to add something of Power and Wisdom to Love if we are to make it effective and reasonable as well as kindly.[154]

To the early 1940s belongs the most entertaining critique of the lack of Cornish within bardic ranks, Peggy Pollard's *Synt Tanbellen: a tryfle in one scene*.[155] This is not just a bard's very funny pastiche of the style of the medieval Cornish plays but a scathing attack on the failure to place Cornish at the centre of the Gorsedd ethos. As has been noted, Nance had some difficulty with this issue. He too felt it essential to maximise the use of Cornish but at the same time was most anxious not to alienate actual or potential allies in the Cornish cause. His knowledge of the language was naturally not in question, but he did not escape Pollard's censure. The playlet's Grand Bard speaks:

Gorowrys Y Gernygow: Lyvrow my re wruk scryfa,
                                        marthus tek, mur aga frys.
                                        Map lyen of, re'm ena,
                                        mur enorys y'n pow-ma.

Synt Tanbellen: Hem yu da, prydydhyon flowr;
                                        mes nyns yu lowr.[156]

[*Little Gilded Horns:*   *I have written books,*
                                         prodigiously fine ones, of great worth.
                                         I am a man of letters, by my soul,
                                         greatly honoured in this land.

St Bombshell: *This is good, flower of poets;*
                                         but it is not enough.]

Trystan hag Ysolt, rendered into Cornish by A.S.D. Smith (who of course also deplored the lack of Cornish within the Gorsedd), is quoted with approval in this work, as a hope for the future.

Cornish-Breton solidarity became even more important to Nance during the war. In a letter to Phillips in 1942 he mentioned that the Cornish Gorsedd had kept in touch with Free-French Bretons and expressed the belief 'that our real links with Brittany and France through the Gorsedd may be of great value by and by'.[157] In the address with which he opened the Gorsedd of 12 September 1942 he spoke at length on the Cornish-Breton display at Penzance on 5 September,[158] on which occasion he had made a speech in Breton, and *Arta ef a-*

dhe had been sung.[159] (He returned to the subject of (non-political) Cornish solidarity with Brittany at the next two Annual Meetings, though little concrete action apparently resulted.)[160]

After three years of hostilities he was still able to be optimistic about the viability of the post-war Gorsedd and the importance of its role:

> If the Gorsedd is to go on, of course it will have to be ready to adapt itself to whatever conditions arise in the future, but it is already so broadly based that if a more really democratic society is the chief alteration to be expected, it will fit into that perfectly. It will become more and more difficult to maintain individuality and local differences as the world is tending, but that will only mean that the Gorsedd and Old Cornwall Societies are more obviously needed to offset the tendency for every place and person to become alike.[161]

The following April he shared some further thoughts as to the new start the Gorsedd might make in rebuilding Cornwall after the war, adding 'Ny-wruk an Orseth mur a dra kens es dalleth an bresel, del won lowr yn ta, mes gwell vyth an gwel rygthy wosa hemma martesen'. [*The Gorsedd did not do much before the war started, as I know well enough, but perhaps the outlook will be better for it hereafter.*][162]

(iii) The post-War Years (1945–1959)

An abbreviated ceremony was retained for the first Gorsedd after the war (1 September 1945), but peace had brought with it the promise of an end to the restrictions on Gorsedd activity. At the Closed Gorsedd in 1946 Nance took the opportunity to urge bards to place more value in people who took a real interest in Cornwall than in mere numbers, and to give every encouragement to young people for the good of Cornwall's future.[163] A full Gorsedd was held on 7 September 1946 on the site envisaged for the 1939 ceremony, Perran Round, and was described as the most successful since 1928.[164] Nance's declared ambitions for the institution were lofty indeed:

> It aims at helping to permeate society with the spirit of brotherhood, cooperation, harmony and racial unity.[165]

The coming of peace had not however pacified Nance's critics. Not only did he feel the need to temper his passion for Cornish because of the possible consequences of too fervent an insistence on its promotion, but he was also concerned to prevent the ceremony itself becoming tedious for participants and spectators. Smith was dubious about this approach:

> I agree that the Gorseth should have a definite shape, and not be too long drawn out. But I am far from agreeing that this can be attained by the exclusion of Cornish speeches.[166]

Cargeeg was also involved in some lively discussion (not reflected in the Minute Book) at the Closed Gorsedd on 4 June 1949. He asserted that the college of bards had failed 'lamentably' to live up to its name. Nance regretfully agreed, but strongly disputed Cargeeg's additional assertion that the college had lacked definition of aims from the outset. The drama then intensified:

> Mr Morton Nance tested the feeling of the meeting with a motion that the Gorsedd be abandoned, but there was no seconder ... The Grand Bard: I made my promise that it should go on, and for that reason I allowed myself to become Grand Bard. I don't like it. I don't like the title. I don't like being Grand Bard. What I do like is the recognition that I have done something for Cornwall or tried to do something for it.[167]

Though part of him no doubt wished to be rid of his leadership responsibilities, this may also indicate that Nance's skills in brinkmanship had not deserted him, and he went on to repudiate Cargeeg's further charge that the study of Cornish history had been largely neglected.

Of all critics of the Gorsedd, the most surprising case is that of A.L. Rowse, who, unusually for him, changed his mind on the subject. Distinguished international scholars had consented to be bards of honour as early as 1930, but when Rowse chanced to learn that it was intended to hold the 1949 ceremony ('These idiotic festivities') in the field next to his house and that as Patron of the local Old Cornwall Society he should be on hand, he wrote: 'But it is unthinkable that I should be there, that I should allow myself to be seen by them'.[168] When he finally consented to become a bard himself, in 1968, 'he had come to recognise that the Gorsedd was not the marginal eccentricity he had suspected but was an important contributor to the cultural life of Cornwall.' In his own words:

> In the interval [since its beginnings] the Gorseth and its bardic organi-
> sation had held on, taken root, done good work and spread. All this was
> largely due to the remarkable work of a man whom I greatly underesti-
> mated: Morton Nance ... He was right and I was wrong.[169]

At the Gorsedd of 1951, held at Tregirls, near Padstow, Nance again voiced one of his primary concerns: 'We are keeping in memory for ever the fact that we are Cornish people and inherit most of our good qualities from Celtic ances-tors'. A unique feature at the Gorsedd was the ceremony of 'Crying the Neck', which Nance carried out, having been offered the sheaf by his six-year-old great-nephew, Peter Robin Morton Nance, who spoke in Cornish.[170] This was also the first year in which candidates for bardship by examination in Cornish could choose to undergo an oral examination, either in addition to or instead of submitting the '500 words' of good, unaided written Cornish which was the usual requirement. It was hoped that this would lead to an increase in Cornish conversation.[171]

A matter on which Nance evidently had mixed feelings was the concert after the Gorsedd:

> We have sometimes had a concert that had the right Celtic flavour...
> when visiting Welsh and Breton contributors took part in an impromptu
> entertainment, but personally I would much rather have had nothing
> after the ceremony than the quite inappropriate music that we are usu-
> ally offered. My Cornish classes were prepared to enact <u>an Tyr Marya</u>,
> taken from the Resurrection play, in Padstow Church between the musi-
> cal items, but the parson seems to be a puritan who objects to anything
> that could be called a "play", or perhaps to words written, in a language
> unknown to him, before the Reformation.[172]

Nance gave a talk at the 1954 Closed Gorsedd 'on the importance of the

[Cornish] Language as the distinctive mark of a Bard',[173] reflecting an anxiety about the state of the language which was to remain with him for the rest of his life. At the 1955 Gorsedd no awards were presented for Cornish poetry or prose. Neither Nance nor E.G.R. Hooper were impressed as judges by the standard of the entries,[174] and Nance again stressed the vital importance of the language in his own 'outspoken' appeal to bards to study it:

> For some time past ... people had become bards through a slight knowl-edge of the Cornish language, and some of them on becoming bards had done no more. "That is not the way we are going to have the Cornish lan-guage revived," he said. "That is the first foot in the first rung of the lad-der and no more than that. There are many rungs yet, many of them beyond my head, and some of them we shall probably never reach. But we are gradually building up a Cornish language as capable of being used as any language in the world, and a lovely language it is, too."[175]

For him a wholehearted, rather than superficial, revival of Cornish was nec-essary for the Gorsedd to achieve its purpose.

C.H. Beer[176] references the 1957 Gorsedd as an example of Nance's desire to keep politics out of the college of bards, in the context of his striving for unity in the Cornish movement:

> To 'Mebyon Kernow' with its rather more political brand of Cornish 'Nationalism', Mordon adopted openly a cautiously non-committal atti-tude as befitted his positions as Grand Bard of the Gorsedd and President of the Old Cornwall Societies and thereby the Leader of so many of varying shades of opinion. We know, however, that he was broadly sympathetic with many of our aims, though anxious that noth-ing should disrupt Cornish unity. This thought must have been in his mind when, at the Gorsedd of 1957 ... he based his message to all pre-sent on "Cres ha Kerensa" [Peace and Love].[177]

Ill health meant that the Council meeting on 26 July 1958 was the last which Nance attended,[178] though he was able to officiate at his final Gorsedd that year, at Perran Round. There were again no awards for Cornish poetry or prose, and, for the first time, no initiation of bards by examination in the Cornish language. Nance lamented that 'the Gorsedd had restored the language, but if it was not learned by the younger generation it would die again',[179] and George Pawley White confirmed Nance's despondency over the lessening of enthusiasm and substantive work within the Gorsedd.[180] P.A.S. Pool however stated that Nance was 'confident that his life's work would be carried on (as it was) by people who believed in it',[181] and it is to be hoped that he did indeed feel this confidence at the end, despite his anxieties over the Gorsedd and the language.

Pool wrote that 'while [*Mordon*] lived the idea of another as Grand Bard was unthinkable',[182] and at the age of 85 he was re-elected for the last time at the Council meeting on 22 November 1958, in his absence through ill health[183] – probably the first occasion on which he had failed to attend a Gorsedd meeting. A letter he wrote to Pool two days later is an affecting tribute to the value he placed on personal friendship and to his stoicism:

> [I]t is hardly likely that I could figure again with a good effect in a Gorsedd procession, or get over rough ground to a Gorsedd site. That being so, my 25th year as Grand Bard is not one to which I can look forward. As to any form of presentation, much as I am bound to feel gratified by the kind wishes of your Committee, I can think of none that I should not find very much more embarrassing than happy ... I hope still to be able to go on with a good deal of my work and to see my friends and make plans with them as in the past.[184]

Six months later, however, on 27 May 1959, Nance died, in his ninth consecutive three-year term as Grand Bard, a period in office which Gorsedd rules ensure can never be surpassed. At his burial service at Zennor, the Sword of the Gorsedd lay upon his coffin and was carried before him as the funeral party left the church.[185] The report in the Minute Book of the first meeting after his death, the Annual meeting on 6 June, already conveys the idea of another new beginning. After the bards had stood as a mark of respect, the book records their reinforcement of the rule stipulating a triennial election for the office of Grand Bard on the grounds that it 'should pass in turn to those qualified to occupy it, and not be regarded as one person's freehold',[186] presumably with reference to Nance's tenure. Minute books are not noted for effusiveness, and this remark is perhaps understandable in context. Its tone is certainly more than counterbalanced by tributes to Nance in the more public arena of printed obituaries and memories, in newspapers and elsewhere.[187] Pool's words are perhaps the most memorable. For him, Nance was simply 'the grandest of Grand Bards.'[188]

Conclusion

Robert Morton Nance was the single most important figure in the history of Gorseth Kernow. Most of the features which form a regular part of the ceremony and the Gorsedd year evolved under his leadership, at his instigation or with his support. He set up the Gorsedd as a visible symbol of Celtic Cornish 'difference', to promote the positive values of Celtic Cornwall and as a defence against trends which he saw as inimical to Cornwall's essential self. These trends are even stronger today, but the consciousness of Cornwall's individuality is likewise more keenly felt among her people and others, and Nance's work has played an important part in bringing this about. Many of the problems he came up against, including some deep-seated issues within the Gorsedd and outside it, are still being encountered by his successors, and the institution still attracts criticism as it did in his time, and as he did as an individual. Yet it survived despite setbacks, difficulties and shortcomings to become an important player in the Cornish cultural scene. This betokens a profound conviction and commitment among the very small group who worked for it over the years and was not the achievement of just one man. However, without Nance's determination to bring it into being and ensure its survival – partly through an anxious balancing act between conflicting tendencies within the movement – it is by no means certain that there would be a Cornish Gorsedd today, and without the Gorsedd the awareness of Cornwall's claim to individual recognition would undoubtedly be far less widely understood than it is. Most lovers of Cornwall would salute him for that at least. It was after all Cornwall itself that he loved, and for him the Gorsedd was only one part of a wider perspective:

> [Y]ma lyes tra a-dal bos gwres adro dhe'n Orseth. Betegens gwell yu un ur war ben onen a'gan menedhyow es del yu myl orseth yn-ta del wodhes.

> [*There are many things which must be done concerning the Gorsedd.*

Nonetheless, a single hour on top of one of our hills is better than a thousand gorseddau, as you well know.][189]

Notes

1. The story of Nance and the Gorsedd has been told before, in e.g. Hugh Miners (1978) *Gorseth Kernow: the first 50 years*, Penzance: Gorseth Kernow; Derek Williams (1997) 'Robert Morton Nance' in *An Baner Kernewek/The Cornish Banner*, no. 88, May 1997, pp. 3, 14–18. Of Nance's own published writings on the institution, the earliest appeared even before he was initiated as a Welsh bard and the last less than a year before his death: R. Morton Nance (1928) 'Cornwall and the Gorsedd' in *Tre Pol and Pen: the Cornish annual*, 1928, pp. 97–99; Nance (1951) 'The Cornish Gorsedd' in *The Cornish Review*, no. 7, Spring 1951, pp. 22–27; Nance (1958) 'Aims of the Gorsedd' in *Cornish Magazine*, vol. 1, no. 7, November 1958, pp. 244–245. The present chapter seeks only to supplement these writings. The wealth of source material available means that a much fuller account might still be written.

2. Nance (1951), pp. 25–26.

3. For Jenner, see especially Derek R. Williams (ed.) (2004) *Henry and Katharine Jenner: a celebration of Cornwall's culture, language and identity*, London: Francis Boutle.

4. Nance (1951), p. 26.

5. Nance (1938) *Wales & the Cornish Language & Gorsedd* (paper read to the Royal Institution of South Wales, Swansea, 24 February 1938), Nance Collection, Courtney Library, Royal Institution of Cornwall, Truro.

6. Ibid. See also C. Morton Raymont (1962) *The early life of Robert Morton Nance*, [Leedstown]: New Cornwall, p. 28.

7. Nance (1938).

8. Ibid. See also *Western Morning News*, 28 May 1959 (Nance obituary).

9. See R. Morton Nance, Letter to Henry Jenner, 29 May 1918, Nance Collection, Courtney Library.

10. Nance (1938).

11. *Western Morning News*, 20 September 1928.

12. Llyfrgell Genedlaethol Cymru / The National Library of Wales, Papers of David Rhys Phillips, 3596–3627, 3629, 3630, 3634–3646 (Letters from R. Morton Nance to Phillips referring to the Cornish Gorsedd); Cornish Gorsedd Archives, Copies of these letters and Letters from Phillips to Nance.

13. NLW, Phillips Papers, 3596. See also 3597.

14. See Henry Jenner (1928), 'The Gorsedd of Boscawen-Un' in *Old Cornwall*, vol. 1, no. 7, pp. 1–6, reproduced in Williams (2004), pp. 182–189. See also William Morris (1974), *The Gorsedd and its Bards in Britain*, Penzance: Gorseth Kernow. The triad is quoted in both these sources, and in Nance (1951).

15. Nance (1928), p. 98.

16. NLW, Phillips Papers, 3597.

17. Nance (1951), p. 27. See also Nance (1938) and his *Symbolism of the Gorsedd*, Nance Collection, Courtney Library (particularly the footnote). Nance had made the first tentative suggestion of this innovation to Phillips in a letter of 7 June 1928 (NLW, Phillips Papers, 3603). Phillips was not keen, but Nance stood firm (3608, letter of 23 July 1928), as he did later when the idea was challenged. (See e.g. Cornwall Record Office, X1104/1, Cornish Gorsedd Minute Book, insert between pp. [124] and 125).

18. Nance (1938).

19. See e.g. Jenner (1928) and Letter to R. Morton Nance, 5 September 1928, Nance Collection, Courtney Library.

20. See D. Rhys Phillips, Letter to R. Morton Nance, 21 July 1934, Cornish Gorsedd Archives.

21. *Western Morning News*, 12 September 1946.
22. Ibid., 29 [?] September 1923 (cutting in box marked 'Gorsedd 1927–1932 only', Courtney Library). In his letter, Nance ascribes membership of the Christian ministry to the majority of modern Welsh druids in general, whereas the ascription applies only to recent Archdruids, as he surely knew. In 1932 the Gorsedd was charged not only with paganism but with advancing 'claims of superiority and isolation' (ibid., 13 September 1932). Nance's reply is an elegant apologia, attempting to allay public concern through reason (ibid., 15 September 1932). In a lively exchange of letters in 1946, Nance's argument elicited the suggestion at one point that the Gorsedd had fascist, as well as pagan, tendencies: 'Do but spell culture kultur and you see the inevitable result' (ibid., 2 September 1946).
23. See e.g. ibid., 27 September 1923. (In a letter to the newspaper earlier the same month he had suggested that performances of Nance's dialect plays might be staged at a Cornish Eisteddfod.)
24. Ibid., 24 September 1928.
25. *West Briton*, 10 January 1927.
26. *Western Morning News*, 7 September 1923.
27. Ibid., 29 [?] September 1923.
28. *Cornish Guardian*, 6 September 1934.
29. Festivals on a smaller scale were held in Nance's time: a 'Blackwater Eisteddfod' was referred to in *Cornish Evening Tidings*, 22 August 1938, and a Launceston 'Eisteddfod Week' was mentioned at the Closed Gorsedd on 5 June 1948 (CRO, X1104/1, p. [259]).
30. The address is transcribed inside the front cover of *Gwarnyans Gorseth Byrth Kernow/Esethvos Kernow/Proclamation of the Gorsedd of the Bards of Cornwall 1983*.
31. *Western Morning News*, 23 April 1928.
32. *Western Mail*, 8 August 1928.
33. CRO, X1104/1, p. 21.
34. R. Morton Nance, Letter to Peter Laws, 20 May 1949, Cornish Gorsedd Archives.
35. This would appear to be the document preserved as NLW, Phillips Papers, 3646, but it is properly an addition to 3610.
36. Note beside *Western Mail* article on Treorchy Gorsedd, CRO, X1104/1, pp. [14]–15. Jenner was not present at Treorchy (NLW, Phillips Papers, 3603).
37. NLW, Phillips Papers, 3602.
38. CRO, X1104/1, pp. 33–[34].
39. NLW, Phillips Papers, 3600.
40. Ibid., 3621.
41. CRO, X1104/1, p. [24].
42. Henry Jenner, Letter to R. Morton Nance, 5 September 1928, Nance Collection, Courtney Library.
43. *Western Morning News*, 20 September 1928.
44. *Cornish Guardian*, 6 September 1951.
45. *Western Morning News*, 8 November 1927. There seems to have been no attempt to involve the Gorsedd of North Staffordshire ('a minor affair', in Nance's words) (*West Briton*, 13 September 1928).
46. Ibid., 20 September 1928.
47. Amy Hale (2005) 'Review article: Rethinking Henry Jenner' in *Cornish Studies*, 2nd series, no. 13, 2005, p. 309.
48. *The Cornish Gorsedd at Boscawen-Un Stone Circle*, Penzance: "The Cornishman" Group of Amalgamated Newspapers, p. 10.
49. Ibid., p. 13.
50. *West Briton*, 27 September 1928.
51. CRO, X1104/1, p. [22].

52. NLW, Phillips Papers, 3614.
53. CRO, X1104/1, p. [36].
54. *Cornish Times*, 11 September 1931.
55. R. Morton Nance, Letter to F.B. Cargeeg, 3 November 1937 (private hands).
56. CRO, X1104/1, p. 37.
57. *Programme of the Gorsedd of the Bards... 1929*, Penzance: [Gorseth Kernow].
58. *Western Morning News*, 31 August 1929.
59. Nance (1938).
60. NLW, Phillips Papers, 3620.
61. *Western Morning News*, 20 February 1929.
62. *West Briton*, 5 September 1929.
63. *Ceremonies of the Gorsedd of the Bards of Cornwall*, [n.p.]: [Gorseth Kernow].
64. *Western Morning News*, 31 May 1935.
65. Undated postcard, probably June 1929, NLW, Phillips Papers, 3619.
66. Ibid., 3620.
67. Ibid., 3625.
68. Hugh Miners and Treve Crago (2002) *Tolzethan: the life and times of Joseph Hambley Rowe*, [n.p.]: Gorseth Kernow, pp. 21–22.
69. R. Morton Nance, Letter to W.A. Pascoe, 28 July 1930, Cornish Gorsedd Archives.
70. There was in fact no prohibition against non-Cornish people becoming bards. The Revd Canon H.R. Jennings was initiated in 1929 as *Saws Degemerys* (Accepted Englishman).
71. *Western Morning News*, 10 September 1930.
72. R. Morton Nance, Letter to W.A. Pascoe, 23 September 1930, Cornish Gorsedd Archives.
73. See e.g. *Royal Cornwall Gazette*, 18 August 1937; *Evening Herald*, 9 September 1946.
74. See e.g. *Western Morning News*, 15 August 1936 and 20 August 1938.
75. Revd Canon G.H. Doble, Note to R.J. Noall, 26 February 1931, Box marked 'Gorsedd 1927–1932 only', Courtney Library.
76. CRO, X1104/1, pp. 55–[56].
77. *Western Morning News*, 8 September 1932. The play was also performed at the evening concert after the 1953 Gorsedd (Concert programme, Cornish Gorsedd Archives).
78. CRO, X1104/1, pp. 57–[58].
79. R. Morton Nance, Letter to F.B. Cargeeg, 29 May 1934 (private hands).
80. R. Morton Nance, Letter to F.B. Cargeeg, 31 March 1934 (private hands).
81. His approach had the opposite effect in at least one case. John Legonna wrote: '*Mordon* offered to make me a bard 'if I would send him a short story in the same language in which I had written to him'... [but] it seemed a bit wrong to me being a bard without a full command of the language'. (Letter to E.G.R. Hooper, 21 January 1972, Talek Papers, Cornish Gorsedd Archives).
82. R. Morton Nance, Letter to F.B. Cargeeg, 29 May 1934 (private hands).
83. A.S.D. Smith, Letter, probably to E.G.R. Hooper, 1939 or 1944, Talek Papers, Cornish Gorsedd Archives (photocopy of p. 2 only).
84. *Cornish Evening Tidings*, 13 September 1932.
85. *Western Morning News*, 25 August 1933.
86. CRO, X1104/1, p. [312].
87. R. Morton Nance, Letter to E.G.R. Hooper, [1935], Talek Papers, Cornish Gorsedd Archives (photocopy of part only).
88. *Western Morning News*, 29 August 1933.
89. CRO, X1104/1, p. 71.

90. NLW, Phillips Papers, 3635.
91. *Western Morning News*, 4 September 1944.
92. For Rowe, see Hugh Miners and Treve Crago (2002).
93. CRO, X1104/1, p. 81.
94. NLW, Phillips Papers, 3636.
95. D. Rhys Phillips, Letter to R. Morton Nance, 21 June 1934, Cornish Gorsedd Archives.
96. See e.g. ibid., D. Rhys Phillips, Letter to R. Morton Nance, 23 June 1934.
97. NLW, Phillips Papers, 3637.
98. Ibid., 3636 and 3639; D.Rhys Phillips, Letter to R. Morton Nance, 23 June 1934, Cornish Gorsedd Archives.
99. NLW, Phillips Papers, 3636.
100. CRO, X1104/1, p. [84].
101. R. Morton Nance, Letter to F.B. Cargeeg, 4 August 1934 (private hands).
102. D. Rhys Phillips, Letter to R. Morton Nance, 21 June 1934, Cornish Gorsedd Archives.
103. This was agreed at the Council meeting on 1 August 1934 (CRO, X1104/1, p. [88]).
104. D. Rhys Phillips, Letter to R. Morton Nance, 21 July 1934, Cornish Gorsedd Archives.
105. *Souvenir Programme of the Gorsedd of the Bards... 1934*, Liskeard: [Gorseth Kernow].
106. NLW, Phillips Papers, 3638.
107. *Western Morning News*, 8 September 1934.
108. *West Briton*, 28 May 1959.
109. *Western Morning News*, 8 September 1934.
110. *Cornish Guardian*, 6 September 1934.
111. *Western Morning News*, 8 September 1934.
112. Ibid.
113. *Cornish Times*, 14 September 1934. E.E. Morton Nance confirmed that he had no help from his uncle (Interview with Chris Blount, undated, Falmouth: Chough Tapes).
114. *Cornish Guardian*, 6 September 1951 and 9 September 1954.
115. Box marked 'Cornish Gorsedd'.
116. For Rowe's ideas, see his Letters to R. Morton Nance, 28 July 1934 and 29 July 1934, Cornish Gorsedd Archives.
117. NLW, Phillips Papers, 3639.
118. R. Morton Nance, Letter to F.B. Cargeeg, 15 November 1934 (private hands).
119. R. Morton Nance, Letter to F.B. Cargeeg, 18 January 1935 (private hands).
120. See CRO, X1104/1, insert between pp. [62] and 63; *Cornish Times*, 14 September 1934.
121. CRO, X1104/1, pp. 105, [108]. Despite the meeting's designation, the press were allowed access. (See *Western Morning News*, June 17, 1935.)
122. CRO. X1104/1, p. [287].
123. Ibid., p. [116].
124. *Western Morning News*, 31 August 1935.
125. See e.g. A.S.D. Smith, Letter to F.B. Cargeeg, 4 July 1937 (private hands).
126. Miners (1978), p. 32.
127. *Western Morning News*, 31 August 1935.
128. CRO, X1104/1, p. 121.
129. *Western Morning News*, 17 August 1936.
130. *West Briton*, 20 August 1936.
131. *Western Morning News*, 20 August 1936.
132. CRO, X1104/1, insert between pp. [138] and 139. This was still an issue in 1942, when a sub-committee, on which Nance was to serve, was set up to work through it (ibid., p. 195).

133. A.S.D. Smith, Letter to F.B. Cargeeg, 4 July 1937 (private hands). Though no action resulted, Nance brought forward Smith's *Kernow* (the first all-Cornish periodical) for discussion at two meetings in 1936 (CRO, X1104/1, p. [124] and insert between pp. [124] and 125).
134. Nance (1938).
135. Charles Taylor [?], Letter to A.S.D. Smith, 12 July 1937, Talek Papers, Gorsedd Archives.
136. CRO, X1104/1, p. [156].
137. *Western Morning News*, 22 August 1938.
138. NLW, Phillips Papers, 3641.
139. *Western Morning News*, 3 August 1938. An addition to this cutting in the Cornish Gorsedd Archives indicates that Nance spoke also in Breton.
140. CRO, X1104/1, p. [160].
141. NLW, Phillips Papers, 3641.
142. Ibid., 3642.
143. *Old Cornwall*, vol. 3, no. 6, Winter 1939, p. 228.
144. W. Crwys Williams, Note to R. Morton Nance, 12 September 1939; D. Rhys Phillips, Letter to R. Morton Nance, 7 September 1939, Cornish Gorsedd Archives.
145. CRO, X1104/1, p. [166]. There is a marginally different version in the Cornish Gorsedd Archives.
146. Trelawny Roberts, Letter to R. Morton Nance, 15 September 1939, Cornish Gorsedd Archives.
147. *Old Cornwall*, vol. 3, no. 6, Winter 1939, p. 245.
148. CRO, X1104/1, p. [172]. The minutes of this meeting are particularly tantalising, giving a glimpse of what must have been a wide-ranging discussion, including the following: 'Mr Ashley Rowe reported that he had received Magazines and paper from Belgium and considered that someone was trying to cause trouble through the Celtic movement. Mr Atchley said he had heard Germany intended to let us retain Cornwall if Hitler won. <u>When</u>. Mr Kinsman … referring to the Disciples thought they might use a Dictionary for their Cornish or be helped by an alien'.
149. R. Morton Nance, Letter to F.B. Cargeeg, 19 November 1942 (private hands).
150. CRO, X1104/1, pp. [182]–183. There is indeed no record in the Minute Book of Nance's re-election as such in 1937 or 1940, though elections to Council (of which he would have been an *ex officio* member) are recorded for those years (pp. [144] and [176]). A newspaper report of the Annual Meeting preceding the 1940 Gorsedd, however, indicates that he was re-elected on that occasion (W.J. Stephens Collection, 36 (Gorsedd news cuttings), Courtney Library, p. 82, cutting of 9 [?] September 1940).
151. The paper is accompanied by an envelope, also marked 'The Symbolism of the Gorsedd', which contains various background notes of relevance to it.
152. *Western Morning News*, 8 September 1941.
153. CRO, X1104/1, p. 189.
154. He gave the same paper, or a similar one, at the Closed Gorsedd on 6 June 1953, on which occasion it was suggested that it might be printed and distributed free to young people. (CRO, X1104/1, p. [301]).
155. Nance Collection, Courtney Library.
156. Ibid. The Grand Bard's name is taken from the medieval Cornish saint's play *Beunans Meriasek*, l. 3396. The word translated 'worth' can also mean 'price', and the usual meaning of 'map lyen' is 'clergyman' rather than 'man of letters'.
157. NLW, Phillips Papers, 3643. See also 3644.
158. CRO, X1104/1, p. [202].
159. Cornish-Breton Committee programme for the event (copy in Cornish Gorsedd Archives).
160. CRO, X1104/1, pp. [214]–215; *Western Morning News*, 4 September 1944.
161. R. Morton Nance, Letter to F.B. Cargeeg, 19 November 1942 (private hands).
162. R. Morton Nance, Letter to F.B. Cargeeg, 20 April 1943 (private hands).

163. *Western Morning News*, 3 June 1946.
164. Ibid., 9 September 1946.
165. *Cornishman*, 19 September 1946.
166. A.S.D. Smith, Letter to R. Morton Nance, 22 August 1946, Cornish Gorsedd Archives.
167. *Western Morning News*, 6 June 1949.
168. Quoted in Philip Payton (2005) *A.L. Rowse and Cornwall*, Exeter: University of Exeter Press, p. 147.
169. Ibid., p. 211.
170. *Cornish Guardian*, 6 September 1951.
171. *Old Cornwall*, vol. 4, no. 12, Winter 1951, p. 470.
172. R. Morton Nance, Letter to Peter Laws, 19 September 1951, Cornish Gorsedd Archives.
173. CRO, X1104/1, p. [310].
174. E.G.R. Hooper, Letter to R. Morton Nance (and annotated by him), 4 August 1955, Cornish Gorsedd Archives.
175. *Royal Cornwall Gazette*, 8 September 1955. See also *Cornish Guardian* of that date.
176. For Beer, see Garry Tregidga and Treve Crago (2000) *Map Kenwyn: the life and times of Cecil Beer*, [n.p.]: Gorseth Kernow.
177. *New Cornwall*, vol. 7, no. 5, August–September 1959, p. 4.
178. CRO, X1104/1, p. [328].
179. *Western Morning News*, 8 September 1958.
180. Personal conversation, 15 October 2005.
181. P.A.S. Pool (1991) 'Mordon Remembered' in *An Baner Kernewek/The Cornish Banner*, no. 64, May 1991, p. 11.
182. P.A.S. Pool, 'R. Morton Nance, 1873–1959: memoir and appreciations' in R. Morton Nance (1963) *A Glossary of Cornish Sea-words* (ed. Pool), Truro: Federation of Old Cornwall Societies, p. 12.
183. CRO, X1104/1, p. [329].
184. R. Morton Nance, Letter to P.A.S. Pool, 24 November 1958 (private hands).
185. R.G. Jenkin (1959) 'Cornwall's Great Loss' in *New Cornwall*, vol. 7, no. 4, June–July 1959, p.1.
186. CRO, X1104/1, p. [334]. It was certainly Pawley White's feeling that Nance should have stepped down from office some years before his death. (DVD, *Interview with Gunwyn... 26th July 2000*, Falmouth: Tower Films). There is also anecdotal evidence that Nance would have done so if he had found a suitable and willing successor.
187. See e.g. *New Cornwall*, vol. 7, no. 5, August–September 1959 (memorial issue); J.L. Palmer (1960) 'Nyns-yu marow Mordon' in *Old Cornwall*, vol. 5, no. 11, 1960, pp. 450–451; Nance (1963).
188. Pool (1991), p. 11.
189. R. Morton Nance, Letter to F.B. Cargeeg, 10 August 1936 (private hands).

Acknowledgements

Personal thanks are due to Audrey Randle Pool and to Angela Broome and her staff at the Courtney Library. The letters of Nance to D. Rhys Phillips are used by permission of Llyfrgell Genedlaethol Cymru/The National Library of Wales, to whom thanks are also due for allowing these documents to be copied and the copies placed for research purposes in the Cornish Gorsedd Archives.

Keeping Cornwall Cornish: Robert Morton Nance and the Federation of Old Cornwall Societies

Brian Coombes

The Gorsedd of Cornwall has become a potent and accepted symbol of Cornish distinctiveness. Its foundation in 1928 was largely due to the inspiration of Henry Jenner, the first Grand Bard, with his successor Robert Morton Nance (*Mordon*) and a talented team of helpers, his principal supports. Earlier in the 1920s the two men had been leaders in the Old Cornwall movement, with the first society being established at St Ives in 1920 and the Federation four years later. In the Autumn 1970 issue of *Old Cornwall*, the Golden Jubilee of the movement was marked, the then Grand Bard G. Pawley White (*Gunwyn*), writing in a letter of greeting: 'The College of Bards remembers that its first two Grand Bards were also the founders of the Old Cornwall Movement, and is grateful for the support of the various societies during its 42 years ... [T]he transformation in the attitude of Cornish people to their own separate identity is largely due to the spirit which the Old Cornwall Societies have engendered...'[1] St Ives was a fishing port and mining town which, through the Hain Steamship Company, had links with the deep-sea, mercantile aspect of Cornish life. It also had a Celtic Saint's cult, could boast involvement in the Prayer Book Rebellion of 1549,[2] was the base of the puritan Joseph Sherwood junior who is thought to have preached in both Cornish and English in the mid 17th century, was near the area where Cornish was last spoken and had links with the Wesleys and other nineteenth century religious sects. It is small wonder, then, that St Ives was where the Old Cornwall movement took shape.

Although the Gorsedd is better known, the Old Cornwall Societies are especially (uniquely?) Cornish and the contribution of *Mordon* to both was fundamental. In 1906, already an established artist and illustrator, and increasingly recognised as an authority on nautical matters, particularly ship models,[3] he left Wales to live in a cottage at Nancledra, a hamlet between St Ives and Penzance. Two years earlier Henry Jenner had published his *Handbook of the Cornish Language*[4] – an event that is credited with starting its revival. In 1909 he retired from the British Museum, settling at Hayle where his wife had a family home. Nance wrote of meeting Jenner that same year in the Penzance (Morrab) Library,[5] when trying to find the Cornish language origins of fishing terms. They formed a close friendship. Different as they were in so many ways, they shared a devotion to Cornwall and to learning; both were always ready to help others. Here we should note the contributions made by each, not only to the Morrab, but also to the Royal Cornwall Polytechnic Society in Falmouth and the Royal Institution of Cornwall in Truro, as both office holders and contributors to their respective journals. This is likely to have helped in gaining acceptance for the Old Cornwall movement – after all, in 1920 Jenner made it clear that it would not be in competition with existing organisations.[6]

From the first decade of the twentieth century the Nances and their young family became part of the Nancledra community, with Robert writing plays in local dialect based on local folklore for acting by local children. Although these *Cledry Plays* were not published until 1956, the Preface outlines their importance to the start of the Old Cornwall movement and the formation of the St Ives society nearly forty years earlier. There is also a grateful – and graceful – dedication to 'my wife … producer and prompter, stage-manager, costume-maker… [who] brought all these plays to life'.[7] It should be remembered that although they moved to a new house, 'Chylason', Carbis Bay in 1914, they kept the Nancledra cottage and their links with the place.[8] It does seem that later there were other performances by adults, possibly for charity, in St Ives, the Arts Club being one venue,[9] and at Penponds, near Camborne. W.M. Symons of Camborne Old Cornwall Society recalled that one of the various functions arranged to raise money for the proposed restoration of Richard Trevithick's

Federation of Old Cornwall Societies meeting, Wadebridge, 1954. Nance and A.K. Hamilton Jenkin 3rd and 4th from left (Courtesy of St Ives Old Cornwall Society/St Ives Museum)

cottage in the early 1930s was 'a memorable production in Church House ... of one of Morton Nance's Cledry Plays: "Duffy and the Devil"'. Among those taking part were A.K. Hamilton Jenkin, a Mrs James and *Mordon* himself.[10]

There were, too, informal meetings for play-reading and discussion. In his detailed exploration of the origins of the Old Cornwall Societies,[11] Brian Stevens tells the story of one such meeting that took place at the home of Mrs Aubrey (Annie) Pool in January 1920, when the afternoon theme was 'Cornish Dialect'. Of the ten or so who took part in that enjoyable session – both the Jenners and the Nances were amongst those present – Mrs [May S.?] James was to the fore in suggesting that it would be good if others could share their enthusiasm and that a society should be formed. The St Ives Old Cornwall Society Minute Book records that at a meeting held in the Council Chamber on the afternoon of Wednesday 21st, it was decided 'to form a society and that it be called 'The St Ives Old Cornwall Society'' and 'to call a public meeting at an early date to enlist Public Sympathy'. In advance of the meeting arranged for 11 February, Nance wrote to the editor of the *St Ives Times* on 30 January, outlining what he hoped it would achieve:

> Sir – Bad results of war are so much in evidence that it is all the more desirable to insist on one good one – the strengthening of our attachment to our own country, and to all the old associations that cluster about the thought of home.
>
> No corner of our country is richer in such associations than Cornwall, and of Cornwall no corner has a better selection of them than St Ives. We have buildings, even … that date back, not hundreds, but perhaps thousands of years, and we have words still in use that are Celtic and almost as old, to say nothing of our tales and traditions.
>
> Learned societies have done very much in pointing out and explaining these things; but unfortunately this has often been done in such a way as to smother up most interesting things in dullness, or what seems dullness to the ordinary person. Many people, too, who know best about our later traditions have been shy of telling what they know for lack of ability to use such learned wrappings for their facts. In the result very little of this old-time knowledge has been handed on to the young people who have the best right to it.
>
> It has seemed to a few of us who are enthusiasts for the things of Old Cornwall that St Ives "Old Cornwall Society" – not a learned society, but one the work of which would be to collect and talk over the old things before they are lost, and to hand them on to the younger folk for preservation – would appeal to all sections of St Ives people. If, as a result of the meeting announced elsewhere in your columns, such a society is successfully launched, meetings of all kinds, grave, gay, with summer excursions, etc., would provide something for 'one and all'.

Details of the public meeting, at which there was 'a fair attendance', were reported in the *St Ives Times*, *Western Echo* and the *Cornishman*, particular mention being made of 'Mr R. Morton Nance's enthusiasm for collecting and preserving things historical' and his 'ambitious programme for the future working of the Society'.[12] Reviewing the Society's progress just over seven months later, the *Royal Cornwall Gazette* and the *St Ives Times* underlined the fact that it was not intended to be a learned society, but 'a popular and social body', whose members would 'meet as friends to discuss the interests they have in common, all to take their share in teaching and learning, and not to preach a holy war against the stranger'.[13] Writing in 1925 concerning the name chosen for St Ives Old Cornwall Society, Nance explained that "Cornish Society" was rejected as being too vague, hardly distinguishing its aims from those of Cornish associations outside Cornwall. "Old Cornish Society", though more specific, was likely to give the impression that the society was one devoted to the language, the term "Old Cornish" being a normal one for the language at that time and not, as now, applied to its early medieval period only.[14]

The society prospered and in September 1920 Jenner gave a Presidential address to the Royal Cornwall Polytechnic Society on 'The Renaissance of Merry England'[15] – an unhappy title for one of the key speeches in Cornish history, but for want of a better one 'counting Cornwall, for this occasion only, as if it were part of England'. The address is full of maypoles, folksy sentiment and red scares, and deals at some length with the "Village Drama Society", of which '[o]ne of our members, Mr R. Morton Nance, whose plays in the Cornish dialect … are well known to some of us' was 'down in the list of "trainers" '. Warning against the dangers of breaking with the past and failing to respect beauty and antiquity, Jenner praises the scheme whereby schools would collect "rural lore". 'A good example of how it may be taken up [by other agencies],' he continues, 'has been given this year at St Ives. In that town a Society called "The St Ives Old Cornwall Society" has been formed, chiefly organised by Mr Morton Nance, for studying, collecting and preserving … Cornish … language, dialect, manners and customs, folk-lore, legends and the like.' Members had been successfully engaged in this work through the summer. Other towns could do likewise. 'Why not have Old Cornwall Societies all over the county?' he asked. Run on different lines, they would not clash with the old existing societies and 'might indeed be worked on lines similar to those of those excellent things, the Women's Institutes, with perhaps eventually a similar collective organisation'. The establishment of the St Ives society set the pattern for the whole movement, stressing the local character of each society – they *were* not, and *are* not, 'branches'.

On 9 June 1922, the second Old Cornwall Society was formed, at Truro, with

Redruth following suit shortly afterwards on 2 July.[16] Nance was closely involved with these new societies, speaking at inaugural meetings on the objects and desirability of establishing societies, or lecturing at early ones, amongst them Helston (1924), St Austell (1925), Penzance (1926), Liskeard (1928) and Newquay (1928).[17] At Penzance, for example, following a preliminary meeting at the Guildhall on 26 February which both he and Jenner attended 'to support and advise', he subsequently gave the first recorded paper on 'The Hearth of Cornwall'.[18] He quickly foresaw a wider role for the fledgling society, mentioning to the former Welsh Liberal MP and political activist, E.T. John just two weeks later, that he thought it should play an important part in preparing the way for the projected – and ill-fated – Celtic Congress at Penzance where accommodation was the most pressing question.[19] Nance continued to support specific societies, particularly those in West Cornwall, often by reading papers such as 'Gleanings in Brittany',[20] 'Cornish Dialect'[21] and 'Dolly Pentreath'[22] (all at St Ives), 'Lights of Old Cornwall' (at Penzance)[23] and 'Old Cornwall Topics' (at Truro).[24]

The role that Nance played in the life of his local Old Cornwall Society at St Ives involved not only giving lectures and leading Cornish language classes, but also creating a museum. Late in 1923 the Society acquired an old fish store at the top of Pudding Bag Lane (Capel Court) in the old quarter of 'Downlong'. Meetings were held upstairs in the net loft which members began to decorate with artefacts, especially those relating to fishing and mining. The Society's first Minute Book records that on 3 October 1924 Nance proposed that authority be given for the purchase of some old farm implements from Tregadgwith in St Buryan,[25] some miles west of St Ives – a conscious decision literally to 'gather up that which remains' and an important precedent. In the early 1930s these premises were lost to a slum clearance scheme and in due course the growing collection was stored in members' homes for safekeeping. At the beginning of 1950 a temporary exhibition staged to re-establish the collection proved such a success that at a meeting of St Ives Old Cornwall Society that October, Nance referred to the possibility of this and subsequent exhibitions held during the summer months becoming a permanent museum in the near future. A further repeat of the exhibition for the Festival of Britain celebrations in 1951 increased the demand for something more permanent and St Ives Museum was duly opened on 14 June 1951 by A.K. Hamilton Jenkin, with Charles Short Murrish as its first Honorary Curator.[26] Seventeen years later the museum moved to Wheal Dream, into a section that is today the 'Nance Room', 'so named after the man who did so much to bring the St Ives Old Cornwall Society and the Museum into existence'.[27] With trustees drawn from both the Old Cornwall Society and the town and district councils, the museum is in an ideal setting for visitors (crucial to the educational and heritage roles of the Old Cornwall movement), a tribute to the sterling work of *Mordon* and his co-workers (Cyril Noall and A.K. Hamilton Jenkin) and a model of what can be achieved by Old Cornwall societies working with local councils. Nanceana at St Ives Museum includes a collection of killicks and a model of a lestercock made by *Mordon*, an oil painting and some drawings of his and some family archive material.

In the meantime, on 24 April 1924, the Federation of Old Cornwall Societies had been formed, with Henry Jenner as President, the Vicar of Penponds, Canon Sims Carah of Camborne Old Cornwall Society as Vice-President, and A.K. Hamilton Jenkin (the distinguished Redruth-born mining historian) as Secretary.[28] Nance held the post of Recorder. From the outset he pressed for the admission of 'the only one [of all Cornish Societies] that aims at fostering a popular sense of Cornish nationality and Celtic sympathies' to the Celtic Congress and successfully negotiated a reduced fee – basically what the Federation could afford – with D. Rhys Phillips, the then secretary.[29] Writing again to E.T. John on 31 March 1926, he felt that the preparations for the Celtic Congress seemed to be going well, with the 'Federation of Old Cornwall Societies … undertaking the first work of organisation', prior to the formation of an all-Cornwall committee and local committees at Penzance.[30] This was a foretaste of the crucial role that the Federation would play two years later when the Cornish Gorsedd was established.

In April 1925 the journal *Old Cornwall* appeared for the first time, with material from the St Ives society and, therefore, with Nance and Hamilton Jenkin as joint editors.[31] Nance was keen for its appeal to be wide, describing it to D. Rhys Phillips as 'the first definitely Celtic journal to be issued in Cornwall'. 'The language of course must be English,' he continued, 'but there is a good deal of Cornish worked in in one way and another. On the cover is our motto ... I won't attempt it in Welsh, but you will find it in S. John. vi. 12.'[32] That first issue was described as 'an experimental one', the first of two journals that would appear that year. 'A quarterly issue may be reached next year,' its editors continued, 'and the ideal at which we aim is a monthly journal for all lovers of Cornwall throughout the world.' Individual societies provided material for the first four issues, with Truro, Redruth and Camborne following the lead taken by St Ives. It was confirmed by the Federation on 13 October 1928, that 'Mr Morton Nance be asked to carry on editorship'. (It should be remembered that, as well as being secretary of the Federation, Hamilton Jenkin was writing his books on mining and social history during this period). In April 1931, in view of the pressures on Nance's time, A.A. Clinnick of Truro Old Cornwall Society was asked to take over as editor.[33] After only a year, however, Nance again became joint editor, with Clinnick, who was preparing for ordination and from 1934 until his death in 1959, he was sole editor.

The journal became an important method of spreading the aims of the Old Cornwall movement and, in the absence of the first Minute Books for societies such as Hayle, is an important record of the earliest days. To the first issue of what Philip Payton has recently called 'an important window into the motives and activities of the Revivalists in this period',[34] Nance contributed an article entitled 'What we stand for'. This sets out the aims of the Federation, laying particular stress on recording[35] – Nance thought that the recorder was the most important post in each society. The Old Cornwall Societies differed from the learned societies that dealt with Cornish antiquities in being 'as much interested in the holiday, workaday and home life of older generations – the festivals, the hearthside tales, the printed dialect literature, and the old songs and words – as in any other side of the past of Cornwall...' Old industries and methods of work on farm, fishing boat, in mine, or at home needed recording. '[H]ere is work that awaits Old Cornwall workers in every parish,' he continued, 'who will look up the details of such things as ploughing with oxen, the seine-fishery, local mining and tin-dressing, weaving, old-time cookery, etc.' The typical Old Cornwall member or "Old Cornwallite" Nance described as 'a person who is first of all on the watch for anything that is not generally known of the words and ways of the Cornish people of old times, with perhaps a preference for those of times not too old; one who never misses a chance of talking over these old times with the right person; who is ready to help with anything that brings Cornish people together as such; is as ready to acknowledge his kinship with a Breton or a Welshman, and who, however able to give the current coin of English speech when it is wanted will be as ready with a good supply of Cornish fashioned small change for familiar use.'

Nance was an assiduous and hands-on editor and co-editor, chivying others, especially recorders, to contribute. *Old Cornwall* contained articles by scholars such as Charles Henderson[36] (who worked in the1920s as an extra-mural lecturer in Cornwall and whose premature death in 1933 was such a great loss to Cornish local history) and Canon Gilbert Doble, the authority on Cornish saints.[37] The extent of Nance's own scholarship was, of course, formidable, and over the years his contributions ranged from 'Cornish Family Mottoes' in the first issue to 'Some Cornish Schools of Long Ago' in the last number to appear in his lifetime. Equally important were the notes on local traditions, dialect, antiquities etc. – 'old scraps gathered together by all the Recorders' – that were often too short or too local for the annual publications of the older societies. In No. 1 there were notes on 'Word Collecting', 'Some Cornish Shibboleths' and 'The Cornish Language in America, 1710'. Although No. 2 covered subjects as varied as 'Draa' Foo'th and Bread your Baasins!', 'Hallan-Apples' and 'Saint Golder', Nance hoped that future issues would include a more varied selection than the Federation Recorder could himself be expected to supply. When, with the Camborne issue of October 1926, the system that involved looking to each society in turn to supply material was abandoned, the need for material, particularly for the 'Notes' section, became more pressing. Already there were complaints about the journal's low circulation, with some societies singled out for not doing enough – Bodmin, for example, had not appointed a magazine officer. The duty of recorders, reiterated the editor, was 'to record such Folklore Scraps, Short Characteristic Tales, Dialect Words, Place-names and Old Traditions or Customs as are mentioned, apart from papers, at meetings. Such things should be directly asked for and collected also, and if written down and initialled by their original tellers, so much the better. Such material, as it accumulates, or immediately if it seems of unusual importance, should be sent to the Federation Recorder. It would then be printed here or filed for future reference.'[38] A year later Nance complained that the journal was 'still living too hand to mouth an existence' and again appealed for more papers read at meetings to be sent in for publication and for recorders to communicate notes on matters that came up in sessions at meetings, so that these could be used in 'The Crowdy-Crawn', which had replaced 'Notes'.[39] By the winter of 1930, things had come to a head and with No. 12, the last issue that he edited before taking a short sabbatical, he felt compelled to issue a six-point Editorial Ultimatum.[40] Although membership of the Federation had doubled over the previous five years, *Old Cornwall*'s circulation had stood still. His recommendations to try to ensure its continued existence included all recorders recording, and submitting their choicest notes, all writers, however inexperienced, sending in anything fresh on a Cornish subject without waiting to be personally asked for it, and all readers 'wearied by serious articles' themselves seeing to it that the equally welcomed lighter dialect tales, verse, songs etc. were sent in. 'If they do not,' he threatened in an outburst that is extraordinary, given his commitment to the Cornish language, 'they may expect to see more notes on Cornish Antiquities, or, still worse, unreadable Kernewek.' An Old Cornwall Society, he reminded the membership, was 'no mere social club for summer outings or winter happy-evenings'. Twenty-six years later he was still waving the stick, it being 'more necessary each year to remind those who read *Old Cornwall* that it is also expected that they will write for it'.[41] It must be admitted that the circulation has remained low (c. 1,200) and subsequent presidents have often echoed *Mordon*'s sentiments. *Old Cornwall*, though, has continued to play a vital part in the Cornish revival.

Despite the criticism inherent in the phrase 'unreadable *Kernewek*', the most distinctive works in *Old Cornwall* were the notes about, and articles in, the Cornish language. These were often written by *Mordon*, himself, although the journal provided a valuable platform for others to do the same. Indeed, the range of the contributions and the accessibility of the scholarship owe much to his outlook and were important in ensuring that the movement was not home to an inward-looking group of academics or escapists from the real world. It is notable that each of the four founding office-holders in the Federation was amongst the thirty-odd contributors to the London Cornish Association's *Tre Pol and Pen* volume of 1928,[42] the first and only issue of what was intended to be an annual publication. *Mordon* wrote on 'Cornwall and the Gorsedd', less than six months before the founding of a Cornish branch – something that gives a visual focus to Cornish nationhood and to our links with Wales and Brittany. The banners of individual Old Cornwall societies not only give extra colour to the ceremony, but also make for the personal involvement of the movement's members, as well as providing an emotional link with the wider Celtic world.

There are two publications which should be mentioned for their influence on *Old Cornwall*. The established quarterly *Devon and Cornwall Notes and Queries* contained short articles, notes and replies to 'queries', but was concerned mainly with family and religious history and, in those days disproportionately, with Devon.[43] It remains a respected and useful journal, though narrower in scope than *Old Cornwall*. And over the years there has been less of a tendency in Cornwall to regard being coupled with Devon as satisfactory – and not only on emotional, Celtic grounds! *Mordon* had been one of the founders in 1910 of the Society for Nautical Research and though not a member of its London-based editorial board, was a frequent contributor to its journal *The Mariner's Mirror* – in those days a monthly, though now a quarterly. His articles and his frequent illustrations for the contributions of others show a mastery of technical terms in various languages and a wide field of interest, including the origin of words. It is interesting that during this period he was taking his first steps in the Cornish language. The scholar, the practical man and the ordinary person alike can continue to feel at home with the Society for Nautical Research and *The Mariner's Mirror*. With his authoritative articles and his 'Answers' to the monthly 'Queries', Nance was part of their enquiring outlook – an outlook that is reflected in *Old Cornwall* and its parent body, giving us cause to trust his judgement in two parallel areas of research.

In the literary field, the Federation also acted as the publisher, under *Mordon*'s leadership and often with the collaboration of A.S.D. Smith, of other Cornish works, including dictionaries and extracts from the religious plays.[44] On a more accessible and popular level the Federation – in particular, the St Ives society – was instrumental in stimulating the revival of the 'Crying of the Neck' and the Midsummer Eve Bonfire ceremonies, and in supporting the revival of church services in Cornish, the first of which was organised by Tyr ha Tavas at Towednack on 27 August 1933. For the latter, *Mordon* played a part in providing a Cornish translation of the Form of Evening Prayer from the Anglican Prayer Book and presumably had a hand in doing likewise for the

hymns and sermon.[45] A contemporary newspaper account of the revival of the
old Harvest custom of cutting the last strand or 'neck' of wheat at Hugh
Dunstan's Churchtown Farm, Towednack in 1928 specifies that it was done
'with the co-operation of the St Ives Old Cornwall Society'.[46] The following year
saw the Old Cornwall movement organising a chain of bonfires across the 80-
mile length of the Cornish peninsula on St John's Eve (23 June). In his *Cornish
Homes and Customs* (1934), A.K. Hamilton Jenkin provides a vivid, first-hand
account which begins: 'As the twilight of a perfect summer's evening began to
fall across the stern, bleak moorlands of the west, the first of the waiting beacon
fires broke into flame upon the rock-strewn summit of Chapel Carn Brea...'[47]
Even the *Times* provided a short account of the ceremony which 'concluded with
the singing of the National Anthem in the old Cornish language'.[48] Such work
helped Cornish to be heard and accepted by the ordinary people of Cornwall –
no mean achievement!

Much of the work of the Federation of Old Cornwall Societies in the 1930s
was concerned with the preservation of Richard Trevithick's cottage at
Penponds. Until 1935, when the formation of an Executive Council reflected
the growth in the number of societies, it held quarterly meetings for all members of the societies, one being the 'annual' meeting.[49] *Mordon* played his part in
this work, helping to arrange pilgrimages and meetings and, as we have seen,
acting as a contact for the Celtic Congress, which was first held in Cornwall in
1932. When Henry Jenner died in May 1934, *Mordon* succeeded him as Grand
Bard and also as President of the Federation. The links between the two bodies
have always been close, with the personalities of their first leaders being important in getting both accepted in Cornwall, in the wider Celtic world and by the
Cornish 'diaspora'.

There is a sense in which the High Church, Anglo (later Roman) Catholic
establishment figure of Henry Jenner was completely different to the vegetarian, teetotal artist Robert Morton Nance.[50] However, they were united in their
love of Cornwall and their very 'untypicalness' may have helped their acceptance. The Old Cornwall movement was thus able to include all classes and
cater for all aspects of study.

Charles Thomas has commented on the resemblance of the Federation to a
Methodist circuit or to a Methodist district and its synod.[51] There are other pos-

sible precursors, such as the debating societies and reading rooms of the 19th century.[52] Cars, coach outings, television, radio and the popular press have all changed the climate in which the Old Cornwall movement operates. There has also been a growth in both professional and amateur involvement in archaeology, in building and wildlife conservation, and in adult education, whilst dialect and language have become specialist fields of study. The fact that *Mordon* was an active member of St Ives Bowling Club meant that he was in contact with the sporting side of Cornish culture and a wide cross-section of local society. *Old Cornwall* was neither escapist nor exclusive! Indeed, to the third issue of its magazine in April 1926 he contributed 'Bowling and the Cornish Language', perhaps showing his belief in 'Cornish for All'.[53] Besides Jenner and Nance, those who made up the team that provided leadership for the Old Cornwall societies had wide connections and interests – mining, for instance, was A.K. Hamilton Jenkin's field, while William Paynter was a folklorist with witchcraft as a specialism, and W. Tregoning Hooper was an expert on Cornish wrestling. The societies and the Federation itself were able to provide a popular base that transcended the Cornish language or Celtic revival, the bonfires at Midsummer or Harvest often being a platform for the language. Nance played an important part and his example meant that the movement was accepted in all parts of Cornwall – a fact born out by the early records of the societies. The Cornish revival is real and the Old Cornwall movement has had, and will continue to have, a special role in it. That is, in large part, the legacy of Robert Morton Nance who, with the involvement of a large number of supporters from all parts of Cornish society, built on the work of Henry Jenner.

Notes

1. Gunwyn (G. Pawley White) (1970) 'Greetings from Gunwyn' in *Old Cornwall*, vol. 7, no. 7, Autumn, p.329.
2. The 2003 reprint of J. Hobson Matthews' *A History of the parishes of St Ives...* (St Ives: St Ives Trust and St Ives Library), which details the town's role, refers to the extensive unpublished notes made by Nance in his personal copy of the book – notes transcribed by Cyril Noall.
3. Mrs C. Morton Raymont (1962) *The Early Life of R. Morton Nance*, [Leedstown]: New Cornwall, p. 30; see also R. Morton Nance (1963) *A Glossary of Cornish Sea-words*, St Ives: Federation of Old Cornwall Societies.
4. Henry Jenner (1904) *A Handbook of the Cornish Language...*, London: Nutt.
5. R. Morton Nance (1958) 'Cornish Beginnings' in *Old Cornwall*, vol. 5, no. 9, p. 369.
6. Henry Jenner (1920) 'The Renaissance of Merry England' in *Royal Cornwall Polytechnic Society Annual Report 1921–22*, p.60.
7. R. Morton Nance (1956) *The Cledry Plays*, Marazion/Penzance: Federation of Old Cornwall Societies, p. 3;

see also appreciations by Amy Baker and C. Morton Raymont in Nance (1963), p. 2.

8. A. K. Hamilton Jenkin (1970) 'How It Started' in *Old Cornwall*, vol. 7, no. 7, p. 289.

9   Amy W. Baker, 'From An Old Friend' in Nance (1963), p. 15.

10. W. M. S[ymons] (1970) 'Camborne O. C. S. – An early project' in *Old Cornwall*, vol. 2, no. 7, p. 299.

11. Brian J. Stevens (2006) 'Gather ye the fragments that are left, that nothing be lost: the origin of the Old Cornwall Societies' in *Old Cornwall*, vol. 13, no. 6, pp. 2–11; see also St Ives Old Cornwall Society Minute Book.

12. 'St Ives "Old Cornwall" Society' (1920) in *St Ives Times* 13 February, the *Western Echo* 14 February and *The Cornishman* 18 February.

13. Stevens (2006), p. 6.

14. R. Morton Nance (1925) 'What We Stand For' in *Old Cornwall*, no. 1, April, p. 3.

15. Jenner (1920), pp. 51–61.

16. Federation of Old Cornwall Societies Minute Book; see also Brian Coombes (2004) 'Gathering the fragments…' in Derek R. Williams (ed) *Henry and Katharine Jenner*, London: Boutle, pp. 166 and 178 (note 27).

17. Society reports in *Old Cornwall*, vol. 7, no. 7, Autumn 1970.

18. 'Penzance O. C. S.', ibid., vol. 7, no. 7, Autumn 1970, p. 312.

19. Letter ETJ 4576, dated 10 March 1926, in E. T. John Papers (GB 0210ETJOHN), National Library of Wales.

20. 'Reports' in *Old Cornwall*, no. 2, October 1925, p. 43.

21. 'Federation of Old Cornwall Societies', ibid., vol. 2, no. 6, Winter 1933, p. 42.

22. 'Old Cornwall Papers and Work', ibid., vol. 2, no. 8, Winter 1934, p. 42.

23. 'Reports', ibid., no. 4, October 1926, p. 43.

24. 'Federation of Old Cornwall Societies', op. cit., p. 42.

25. Cyril Noall (1968) *The St Ives Museum – A Short History*, St Ives: St Ives Museum Joint Committee, p. 1.

26. Ibid.

27. Brian Stevens (ed) [c. 2003] *St Ives Museum*, St Ives: St Ives Printing and Publishing Company, p. 7.

28. Federation of Old Cornwall Societies Minute Book.

29. Letters 3591 and 3592, dated 22 and 27 January 1925, in D. Rhys Phillips 2 Collection, National Library of Wales.

30. Letter ETJ4585 in E. T. John Papers.

31. 'Editorial Note' in *Old Cornwall*, no. 1, April 1925, p. 2.

32. Letter 3595, dated 21 April 1925, in D. Rhys Phillips 2 Collection.

33. Federation of Old Cornwall Societies Minute Book.

34. Philip Payton (1996) *Cornwall*, Fowey: Alexander Associates, p. 268.

35. Nance (1925), pp. 4–5.

36. See, for example, Charles Henderson (1928) 'The Bounds of Zennor' in *Old Cornwall*, no. 7, April, pp. 13–15.

37. See, for example, G. H. Doble (1926) 'Scraps of Penwith Folklore', ibid., no. 3, April, pp. 5–9.

38. R. M. N. (1926) 'Notes', ibid., no. 4, October, p. 26.

39. 'Editorial Note', ibid., no. 6, October 1927, p. 30.

40. 'Editorial Ultimatum', ibid., no. 12, Winter 1930, p. 44. In a letter to W. A. Pascoe, dated 19 November 1930, Nance expressed the view that *Old Cornwall* would not appear again 'unless it changes its character under different editorship' (Cornish Gorsedd Archives).

41. 'To our Readers', ibid., vol. 5, no. 7, 1956, p. 325.

42. Trelawny Roberts and Charles Henderson (eds.) (1928) *Tre Pol and Pen: The Cornish Annual 1928*, London: Dodsworth.

43. In volume 17 (1932–33), for instance, only 55 of its 384 pages are concerned with Cornwall.

44. See for example R. Morton Nance, *Cornish for All* (1929), Nance and A. S. D. Smith, *An English-Cornish Dictionary* (1934), Nance, *A New Cornish-English Dictionary* (1938) and the booklets, in unified spelling with amended translation by Nance and Smith, in the series *Extracts from the Cornish Texts* (1949 onwards).

45. He also translated many of the hymns in the *Lyver Hymnys ha Salmow* [Book of Hymns and Psalms] of 1962.

46. Charles Howard Jewell (n.d.) *The Crying of the Neck*, [n.p.]: Federation of Old Cornwall Societies, p. [1].

47. A. K. Hamilton Jenkin (1970) *Cornwall and its People*, Newton Abbot: David and Charles, pp. 439–440.

48. *The Times* 26 June 1929; see also Cyril Noall (1963 and 2003) *The Cornish Midsummer Eve bonfire celebrations, with additional notes by Yvonne Gilbert*, [n.p.] and Pentewan: Federation of Old Cornwall Societies; Nance (1953). *Cornish in Song and Ceremony, with English translations*, (Marazion: Federation of Old Cornwall Societies, [1953]), which was printed in response to repeated requests for a collection of the Cornish words most often wanted for use at various Old Cornwall gatherings, includes *Mordon*'s 'Prayer for the benediction of the Midsummer Bonfire', his prayer of thanksgiving before cutting the neck and the form of words used after the ceremony.

49. Federation Minute Book, op. cit.

50. Charles Thomas (1963) 'An Dasserghyans Kernewek [The Cornish Revival]' in *Old Cornwall*, vol. 6, no. 5, Autumn, p. 197.

51. ibid., p. 198.

52. See, for example, L. E. L[ong] (1970) 'Bodmin's Old "Lit."' in *Old Cornwall*, vol. 7, no. 7, pp. 333–334.

53. See Raymont (1962), p. 17 for *Mordon*'s lack of interest in ball games compared to his brother Ernest who was a Cambridge tennis blue.

Acknowledgements

I did not know *Mordon* well, being an 'exile' in his day, but I am aware of the courtesy he extended to everyone. The regard and devotion of his friends and pupils, as well as the legacy of his works, enable us to know him in a special sense. There are many who have helped in the writing of this short study, some with specific information, others – many now departed – with general background over the years. To each of them I am grateful and many others, besides myself, will feel gratitude to such workers for Cornwall. They are:

Angela Broome of the Courtney Library, Royal Institution of Cornwall, Truro; Terry Knight and the staff of the Cornish Studies Library, Redruth; Annabelle Read and the staff of the Morrab Library, Penzance (formerly the Penzance Library); the staff of the Bennett Library, National Maritime Museum, Falmouth; Audrey Randle Pool; Ann Trevenen Jenkin; Brian Stevens of St Ives Old Cornwall Society; George Hogg; Hugh Miners; Brian Sullivan; G. Pawley White; Arthur Lyne; Wyn Cothey; Charles Thomas; E.G. Retallack and Bertha Hooper; Joan Petchey; E.E. Morton Nance; R.C. Jennings; Susan Hosking; R.G. Jenkin.; and P.A.S. Pool.

Sea-Stones and Killicks in West Cornwall

R. Morton Nance

Where rocks and boulders are plentiful and trees are scarce, the conditions usually found in West Cornwall, it is not surprising to find wood and iron supplanted in many of their uses by stone. Where hedges, stiles, gate-posts, rollers, pig-troughs, linhay-posts and loft-steps are all of stone: where the rick-thatch and house-roof, and even the "week's wash," are held down against the wind by stones, and miller, blacksmith, and cobbler find stones to their purpose without leaving their parish, the stone-age has never quite ceased to be; and Cornish fishermen, heirs of a set of craft mysteries that date back beyond history, find many uses in their work for stone.

First, intermediate between land-stones and sea-stones, comes the "pressing-stone" (Fig. 1, see page 240). This, just a large boulder, or "bully," has, with its iron crook, a rough likeness to the "curling-stone" of the Scot; but in this almost frostless land its use is, or was, severely practical. Hooked on at one end of a beam, the other end of which rested in a hole in the fish cellar wall, while its middle had a barrel of "fermades" (pilchards, salted for the Italian market) as its fulcrum, these stones supplied the force by which the train-oil was pressed out of the fish, through the chinks of the barrel, to be collected in a pit in the stone-paved floor.

Pickling-vats and screw-presses have thrown the "pressing-stone" out of work, and no more does the rumble of these, dancing and trundling themselves about in the cellars, in the "dead waste and middle of the night," proclaim the speedy arrival of fish, as, we are told, was once the case; but they are still to be seen, gathered in idle clusters at street corners, or serving as door-stoppers in the fishermen's fore-doors in every fishing village.

In connection with the Seine fishery for pilchards or mackerel, as carried out in Mount's Bay, a stone of another sort is still used, and still keeps the Celtic name, *caboolen, camboolen,* or *cabooly-stone,* which, with its likeness to the Wesh *cabolvaen,* a sleek-stone, and *caboli,* to polish, seems to suggest that its bearer was once an amphibious stone, borrowed for the occasion from a village trades-man when the old cry, "*Heva!*" had announced a school of fish, and at the call "*Tola roos!*" "Cast the net!" the catch was being secured.

Fastened to a rope, this *caboolen* is repeatedly dashed into the water to fright-en back the fish that attempt to break out at the still unjoined ends of the seine. So that it may be still more alarming to the fish, this blustering visitant from the upper realms, whose Marazion name of "bully-stone" must seem most appropriate from the pilchards' view-point, is chosen of as light a shade as may be, and through the middle of its disc a large hole is bored, so that by no chance can it slip from the rope (Fig. 2).

The *camboolen* from Mullion (Fig. 3) is of another pattern and, except that a ring-bolt takes the place of a hook, it is just a smaller "pressing-stone." At St Ives and on the North Coast, a stamping of boots on the boats bottom-boards, is used to prevent the pilchards from stampeding into safety; but at Cadgwith, round the Lizard, a stone is still used for the purpose. This, however, called a "plumping-stone," is of the same shape as that of the next class of sea-stone to be considered, the *minyz,* or *mennaz.*

This is the name, apparently meaning simply "small," that from Lamorna to the Lizard, and round it, is still given to the stone used in mooring the Cornishman's long-lines, the big "bulter" and small "spiller." For this purpose he makes choice of a "bully," wave-worn to a roughly cylindrical shape. Where granite can be had for the picking up, he has no difficulty in finding a suitable *minyz;* but it still has to be made ready for the strop with which it is to be girt, by being grooved about its middle. The groove is hammered out, or sometimes beaten out in more primitive fashion with another stone, and when made is called a "grove" or, at Penberth, a "raow," a name that at the next cove, Porthgwarra, is given to the strop itself, but seems to be a form of English

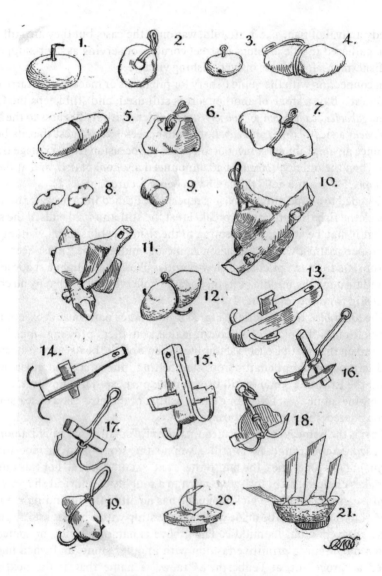

Sea-stones and Killicks in West Cornwall

"rough." At Dolly Pentreath's Mousehole, however, where, more than any-where, old Cornish still lingers, the name *droke*, the Welsh *trwch*, is still in use for it. When the boulder is very hard and of a regular shape, this *droke* may be more carefully worked, as in the *mennaz* of serpentine from Coverack (Fig. 5). A very large stone of exactly this shape was dragged up from the bottom of Mount's Bay some years ago and is still preserved at Marazion. This, too heavy for a fisherman's *mennaz*, is thought to have been used by smugglers in mooring their sunken tubs of "moonshine."

The hard-stone *mennaz* of Coverack, is now most often made roughly wedge-shaped and bored through with a strop-hole at its thinner part, as in Fig. 6, forming a stone implement of quite a distinct pattern. Alongside of these two Coverack forms of *mennaz* is to be seen yet another; this, made of flatter stone, has merely two nicks worked in the edges of its longer sides. At Cadgwith, where the nicks are named "jaws," this is the commonly-used type of *mennaz* (Fig. 7).

Differing from the last-mentioned type of *mennaz* in size only, are the stones, "side-stones," "crabpot stones," or, at Cadgwith, "jawen-stones," as they are var-iously called (Fig. 8). These are lashed at opposite sides of the bottom of the crab-pots, as ballast. At Mullion I found these being made by nicking with a bricklayer's hammer, a modern, time-saving improvement upon the improvised hammer of stone.

Before the introduction of lead sinkers for lines and nets, stones must have taken their place. Stephen Graham, in *Undiscovered Russia*, p. 123, tells us how he fished in the Dwina with a stone-weighted seine, and net-stones must, at however long a distance, have once been used in Cornwall. Whether the small grooved stone (measuring, to be precise, 3½in. by 2½in.) is such a net-stone or sinker; or whether it is a pre-historic hammer, or even the weight of a primitive loom, I know not. Found on the cliffs, it may be either a land-stone or a sea-stone; it is, at all events, of a kind not known to-day on land or sea.

The use of stones as ballast, giving place gradually to fire-bars, pig-iron and iron weights, is still, as it has been from the beginning, universal; but in enu-merating the sea-stones of Cornwall we must not forget the ballast-stones.

Not less ancient than as ballast, is the use of stones as anchors, and here in Mount's Bay we have, still existing, practically all the stages of development of an iron anchor from the primæval mooring-stone.

This parent of anchors, under the name of "strop-stone," is the common means of mooring boats around the Land's End, where the rough ground claims so heavy a toll of lost anchors that more expensive killicks could hardly be afforded. Iron anchors must, of old, have been still rarer than they now are at Sennen, if the old tale of the fishermen there is not entirely what they would call a "ky-widdle." According to this yarn some Sennen men once drew up from the Kettle's Bottom, off the Land's End, where it had been dropped as the last vain effort of a foreign crew to escape wreck, an old, rusty, stockless anchor. All declared that none of them "never seed no such thing afore," and they long and deeply puzzled over it. At last the oldest and wisest inhabitant was thought of. "If he don't know, nobody don't know," they decided, and he was brought tottering from his warm chimney-bench to pronounce judgment.

"Well, boys," said this old Uncle Billy, "you do ax me, do I know what a es; and I'll tell 'ee, I *do* know what a es. 'Tes a oogly, g'eat, awvergrawed *pick*. Tha's what a es!" And back he went to his chimney corner.

Anchors and, still more, grapnels, these still called by their Celtic name, *gra-bel*, are to be seen in Sennen to-day; but these are used only for the larger boats that are moored in the sandy Whitesand Bay, and the usual killick for the smaller boats of all the western coves is still a grooved boulder, like the *minyz*, of Fig. 4, which, at the Land's End, would also be called a "strop-stone."

About forty years ago, several words of the old Celtic language, traditionally known to them, were taken down from the lips of two or three old men of Newlyn and Mousehole. Among these occur the names:– *ake*, *ludras* and *Kentepathengy*, of parts of a stone anchor; the *ake* being a groove in its stone, the *ludras*, its wooden frame, and the *Kentepathengy*, pegs belonging to it in some way. I have talked of old times with several very old men in these places, men who not only knew the other words in this forty-year old list, but could add to them with hitherto unrecorded Cornish; but I cannot find that these three words, or even the memory of a stone-and-wood killick, are left now on the Western side of Penzance. At Porthleven, however, the stone anchor had a longer life, and at Bessy's Cove, between that place and Marazion, which was probably its last holding-ground, I succeeded in finding a fisherman who had made many of them, and was kind enough to show me how it was done. The first requisite was, of course, the stone itself. For this a dressed quoin from a ruined wall was preferred; if this was not available, an angular boulder might do. This would, if necessary, be grooved a little at the sides, but no more work would be spent upon it. Next, the timber must be found and the small amount of this that was needful was obtained, like the stone, as a free gift of Heaven. Going "up the land" from his cove, the fisherman would choose out, as they grew, the first two boughs that he could find to suit his purpose; one of them forked, and the other a larger, straight or curved piece, such as might be lopped from the same limb, nearer to the trunk of the tree. The latter being, for choice, a tough, storm-beaten Cornish-elm. Returning with the timber portions of his anchor, to the stone, he would assemble all together, after drilling two holes in the thicker bottom-piece, by inserting in these holes the two arms of the fork with the stone within their angle. When the bottom-piece was driven up as tightly as possible upon the arms of the fork, and wedged in place, the result was a stone anchor such as I have drawn in Figs. 10 and 11. The upper angle, not quite filled by the stone, makes a convenient hole through which to pass the strop, unless, as in Fig. 11, a special hole is bored for this. The stone itself, besides giving weight, forms a sort of anchor stock. The flukes are made by the projecting ends of the bottom piece. Until the stone itself was lost, such an anchor could be re-made over and over again, the stone nucleus passing down as an heirloom in the fisherman's family. At Bessy's Cove the wooden frame of this anchor was called, not a *ludras*, but a "yoke," and it is so like to a single ox-yoke with its ox-bow turned upside down, that no better name could be found for it; and of "yoke," *ludras* may possibly have been a now forgotten Cornish equivalent. The *ake* would be the slightly hollowed part of the stone that fitted closely to the sides of the fork. The *Kentepathengy*, probably *kenter-parth-an-gy*, peg-beside the-*gy* (*kentrow* would be the plural) would perhaps be a wedge or pin that held the fork in place, *gy* naming either a part of the *ludras* or the complete anchor, and meaning literally "dog."

From this anchor of stone and wood, killicks seem to have taken at least two lines of evolution. At Mousehole the *ludras* was given up in favour of a rude "frame" of iron, a mere band about its middle, with ends that, projecting hook-like, served as flukes. This iron-bound stone, still used there, has made no further progress. (Fig. 12)

On the eastern shore of the bay, as we have seen, the wooden killick lasted longer; and the stone itself, not the wood, was there the first to give place to iron. Fig. 11 shows how a strop-hole was sometimes made at the head of the "yoke" of a stone anchor; and by this hole alone can we recognise the wood-and-iron killick of Fig. 13 as its descendant. Here the weight, a fire-bar from some wrecked steamer, too small and thin to be set in a "yoke," is mortised and wedged into a bottle-shaped log, the upper end of which has a strop-hole, and the place of the now impossible bottom-piece is supplied by a bent bolt of iron that forms the flukes.

This particular form of killick has now given way to an improved form in which the flukes are made of flat soft iron that, bending under great pressure, allow of its recovery even when it has hitched in a crevice of the rocks below. Such killicks are still used at St Michael's Mount and Bessy's Cove, where Figs. 14 and 15 were sketched; but already others are to be seen in which neither stone nor wood are used. Of these I give three examples. Fig. 16, from Marazion, shows how the flat, iron flukes, creeping up the wooden shank, have at length met at its head and agreed to oust the timber that once supported them. A rivet takes the place of the wedges that fixed the bar in its place, an iron ring is fitted to make an improved attachment for the mooring line, and wood is now unwanted.

Fig. 17 shows another type of all-iron killick from Bessey's Cove. Here a round rod of iron has been bent by the blacksmith into the shape of an anchor, an opening is left at the top to serve as a ring or strop-hole, then the two parts, after being welded together for a little distance, open out to enclose a fire-bar; this bar is held firmly in place by a ring that binds the two parts together just before they curve away from one another to form the flukes with their flattened tips.

The latter iron killick would, at Porthleven, be called a "jinny-lin." Perhaps its partly-wooden ancestor was introduced at a time when the name and fame of Jenny Lind[1] had reached even the remotest parts of the country; but it is as likely that some Celtic meaning is hidden in its name; for a "jinny-lin" it has certainly been for over half a century, during which time it has passed through some such changes as we have already traced, and evolved into the present-day form shown in Fig. 18. This, in principle, is the same as that of Fig. 17, but there are some differences – a galvanised thimble is added at the top, the fire-bar being of a different shape is fastened to the twin shanks with a twist of iron in two places, while the fluked arms are less hooked.

At Mullion I sketched the stone anchor of Fig. 19, not a traditional Mullion killick, but the home-made "jinny-lin" of a man from Porthleven, who used the first materials that came to hand. The stone served instead of a fire-bar. Round this a thin iron rod was bent without heat into the required shape, and then, to bind these together, a scrap of wire-rope above the stone and, below it, a strip of sheet iron, were wound about the rod. Its likeness to the iron-bound strop-stone of Mousehole (Fig. 12) is striking, and it provides a good specimen of atavism in killicks.

Of another stone once used by Cornish fishermen, the name alone is left. This was the *mean-ollas*, the hearth-stone; in Welsh *maen aelwyd*, in Breton *men oaled*. In the sardine-boats of his cousins in Brittany, the hearth is still a flat stone, as, no doubt, was the Cornishman's in the days when he spoke his own language. At Mousehole and Newlyn the name forty years ago was given to a fire-box built of stones and clay. It is still in use for any such makeshift hearth other than the iron "caboose"; a fire-bucket, even, might be called a *mean-ollas*.

Of yet one more sea-faring stone I should like to say something, although, strictly speaking, it does not concern the fisherman, except during that part of his apprenticeship that is spent among the rock-pools, fishing for the *bulgranack* and the *pedn-y-borbas*; as with the conservatism of boyhood, he still, in old Cornish, calls the father-lasher and the rockling.

This is the *tol-y-mean* of the young marine architect of Mousehole and the *leu* or *loo* of the St Ives quay-boy. The Mousehole boy builds boats of two kinds. One, the "kiskeyman," is made of a split hemlock stem, a "kiskey," with thwarts of the same and, carrying inside ballast, is able to bear a sail of ivy-leaf or paper. The other, the *"carker"* is fashioned from a net-cork, and to allow of its bearing similar sail carries outside ballast in the form of a bit of slate, "helling-stone" he calls it, stuck in the bottom.

This slate (Fig. 20) is the *tol-y-mean*; although meaning literally "hole of the stone" the name, like that of the Penberth and Porthgwarra "raows," seems to have been applied to two things, the hole, first, in which the stone was stuck, and then the stone itself.

At St Ives the quay-boys have a far more scientific traditional boat that, if well-made, will point up to the wind like a schooner and sail on any tack; and has the additional advantage that it can be hurled out beyond the breakers without injury.

A carefully shaped hull, deep and narrow, is cut from half a cork float, and into a deep score below a "helling-stone" is driven (or hoop-iron it may be in these latter days) forming an effective centreboard. The "deck" is criss-crossed with the knife in two or three places and is given another lengthwise cut at the bow. Into the diagonal cuts high-peaked lug-sails of chip are firmly fixed, on the desired tack, and at the bow another chip makes the "jib." This sail plan, Fig. 2, quite unlike that of the modern lugger, resembles that of the old three-masted boats of long ago; but even more interesting is the survival on the quay-boys tongue to-day, of the old Celtic names, firstly of his boat, which he calls a *cok-an-baba*, boy's boat, and secondly, of the slate centreboard, which he calls the *leu*, the old Cornish for "rudder." In the old tongue a sailing boat was a *cok*, Welsh *cwch*, distinguished from the *scath* and the *scath-roos*, or seine-boat, which were rowed; but, except in the name of the Cock Bank, a sandspit outside the harbour, it is doubtful if the word has been used at St Ives for two centuries, while the time that has passed since the full-grown St Ives fisherman called his rudder *leu*, may be judged by the fact that he now names it, in mediæval English, the "rother."

These are the sea-stones and killicks of Cornwall. Scandinavia, Russia, Normandy, Brittany and our own "Celtic fringe" may still have these or others. The Chinese anchor is still a wooden "jinny-lin," and Jal[2] illustrates a stone anchor from the Far East that, he says, resembles those of Iceland and Norway. This, with a double "yoke" is, unless my memory is at fault, very similar to one sketched by Callow[3] in the Channel Islands long ago, and now enshrined in the pages of a school copy-book of the *Vere Foster* series. Much more of such sea-lumber must have gone, unrecorded, into Davy Jones' locker.

Editors' Notes

1. Jenny Lind (1820–1887) was a Swedish soprano who achieved great popularity everywhere.
2. Auguste Jal (1795–1873), compiler of the *Glossaire Nautique*.
3. The marine painter and drawing master John Callow (1822–1878) produced a large number of illustrations for school textbooks published by the Irish educationist Vere Foster.

Acknowledgement
This article was published in *The Mariner's Mirror* vol. 3 (1913) and is reproduced with the permission of The Society for Nautical Research.

Reawakening Cornwall's Celtic Consciousness

Ann Trevenen Jenkin

The Background

Robert Morton Nance was brought up in Wales, his country of birth, and this gave him plenty of opportunities as a young man to study the effect of a non-English culture on someone with an enquiring Cornish mind. Robert's grand-parents, Henry and Hannah Nance – she was from St Ives – spent much of their married life in Padstow, Cornwall, where Henry was an agent for the Express Steam Packet, plying between Padstow and Cardiff. In the 1850s, before the more extensive development of the railways, travel by sea to and from Cornwall was still the norm. Not only did passenger ships come across the Bristol Channel to Padstow, but cargo ships brought trade across the high seas. Henry was also an agent for the worldwide Packet Service, and many Cornish people were, at that time, emigrating from Padstow, seeking work and a better life over-seas.[1]

William Edwin Nance, the eldest of the ten children of Henry and Hannah, went to Wales by sea in 1857, aged 19, to begin a business career in Cardiff. As he was a member of a very large family living in an area of high unemployment, this route was almost inevitable. He left behind his devoted parents and broth-ers and sisters for a new life in industrial Wales. As Donald R. Rawe put it, 'Cardiff must have been to Padstow what Plymouth or Truro is these days: the place where you could get nearly anything and where many Padstow people had relatives or friends...'[2] In 1862, following a slump and economic depression, Hannah and Henry also moved to Cardiff, where William was doing very well, due to the expansion of industry and the steam coal trade in South Wales. In 1867 William married. It was also the year his mother died. Most of his brothers and sisters also moved to Cardiff, though some went to sea, and Charley eventually settled and did well in Australia. William himself lived till 1932, dying at the advanced age of 94 in Cornwall, having eventually come back to live with his son Robert in Carbis Bay.

Early Life in Cardiff

Robert Morton Nance was born to William and Jane (Morton) Nance in Cardiff on 10 April 1873, although the family moved to Penarth in 1878. Apart from the strong Welsh and Cornish influences, his great-grandfather, a soldier, had come from Ayr in Scotland. Robert grew up with a love of ships and the sea – there were generations of sailors on both sides of the family, and also many shipbuilders. However, there were other influences:

> Our mother read to us often ... She had a pleasant voice, and read beautifully, and I am sure helped us to form our taste.[3]

Books were imaginative, about stories and legends; Ruskin's *King of the Golden River*, Kingsley's *Greek Heroes* and *The Water Babies*, and George Macdonald's *The Back of the North Wind* were enjoyed. A special favourite of Robert's was a large volume of English songs set to music and illustrated by Walter Crane, called *Pan Pipes*.[4] The children all sang standing round the piano. Robert himself invented stories. 'Also I remembered how he and I would go into the Dingle – now a part of the park – at Penarth and play at wonderful fairy stories with tiny wooden farthing dolls, dressed as witches and fairies.'[5] The children all wrote stories and edited a family journal called the *Penarth Magazine*, which included a poem by Robert entitled 'The Merry Ballad of the Cornish Pasty', later printed in Quiller-Couch's *Cornish Magazine* of 1898. 'We certainly made our own pleasures,' recalled his sister, 'and I never remember any of us being at a loss about what to do next; but it was Robert who thought of interesting things to do, and who was our leader...'[6] Robert was also fascinated by fire –

an indication, perhaps, of his later interest in the re-establishment of the Midsummer Bonfires in Cornwall, which he loved, and his knowledge of the Beltane fires which he would have read about.

The sea was always present and in 1875, when Robert was only two, the family travelled back from Cardiff to Hayle on a friend's ship. Their life seemed to be divided between living in Penarth and for some six to eight weeks in the year at St Ives, his grandmother's home. The railway also became important, especially journeys to Cardiff, to the Welsh hills and later, when they no longer travelled by sea, to St Ives.

Education

School influences were strong, first Mrs Fisher's Kindergarten, then private lessons with a clergyman called Powell, and after that at the Cardiff Proprietory School. Robert was grateful to his English teacher, and quickly developed an aptitude for drawing and map-making. He also soon became interested in languages, especially French. His French teacher, later Professor Barbier, whom Nance afterwards met at the Celtic Gathering of 1899, was a great influence:

> As his pupil some ten years earlier, I remember how apt his lessons were to run into comparisons of Breton words with the Welsh of some boys and the small amount of Cornish that I could muster myself – how for instance we all agreed on crow mogh – and how sometimes the French class stayed long after its time listening to his dramatic telling of some Breton folk-tale, much more thrilling and memorable than French verbs. But these are perhaps memories more interesting to myself than to others, though they may have some bearing on the Celtic Movement in Cornwall, too.[7]

According to his sister, 'Later, when he had begun his study of Cornish, he remarked on the opportunities he had missed when sitting next to a Welsh boy.'[8] However, he listened carefully to the Welsh dialect all around him, and assimilated much of the Welsh construction of sentences and the everyday speech of his Welsh companions.

His artistic ability took him to Cardiff Art School, and from about the age of 18 or 19, wherever he was at the time, he began to sketch Welsh miners and

Cornish fishermen. His mother thought he would take up book illustration and correspondended with Herkomer, one of the best artists of the age. On her death in 1893, he went to Herkomer's School at Bushey in Hertfordshire. Following his marriage to Beatrice Michell, a very gifted fellow student, in 1895, he went back to Penarth, after six months in St Ives where their daughter Jeniver was born. When the National Eisteddfod of Wales was held in Cardiff in 1899, Robert and his wife, who ran a studio together, won prizes for painting. 'It may have been at this time,' remembered Christine Raymont, 'that he became interested in the Eisteddfod, as some of our friends were Bards, and later when the Gorsedd was instituted in Cornwall, it was very much on the same lines.'[9] He also met met John Hobson Matthews, a Welsh-speaking Cornishman with a smattering of Breton and Cornish who was living and working in Cardiff, and who was influential in bringing over a party of Bretons to the Pan-Celtic Congress that was held during the Eisteddfod. Hobson Matthews was made a Welsh Bard by the Revd Rowland Williams (*Hwfa Môn*), taking the name *Map Kernyw* (Son of Cornwall).[10] Another influence was T.H. Thomas, *Arlunydd Penygarn*, the Herald Bard of the Welsh Gorsedd, who was instrumental in setting up Celtic co-operation with those from other countries. Nance put Thomas's influence on his own interests and Celtic aspirations as second only to that of Henry Jenner.[11]

The Intervening Years

Before his wife's early death, Beatrice designed and Robert executed some murals of children playing for the front of Albert Road Board School, Penarth, as well as attempting to set up a School of Painting. As a young widower, Robert went off to Paris for a short while to study, but soon came back to Penarth to be with his young daughter. He set up several exhibitions of medieval ship models and illustrated several books.

In 1906, he married Annie Maud Cawker, another student at Bushey and a great friend of his first wife. After living initially in Nancledra, in 1914 they moved to Carbis Bay, which remained his home for the rest of his life. Here, Nance painted for many years, mainly works associated with the sea, and the couple brought up three children. In 1916 he joined the Duke of Cornwall's Light Infantry Volunteers, as he was too old for active service. Eventually, how-

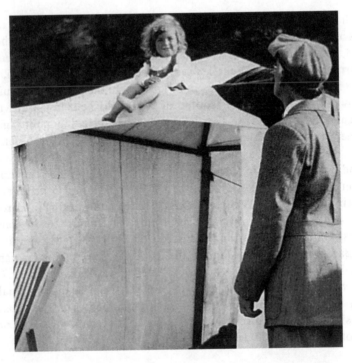

Robert Morton Nance with his daughter Phoebe, c.1916/1917
(Courtesy of Carola Nance Scupham/Gorseth Kernow Archive)

ever, his interest in painting became subservient to his growing interest in the Cornish language, the development of the Old Cornwall Societies and the Gorsedd. His friendship with Henry Jenner, the first Grand Bard, and with many others involved in Cornish, encouraged him, and in 1929 he produced *Cornish for All*. Parallel with all these interests was his increasing support for and involvement in the Celtic world, particularly the Celtic Congress.

Celtic Beginnings

The seeds of this involvement were sown during his boyhood in Wales and his early connections with the Welsh Eisteddfod. In 1901, 'a wave of the Celtic revival at last reached Cornwall and the *Cowethas Kelto-Kernuak* was formed'.[12] This 'Celtic-Cornish Society' had a short and chequered career, but many of the names suggested the wide interests of its members. In particular, in his *Handbook of the Cornish Language* which was published in 1904 under its auspices, Jenner put into words what many were thinking. He stressed that the Cornish, too, should have a chance to learn their own language for a Cornishman was 'as much a Celt as any Gael, Cymro, Manxman or Breton' and Cornish was necessary to him as 'the outward and audible sign of his separate nationality'.[13] Cornwall was admitted to the Celtic Association in Caernarfon in 1904, when Jenner pleaded Cornwall's case in Cornish. She thus became a member of the Celtic group of nations, and as such, 'entitled to representation at all such Celtic gatherings – a status that has been allowed it ever since'.[14] Jenner, with whom Nance had a twenty-year close association, inspired him to be involved in all these concerns, but above all '[we] were inspired by his ideal of Cornwall as a Celtic Nation...'[15] Nance picked up many of Jenner's ideas and moved them forward.

In 1924 Robert went to Brittany with Charles Henderson and the Revd Gilbert H. Doble, forming a memorably strong delegation that attended the Celtic Congress in Quimper. On 21 October 1924, he read a report at the autumn meeting of the Royal Institution of Cornwall, a report which was later printed.[16] In a full and personal appreciation of what it meant to Cornwall to be represented, Nance referred to the fact that the Cornish language was almost extinct. However:

> The Celtic Congress has ... settled the question generously for us; allowing that the continued use of the Cornish language, by even the merest handful of people and to the most limited extent, does, with the real Cornish sentiment that still exists, justify the admission of Cornwall to this gathering of the Celtic clans, and at it we are granted the same representation as is given the Isle of Man, our greater numerical importance being fairly balanced by their stronger position as still having a small number of habitual Manx speakers.[17]

Nance hoped that the Celtic Congress might come to Cornwall in 1926 and that the full week of lectures, sight-seeing, concerts, processions and plays in

Brittany could be replicated in Cornwall. He enjoyed the plays which reminded him of the close links between Cornwall and Brittany, especially in the play of St Noluen (possibly St Newlyn) and the village's proximity to the tomb of St Meriasek, patron saint of Camborne, which he visited. The Cornish delegates were already speaking up for the cause of the Breton language 'which, thanks to an over-centralised government, is still a proscribed one in the Breton schools; [but] by the use of Breton in church and Sunday-school, and especially by the printing of cheap Breton books and the acting of Breton plays, serious and farcical, the national sentiment of Brittany in spite of all opposition is being encouraged and preserved alive by a comparatively small number of active workers'.[18] All this was further inspiration to the Cornish delegates, especially Nance, who were already attempting to form a branch of the Celtic Congress in Cornwall and facing many obstacles. He visited Brittany again in 1927.

In 1926 plans to hold a Celtic Congress in Cornwall for the first time were cancelled, largely because of industrial unrest, but strong links were maintained, especially with both Wales and Brittany. The extensive correspondence between E.T. John, an expatriate Welshman who became involved in Welsh politics and culture on his retirement, and Robert Morton Nance[19] shows the earnest desire of the Welsh in particular to include the Cornish in their actions and deliberations. Nance spent months encouraging many in Cornwall to follow his dream and it was ironic that the poor exchange rate of the franc for the Bretons, the dilatoriness of some Congress officers, the shortage of accommodation in Cornwall in July (the high holiday season) and ultimately the General Strike led to the Congress efforts to visit Cornwall coming to naught.

However, links between Wales and Brittany continued to be established and strengthened through the setting up of Gorseth Kernow in 1928. In that year Wales was instrumental in establishing the Cornish Gorsedd by initiating eight bards, including Robert Morton Nance, at Treorchy. A Welsh delegation then returned to Cornwall with the Archdruid, for the first gorsedd at Boscawen-Un. Henry Jenner was instituted as Grand Bard with Robert Morton Nance as his first deputy. While there were no official Breton links in 1928, a huge delegation came over the following year to take part in Cornish and Breton wrestling tournaments and to participate in the 1929 Gorsedd on Carn Brea. They appeared in Breton costume and provided a colourful spectacle. Since 1929, both Welsh and Breton delegates have attended and spoken in their own languages at virtually every Gorseth Kernow. They have always been treated as honoured guests.

The Arthurian Congress (1930)

In 1930, several Bards of Honour who had been attending the Arthurian Congress in Cornwall were admitted at the gorsedd that was held at The Hurlers. They included Dr Mary Williams (*Rhiannon*, a Welsh legendary name), Professor R.S. Loomis, the well-known Celtic scholar (*Gwas Gerrans*, Servant of Geraint), Mrs L.H. Loomis (*Myrgh Enyd*, Daughter of Enid) Dr A.G. van Hamel (*Map Yseldyr*, Son of the Low Countries) and Dr E. Vinaver (*Gwas Gwynear*, Servant of Gwinear) – illustrious names indeed. Nance supported Henry Jenner in his efforts to get distinguished Celtic scholars from all over the world to visit Cornwall, and the topics presented at the Arthurian Congress make interesting reading now. Serious, but occasionally somewhat whimsical, lectures were attended by many local people, emphasising for the first time, perhaps, the fact that Cornwall had once been part of a much wider, more prosperous, more intellectual and more creative Celtic world.

The visitors were delighted with all they saw and heard, including visits to the places of Arthurian and Celtic interest. On being made an honorary bard, Professor Mary Williams of Swansea University said that '[s]he wanted to do her utmost to unite Cornwall and Wales as much as possible, because Cornwall, like Wales, was a small country, and in unity [there] was strength'.[20] When he was made an honorary bard, Dr E. Vinaver, the President of the Oxford Arthurian Society, also spoke of Cornwall as a country, with the Arthurian Round Table 'the symbol of unity, of love and fraternity ... I think it is best represented by our union here, people of various countries who have come down here... Let that Round Table be a symbol of our unity...'[21]

The first Celtic Congress in Cornwall (1932)

All these links with international Celtic scholars and other representatives of the Celtic countries laid the foundation for the first successful Celtic Congress in Cornwall when it was eventually held in Truro in 1932. Nance wrote of the reasons for the visit:

Among the fundamental and accepted objects of the Old Cornwall Movement we have in plain print, *The encouragement of an interest in the old Celtic speech of Cornwall ... and with this of a more lively sense of our kinship with other Celts...*[22]

The Gorsedd also had – and still has – as one of its accepted aims: *To link Cornwall with other Celtic countries.*[23] Nance, by now Secretary for Cornwall, was effusive in his praise for the Truro Congress:

[I]t has been a complete success from beginning to end – its papers and discussions were of a very high order of interest, and, better still, a warm inter-Celtic friendliness was the note of every one of its meetings.[24]

The congress included a Presidential Address by Henry Jenner who, in 'The Awakening of Celtic Cornwall', provided a masterly summing up of Cornwall's claim to Celtic nationality. He concluded by saying that 'thanks to the Old Cornwall Movement, no intelligent person can remain utterly ignorant of his or her Celtic nationality, and thousands take a real pride in it.'[25] With Nance's support, involvement and encouragement, this was a huge stride forward for Cornwall, which continued to gain allies among the Celtic countries who wished to support their own aspirations.

Especially interesting was a discussion on 'The Best Means of Reviving the Celtic Languages', each speaker using his own Celtic speech. No less than eight people rose one after another and spoke in Cornish, 'a dramatic surprise... this little demonstration [being] regarded as a most hopeful sign'.[26] There was also a Celtic Concert, which took place under the direction of Ralph Dunstan. Songs in Cornish were sung by a children's choir from Daniell Road Council School, and by Mrs Russell Mitchell and Tom Robins. An Old Cornwall interlude, *An Balores* (The Chough), was written by Nance for the occasion. With a cast of seven, only four of whom had spoken at the previous discussion on the Celtic languages, the play featured the return of the chough, a symbol of Cornwall's resurrection from the dead as a Celtic people, and linked with the idea of King Arthur in the guise of a chough returning to fight for Cornwall. The idea was later incorporated in the gorsedd song 'Arta ef a dhe/He shall come again'. 'As the first Cornish play to be given since the early 17th century,' concluded its author, 'even so short an interlude was something of an historical landmark.'[27]

Excursions of Celtic Congress and Old Cornwall members included a visit to the Gorsedd at the Merry Maidens Stone Circle, which featured the initiation of several Bards of Honour who had attended the Congress. These were Professor Agnes O'Farrelly of Dublin, (*On Enys Ywerdhon*, Lamb of Ireland), Professor Douglas Hyde, Ireland (*Scorennyk*, Little Branch), Revd John MacKechnie, Scotland (*Gwas Alban*, Servant of Scotland), Mr Percy Kelly, Isle of Man (*Map Enys Manow*, Son of the Isle of Man), Revd G. Hartwell Jones, Wales (*Map Trevaldwyn*, Son of Montgomery), and M. François Gourvil, Brittany (*Baren Ydhyow*, Ivy Branch). Other Bards of Honour included Mrs Ethel Paynter from Cornwall (*Offrynores*, The Offerer) and The Master of Sempill/Lord Sempill (*Edhen an Ayr*, Bird of the Air), a kilt-wearing Scottish peer with Welsh connections, who flew to Cornwall to attend the Gorsedd! An article in the *Daily Telegraph* described him as having 'the heart of a boy and the instincts of a highland chief – a feudalist, a romantic and a bit of an eccentric'.[28] A Gaelic speaker who later, on the death of his father, became the eighth Baron of Craigevar in Aberdeenshire, he showed disdain for authority all his life and a wish to be a part of those who were different. (Was this why he became interested in the early Cornish Gorsedd?) His love of flying and his skill as a pilot meant that '[w]hat he most enjoyed was touring the British Isles by seaplane, landing on lakes, rivers or coves offshore'.[29] Before the Second World War he was accused of being a spy for the Japanese whose air force he had revitalised, but this was not proven. I wonder what Nance made of him! I'm sure he was unfailingly courteous.

After the Gorsedd, a paper was read by Miss Maud Quayle from the Isle of Man on the youth movement there. This led directly to the establishment of Tyr ha Tavas/Land and Language among the young people already active in Cornwall or outside. They took as their aims ones very similar to those of the Isle of Man, which were 'To promote the study of the Manx Language, and to foster in the youth of the Island a love and knowledge of their Country, and a realisation of their kinship with other Celtic nations.'[30] This was heady stuff to the young people of Cornwall, and from that time onwards there have been many initiatives to link up with young Celts from outside Kernow. Nance mentioned one problem in Cornwall at that time – and one shared by most Celtic countries – the emigration of many of the young people each year to attend university and often not return: what in modern parlance is called the "brain drain". Tyr ha Tavas was particularly busy for some years in London, rather than in Cornwall.

A Cornish Homecoming

Henry Jenner had died in 1934. He had not been particularly active since presiding over the first Celtic Congress in Cornwall in 1932 and Nance had gradually assumed the mantle of responsibility for all things Cornish and Celtic. In 1935 he was involved with Sir Arthur Quiller-Couch in the first attempt to set up a Cornish Homecoming Scheme to invite Cornish exiles and descendants of emigrants from all over the world to come back to Cornwall. Indeed, the original idea had come from Nance. The Federation of Old Cornwall Societies and the Cornish Gorsedd had both offered their support through him, and not only local people in Cornwall but also the Cornish overseas were enthusiastic. However, 'Q' was elderly and the logistics of organising such a big event in Cornwall, with its financial implications, proved overwhelmingly difficult.[31] Then, in 1939 war came along and the project was shelved. The idea was not realised until the first Dehwelans Festival with its homecoming of Cornish exiles at Pendennis Castle in 2002, under the chairmanship of the present writer. Sixty years later, with all the modern means of communication, it was still a complicated project to organise!

Wales & the Cornish Language & Gorsedd (1938)

In February 1938 Nance gave a seminal lecture for Cornwall to the Royal Institution of South Wales in Swansea entitled 'Wales & Cornish Language & Gorsedd'.[32] In a long and detailed summary of Cornish aspirations and the close links still remaining between Cornwall and Wales, he particularly emphasised the debt Cornwall owed to Edward Lhuyd who came to Cornwall when the language was in decline and saved many Cornish words for future scholars. He stressed the close links through place names, history, stories and legends as well as the journeys of the Celtic saints. King Arthur comes in for a mention, as Nance tells the tale of a riot in Bodmin, when a doubter said that Arthur would not come back to save his people in their hour of need and was punched by members of the crowd! There is a similar story in Wales about King Arthur's powers. He also referred to A.S.D. Smith, who had first studied Welsh and written a booklet called *Welsh Made Easy*, before embarking on *Cornish Simplified*. Lastly, he praised the work of Henry Jenner who had been instrumental in the revival of Cornish, ending with an impassioned plea for support from the Welsh in the Cornish struggle to revive the language. It emphasised again the importance Nance placed on Celtic links, particularly those with Wales and Brittany:

> I have said a great deal about our little attempts to revive Cornish, not because I have no sense of proportion but because I cannot help thinking that the struggles of any Celtic community, or even of a tiny minority in such a community, to retain its Celtic character to the utmost possible, ought to be interesting at least to those in Wales who are not indifferent to the national language and individual character of the country to which they belong...[33]

In July that same year, at about the time that he was teaching Cornish and Breton to his little granddaughter, Nance also represented Cornwall at a Breton Festival at Châteaulin and at the Breton Gorsedd. The Gorsedd Minute Books reveal that among the party from Cornwall that travelled to Brittany by steamer from Falmouth were the organiser Mrs Ashley Rowe (*Cares an Mowysy*), the Grand Bard *Mordon*, Miss Ada Williams (*Myrgh Ludewon*) who took her camera with her and left some fine photographs of the visit, Canon Doble (*Gwas Gwendron*), and W. Tregoning Hooper (*Bras y Golon*), who was involved in Cornish and Breton wrestling tournaments. The tour was conducted by Canon Doble, whose knowledge of Brittany and the Celtic Saints was placed at the disposal of the visitors.[34]

Wartime (1939–1945)
This bond between the two Celtic nations was to prove important after the outbreak of war in 1939. At a Closed Gorsedd at the Royal Institution of Cornwall in Truro on 1 June 1940, it was reported that '[t]he visit paid by the Cornish people to the Breton Gorseth bore fruit after the outbreak of war, by offers of hospitality to Cornish soldiers on leave in France'.[35] In 1941 Lieutenant Jean de Cadenet was made a Bard of Honour at a Closed Gorsedd, taking the bardic name *Ab Soniou* (Son of Songs), and the Grand Bard, *Mordon*, announced that

they were not only honouring the officer, but also Brittany.[36]

A reciprocal arrangement was made in Cornwall in September 1942 when a 'demonstration' was held in Penzance in support of the Bretons. The Friends of Brittany Society was later formed under the auspices of Mr and Mrs Ashley Rowe.[37] In the Morrab Library at Penzance a Breton magazine, paid for by Gorseth Kernow, was available for Breton readers from as early as 1935[38] and competitions were suggested between the two countries.

During the war many Cornish activities, including the Gorseth ceremonies, were not held in their normal form, but there was a flourishing 'Kelgh Keltek' a Cornish Correspondence Circle with writers in many parts of the world, including the other Celtic countries. I gather that the army censors had some difficulty in determining whether or not Cornish was a subversive language, as none of them could read the language except Edwin Chirgwin and he was also the writer of letters home in Cornish! Nance was by no means inactive, and in 1943 he gave a lecture entitled 'The Spirit of the Celtic Movement', which symbolises the upbeat attitudes of himself and others to the re-establishment of the Cornish language and of Celtic links after the war.

The Spirit of the Celtic Movement (1943)

Nance wrote this paper two years before the end of the Second World War. In it he stresses the wisdom of thinking of the future of Cornwall, its language and its Celtic links:

> All around us we hear post-war plans being discussed … [I]t is surely a helpful thing to consider all possible means of keeping our freedom and peace whenever they are won back, and along with any new plans that may be devised it is well to reconsider the older contributions towards making the world fit for peace-loving and freedom-loving people to live in.[39]

Nance saw the development of Celtic links as providing this stability, writing of the modern Celtic Movement that 'in each of the Celtic countries it has had the effect of lifting national sentiment above the political or religious differences that separate the people of Wales, Brittany or Cornwall, North and South Ireland, Scotland or the Isle of Man'.[40] He takes this vision much further and sees this attitude of tolerance stretching far beyond the Celtic countries:

> [I]t cannot stop short at fellow-feeling among Celts only, for once a narrow, exclusive love of country, which in itself is such a danger, has been rendered safe by being made to include a wider and more generous sentiment towards all Celtic countries, it becomes easy to extend it to non-Celtic countries, and especially to all those where love of freedom and peace is as strong as in our own, and where a similar struggle is needed to preserve from oblivion national ideals, history, language, traditions, literature and music, not merely because these are vital to one particular little nation, but because each fits into its own place in the great scheme of world-culture, to which diversity is as necessary as unity.[41]

Nance was no political activist, although he could count many members of Mebyon Kernow, founded in 1951 eight years before his death, among his friends, especially E.G. Retallack Hooper and G. Pawley White, both future Grand Bards. He had certainly supported Tyr ha Tavas, which had also had some political aspirations. However, his view of cultural nationalism and the nationhood of Cornwall was one still embraced by Gorseth Kernow and one which I myself grew up with and was comfortable with. It was certainly relevant at the time and provided a secure basis for the development of Gorseth Kernow and the Celtic Congress. Mebyon Kernow and the Cornish Branch of the Celtic League, founded in the early 1960s after Nance's death, provided a more political approach, although they did not forget the cultural and linguistic aspects. It was all a question of emphasis. Nance realised that the struggle for Cornwall and the other Celtic countries would not be easy, but he also acknowledged the toughness and resilience of their rejuvenated peoples:

> One thing ... is shown as found among them all, and that is the capacity to blow on patiently until below dead ashes a kindling spark is reached again. Another thing ... is the mind that never grows old, cynical and disillusioned. The great Chinese philosophers of thousands of years ago knew the value of this, when they argued that the greatest essential of the noblest mind was that it must be child-like, which is not at all the same as being childish.[42]

Post-War: The Inter-Celtic Festival, St Ives (1949)

It is impossible to refer to everything in which Nance was involved in connection with the Celtic world after the Second World War, so I have concentrated on the highlights. One of these was the Inter-Celtic Festival in St Ives in 1949. This was an interesting initiative in that it was arranged by the St Ives branch of the Gaelic League in Cornwall, itself an offshoot of the St Ives Catholic Irish Association. The festival ran for a week from 23–30 April, with the official programme costing 1/- [5p].[43] St Ives at that time was still full of hotels, and many Irish people had come over to work in them, so there was a huge Irish Catholic population and the Revd Father Delaney was an active Irish speaker in charge of a flourishing Catholic congregation. Bretons often came to the port as fishermen or passengers on the boats. Dancers and musicians were among those sojourning in Cornwall, and Irish dancing was taught to the locals. As a student about to attend university, I was one of those attending classes and trying to master the intricacies of Irish jigs and Breton processional dances! At the same time, I was studying Cornish at 'Chylason', Carbis Bay, with Nance. As our horizons widened, it was a euphoric time for young Cornish people.

Through that Irish Association links were developed with other Celtic bodies in Cornwall, so that discussions were held with the Federation of Old Cornwall Societies, the Gorsedd and the Celtic Congress. At a meeting on 6 March 1949, two members of the St Ives Catholic Irish Association, P.J. Courtney and E.C. Curnow, were elected to the committee of the Celtic Congress. All these organisations included Robert Morton Nance who had already worked closely with the Irish in St Ives to foster deeper Celtic links in Cornwall.[44] Nance had added the post of hard-working Committee Chairman for the Festival to an already full schedule:

> Already well into his seventies, he still retained the office of Grand Bard of the Cornish Gorsedd, which he had held continuously since 1934. One would imagine it was his enthusiasm and leadership that presented such a feast of opportunities to one and all to compete in the prestigious events which the programme presented.[45]

Brian Stevens' article tried to recapture the excitement of the time. The Festival programme included poetry competitions, literary competitions, dance competitions of various types, including Irish and Breton, a Manx section and a large, non-competitive Cornish arts and crafts exhibition. Many of the young artists and craftsmen of St Ives were supporting members, including Bernard Leach, Guido Morris and Dicon Nance, Robert's son. The festival became a showcase for Celtic excellence, with entrants from all over Cornwall and many from the other Celtic countries. The cover of the programme featured the shields of all six Celtic countries, against a background of ivy leaves. While I hold no brief for Celtic-only entertainment, it is sad that the 2006 St Ives Autumn Arts Festival – with one exception, a lecture on Alfred Wallis by Cornish Bard Robert Jones (*Den Awenek*) – contained only a little that was Cornish or indeed Celtic, and paid scant homage to our Celtic roots and to the illustrious history of St Ives.

The Celtic Congress, Truro 1950

The following year, the International Celtic Congress came to Cornwall for a second time after a long gap of 18 years. Its patron was the Lord Bishop of Truro, with Nance as the President of the local branch, Henry Trefusis as its chairman, Ashley Rowe as secretary, and Audrey Humphris, who as Audrey Pool still serves the Congress faithfully after 57 years and is now one of two Life Presidents, as hospitality organiser. The Congress President, Professor Agnes O'Farrelly, was eighty and unable to travel, but sent her good wishes:

> In Cornwall, where you meet in congress, there is again, as there was when the congress last met there under Dr [*sic*] Jenner … an upsurging of Celtic spirit. You are fortunate in having Dr [*sic*] Nance, one of the pioneers and a noted authority on the language and traditions of the county with you at the congress…[46]

> It has been heartening during the year to hear of the enthusiasm of a small band of workers throughout Cornwall. Their efforts in song and story and drama will be judged – favourably I have no doubt – during Congress week.[47]

The programme included a reception and civic welcome given by the Mayor of Truro, greetings from national delegates, a talk on 'Welsh Saints and their

Celtic Communities' that was chaired by Nance, and various lectures from other Celtic delegates, including 'Celtic Migrations'. There was also an outstanding presentation on 'The Last Phase of Celtic Art' by Sir Cyril Fox, Director of the National Museum of Wales, which made the audience, including this writer, realise how important and creative as craftsmen the Celts had been. It certainly gave me a sense of pride in that aspect of our Celtic heritage. Visits to Truro Museum and to a Polytechnic Exhibition at Falmouth with a return journey to Truro by boat, and an expedition to St Michael's Mount on the Saturday gave delegates a flavour of Cornwall. There were also concerts and services, the one in Truro Cathedral on the Sunday being in Cornish.

Other features of the packed programme included discussions in the Celtic languages, with the 'p' Celts in one group and the 'q' Celts in another. There was a fine production in Cornish of part of *Bewnans Meryasek* (The Life of Meriasek), which the following year was part of the Cornwall Drama Festival contribution to the Festival of Britain, and a visit to the annual gorsedd at Boscawen-Un. Everywhere, as Cornish President, Nance was much in evidence, and a photograph taken outside the Royal Cornwall Museum shows him as an old man, wearing the inevitable plus fours, but upright and distinguished in the centre of the delegates.[48]

The Celtic Congress, Truro 1956

The congress of 1956 was the last that Nance attended as President of the Cornish Branch. The official photograph on the steps of the Royal Cornwall Museum shows him as I remember him: a frail, elderly but still upright man with a strong determination to continue speaking up for Cornwall and the Celtic world. He never gave up.[49] Delegates were welcomed by Nance as Grand Bard, President of the Federation of Old Cornwall Societies and President of the Celtic Congress in Cornwall. Like Henry Jenner, the first Grand Bard, he was a tripartite leader whose energy had been inexhaustible. Some of the Bretons had arrived by fishing boat and twenty young people from the first Celtic Youth Camp at Castle Gotha attended some of the proceedings. Also present were the Chief Justice of Ireland and Michael Yeats, son of the famous Irish poet, W.B. Yeats. Cornwall's own Richard Jenkin was the International Secretary. The Reverend D.R. Evans, a Welshman living in Cornwall who had

Celtic Congress delegates on the steps of the Royal Cornwall Museum, Truro, 1956,
Robert Morton Nance, front row, 4th from left
(Courtesy of Archive of Celtic Congress – Cornwall)

been Deputy Grand Bard, was reported in the local press as follows:

> The Celtic tongues are difficult, but for true Celts that only strength-
> ened their moral fibre and bound them closely together in the feeling
> that they had a distinctive place in the British Isles. The Celtic spirit
> had something far from materialistic, whereas materialism broke down
> the unity which should exist through human nature.[50]

The general atmosphere in 1956 was one of harmony, tolerance and a desire on the part of the Celtic peoples to learn from one another about their lives and languages. The congress further stimulated Cornish cultural activists to pursue their aims for a more Celtic Cornwall.

Final Tributes

Robert Morton Nance died on 27 May 1959 at the age of 86. He had been active almost to the end and, together with Henry Jenner, had steered Cornwall through various vicissitudes to a position of some respect in the Celtic world. It had not always been thus. Proof of his own position in that world came in the form of tributes to him from other Celts.

Oscar MacUilis, who could speak all six Celtic languages, was chairman of the Irish Branch of the Celtic Congress, a former general secretary of the Congress and an Honorary Bard of the Breton Gorsedd, wrote:

> The name of Morton Nance was very familiar to me long before I met that grand old man. Miss O'Farrelly ... used often to speak of him and his work, and of having seen "An Balores" performed in Truro.
>
> When Morton Nance replaced his old friend and colleague, the almost legendary Henry Jenner, as Grand Bard he had a difficult task indeed, that of living up to so great a predecessor. Yet *Mordon* lived up to him, brought new and different qualities to the office, and adorned it not only with scholarship, but also with art and music and humanity.
>
> All this he brought, and something more. He brought patience, the will to continue for years to write in Cornish, to teach Cornish, to encourage the few who came to study Cornwall, though the task must have so often appeared impossible, the object quite visionary.
>
> This is where *Mordon* is such an example to us Celts outside Cornwall. Having once put his hand to the plough he never looked back. His was a labour of hope, a labour of love. He would not personally see the harvest nor could he judge the ultimate achievement, but he held on. Would that we had more like him among us.
>
> *Mordon* I personally remember with affection. He had a great interest in people, and a wonderful memory for them. With sorrow I bid him farewell, with gratitude I can say I knew him as a friend.[51]

The Reverend D. R. Evans, chairman of the Cornish Branch of the Celtic

Congress, Deputy Grand Bard of the Cornish Gorsedd and a Welsh speaker had this to say:

> I consider it a privilege to be asked to give my testimony to *Mordon*; for he did so much for Cornwall during a period of re-awakening of the consciousness of its individual life as a part of Britain where Celtic life and culture prevailed, in spite of Roman, Saxon and Norman political counter-influences.
>
> During his lifetime *Mordon* was one of the finest fighters against those effacing tendencies which the Celts have had to withstand. In this way he stood for the freedom of the spirit of man – that spirit that defies the fettering of private judgement by church or state or both combined.
>
> *Mordon* helped us to feel that the Celts have yet their part to play in the life of Britain. He was a worthy successor to all those who thought that Cornwall was not just a part of England...[52]

From Roparz Hemon, chairman of the Breton Branch of the Celtic Congress, came the following:

> R. Morton Nance was one of the most prominent workers for the revival of Cornish in this century ... There are some who think that those who are willing to revive Cornish are nothing but dreamers, but there are others who think the same about all who are maintaining the Celtic languages. Such dreams, though, are sometimes sources of priceless spiritual life, often, at least, sources of enjoyment and pleasure. He who will listen to Morton Nance's call, will not be sorry: "Gwreugh dysky Kernewek, na vo gesys dhe goll puptra es gwres dheugh gans re erel." – Learn Cornish, so that everything shall not perish, which has been done for you by others.[53]

Nance never weakened in his resolve to support his beloved Cornwall. L.R. Moir, Honorary Secretary of the Federation of Old Cornwall Societies and a Bard, painted the following picture of Nance in his last few weeks, still chasing Celtic connections:

> It was with reluctance that he loosened his grasp on his life-work; so

much remained to be done, as he said with a hint of exasperation in his voice, and yet he had done so much.

To the end his mind was scholarly and lucid. While in hospital he was delighted to find that his Irish nurse spoke the language of her native land; here, to his way of thought, was another opportunity to elicit facts, clear away doubts and make himself better acquainted with one more Celtic language. But it was not to be.[54]

Conclusion

Robert Morton Nance was of his time. Ways of behaviour and attitudes change over the years, but his contributions to the development of the Celtic aspirations of Cornwall are self-evident. It is why the Cornish Branch of the Celtic Congress, (now Celtic Congress – Cornwall), just over 100 years since Cornwall was recognised at Caernarfon, is still advancing and developing. Certainly, the Congress has, perhaps, become less academic and more populist, less middle-class, less religiously based, more political without being party political, and through many subjects and themes, is reaching out to the wider Celtic world of the twenty-first century.

For instance, the International Celtic Congress which came to the University of Exeter in Cornwall Campus at Tremough, Penryn in July 2007, looked at the Celtic World today, specifically 'The Contribution to the World of Arts, Science and Industry by the Celtic Diaspora'. The Institute of Cornish Studies, under Deputy Director Dr Garry Tregidga of the Exeter University Campus at Penryn, ran a very successful conference on 21st Century Celts in September 2006. Some broad themes explored included 'Modern Celtic Identities', 'Space and Celtic Identities', 'Place, Monument, Artifact and Celtic Identities', 'The Performance of Celtic Identity' and 'The Language of Celtic Identity'.

While Nance might not necessarily have considered some of these subjects the proper stuff of research, his appreciation of a wide range of ideas, his vision for the future, his interest in worldwide tolerance, his sense of fun, and his innovative mind, would have ensured that he enjoyed and supported both conferences.

Notes

1. Christine Morton Raymont (1989), *Padstow in the mid-Nineteenth Century with Foreword and Epilogue by Donald R. Rawe*, Padstow: Lodenek Press, p. 1.
2. Ibid., p. 3.
3. Mrs C. Morton Raymont (1962), *The Early Life of R. Morton Nance*, [Leedstown]: New Cornwall, p. 10.
4. Ibid.
5. Ibid. p. 11.
6. Ibid. p. 19.
7. R. Morton Nance (1943), 'The Spirit of the Celtic Movement', Nance Collection: Nance Essays and Lectures, Courtney Library, Truro.
8. Raymont (1962), p. 24.
9. Ibid. p. 28.
10. Nance (1943).
11. Ibid.
12. R. Morton Nance (1934), 'Gwas Myghal and the Cornish Revival', *Old Cornwall*, vol. 2. no. 8, p. 3.
13. Ibid.
14. Ibid. p. 4.
15. Ibid. p. 5.
16. R. Morton Nance (1925), 'The Celtic Congress, Quimper 1924', *Journal of the Royal Institution of Cornwall*, vol. 21, pt. 72, pp. 451–454.
17. Ibid. p. 451.
18. Ibid. p. 454.
19. E.T. John Papers (GB 0210ETJOHN), National Library of Wales, Aberystwyth.
20. *Royal Cornwall Gazette*, 3 September 1930.
21. Ibid.
22. R. Morton Nance (1932), 'Old Cornwall and the Celtic Congress', *Old Cornwall*, vol. 2, no. 4 (Winter), pp. 21–22. The aims and objectives of the Old Cornwall Movement are quoted in this article.
23. The Gorseth Rule Book.
24. Nance (1932), p. 22.
25. Ibid.
26. Ibid. pp. 22–23.
27. Ibid. p. 23.
28. Pearson Phillips (2002), 'The Highland Peer who prepared Japan for War', *Daily Telegraph*, 6 January.
29. Ibid.
30. Nance (1932), p. 24.
31. Biographical file and other material on Arthur Quiller-Couch, Cornish Gorsedd Archives.
32. R. Morton Nance (1938), 'Wales & the Cornish Language & Gorsedd', Nance Collection, Courtney Library, Truro.
33. Ibid. p. 33.
34. Cornish Gorsedd Minute Book covering 1938, Cornwall Record Office, Truro; R. Morton Nance (1938), 'Cornish Delegations', *Old Cornwall*, vol. 3, no. 4 (Winter), pp. 157–159.
35. Cornish Gorsedd Minute Book covering 1940, Cornwall Record Office.
36. Bardic List in Cornish Gorsedd Archives; Cornish Gorsedd Minute Book covering 1940, Cornwall Record Office.
37. Annual General Meeting 1943, Gorsedd Minute Book, Cornwall Record Office.
38. Cornish Gorsedd Minute Book covering 1935, Cornwall Record Office.
39. Nance (1943), p. 1.

40. Ibid.
41. Ibid.
42. Ibid. p. 4.
43. St Ives Catholic Irish Association leaflet, 1948; Archives of Celtic Congress – Cornwall. Officers of the St Ives Catholic Irish Association were President Father Delaney, Vice President Revd Father Healy, honorary treasurer Mrs E.C. Curnow, honorary secretary E.C. Curnow and joint honorary secretary and organiser P.J. Courtney.
44. Ibid.
45. Tre Pol Pen [Brian Stevens] (1999), 'A look back at the 'Inter Celtic Festival' of 1949', *St Ives Times & Echo*, 23 July.
46. Archives of Celtic Congress – Cornwall.
47. Ashley Rowe (1951), 'An Guntelles Keltek (The Celtic Congress)', *Old Cornwall*, vol. 4, no.12 (Winter), pp. 473–476.
48. Archives of Celtic Congress – Cornwall.
49. Congress Group outside the Royal Cornwall Museum 1956, Archives of Celtic Congress – Cornwall.
50. Unidentified Cornish newspaper, 1956.
51. Richard and Ann Jenkin (eds.) (1959), *New Cornwall*, vol. 7, no. 5, August/September.
52. Ibid.
53. Ibid.
54. L. R. Moir (1963), 'His closing years', in R. Morton Nance, *A Glossary of Cornish Sea-words*, [Truro/Marazion/St Ives]: Federation of Old Cornwall Societies, p. 22.

Acknowledgements

My thanks to Angela Broome, Courtney Library, The Royal Institution of Cornwall, Truro; Terry Knight and the staff of Kresenn Kernow/The Cornwall Centre, Redruth; Derek Williams for information on material available in the National Library of Wales, Aberystwyth; The Celtic Congress – Cornwall for the use of its archives; The Cornish Gorsedd for the use of its archives and of its Minute Books in the Cornwall Record Office, Truro.

The Spirit of the Celtic Movement

[A paper read in 1943]

R. Morton Nance

All around us we hear post-war plans being discussed. To some minds this seems premature, but as long as no-one acts as though the war were already over, it is surely a helpful thing to consider all possible means of keeping our freedom and peace whenever they are won back, and along with any new plans that may be devised it is well to reconsider the older contributions towards making the world fit for peace-loving and freedom-loving people to live in.

One of these has been the modern Celtic Movement to which the Cornish Gorsedd owes its existence, and of which it forms a part. As far as its influence has been felt, in each of the Celtic countries it has had the effect of lifting national sentiment above the political or religious differences that separate the people of Wales, Brittany or Cornwall, North and South Ireland, Scotland or the Isle of Man, and by concentrating on the things which are common interests of the mind and spirit in them all it has promoted tolerance, mutual respect and understanding and brought about many helpful friendships among those who without it would never have met. More than this, when such a movement succeeds in its first object it cannot stop short at fellow-feeling among Celts only, for once a narrow, exclusive love of country, which in itself is such a danger, has been rendered safe by being made to include a wider and more generous sentiment towards all Celtic countries, it becomes easy to extend it to non-Celtic countries, and especially to all those where love of freedom and peace is as strong as in our own, and where a similar struggle is needed to preserve from oblivion national ideals, history, language, traditions, literature and music, not merely because these are vital to one particular little nation, but because each fits into its own place in the great scheme of world-culture, to which diversity is as necessary as unity.

From its beginnings the Celtic Movement has taken this wider view. Perhaps it could be said to have started with the Celtic saints, who took their message of peace and goodwill from their own to other Celtic countries and thence to non-Celtic countries, bringing their light into the Dark Ages; or with Edward Lhuyd's first recognition that Welsh studies were only to be completed if Gaelic, Breton and Cornish, and other, non-Celtic, languages, were compared with Welsh. The date from which continuous progress can be traced, however, is 1807, when le Gonidec[1] printed his Breton grammar, which led to, or intensi-fied, a revived interest in the Breton language and literature. Bretons have noticed that great events three times followed this at intervals of three decades; almost as if there must be something in the magic of the Bardic triad. At all events it was 30 years later that, owing to the desire of Villemarqué, the leading Breton poet, to get in touch with the bards of Wales, the first of all inter-Celtic meetings was held at Abergavenny in 1837, attended by a little band of five lit-erary Bretons, and it was after another 30 years that the return visit of Welshmen to Brittany was made at the congress of St Brieuc in 1867. Cornwall was then represented only by the presence of the Rev W.C. Lukis,[2] who though interested in Cornish antiquities was not himself a Cornishman. A Breton Miracle Play, *Le mystère de Sainte Tryphine*, was one feature of this. During the next 30 years interval a Penzance party chartered a steamboat and went to Brittany, but their main object seems to have been to compare Breton and Cornish megaliths, and this does not seem to have been reckoned as an inter-Celtic mission. Some flamboyant attempts to unite all Celts in a political move-ment were made without any success at all during the same interval, and these, too, are left out of account, but a speech by an Irishman, Wm. O'Brien,[3] in 1892, proposing a "Celtic League" with a purely cultural purpose, may have had its effect although no such league was formed. It seems to have taken just another 30 years before the Celtic Movement woke up once more, and this time it was the Red Dragon of Wales that fulfilled its ancient boast, *Y Ddraig Goch a ddyry*

Gychwyn, "The Red Dragon will set things moving". Representing the Welsh National Eisteddfod, in 1897 the then Herald Bard of the Gorsedd, T.H. Thomas,[4] *Arlunydd Penygarn*, attended the ceremony of the foundation of the *Feis Ceoil*, the Irish National Musical Festival, the nearest thing in Ireland to a National Eisteddfod. No-one better fit to set going a movement for Celtic co-operation could have been found. *Arlunydd Penygarn* was a man of wide culture who had studied art in Rome in his youth, and without losing any of his enthusiasm for Wales and Welsh he could take a very real interest in other countries and languages, especially if they were Celtic. The Gorsedd ceremonial owes many improvements to his artistic guidance; in other ways the Cornish Gorsedd may be said to owe something to him, too, for in my own youth, to me he was one of the kindest of friends, and it would have been strange if he had not passed on to me some of his enthusiasm. I remember, for one thing, how interested he was in the Glamorgan dialect of Welsh, which he found sometimes to approach more nearly to Cornish and Breton than the other dialects. Next to *Gwas Myghal*[5] as an inspiration I think I shall always put *Arlunydd Penygarn*.

He seems to have broken the 30 years charm, or perhaps with three recurrences this had worked itself out. Following his example, representatives of Wales, Scotland, the Isle of Man and Brittany attended the next Irish National Musical Festival, held at Belfast in 1898, and this opportunity was taken to form a committee to organise future Pan-Celtic gatherings. The first such meeting took place in connection with the National Eisteddfod held at Cardiff in 1899. To this Brittany sent a large delegation of 22 of its leading men, the youngest of whom was *Taldir*[6], and they had a marvellous reception. The result of this visit was the setting up of the Breton Gorsedd a year later. Ireland and Scotland were well represented at Cardiff, too, and there was one Manx delegate, but Cornwall was not included, and this in spite of the fact that J. Hobson Matthews,[7] the historian of St Ives, who had more than a smattering of Breton and Cornish and spoke Welsh, had been one of those most useful in bringing the Breton delegation over. At least I had the pleasure of seeing him then made a bard by *Hwfa Môn*[8] in the name of *Mab Cernyw*, "Son of Cornwall". Among the Bretons, too, was one in whom I had a great personal interest. This was Prof Barbier,[9] who taught Cardiff French at the time. As his pupil some ten years earlier, I remember how apt his lessons were to run into comparisons of Breton words with the Welsh of some boys and the small amount of Cornish that I could muster myself – how for instance we all agreed on crow mogh – and how sometimes the French class stayed long after its time listening to his dramatic telling of some Breton folk-tale, much more thrilling and memorable than French verbs. But these are perhaps memories more interesting to myself than to others, though they may have some bearing on the Celtic Movement in Cornwall, too.

After this meeting at Cardiff the Pan-Celtic Congress began to meet independently of the Eisteddfod or the Feis Ceoil. Convened by what now called itself the Celtic Association, it met at Dublin in 1901. Among its decisions were that a Pan-Celtic Congress should be held again in 1904, and that as a common symbol of their unity, the heather-bloom should be adopted as the Celtic flower, since it is characteristic of all the Celtic countries alike. A "Song of the Heather" was written and was translated into most if not all of the Celtic languages. After having turned it into Cornish verse myself, I of course found that *Gwas Myghal* had a Cornish version ready long before, though for some reason this song, to the tune of "Brian Boru's Lament", has been neglected, and his was never used. Perhaps this was because the Celtic Association, as such, faded out after a few years, and with it unfortunately the monthly journal *Celtia*, which had been so useful while it lasted, as a literary link between all the Celts. It was still going strong, though, in 1904, when it arranged for a Pan-Celtic Congress to coincide with the National Eisteddfod held that year at Carnarvon [*sic*]. This started on the first day as a gathering of the *five* Celtic nations, but a claim for the inclusion of Cornwall had already been made on behalf of the old Celtic-Cornish Association, founded in 1901, and a vote on the recognition of Cornwall as a Celtic nation was down on the first day's agenda. Probably the printing of Cornish poems by different persons in *Celtia* had prepared the way, but we all know that a speech by *Gwas Myghal*, who had been made a bard in this name, or rather the Breton of it, *Gwaz Mikael*, in Brittany a year before, and who had just published his *Handbook of the Cornish Language*, won the day for Cornwall, so that the congress ended as one of *six* Celtic nations. We also know how ready the other five have always been to take us as we are and give us full credit for the little we have been able to accomplish. As illustrating that it is natural for those who love their own Celtic nations to carry this on, first to Celts who speak other Celtic languages, or to those who speak none, and then to all small nations, irrespective of language or race, at this Carnarvon congress one afternoon was given to a paper on all the minor languages of Europe.

It has been in this generous spirit of sympathy and co-operation that the Celtic Congress has always met, and on the whole it has been extraordinarily successful, for the reason that among its members love of their own countries and institutions has led to respect and toleration if not admiration for those of other people. The Celtic fire instead of becoming a destructive flame has thus become an enlightenment and has brought genial warmth for mind and spirit.

In our own Old Cornwall Movement and in the Cornish Gorsedd, set going for us by the Arch-Druid Pedrog[10] and a Welsh deputation in 1928, we have had a similar experience. Cornish people have often been said to prefer the individualistic outlook to the co-operative, and Cornish towns to prefer to look on one another as rivals rather than friends. The history, geography and geology of Cornwall have separated its people into groups with different ways of life and speech, yet in "Old Cornwall" we find a common love of country to form a bond that unites us all, and especially in the Gorsedd we have widened that bond to include the bards of Wales and Brittany, with those who remember, as Gaulish bards, the Celtic past of France, and finally not only all Celts, but those of all nations, small or great, European or otherwise, who value freedom and peace as we do ourselves.

As Cornish bards we certainly have our useful place in any order of things that is based on a desire for worldwide peace and goodwill. The Gorsedd ideal of perfection as combining Power, Wisdom and Love will never become old-fashioned. In the Gorsedd motto *An Gwyr erbyn an Bys*, "The Truth against the World", too, we have something that should help us to shed any of our accepted ideas that are no longer useful and may stand in the way of those that are more universally true.

Some may have wondered, seeing how many of the things I have mentioned are of the past, or now swept away by the war, whether such talk is of any present value. If so, I will ask them to go back to my first date, 1807, and think what had happened so shortly before in Brittany, during the fury of the French Revolution. [Nothing worse can have happened there now, bad as we know it is, and nothing much worse could happen even if Brittany becomes again a battleground.][11] Yet out of all that destruction came a rejuvenated Brittany, and final-ly, as you see, a movement that included all Celtic peoples. One thing, too, is shown as found among them all, and that is the capacity to blow on patiently until below dead ashes a kindling spark is reached again. Another thing that has shown itself among all the leaders of this Celtic Movement to a greater or lesser degree is the mind that never grows old, cynical and disillusioned. The great Chinese philosophers of thousands of years ago knew the value of this, when they argued that the greatest essential of the noblest mind was that it must be child-like, which is not at all the same as being childish.

Editors' notes

1. Jean-François Le Gonidec (1775–1838), a Breton linguist who, in the 1830s, created a modern phonetic system for the language.
2. Revd William Collings Lukis (1817–1894), a Guernsey-born antiquarian who carried out research in Cornwall (with W.C. Borlase), Wiltshire and Yorkshire, particularly into megalithic tombs.
3. William O'Brien (1852–1928) was one of the first Irish politicians to make a serious case for Pan Celticism.
4. Thomas Henry Thomas (1839–1915), an artist and naturalist who was closely associated with all aspects of Welsh culture.
5. Henry Jenner (1848–1934), author of *A Handbook of the Cornish Language* (1904) and first Grand Bard of Gorseth Kernow.
6. François Jaffrenou (1879–1956), the Breton journalist, scholar and poet, was an influential member of the Breton nationalist movement, and founder of the Breton Gorsedd.
7. John Hobson Matthews (1858–1914), a Croydon-born solicitor, historian and archivist who learnt both Cornish and Welsh and contributed to many aspects of life in South Wales. He was barded in 1899.
8. Rev Rowland Williams (1823–1905), the Angelsey-born poet and Nonconformist minister, was Archdruid between 1895 and 1905.
9. Paul Barbier (–1921), a teacher and lecturer who devoted himself to forging closer links between Wales and Brittany.
10. Rev John Owen Williams (1853–1932), the Welsh poet and editor who worked as a gardener and salesman in Liverpool before becoming a Congregationalist preacher. He was Archdruid between 1928 and 1932.
11. A note in Nance's hand, presumably added later, reads: This was proved too sanguine.

The manuscript of this lecture may be found in the Nance Collection at the RIC, in an envelope marked 'The Symbolism of the Gorsedd'. It is reproduced with the permission of The Royal Institution of Cornwall, Courtney Library.

Splinters of a great wreck: *Mordon* and some relics of Cornish folklore and dialect

Donald R. Rawe

As a polymath interested in all aspects of Cornwall, especially linguistic and historical, Robert Morton Nance was from an early age fascinated by folklore. His sister, Mrs Christine Morton Raymont, recounts in her booklet *The Early Life of Robert Morton Nance* how he would devise plays for her and her two older brothers, using their breakfast table as a stage, enacting some of the old folk tales from Robert Hunt's *Popular Romances of the West of England* and other books. 'When I first saw the Nancledra Plays,' she continues, 'I remembered the plays my brother invented ... No words were written, but the plot was given to us, and we made up the words as it went along. Most impassioned speeches were made, and exciting events took place ... Also I remembered how he and I would go into the Dingle – now a part of the park – at Penarth and play at wonderful fairy stories with tiny wooden farthing dolls, dressed as witches and fairies.'

Later in life, married and settled at Nancledra, Nance wrote and acted in his own dramatic versions of some of these legends: 'Duffy', 'The Kite in the Castle' and 'Sally's Shiners', which he and his wife produced, other actors being such well-known figures in the Cornish revival as A.K. Hamilton Jenkin and Kathleen Frazier. In this age of deteriorating Cornish dialect, when what passes for 'dialect' is often no more than slipshod and misspelled English, it may be salutary to quote some of the rich speech then heard in West Penwith. The following is an extract from 'Duffy', where the old housekeeper Joan gives her opinion of the Squire's choice of a housemaid:

> Duffy 't would ha' ben, as like as not, ef I hadn' a-tould un of her idle waays – foriver down to mill, lookin' to see for folks sa idle as hersilf while their carn's a-grindin' – Skeeze about, daancin' of rounds, there, she will, weth the nixt; but to bait up the time 'pon the crowd for the rist to daancy – Aw! That's too hard woork for she! – Set there couzin' for hours, she will, too, harkin' to ivery ould whiddle as ivery ould wumman mind to tell her; but niver knawed yit to take and serge their flour for arra wan o' them, not she! ... And weth et all, she caen't mind a arrant – not from the hale to the heps; nor do more woork en the house nor a six-months' cheeld! – Axin' of her they was, wan time, "Can 'ee milky, Duffy?" "Can 'ee spenny?" "Can 'ee baakey, Duffy?" "Can 'ee darn the stockens?", and she niver had but the wan answer:– "Aw, mawther b'long do that" ... Squire, bless his heart, 'ud niver ha' gone paast her, not wethout I'd a-left 'n know, I wudn' have she about the plaace – not ef there wadn' anawther maaid to be got, from the Mount to Tol Pedn!

(*Note*: to skeeze – frisk; couzin' – talking, Cornish *cows*, to talk or speak; whiddle – tale, nonsense, Cornish *whethel*; to serge – to sift flour; hale – a best parlour; heps – a half-door; arrant – an errand; cheeld – a girl child.)

Amusing and effective as they evidently were, and intelligible to the old people in the audience at that time, the Cledry Plays would hardly be understood by us today. The Cornish dialect of the late 19th and early 20th centuries in which Nance took such delight, would surely mystify us. The plays themselves are set in the late 18th century and would no doubt have appeared as antiques to his audiences in St Ives and West Cornwall when performed. But they are a rich repository of dialect terms and speech, and relics also of the late Cornish language last spoken in West Penwith. As Nance suggested in his Preface, 'They are only a slight extension of the music that West-Penwith voices will put into the dialogue.'

Many of the terms that might puzzle us today are explained in the Glossary which Nance published with the plays themselves (Federation of Old Cornwall Societies, 1956). A few choice examples will serve to show what we have lost in the age of mass-communication:

THE CLEDRY PLAYS

Drolls of Old Cornwall
For Village Acting and Home Reading

BY

R. MORTON NANCE

Three of these Plays, written by its President in Cornish Dialect and based on Local Traditions, have now been printed for the Federation of Old Cornwall Societies in an attractive form which recalls a period when Plays, as well as being acted, made the favourite Light Reading.

Each thus has its Prologue and its Epilogue; each its Full-page Picture, Headpiece and Tailpiece, and in the text the Music of its several Airs, without which no Cornish Droll could be complete.

As the dialogue contains many words that are too deeply Cornish to be as familiar now as once they were, a full Glossary is also given.

Price—
In Stiff Paper Covers   –   –   8/6

A limited number will also be available Bound in Cloth, at –   –   10/6
   (Postage extra)

OLD CORNWALL MEMBERS should order through their own Society's Journal Secretary, and all others from:

BRIDGER'S BOOKSHOP (G. Linfoot, Proprietor),
112a and b, Market Jew Street, Penzance.

Prospectus for The Cledry Plays,

Balscat – abandoned mine [Cornish *bal*, mine and *scattya* (variant of *squattya*), to break].

Bannel – broom plant [Cornish *banal*]

Biskan – a finger-stall [Cornish *bys*, finger and *gon*, sheath or scabbard].

Brandis – an iron tripod for cooking on the hearth.

Breal – a mackerel [Cornish *bryel* or *brythel*].

Bucca – a hobgoblin; hence a fool, a scarecrow.

Bulorn – a snail [bullhorn].

Chack-pie – scolding.

Clunk – to swallow [Cornish *collenky*, to swallow].

Condiddle – to get anything away by stealth [cf. modern 'diddle' and 'con', confidence trick].

Conkerbell – an icicle [Cornish *cloghy?*].

Crowd, crowdy-crawn – a sheepskin-bottomed corn-measure, used as a tambourine, etc.

Cuzzle ha tayg – soft and fair [Cornish *cosel ha tek*].

Daggin' – borne down, longing, trailing.

Drilgey, drilzey – a wearisome noise.

Gambern – an animal's hock, a crooked leg [Cornish *cam*, crooked and *ber*, leg].

Garm – to scold, to cry out [Cornish *garma*, to shout out].

Gozzan – rusty earth (often tin-bearing), rust colour.

Hedheugh e genough! – "Fetch it with you!"; Cornish cry to oxen [Cornish *hedhes*, to fetch].

Mun – fish manure [Cornish *mun*, ore, mineral].

Muryans – ants [Cornish *muryon*].

Nag'os a beej – not for the world! [broken (late, debased) Cornish].

Raglen – a fisherman's apron.

Rid-leg chawk – a chough.

Scavel-an-gow – noisy talk; an ill-behaved crowd [Cornish for a scandal-party or gossip, literally 'bench of lies'].

Smeech – a burning smell; to smoke unpleasantly.

Tantarabobus – the devil.

Teen – to set alight.

To-wanst – at once.
Whitneck – a weasel (or stoat).

How many of these terms have survived into everyday speech? Very few, no doubt. Some dialect phrases may still be heard, for instance: 'They that can't schemey must louster' (schemey – to plan or think out; louster – to labour manually) and 'All of a motion, like Mulfra toad on hot showell' (… a Mulfra toad on a hot shovel).

As to the origins of the plays themselves, 'Duffy' is a Cornish version of Rumpelstiltskin, with local Penwith characters: Squire Lovel of Trove (Trewoofe); Duffy, a 'giddy giglet' who marries him and becomes Lady Duffy; Joan the housekeeper; and Terrytop, a deluding imp. 'Sally's Shiners' is a smuggling tale involving two characters from the Helston Furry or Hal an Tow – John the Bon and Sally Dover. (*Mordon* notes that a John le Bon was MP and Reeve of Helston in the 14th century, but who Sally Dover was, has not been established.) 'The Kite in the Castle' is the Faustian tale of how Ezekiel Lenine, a miserly cobbler, sold his soul to the Demon Mason in return for a fine mansion in which to end his days.

Mrs Morton Raymont tells how *Mordon* himself played Jack (John the Bon) in 'Sally's Shiners' and deceived the Searcher who was looking for the goods he had smuggled in:

> He [my father] went on to say that Robert had so disguised himself as an old Cornish woman that he had not discovered him at all, although he [Robert] had had a good deal to say through the two hours of the play.

Mordon also took the part of Squire Lovel in 'Duffy'. Both he and his wife were very much involved, the dedication to the published edition of the plays reading: 'To my wife, who as producer and prompter, stage-manager, costume-maker, critic and encourager, brought all these plays to life.' Their influence was far-reaching.

Nancledra in those days (c. 1903–1920) was a friendly little village, a small world of its own, and Nance enjoyed and extolled its many virtues in his introductory poem 'Little Cledry':

From all the world to Cledry
You're forced to trudge up-hill,
And worldlong back from Cledry
The roads are steeper still.
In Summer's sun, who trudge for fun
Will leave our lanes alone,
In Winter's wet, they're shyer yet,
And Cledry's all our own!
Hid at the bottom of a peeth,
They say you may find Truth –
Down in a bottom, too, beneath
Lies Cledry, in the looth.
Around her stand hills great and grand
To all seafarers known;
But few men know where she lies low,
And Cledry's all our own!

        ★ ★ ★

Oh! Cledry, little Cledry!
Fine folk may think you mean,
Nor ever care at Cledry
To halt their speed-machine.
With smeech and blast they scurry past,
But when their dust has blown,
D'you think we grieve that they should leave,
And Cledry's all our own? ....

(*Note*: peeth – a well; in the looth (lew) – out of the wind.)

A feature of the dialect recorded in these plays is the former Cornish pronunciation of words containing the elements gh: for example, 'broft' for brought,
'thoft' for thought etc. Even as late as the period 1890 to 1910, the rural Cornish
of West Penwith were still retaining the guttural gh sound of Elizabethan
English, which must have been abandoned across England itself centuries earlier. But then, of course, West Cornwall was, as *Mordon* himself realised, well

A performance of 'Duffy and the Devil', with Nance standing on the right, with A.K. Hamilton Jenkin on the left of the picture; seated are Miss R. Frazier and Mrs Stanley R. James
(Courtesy of Carola Nance Sculpham/Gorseth Kernow Archive)

and truly beyond England.

One of his passions was researching and recording the traditional Cornish names for birds and animals – research that produced articles in *Old Cornwall* such as 'Cornish Names of the Seal' and the two-part 'The Celtic Bird-names of Cornwall'. The latter, which was probably written in the late 1920s, was published in vol. 6, nos. 8 and 9, Spring and Autumn 1965, with notes by Dr Eugene

Graves and E.G. Retallack Hooper (*Talek*). Preserved in several ways, as Nance points out, from the Cornish Vocabulary in the Cottonian Library, the Miracle Plays, and the writings of Edward Lhuyd, John Ray and other later recorders down to more recent or 'present day' dialect speech and place-names, are the Cornish names of a choice selection of birds. Beginning with farmyard and tame birds, Nance includes *mabyar* ('hen's son'), chick; *yar Gini* and *cok Gini* ('hen of Guinea' or 'cock of Guinea'), turkey; and *kelyok goth* ('cock goose'), gander. Of the several game birds named in sources, he chooses, for example, *gavar hal* ('moor goat'), jacksnipe; *grugyar* ('heath hen'), partridge; and *kevelak*, woodcock. As one might expect, sea birds are well represented. 'Scarraweet', a name 'still used at St Ives' for the black-headed gull, Dr Graves thought likely to be of English origin. More successful is *saithor*, gannet, with Graves describing Nance's interpretation of its derivation from *saith, seth, saeth* (arrow) as 'brilliant'. Alongside *morvran* ('sea crow'), cormorant, is considered *spilgarn*, a Mousehole name that included both shag and cormorant and that may mean 'carn-hoverer', 'from their habit of spreading their wings to dry while perched on sea rocks'. *Morwennol* ('sea swallow'), meaning tern, is the name that Nance's daughter Phoebe would take on being made a bard in 1932. He thought 'cockathodon', which was recorded alongside *skithen* as a Cornish name for the Manx Shearwater, might 'with its suggestion of *ton*, a wave, in its final syllable … have something Celtic about it, although guesses [were] all that [were] possible here'. Birds of prey he singled out for examination included *bargus*, buzzard, Carn Bargus as a place-name being frequent in West Cornwall and always naming a rock that formed an ideal watching-place for a buzzard; *cryssat* or *taw kyryll* ('still hawk'), kestrel; and *berthuan*, screech owl, possibly from *perth-whuan*, 'bush owl', or *beth-whuan*, 'grave owl'. Other birds of whose Cornish names Nance explored the derivations included *pyscador* (or *pyscaderyn*) *an myghtern*, 'fisher (or 'little fisher') of the King'; *molgh los* ('grey-bird'), thrush; *molgh las* ('blue-bird'), fieldfare; *troet*, starling; and *stenor* ('tin streamer'), wagtail (or 'dishwasher'). 'It remains remarkable,' he concluded, 'that birds as familiar and conspicuous as the jay and the bullfinch have left us no recorded Cornish names. When we remember how many of the names here gathered together have survived only because Lhuyd happened to note them, or because they have been traditionally handed down as dialect words, we are bound to recognise that very many once familiar names have been lost only since Cornish ceased to be spoken.'

A perusal of Nance's *A New Cornish-English Dictionary* of 1938 gives us animal names such as *brogh* (from English brock), badger; *dowrgy* ('water dog'), otter; *conna gwyn* ('white neck'), stoat and weasel; *morhogh* ('sea pig'), porpoise; *eskelly greghyn* ('skin-wings'), bat; and various eels: *sylly*, conger, *sylly dowr er*, fresh water eel, and *lavyn*, sand eel. Some of the plant names he recorded are *scaw cough* ('scarlet elder'), *morel*, deadly nightshade; *penduen* ('black head'), bulrush; *ygor Dew* ('God's Ope'), field daisy; *spernen wyn* (whitethorn), hawthorn; *spernen dhu*, blackthorn; *losow mogh* ('pigs' plants'), hogweed or cow parsnip; *ughelvar* ('high bunch'), mistletoe; and *madere bras* (cognate with Breton *'madre'*), ragwort.

Nance's folklore interests naturally led him to the study and performance in Cornwall of the old Christmas plays, which were then dying out. These popular, knockabout entertainments based on the legends of the Crusades were played across Britain, and usually involved Father Christmas, St George the Christian Knight (adopted as Patron Saint of England by Edward III), the Saracen or Turkish Knight, the King of Egypt and his daughter Princess Sabra, a Dragon and a comic Doctor. In the St Ives version, Father Christmas (certainly not St Nicholas), a forbidding figure with a huge club, would begin the proceedings thus:

> Here come I, old Father Christmas,
> Welcome or welcome not:
> I hope old Father Christmas
> Will never be forgot.

The Padstow and other versions continue as follows:

> Room, room, brave gallants, Room!
> No money will I pay:
> Step in, St George the bold,
> For I've swept the room away!

Then enters St George, who rescues the fair Princess from the clutches of the Turkish Knight by running him through with his sword; Father Christmas calls for a doctor, who revives the Saracen with a wonderful concoction called Elecampane, saying: 'If there's seven devils in him, I'll drive 'em out again'. These plays varied very little from place to place. Indeed, there was a very similar version to that recorded by Nance enacted in Padstow until about 1880, when it appears to have been supplanted by the 'Nigger Minstrels' on 'Darkie Day' (the subject of considerable controversy recently). But one particular speech in the St Ives version – that of the Doctor, beginning 'I've travelled far that Light to gain' and ending 'Till Hell's Mouth yawned, and I, upon its brink' – appears to be an invention of Nance himself, recalling King Solomon's gifts of well-known Cornish landmarks to his courtiers in the *Ordinalia* play *Origo Mundi*.

Nance also noted the St Keverne Guise Dance Play, recalled imperfectly by Mr William Mitchell in the mid 1850s. Here St George had become 'King George', a change which probably went back to the late 18th century when George III had been on the throne for many years. One might note here that in the Padstow May Song St George was formerly 'King George', again no doubt recalling that same period in history. As Nance observes, there is some confusion in the Doctor's part in the St Keverne version. Usually, being asked, "What can you cure?" he would reply, "If there are *nineteen* devils in, I can drive *twenty* out," before showing the little bottle, "in the *waistband* of my breeches," and curing the slain man. Here, on being asked by Father Christmas what he can cure, the Doctor replies:

> The hesick, pesick, pox and gout,
> If there are ninety-nine devils in,
> I can drive them out.

Another character is Little Man Jack, who carries his 'wife' – a wooden effigy – on his back. Nance notes that he has apparently lost the family of wooden dolls that should have accompanied him.

Another of Nance's researches took him to Mousehole where Tom Bawcock's Eve was – and still is – celebrated on the night before Christmas Eve:

> A merry plaace, you may believe,
> Was Mouzel 'pon Tom Bawcock's Eve.
> To be there then who wudn' wesh
> To sup o' sibm [seven] soorts o' fesh.

Tom Bawcock was said to be defying custom in fishing on that night, which, according to Nance, was already a feast. As a consequence, he caught nothing but 'cuttifers' – the Mousehole dialect word for dogfish. In the view of Nance, who had it from one J. George of Mousehole, this term derives from the French *les quatres fers d'un chien*. *Mordon* comments:

> The "irons" of the dog are I suppose, shoes, like the *fers* of a horse, for which it has "no more use than a toad for side-pockets," and for which a *chien de mer* would have still less, but cuttifer can hardly be actually connected with quatre fers. "Cultifer" is a possible name for a "picky dog," meaning "knife-bearer." The nearest Cornish to "cuttifer" seems to be *cot e ver*, "short-shanked"; or "short-spiked," possibly, for *ber* has both meanings.

As Nance himself concedes, though, there is too wide a choice for any of these meanings to be accepted as the true one. He speculates that Tom Bawcock himself was a substitution for a local fishermen's saint, citing various other ports where such saints were honoured about that time of year. As for the seven sorts of fish, he concludes that 'this prodigality was probably held to ensure a bountiful supply of fish of all kinds during the coming year'.

Even more speculative, perhaps, is his view of the pisky-led child. Commenting on Thomas Tonkin's 1727 account of one Agnes Martin, aged seven or eight, who disappeared for a time and then came home again, protesting that she had been carried away by the small people, Nance thought Tonkin's explanation – that her tale was put into her head by gypsies – 'quite unnecessary when one knows that it was generally believed at the time that young girls might be taken away by the Small People to look after their children'. According to Nance, the story of Anne Jefferies of St Teath, who had been immured by Justice Tregeagle and, denied food, claimed to have been fed by the fairies for forty days, was known throughout Cornwall. Like Agnes, Anne was supposedly granted healing powers by the small people.

Probably the most thorough topic of Nance's investigations is the subject of a long letter he wrote in 1949 to E. M. Cunnack of Helston, who was gathering material for his book on the Helston Furry Dance and celebrations. What Helston people thought of Nance's historical research and his conclusions can only be guessed, but a good many of his ideas were incorporated by Cunnack in his *The Helston Furry Dance* (1951).

The festivities, Nance saw, fell into two distinct sections: the early morning Hal an Tow when the celebrants go out into the 'greenwood' to gather leaves and branches to welcome the coming of summer, then return to the town to enact the conflict between St George and the Dragon; and the Dance or 'faddy' itself, which goes around the town led by the band, into and through houses and gardens. Nance saw that the English St George had supplanted St Michael (Patron Saint of Helston and, under the Normans, of all Cornwall) in the Hal an Tow. 'Strange indeed that there is no mention in the Hal an Tow of St Michael, whose feast was being kept and [who was] a renowned dragon slayer long before St George was ever heard of,' he wrote. 'The full explanation is of course that the Hal an Tow was originally not a Furry Day but a May Song at the same time as at Padstow, and more or less like many others such sung all over England; though it is only in Cornwall, [where] when it was first introduced St George would have been to the majority a strange saint, and English a foreign language, that it has happened to survive.'

What does this mean? Nance noted that Nicholas Boson reported (c. 1660) that 'in Newlyn the Maypole was set up by men singing 'Haule and Taw' and 'Jolly Rumbelow''. Haul and Taw (Hal an Tow) seem to be derived from a Dutch chant sung whilst handling a rope, to moor a ship or bring up an anchor; and 'Jolly Rumbelow' means to stir actively. Nance compares the Helston chant:

Where are the Spaniards, that made such a boast O?
They shall eat the grey goose feather, and we shall eat the roast O!

to the Padstow version formerly sung on May Day:

Where are the French dogs that make such a boast O?

They shall eat the grey goose feather, and we will eat the roast O!

and concludes that these chants originated in Elizabethan times, after the Armada had been defeated, although Padstow changed 'Spaniards' to 'French Dogs' after the Napoleonic Wars.

In the past the Hal an Tow has been an over-lively and sometimes objectionable affair. Nance quotes a certain 'Durgan' who, in a letter to the *Gentleman's Magazine* of 1790, wrote: 'The Hal an Tow has lost its dance and become mixed up with the electing of a mock mayor, known as the Mayor of St John's [an outlying part of Helston on the River Cober].' This mayor 'formerly had a rowdy procession of his own, and no doubt ended his brief day of glory by being made gloriously drunk and finally pushed from his state wheelbarrow into the river'. Nance insists that the title of Flora Day, which goes back to the 18th century, is not a survival of the Roman festival Floralia. Nor was the Furry (Cornish *fer*, feast, from Latin *feria*) confined to Helston. He notes that in 1700 Edward Lhuyd recorded of Illogan, 'Their feast or Furry Day is the first Sunday before or after St Luke's, October 10th.' Penryn formerly kept Furry Day on or near St Gluvias feast, May 3rd. He also notes that, according to Richard Polwhele, the Lizard held its Furry on May 1st, although in his *A Tour through the Whole Island of Great Britain* (1724–27), Defoe puts Landewednack Feast in June.

The dance itself was known as the 'faddy', and was thought by Polwhele to be a Cornish version of the Irish *Rinnce Fada*, a processional Morris long dance. Nance speculates that it may have been brought from Ireland in Elizabethan times. He goes on to quote 'Durgan':

> In my day the gentility went to some farmhouse in the afternoon, there to drink tea and eat syllabubs, etc., and returned in a Morris dance to the town, where they formed a "faddy" and danced through the streets till dark; this distinguished the May Morris from the Furry Dance.

Nance records that by 1860 the whole affair had lapsed altogether, but that the Helston Old Cornwall Society had revived it in 1930, without its drunken tradition. This certainly accords with Wilkie Collins' report, in *Rambles Beyond Railways* (1851), that the whole of Flora Day [*sic*] was a desperate spectacle.

Comparing the Helston proceedings to the Padstow May Day celebrations, Nance remarks that the Padstow May Song had a similar slowed-down portion. 'This is the only part now remembered there at all,' he writes, 'although the tune as it was sung a hundred years ago [c. 1840] is fortunately preserved in print with some verses of the words. The fact that these May Morris dance tunes were sung usually by dancers in a drunken condition has probably much to do with the imperfect transmission of them to posterity, the nimble steps of the dance itself being the first part to disappear in each place.'

The present-day dance tune, Nance remarks, is quite distinct from the Hal an Tow or Morris tune. There are no words that properly belong to it, though some unofficial ones are sometimes used:

> John the Bon was marching on
> When he met Sally Dover.
> He kissed her once, he kissed her twice
> And kissed her three times over.

> My young man said to me, "Can you dance the Flora?"
> "Yes I can, with a nice young man,
> All the way to Trora."

During the late 19th and early 20th centuries the Hal an Tow began at 6 a.m., using a regular route out of the town to gather the may (actually hawthorn in bloom) and bring the greenwood, usually sycamore, to decorate the town – something that is still done at Padstow. On the way back they called at the old Grammar School to beg a holiday for 'the Latin boys', and then at the inn from where they had started, for breakfast. Nurses from the Cottage Hospital took part in 1946. 'Nowadays [1949],' Nance noted, 'this is replaced by the children's dance around the town.'

He lists the hierarchy of the various dances, the chief dance being appropri-ated by the gentry and principal inhabitants and visitors. The beadles with their wands of office escorted the band which led the procession through the streets and in and out of houses and gardens, thus bringing a blessing upon each property, something welcomed everywhere. Nance compares this with the

'Right of entry' accorded to the Hobby Horse at Minehead.

In the past, the gentry's midday dance would be followed by one for the tradesmen of the town, their families and their friends. During the evening, separate balls were held at the Angel Hotel and at the Star (this was an innovation in 'Durgan's' time). Nance comments that the gentry's main dance (in formal dress) now upholds standards and prevents the event from deteriorating:

> If we were more in touch with the faith of our primitive sun-worshipping ancestors we should better be able to feel like them that such May games were really able by some sympathetic magic to help Nature to perform her annual miracles. Still the custom elsewhere to leap into the air, the highest leaf reached fixing the limit to which the corn will grow, helps us to realise that the strenuous activities of Furry Day had their beginning not as idle sports but as a most important fertility ritual, and that Helstonians in taking it as a duty to themselves and their town to display as much agility about it as possible, are only carrying on a tradition almost as old as the human race.

It appears that both Helston and Padstow, both of whose saints were noted dragon vanquishers, have lost their local folklore commemorations as such, through the imposition of the English St George, also a dragon slayer. Nance ends his survey of Helston and the Furry with a recital of the legend of the town's wonderful escape from a fiery dragon which threatened it. The green boughs are deemed to recall the inhabitants' enforced sojourn in the woods outside the town, a sojourn that lasted until the monster had been vanquished by St Michael. In commemoration of this mythical event, the Angel Hotel got its name, and the Hell's Stone with which the archangel quelled the dragon was formerly to be seen in the hotel yard. Intact in 1783, it has since been broken up, part of it being built into the wall of the inn. Evidently, in that unwittingly vandalizing age, it met with the same fate as the great Tolmen in Constantine parish, broken up for building stone.

Sources
R. Morton Nance (1951), *The Cledry Plays*, Marazion/Penzance: Federation of Old Cornwall Societies.

Nance Collection, Courtney Library, Royal Institution of Cornwall, Truro.
Old Cornwall (1925 –), St Ives: Federation of Old Cornwall Societies.
Mrs C. Morton Raymont (1962), *The Early Life of R. Morton Nance*, [Leedstown]: New Cornwall.

Mordon and the West Cornwall Footpath Preservation Society

Hugh Miners

One of the least chronicled of *Mordon*'s activities is his connection with, and work for, the West Cornwall Footpath Preservation Society. Initiated in October 1953 by Mrs Winifred White of Crowlas (later *Cares Hensy*, 'Lover of Ancient Ways'), the minutes record that at the Society's first public meeting, at Penzance on 3 December 1953, the Vice Chairman of the County Highways Committee was supported by, amongst others, 'Mr R. Morton Nance, Grand Bard of the Cornish Gorsedd'.

He was not then elected either as an officer or Committee member, but his name next appears in the minutes of a General Meeting held on the 28th of the following month when it was recorded that 'in the absence of the President and Chairman, it was resolved to ask Mr Morton Nance to take the Chair'. He was simultaneously elected 'as a member of the Committee' to enable him to preside at the Meeting 'since he had been keenly interested in the Society since its inception'.

At that meeting he reported several diversions of footpaths in the St Ives area, including one which – unsurprisingly – seems to have been particularly near to his heart, namely 'the obliteration of a path from Towednack Church past a culverhouse'. (It may also be of interest that, at the same meeting, 'Mr E.G. Hooper of Camborne was cordially welcomed', having previously corresponded with the Secretary 'for advice as to how to start a branch there'.)

Mordon appears to have taken little active part in the work of the Committee, attending only one meeting during the next year and not sending apologies for absence from the others. Nonetheless, when the President's death was announced at the AGM of November 1955, *Mordon* was present and was nominated, and duly elected, as the new President, a post he held until his death in 1959.

Again, he appears to have played only a small part in the Society's activities, adopting a rather magisterial role, perhaps, as President, although his term of office coincided with probably the most acrimonious dispute over blocked and diverted pathways ever experienced by the Society before or since. According to the minutes, his single specific intervention showed that, in 1956, he was still concerned about a footpath past the culverhouse near St Ives, although 'the Society did not press' an appeal to St Ives Council. He was not deterred, however, but seems to have tried another tack because, at a meeting in March 1957, it was reported that the St Ives Old Cornwall Society had appealed to the Borough Council who had agreed to provide a special access to the site. *Mordon* had got his way! (It will be recalled that one of the aims of the Old Cornwall movement – very much *Mordon*'s brainchild – was the preservation of the integrity of public rights of way).

It was, almost certainly, his last act to improve the network of footpaths in West Cornwall for, at the meeting of 18 March 1959, it was reported that he was seriously ill. This was followed in July by the announcement of his death.

'[Another] well-known and revered man had passed away (on 27 May) whom our Society had the honour to have had as its President since 1955 ... For generations to come he would be revered for his monumental work on the Cornish language and he had been in closest sympathy with our footpath work and had presided with great dignity and effect at our Annual Meetings...' The Meeting stood in his memory and resolved 'to send £1. 1. 0. to the......... in accordance with the wishes of the relatives'. Intriguingly, there is a gap as shown above, so that we shall probably never know just how the Society did mark his death.

Records of those who actually walked the paths were not kept, so it is not possible to say whether *Mordon* ever joined in these or not.

As has already been noted, he appears to have adopted a rather benevolent, magisterial air over the Society's proceedings and those few of us still alive who had met *Mordon* personally will probably recognise this stance!

Worshipping 'at the shrine of St Jal': Robert Morton Nance, artist, ship modeller and maritime researcher

Derek R. Williams

Introduction: The Nance Memorial

In April 1904, E. E. Speight and R. H. Walpole published at Teignmouth, in a limited edition of 300 copies, a reprint of Richard Jobson's *The Golden Trade or A Discovery of the River Gambra, and the golden trade of the Aethiopians* (1623). The illustrations – woodcuts in the form of a magnificent frontispiece and decorated initial letters and borders based on West African designs – were the work of 31-year-old Robert Morton Nance. This was, to my knowledge, his first published work since contributing to Arthur Quiller-Couch's *The Cornish Magazine* five or six years earlier. As he would indicate in a letter a month later, Nance was still feeling his way as a professional artist, and book illustration was just one avenue that he was exploring. The letter in question was written on 5 May to George W. Nance of Floyd County, Indiana, who, making extensive use of correspondence with the various Nance 'clans', compiled *The Nance Memorial*, which was published that same year.[1] In a preamble to the letter, George Nance describes his 'old country cousin' as 'a young man who is gaining some notoriety as an artist' but was too modest to speak much of himself and would not consent to his father speaking for him. After several attempts, though, George Nance managed to get Robert's consent to use the letter as 'Exhibit "K": Art in the family' in his history of the Nance family. The letter reads as follows:

Dear Sir:

My father has asked me to write out a few facts concerning my work, which you apparently think would come into the scope of your family history.

I hope I am only yet at the outset of my professional career, and there seems very little to say. I have had the usual experience among artists of feeling my way to the type of work that is most congenial, and after a few years of varied work, book illustrations, figure painting and various kinds of decorative work, I seem to have found in painting subjects taken from the old romantic days of seafaring, I had an outlet for the slowly accumulating knowledge of old shipping that I had, and also for a love of decorating lines and colours. I have since then devoted myself almost entirely to that class of work, exhibiting it mostly in London, though I was represented at the Turin Exhibition by a screen, "The Three Ships of Columbus" (which you may be interested to know was sold to an American), and I am also showing a screen at St Louis, in the English Applied Art Section, the subject being "Blake and Van Tromp."

Yours very truly

R. Morton Nance

In addition to substantiating the claim of his sister Christine and others that young Robert was a very modest, unassuming man, the letter indicates that the early twentieth century was a very busy time for the young artist. I propose in this chapter to examine firstly, the origins of the 'varied work' that he was undertaking from about 1890 to 1910, during what is generally acknowledged to be his most consistent period as an artist,[2] and to look in some detail at the work itself and the legacy of its creator; and secondly, the growing pull of nautical research and ship modelling, which would lead to his being viewed as one of the fathers of modern maritime research.

The View from Hawthorn House

To explain Nance's artistic skills, we need look no further than his sister Christine who, in *The Early Life of Robert Morton Nance*, explored the close and loving family background that fostered them.[3] Although he was born in South Wales, he spent a great deal of his boyhood in St Ives, learning about the sea and sailing ships from his maternal grandfather, Capt Robert Morton. Given, too, that from the houses occupied by the family in Cardiff and then Penarth, he could constantly see sailing and steam ships in the Bristol Channel, and that Penarth Docks was a favourite destination on Sunday afternoons, it is not surprising that his early drawings were largely of maritime subjects.[4] The sea and the ships that plied it were an early and abiding interest. Christine Raymont recalled the shabby and ink-stained breakfast room table at Hawthorn House at which she and her three brothers would draw and paint, in particular some attractive magic lantern slides produced by Robert.[5] She regarded his failure to pass the arithmetic section of the Junior Oxford and Cambridge Examination when he was about thirteen as one of the chief reasons that he took seriously to drawing, although a contributory factor was the time that he was able to devote to it when convalescing from scarlet fever. It was after either this or another spell of illness that he paid an extended visit to 4, The Terrace, St Ives where he spent most of his time in the company of Capt Morton.[6] Interestingly, among the many items of Nanceana held by St Ives Museum is 'Robert Morton's Book', a kind of commonplace book begun on 8 December 1850 containing writings on a nautical theme, plans, drawings and poems. I don't think that it is too fanciful to suggest that Robert may well have looked through this book with his grandfather, and that it may well have inspired him and his brothers and sister to produce their own magazines. Certainly the issues or part-issues of 'The Penarth Magazine' that have survived[7] are beautifully produced and obviously involved nearly the whole family. Robert would invariably do the illustrations and cover designs, with Ernest, the eldest, contributing a translation of 'a story from the German', Christine a story, their mother and father a poem and a painting of a flower respectively, and Alwyn doing the binding.[8] What is probably the earliest, though undated, surviving example is entitled 'The Penarth Arms' and consists of handwritten pages numbered from 1 to 31 (six of which are blank) containing such pieces as 'Mr Mackintoshes Christmas Ghost' and 'A familiar cry, Nonsense story', and news items on the weather, school and holiday fun. Between the card covers of 'The Penarth Magazine Christmas 1885' are 28 pages of stories, poems and drawings edited by A.M. Nance. Of 'The Penarth Magazine Christmas 1890', produced when Robert was 17, only the card covers, with holly and ivy decoration presumably by him, survive.

It is clear that Robert's output as a boy and young man was heavily influenced by his reading and by the works of the artists that he had access to at home. His sister cites *Pan-Pipes*, a book of old songs by Théophile Marzials, with illustrations by Walter Crane, as a particular favourite. Influenced by Edward Burne-Jones and the pre-Raphaelites and associated with William Morris, Crane (1845–1915) was at the forefront of the Arts and Crafts movement. His own considerable influence on young Nance can be seen when we compare, for example, his 'The Horses of Neptune' (1892) or 'Poppy Time' (1893) with the latter's screen paintings. Similarly, Nance's cartoon-like work for *The Cornish Magazine* is stylistically not unlike Crane's illustrations for children's books. In the early 1900s Nance would make Crane's acquaintance at an Art and Crafts Exhibition. Nance himself would later underline the importance to him of copies of the *Art Journal* and *Graphics* which 'gave me so much as a child'.[9] Another factor in the shaping of his tastes was undoubtedly his mother, who had decided views on clothes and house furnishings, having in her reading come under the influence of William Morris, one of whose designs may well have graced a dado in the family's breakfast room.[10]

At some stage the nursery at Hawthorn House, Kymin Terrace, Penarth, the large, semi-detached house to which the family moved in 1878, became a studio for Robert. And when it became clear that her youngest son's artistic leanings were likely to pay dividends professionally, Jeannie Nance wrote to the artist Hubert Herkomer about the possibility of him attending his art school in Bushey. In the meantime, on leaving school, Robert went to the Cardiff Art School and developed 'an early discipline in pencil drawing which paid dividends in Bushey where Herkomer was a great advocate of pencil drawing as an art form'.[11] Some of his earliest surviving work was done in St Ives in about 1892 when he sketched the old streets, the harbour and some of the fishermen and well-known characters.[12] Six of those fine sketches were later reproduced in *The Studio* as 'Leaves from the sketch-book of R. Morton Nance'.[13]

An aspirant to a niche in the temple of artistic fame: the Bushey years

Bavarian-born Hubert von Herkomer, RA settled in Bushey in 1873 and ten years later opened what he described as "an art school after my own heart",[14] a school that had for its object 'to promote the education of a limited number of persons of both sexes in painting, drawing and the kindred Arts'.[15] It became a large and influential establishment, with more than a hundred students at any given time, from countries as far flung as Sweden, South Africa, America and Australia. Although the school was incorporated in 1886, Herkomer served as its sole principal until 1904 when he closed it, partly because it was denied a Royal Charter, but more probably because its debts had become a drain on his personal finances.[16] Exactly a year before young Robert Morton Nance was to leave Cardiff for what was still a Hertfordshire village, a writer in the *Art Journal* highlighted what Herkomer himself considered one of the school's unique assets – its semi-rural situation, with 'all the attraction of nature for the students after school hours':[17]

> Bushey itself, where the students are billeted, is just outside – and only just outside – the far-reaching suburbs of London. "Town" stretches a long way out, with fringes of coal yards and regions of gas, on the side of Willesden Junction. That great *rendezvous* of railways, however, once passed, things assume a more frankly rural aspect; and but for the inevitable London-brick group of houses that spring up close to all stations for many and many a mile farther out than this, but, also for the high-level arches from which the trains dominate the village, Bushey might be anywhere in the country, north or south – anywhere in the fresh monotony of English fields and hills. It has the pure light, the air tempered with plenty of atmosphere and no smoke that is the distinctive air of rural England, and is unlike the air of the town or the air of the Continent. And the 13 miles of rail that divide the village from London are brief enough for the spending of the students' Saturday holiday among the pictures in town. Five days' work in a village workshop, and a sixth day in the National Gallery, should make good painters, and what is better, men and women of strong and equal life.[18]

Used as we are to photographs of *Mordon* in his Bardic robes and to the image of him as a teetotal, non-smoking vegetarian who advocated the simple life, it comes as something of a shock to learn that he was something of a dandy as a young man and cut quite a dash when he arrived at Bushey in October 1893. '[H]e was so dark and handsome in a romantic style,' recorded his sister, 'and his dress was so unusual in those days, when most young men were conventionally dressed in suits with trousers and bowler hats. His dark hair, too, was worn longer than was customary.'[19] Although Herkomer's school was progressive by then-current English standards, its head was autocratic by nature[20] and one wonders what initially he made of the young man who would come to be considered the best draughtsman of his time at Bushey.

The profile of Herkomer's school was very high in the late 1880s and throughout the 1890s, and there are numerous contemporary accounts in such journals as *The Studio* and *Art Journal* of both the educational methods and the domestic regime that were in operation there. Herkomer's mission was to coax out each student's individuality, which meant, paradoxically, 'the *suppression* of the art student'. He endeavoured 'to make them feel what I aim at, but never to encourage them to copy the results of my aims'.[21] To be considered for admission, a student needed to be 'no mere beginner still at the pothook-and-hanger stage of his education', but someone who fully intended to make art his profession.[22] Applicants were required to send at least three studies in colour or black and white (charcoal on white paper) either of the human figure (nude) or of the head from life.[23] In Herkomer's own words, 'a fairly drawn head from the life in charcoal', which he alone would judge, was usually sufficient to admit a student to the preliminary class. In 1889 the number at the school was limited to seventy, of whom this preliminary class took at least twenty-five on average. The school fees were fixed as low as possible, six guineas for a three-month term. 'My best student,' continued Herkomer, 'presides over this class, where they paint from the living head, or draw from the cast in a free and bold way, treating the plaster figure as if it were a living thing. Twice in the term (of three months) the students of the preliminary class draw from the nude figure, and these drawings are submitted to me without a name attached. I then mark the drawings that have passed students into the life class. The average is three drawings out of twenty. Sometimes none are good enough. This method works admirably, for it prevents a really able student from wasting time in that class, and at the same time gives the first turn of the screw in the system of suppression, as many fail, even after endless trials, to pass into the life class. To this latter I alone attend, going at no fixed time, but always seeing every study that is painted each week. I also give much thought to the students when I am not at the school, which enables me better to judge results, and to fathom the *meaning* of the work when I visit the class.'[24]

Unless he or she was specifically excused, daily attendance was expected of the student in the life class, who during the winter months (October to March) painted from 9.30 to 3 o'clock and returned to his or her studies between 7 and 9 o'clock in the evening to draw. In the summer, the working hours were from 8 till 4, an arrangement that left the students free to paint out of doors from 4 until dusk. Herkomer's students certainly worked 'in no half-hearted manner', as one critic so tellingly put it![25] 'The great advantage of this combination,' continued the school's head, 'is that it prevents the transition from the *student* to the *painter of subjects* being really felt. These outdoor studies and subjects are always shown me at all stages, but privately in my studio, where students can always see me by appointment.'[26] Students were required to live in Bushey, or within easy distance of the school, the majority lodging with villagers.[27]

The Nance family donated a large collection of Robert Morton Nance's pencil drawings to the Bushey Museum Trust towards the end of the twentieth century. Relating particularly to his years in Bushey and immediately after, they include sketches of Bushey and Watford, portraits of local people, still lifes and, more interestingly perhaps, sketches such as 'Penarth, Aug 95', 'From windows at Hawthorn House, Kymin Terrace, July 7th 95', 'Fishing Boats in St Ives, Cornwall' and 'St Columb from the Churchyard Path'. To the Special Winter Number of *The Studio*, 1896–1897, Nance himself contributed 'Bushey Models', consisting of five lead-pencil drawings, together with an introductory text that constitutes a first-hand account of some aspects of student life at Herkomer's school. It is reproduced in full at the end of this chapter.

Although the students worked very hard, they played hard, too, having the use of a tennis court attached to the school and, in the winter, organising impromptu dances in their studios.[28] Herkomer also wrote and composed music for the 'pictorial-music-plays' he performed at his private theatre, with up to 1,500 friends being invited to attend the annual or biennial drama festivals.[29]

Such private theatricals, though on nothing like such a grand scale, would later become an important ingredient of Nance's early Cornish years. Equally impressive as far as the young art student was concerned, were the bardic robes and regalia that Herkomer designed for Rowland Williams (*Hwfa Môn*), who was elected Archdruid of the Welsh Gorsedd in 1895. Nance told the writer Maxwell Fraser how he watched Sir Hubert copy the breastplate from the Bronze Age gold 'cape' which had been found at Mold, North Wales in 1831. 'I ... well remember,' he recalled elsewhere, 'going with his other Bushey pupils to see the oak-leaf crown that had just been made under his directions for the Archdruid. The real oak leaves that served as model for the metal ones, were still in the workshop, I remember.'[30]

Herkomer's system of treating each student as an individual necessarily precluded any idea of the students competing for prizes. Furthermore, his insistence that their progress was his business alone meant that no visitor was permitted to enter the rooms when they were at work and that, initially at least, he regarded 'work done during this process of development' as 'quite unfit to show to the public, however full of meaning it may be to the student's career'.[31] However, there does appear to have been an exhibition of students' work at the Fine Art Society in New Bond Street in 1892 when, interestingly enough, one of the paintings on display was one familiar to many Cornish people – W.H.G. Titcomb's 'Primitive Methodists'.[32] This apparent change of heart may well explain the presence of three of Nance's paintings – 'Portrait of a Woman', 'Old Bowers' and 'Study of a Rustic' – at the Royal Academy Summer Exhibition of 1895.[33] It would also help explain his movements during that year and the following one.

In 1892 two young ladies who would both become Mrs R. Morton Nance had entered the rarified, if progressive, world of the Herkomer Art School. Beatrice E. Michell became a student at the beginning of the year and Annie Maud Cawker that October.[34] Nance became very friendly with Beatrice soon after enrolling the following October and the two were married on 3 December, 1895, living at 5, Carlton Cottages, Bushey until the summer vacation of 1896, thus enabling Robert to complete his three-year course.[35]

St Ives drawing from 'Leaves from the sketch-book of R. Morton Nance',
The Studio, *1898*

SHIPS – Artist (decorative painting of antique shipping a speciality…)
By 1905, when a small advert beginning with these words appeared in *The Studio*, Robert Morton Nance had already chosen the artistic path that he wished to follow. Back at Bushey, a feature of the close, if rigorous, control that Hubert von Herkomer exerted over all his students was his ability to put commissions in the way of successful ones, thus starting them on the road to earning their own livelihood. Although an early marriage may not have been what he would have wished for a star pupil, he apparently suggested that the newlyweds should be 'the founders of a new school of Painting',[36] and whether in Penarth, Cardiff or Newton Nottage, near Porthcawl, to which they probably moved shortly after the birth of their daughter Jeniver at St Ives in December 1896,[37] they seem to have occupied joint studios where they took in pupils.

The period from 1896 to 1906 is the least well-known and least explored phase of Nance's life, although paradoxically it was when he was most prolific as a commercial artist. There are tantalising glimpses in *The Early Life of R. Morton Nance* of the few years that Robert and Beatrice enjoyed together, with 'both painting continually' and Robert's work 'becoming more decorative and less realistic'.[38] At Penarth they collaborated on some panels of children playing that were used to decorate the front of the new Albert Road Board School designed by John Coates Carter, the architect with whom Robert worked. And in 1899 they both submitted entries to competitions when the Welsh National Eisteddfod was held in Cardiff. While the 19th Annual Report of the Eisteddfod Association lists Mr Morton Nance as collecting the 2nd prize of £10 for 'Oil painting of any subject' and the 2nd prize of £2 for 'Study from life', but makes no mention of any female competitors, a report of adjudications in the *Western Mail* for 19 July lists Mrs Morton Nance as taking 2nd prize for 'Oil painting of any subject' and Mr Morton Nance 2nd prize for 'Study from life'.[39] Grant Longman rightly makes the point that Nance's artistic inspiration was most closely associated with Beatrice,[40] and it is certainly the case that the focus of his work seemed to shift with her premature death in 1901. At Bushey Museum and Art Gallery is a black and white photograph of a painting entitled 'Princess and Page' that is reputedly by Nance of Beatrice and himself. Painted à la Burne-Jones, it is an idealised, pre-Raphaelite representation of a medieval scene, with Nance as the page on bended knee holding the train of his princess's robes.[41] The museum also holds a pencil sketch by Nance entitled 'Girl in a smock sitting on a wall' and dated 8 June 1894 that is thought to be his first wife. Although Beatrice's own life was short, it was artistically productive, with romantic pictures, invariably including children, something of a speciality. Examples of her work held at Bushey include two oils on canvas entitled 'Ode to Spring' (1901) and 'The Lantern Girl', and a couple of pen and ink sketches.[42]

Nature and the past were the twin leitmotifs of the nineteenth-century imagination that turned its back on the city and the modern. From its beginnings in the period 1860–1880, the Arts and Crafts movement, in which anti-modernism also ran deep, had by about 1900 become the principal progressive movement in British architecture and decorative art.[43] Indeed, its apogee coincided neatly with Nance's own flourishing as a commercial artist. Herkomer himself was, as one critic put it, 'among the first to preach by example the necessity of the reunion of arts and crafts, to proclaim that the modern limitation of the artist to a speciality, the modern disdain of the painter for the craftsman, is a symbol of feebleness, not of power'.[44] Nance took this philosophy very firmly on board throughout his life and, particularly in the closing years of the nineteenth century and the opening decade of the twentieth, worked hard as a book illustrator, a painter per se and as a producer of painted screens. He would be instrumental, too, in passing that philosophy on to his sons.

In his examination in this volume of Nance's writing in both Cornish and Cornu-English, Alan Kent underlines how important was the opportunity to contribute to Arthur Quiller-Couch's *The Cornish Magazine* in giving the young artist a chance to make his mark as an illustrator. The drawings he produced to accompany the old Cornish ditties and ballads that appear in both volumes are very stylised and cartoon-like, but fit the subject matter well. (He may well have imagined himself back at Hawthorn House helping to produce *The Penarth Magazine!*) Rather more universal are the illustrations for W.E. Henley's poem 'Home, Dearie, Home', the decidedly pre-Raphaelite scenes produced to accompany the 'old carol' 'The Seven Virgins' and the motifs that appear at the end of this and other contributions.[45] The emphasis in all these illustrations, though, is on the past, with many featuring ships and the sea in some form or other and thus foreshadowing sketches that he would include years later in the pages of *The Mariner's Mirror* and in his own *Sailing-ship Models*. It is interesting to note that among the other illustrators who helped make *The Cornish Magazine* such a splendid, albeit commercially unsuccessful, publication was none other than Walter Crane.[46]

Beatrice's death seems to have led to a narrowing of Nance's artistic horizons, with sailing ships henceforth dominating his output. His next venture as a book illustrator involved working, as we have already seen, with E.E. Speight on a reprint of *The Golden Trade*. A year later, in 1905, he teamed up with Speight yet again, co-editing *Britain's Sea Story*, which its editors believed was 'the first [book] to give a simple concise account of British ships and sea-exploits from early times to the great day on which our sovereignty of the sea was assured...'[47] In addition to providing a full-colour frontispiece, 'The Last Fight of the *Revenge*', Nance contributed fourteen more full-page illustrations, as well as sketches to accompany the editors' essay, 'The Building of the Ships'. That same year he provided illustrations and maps for an English version of *Hakluyt's Voyages* and in 1906 worked yet again with Speight, contributing paintings such as 'Frobisher's men and the Eskimo old woman' and 'Sir Thomas Roe and the Great Mogul' to *The Romance of the Merchant Venturers*, a collection of essays that dealt with 'the wonderful adventures and brave exploits of the men of Elizabeth's time'.[48] The considerable variation in the style of the dozen or so paintings shows that Nance might have made a name for himself as a book illustrator, had not his interest in ship models and, of course, his Cornish studies become all-consuming. With the exception of the numerous sketches bearing his characteristic and highly distinctive monogram that graced the pages of *The Mariner's Mirror* from its first appearance in January 1911, there was nearly a twenty-year gap before Nance's next book – his own *Sailing-ship Models* in 1924, for which he began collecting material as early as 1902, if not before. The first edition was limited to 1,750 copies; a second revised edition was issued in 1949 and Dover Publications have recently reprinted it as *Classic Sailing-ship Models in Photographs*. The following year he illustrated *Last Days of Mast and Sail* by Sir Alan Moore, with whom he had helped to found The Society for Nautical Research. In his preface, Moore paid tribute to his illustrator's 'unsurpassed knowledge of ships and boats of all ages and nations', with authorial modesty expressing the opinion that readers would 'turn with relief from the dry descriptions of my text to the lively presentments which illustrate

it'.[49] Someone else who rated Nance's artistic skills very highly was a Mr J. de
M. Jehuson (?) at the Clarendon Press who sent the book's illustrator an
advance copy a few weeks before its publication. In an accompanying letter
dated 7 April 1925, the editor wrote:

> I am never tired of admiring your beautiful drawings in the text. It is
> wonderful with what economy of line you achieve your result. I enclose
> an illustration which I have just made from an 18th Century book of
> Nautical design, very beautiful but, I think, work not so beautiful as
> yours.[50]

Clearly Nance was, in the mid 1920s, in a class of his own as a nautical artist
and ship modeller, but at the turn of the century, only three or four years after
leaving Bushey, he was clearly keen to turn his hand to whatever would ensure
an income for his wife and child. During the first decade of the twentieth century, therefore, he would exhibit when and wherever he could, although it was
with the Arts and Crafts Exhibition Society, which represented the interests of
what around 1900 was the principal progressive movement in British architecture and decorative art,[51] that he probably made the greatest impact. Although
they were not members in 1899 – Robert would join two years later and remain
on the society's books for the rest of his life – Nance and his wife exhibited that
year at the sixth exhibition, which opened at the New Gallery, Regent Street on
Monday 9 October. As 'Mrs Nance' Beatrice showed a portion of a frieze for a
nursery, entitled 'The Children's Journey to the Moon', while her husband's
presence in the North Gallery was represented by a painted corner screen entitled 'The Sea Serpent' and a second painted screen, 'The Spanish Armada'.[52]

Folding screens existed in the East before the beginning of the first millen-
nium and were a Chinese invention that was later adopted by the Japanese.
With the development of trade between the East and the West early in the seventeenth century, they became favourites as imports, appreciated for both artistic and practical purposes. Western artists introduced European motifs and
styles into this ancient Eastern art form and the fashion for screens was enjoy-
ing another of its periodic renaissances at the end of the nineteenth century,
when they were particularly favoured by both Les Nabis in Paris and by the
Arts and Crafts movement worldwide.[53] Indeed, in the nineteenth and twenti-

Nance's cover for The Romance of the Merchant Venturers *(1906)*
(Courtesy of the Morrab Library)

eth centuries major artists and designers began to see the screen as an artistic medium worthy of their most serious efforts,[54] with the result that artists such as William Morris, Edward Burne-Jones, Charles Rennie Mackintosh, Paul Klee, Pierre Bonnard and James McNeill Whistler would each produce one or more folding screens in the years between 1870 and 1910.[55]

Young Nance, then, was in rather exalted company and it is not therefore surprising that he is not mentioned in any of the books about screens that I have consulted. The demand was there, though, for by the turn of the century '[t]he desire, even demand, for folding screens had spread from its centers in London and Paris throughout western and eastern Europe, and as far as Australia. There was hardly a single middle- or upper-class home that did not have at least one of these versatile pieces of furniture ... [in what] was a virtual golden age of screen making...'[56] The three-panelled screen entitled 'The Sea Serpent' shows a boatload of sailors struggling frantically to cope with a monster whose scaly and serpentine body encircles them and threatens to suck them down into the vortex of its own making. The mother ship, its sails billowing, waits in the background. A striking feature of the screen, which is currently in private hands, is the colour – a turquoise-green that contrasts markedly with the dark sky, a colour so intense as to appear at first sight unnatural, but natural enough for someone acquainted with the sea at Porthcurno, say, or Whitesand Bay. Indeed, I agree wholeheartedly with Graham Gadd who, having researched the 1899 Arts and Crafts Exhibition, is of the opinion that 'Mr Nance never worked in quite this style again', and that 'this screen was deeply influenced by the current art ideas of that particular year'.[57] Four years later Nance again exhibited with the Arts and Crafts Exhibition Society, specifically an overmantel entitled 'Westward Ho!', based on the model of a Dutch man-of-war of c. 1730, and 'Blake and Van Tromp', a screen which *The Studio* described as 'a little turbulent in line', but which 'attracts attention by its breezy strength and buoyancy of composition'.[58]

The Society's catalogue for the 1899 exhibition does not give prices, but the catalogues for subsequent exhibitions that I have had access to – they were held every three to four years after 1890 – reveal that in 1906 painted screens entitled 'The Battle of Sluys, 1340' and 'The Revenge' were valued at £50 and £30 respectively, with a painted overmantel, 'Homeward Bound. East Indiamen,

1640', listed at £50. *The Studio*, which was for about twenty years the principal showcase for British Arts and Crafts, reproduced 'Homeward Bound' and some detail from 'The Great Sea Fight off Sluys in Flanders 1340', although it limited any comment on what it describes as 'romantic decorations' to the fact that the artist had again successfully taken the sea and the old three-decked ships as his motif.[59] 'The Revenge' was a joint-production, the hand-woven back being by Maud Carter [*sic*], surely the Annie Maud Cawker who, ten days after the Grafton Galleries exhibition closed on 17 March, would become Nance's second wife.[60] Four years later, at the Society's ninth exhibition, Nance showed 'Outward Bound', a decorative panel selling for £20, and 'The King: his ships', a 5-panelled, painted screen priced at £30.[61] Unless he submitted work for the tenth and twelfth exhibitions, there would be no more input by Nance into the Arts and Crafts Exhibition Society until 1928, when he entered a model of a Dutch Fluitschip, c.1650 that he had designed and which his son Dicon had made. This was priced at £105.[62] There are no further listings of works by Nance at the Society's exhibitions, although he continued to appear as a member in the catalogues.

On the death of his wife Beatrice in the final quarter of 1901 after a long spell of illness, Nance returned to Penarth with his little daughter Jeniver. There would have been a great deal of soul-searching, I imagine, about the course his life should take before, early in 1902, he left Wales for Paris. 'I am beginning to settle down to work again,' he wrote to his sister Christine in February, 'and I am sure it will do me heaps of good to study for a few months. I have got very rusty in charcoal work, and in fact all round, but the average of work here doesn't strike me as being even as good as Bushey, although there are so many students that of course many are ahead of that standard. Still there is always the Louvre.'[63] Indeed, it is clear that he spent much of his time there studying and drawing sailing ship models – something that sometimes involved persuading the authorities to get models out of storage.[64] Some of the resulting pencil sketches would be exhibited in London the following year[65] and many would in due course find their way into his book on the subject.

Over the years the Arts and Crafts Exhibition Society received invitations to organize contributions to an increasing number of exhibitions abroad, notably the Turin International Exhibition of Modern Decorative Art of 1902 and the

Louisiana Purchase Exhibition of 1904. At the former Nance exhibited a screen entitled 'The Three Ships of Columbus', which was subsequently bought by an American.[66] Closer to home, that same year he joined the South Wales Art Society which was founded in 1887 and which still stages an annual exhibition at the Turner House Art Gallery in Penarth. In 1903 he exhibited four oil paintings with them: 'In the Spanish Main', 'A Genoese Carrack', 'A Spanish Galleon' and 'Sir Richard Grenville's last fight'.[67] That same year he also exhibited 'Across the Western Ocean' at the Liverpool Autumn Exhibition.[68] The Louisiana Purchase Exhibition, informally known as The Saint Louis World's Fair, was a very grand affair which opened on 30 April and closed on 1 December 1904. Probably the grandest of the old-style pre World War I fairs, it covered some 1,200 acres, with the British Pavilion being a reproduction of Wren's Orangery at Kensington Palace. Of the British exhibit, which occupied nearly 21,000 square ft. and comprised 292 paintings plus rooms devoted to arts and crafts, *The Times* considered that it would 'make a more complete and comprehensive showing for every branch and division of British art, including arts and crafts, than has hitherto been attempted at an outside exhibition'.[69] Although he may well have contributed other works, Nance certainly exhibited 'Blake and Van Tromp' a painted screen that had formed part of the Arts and Crafts Exhibition Society's London exhibition the previous year.[70]

Another major exhibition that featured some of Nance's work was Naval Portraits and Battle Pieces at Earl's Court in July 1905, under the aegis of the Historical and Relic Loan Collection. *The Times* considered that, of the paintings and pictures illustrating the earliest periods – Tudor and Stuart times – probably those of sea battles would attract most attention and amongst the several modern paintings, those by Mr Morton Nance of battles with the Dutch were particularly noteworthy.[71] To tie in with the exhibition, *The Studio* devoted a section of its 'Studio-Talk' feature to the place of warships in the history of decoration and reproduced Nance's 'The Flying Dutchman', 'A Sea Fight' and 'The Revenge', a painted screen that would be exhibited with the Arts and Crafts Exhibition Society between January and March the following year. In bringing to his drawings a great knowledge of the designs of the old battleships, Nance had been 'wide-awake to the possibilities for decoration contained in the highly ornamental turreted decks, the rows of projecting cannon, the large bellying sails, the bright, sharp-contrasted colours of the quarterings of the flags'. The magazine quite rightly considered that in many of his designs the artist stepped 'into the land of fancy – a short step, for the beautiful turreted vessels of those old times are as much a part of the strange waters known only to imagination as they are a part of the history of the sea'.[72] It is interesting to note that many years later Nance's artistic temperament – his tendency to regard his subject through an atmosphere of romance – would be seen by one critic of *Sailing-ship Models* as standing between the subject and what he called 'the dry light of history, or antiquarian research'.[73] For *The Studio* in 1905, though, the artist's thorough knowledge of his subject was no impediment. 'Technically,' it continued, 'Mr Nance disposes of his favourite subjects in the manner of a natural designer. The screen we reproduce ['The Revenge'] shows how thoroughly he commands his knowledge for the purpose of design. The *Flying Dutchman* is mysterious, it is a picture with sentiment. The screen is a scholarly marshalling of his facts and an arrangement of their decorative virtues. Easy freedom of design he seems to have obtained through his understanding of how to approach his subject as a decorative *motif*. His pictures aim at pure decoration, as decoration they are a revelation of mastery; but they reveal also the fascination of the history of the things he has depicted.'[74]

Tasks fit for the finger-tips of fairies
With the exception of such early watercolours as 'Seine-boats at St Ives' and 'Evening St Ives Bay – Pilchard and Seine Boats' (1900), and some early sketches, Nance would never really produce much in the way of representational art. Instead, he chose to devote his twenties and thirties to painting highly stylised scenes of sea battles or sailing ships *per se* – scenes where the sea can be a highly effective ingredient, as in 'The Sea Serpent', but not the main subject. With the move to Cornwall, his spiritual home, and his increasing absorption in ship modelling and nautical research, he would slowly lose interest in painting, so that his sons Robin and Dicon would grow up very much as craftsmen-artists rather than artists *tout court*, exhibiting hand-made furniture with the Arts and Crafts Exhibition Society and elsewhere.[75] Nance believed that there was nothing of man's creation that so closely resembled a living organism as a sailing ship and in the introduction to his seminal *Sailing-ship Models* described ship

modellers as 'craftsmen who [take] upon human hands tasks more fit for the finger-tips of fairies'.[76] His marriage in 1906 to former fellow art student at Bushey, Annie Maud Cawker, and their move to Cornwall marked the beginning of the long final stage of his life. Nance did not, like his mentor Henry Jenner, turn his back on most of what had gone before.[77] As the advertisement that he placed in *The Studio* in September 1905 makes clear, he was and would remain a professional artist, but the emphasis would change over the years until ship modelling would take precedence over any other form of art, and painting *per se* would cease to be of interest. His second wife was an excellent weaver and at the cottage that they rented at Nancledra, near St Ives, Nance did the designs for some attractive pieces that she produced.[78] Amy Baker recalled that he was still painting at Nancledra, one of his orders being for a frieze of Elizabethan ships for Dartmouth Naval Training College. This semi-circular 'triptych in oil' was almost certainly made to fill the space over the fireplace in the Wardroom, where it can still be seen.[79] Ms. Baker was herself the proud owner of a three-panelled screen depicting a piece of rocky coast, a church, a special bathing-place for one, and four of the great Venetian or Florentine galleys that Nance loved to paint. Of his paintings from this period, she remembered particularly 'The Golden Ship goes down the River'.[80] Although there was a studio in the garden of Chylason, the house in Carbis Bay to which the family moved in 1914, Christine Raymont could not recall whether or not her brother was still painting, only that his other interests seemed more important. Indeed, in due course the desire to paint seems to have deserted him entirely, so that when asked why he did not paint the sea, he replied that the real thing was there for all to see and was much better than any painting of it.[81]

The blending of Nance's artistic skills and nautical expertise that would reach its apogee in 1924 with *Sailing-ship Models*, began back in his childhood when drawing sailing ships went hand-in-hand with making models of them. On the old breakfast-room table at Hawthorn House young Robert would build a pier and harbour of bricks and he and his brothers and sister would play with the little ships for hours. Later models, made by both Robert and his father, were large enough to be sailed in the beach pools at Penarth.[82] Just as the guiding hand of both his father and grandfather Morton were instrumental in fostering Robert's own interest in model ships, so he, in turn, would pass that interest and his practical skills on to his sons. Robin, the elder, recalled, for instance, being encouraged at a very early age to cut odd pieces of packing cases to make toys, mostly model boats,[83] while Dicon would, under his father's instructions, make models in his teens – models which, after his father's death, he would offer to the Science Museum in London.[84] Some of Robert Morton Nance's own work as a ship modeller can be traced through reference to both his and Dicon's dealings with the museum, to which *Mordon* bequeathed an English man-of-war, an English hoy, a Flemish carrack (see page 316) and a Dutch man-of-war.[85] The earliest record is of a late 17th-century Dutch First Rate being loaned to the museum after being exhibited in Whitechapel at the Shipping Exhibition of 1903. Thereafter, models loaned to the museum were exhibited at such events as the Japan-British Exhibition of 1910, the Royal Cornwall Polytechnic Society Exhibition of 1920 and the Soldiers', Sailors' and Airmen's Families Association Exhibition of 1943.

Something of the passion which Nance felt for this skilled craft came across in 'Ship-Modelling as a Craft', in which, with some wit, he deplored the fact that the ship model was 'now [1920] regarded generally as either a domestic nuisance, a monument of wasted time, to be smuggled up like the stuffed canary, the murdered butterflies, the plaster vase of feather flowers, wax fruits or other dismal relics, under a glass case, or at best as a mere museum exhibit, still glass-cased, and looked upon as an "instructive object" suitable perhaps for the inspection of schoolboys'.[86] Four years later, in his magnum opus on the subject, he would trace the growth of the ship modeller's craft. Before doing so, however, he emphasised the importance for him of the romance inherent in it, stressing that a sailing ship was an expression of human thought and feeling, a true work of art. The same was no less true of a ship model, 'made for the pure love of ship form and ship character, and without even the ship-builder's care for any lower consideration of practical utility'. 'To have made... a model for oneself,' he enthused, 'is ample repayment for the time spent on it; the slow digging out of one's facts, the sacrifice of one's leisure moments, even the monotonous "rattling down" of the shrouds that makes the least exciting part of the work of rigging, weigh as nothing against the comradeship to one's sea-fancies that the finished ship affords as one sets and furls its sails in all possible ways and looks at it from all possible angles.'[87] It is clear that this atmosphere of romance through which Nance viewed his subject did not detract from the thoroughness of his research. As well as spending time at the Louvre, in Paris, he visited Copenhagen and, possibly, Amsterdam – Holland was something of a Mecca for ship models – where the Dutch Shipping Exhibition opened on 5 June 1913. Here the British section included documents, prints, charts or photographs lent by, amongst others, R.C. Anderson, R. Morton Nance and the Society for Nautical Research.[88] He corresponded, too, with both European and North American collectors and the principal museums and other institutions on both continents that held ship models. Of the 120 or so plates in the lavishly illustrated *Sailing-ship Models*, four were of models that Nance himself had made. A Flemish Carrack, c. 1450, after the print signed WA, was used as the frontispiece, and later appeared on the front cover of *The Connoisseur* (August 1936) before being bequeathed to the Science Museum. The English Hoy, 1700–1730, was also bequeathed to the museum. Plate 8 was a hanging model of a 16th-century French Galleon that had been made for R.W. Mackenzie of Earlshall, Fife and Plate 10, that of an Elizabethan ship, 1590–1600, made for Colonel Gascoigne of Lotherton Hall, Yorkshire. The Robert Morton Nance file at the Science Museum contains a large number of requests to him, via the museum, for permission to use photographs of his models in publications ranging from school to university level.[89]

A very father of modern maritime research

Nance, then, was not just a passionate ship modeller, but someone with a much wider interest in maritime research who would, in due course, come to be regarded as a master of nautical archaeology. Until the founding of the Society for Nautical Research in 1910, he and other researchers were working very much in the dark and it cannot be stressed enough the extent to which the society and its journal, *The Mariner's Mirror*, became a point of reference or – given Nance's interest in sea-stones and killicks – an anchor for his burgeoning involvement in this field.

    The story of the formation of the Society for Nautical Research was told in the pages of *The Mariner's Mirror* by Sir Alan Moore, whose *Last Days of Mast and Sail* Nance would, as we have already seen, illustrate. The prime mover was Leonard Carr Laughton, son of the naval historian Sir J.K. Laughton. The dif-

'A Flemish Carrack', c.1450, a model by Robert Morton Nance
after a print by 'W.A'

ficulty, as Moore saw it, of getting Laughton to move was overcome by a letter from Nance some two years after they (Laughton and Moore) had first begun to consider that a nautical antiquarian society – tentatively named 'The Jal Society', after Auguste Jal, the compiler of the *Glossaire Nautique* – might be founded.[90] On 9 March 1909 Nance had begun a correspondence with Moore by responding to an article on 'The Ship, 1485–1515' which the latter had contributed to the *United Services Magazine*. 'I must tell you,' he wrote, 'that for many years now I have never missed an opportunity of getting hold of any shipping material of the period before 1700 and I have always had the habit of making sketches and comparing them, so that now anything I can get hold of dovetails in somewhere.' He confessed, though, that the feeling of ramming his head against an impenetrable wall of darkness came at times and that any new ray of light was welcome.[91] On 12 October, seven months into what was by then quite a technical correspondence, Nance wrote from Nancledra a letter which included the following:

> I was very glad to hear of your circle of Jalites [Michael Oppenheim, Leonard Carr Laughton and Gregory Robinson] ... It seems such a pity that people like ourselves should be gathering material and working in a more or less aimless way when by working together we could do so much more ... If only we could form a society however small we could do and ask things that a private person hardly has the cheek to do.

He concluded his letter with the apparently throwaway and rather self-deprecating 'I hope this is not all wildly Celtic and unpractical – Cornwall is such a long way from London.'[92] With hindsight, we can view this statement as Nance nailing his colours to the mast, staking a claim to a maritime expertise, tinged with a growing awareness of Cornishness and Celticity. By 1944, after contributing to *The Mariner's Mirror* for over thirty years, he would show no such reticence in flagging up Cornwall's language, culture and identity, writing in an article on Cornish fishing luggers that 'down to the middle of the sixteenth century, when Cornishmen and Bretons still had practically a common language, intercourse was very closely maintained between the two countries...'[93] Meanwhile, Nance's letter was just the spark that was needed. Having read it, Laughton agreed that the time was indeed ripe for such a project, and over the next few months moves to form what in the interim was referred to as either 'the Jal Society' or 'the Proposed Society of Naval Antiquaries' gathered momentum, with Laughton as acting secretary. Finally, at a meeting at the Royal United Services Institution, Whitehall on 14 June 1910, the society which in due course a provisional committee that included Morton Nance would decide should be called the Society for Nautical Research, came into being. It was felt at the meeting that a periodical in which views might be exchanged, discoveries put on record and questions answered was essential, and on 11 January 1911 the first issue of *The Mariner's Mirror*, with Laughton as editor, was published.[94] As R.C. Anderson would reiterate at the society's AGM nearly fifty years later, no doubt some kind of association of those interested in nautical antiquities would have come about sooner or later, but without the bringing together of Nance and Laughton, with Moore as an intermediary, the foundation of the Society for Nautical Research would not have come so soon or started so successfully.[95] Nance sat on the society's council from at least 1913 until about 1922.

From the beginning, it was intended that *The Mariner's Mirror* should cover the many interests of the Society for Nautical Research's membership and its pages included articles on antiquities, archaeology, art, biography, equipment, folklore, laws and customs, organisation and technology. As well as writing or co-writing over forty articles over the years, Nance contributed extensively to such regular features as 'Notes', 'Queries' and 'Answers'. In the fourth issue, for instance, he enquired:

> Polacca – Can anyone send a good picture of a Bideford Bay "polacca"? The rig is now extinct since about 1870 I believe, although some of the old "pole hacker" are still afloat as ketches.[96]

Generally, Nance had an intimate knowledge of the Dutch nautical scene and was particularly good at responding to queries about the meaning of technical terms. He certainly left no stone unturned in his efforts to research and promote Cornwall's place in naval archaeology, frequently bringing his knowledge of the Cornish language to bear on a particular theme. In the note 'Captain Richard Keigwin', for example, he drew the attention of the journal's readers to its importance in determining the correct meaning of Keigwin – 'white hedge'.[97]

The study of killicks – home-made boat-anchors, often constructed of wood and stone – held a particular fascination for him, so that 'Sea-stones and killicks in West Cornwall' (see pages 238–247) and 'Killicks again' were both published in its pages,[98] whilst 'Killicks: a study in the evolution of anchors' was the title of a paper which he presented to the Cambridge Antiquarian Society on 23 May 1921 and which was published in its journal the following year. Furthermore, there are collections of model killicks and early anchors made by Nance at both the National Maritime Museum, Greenwich and St Ives Museum. Something that often distinguished his articles from those of other contributors was his propensity for waxing lyrical, as in the following extract from 'Trows, past and present':

> The typical trow is no snowy-pinioned sea bird – no butterfly bark of romance. See her, sprawled helplessly across the mud pillows on which the ebb has left her, in some turbid estuary; her tar-thirsty flanks all water-marked with drying ooze; her coal-smirched, threadbare canvas showing with each lazy flap some new detail of its intricate, grey patch-work. Could anything with sail show us such another picture of grimy toil and ignoble ease?[99]

Another – and, perhaps, less idiosyncratic – feature of his articles was that he could and did illustrate his writing with what H. Oliver Hill described as 'charming little sketches, which were not only extremely pleasant to look at but were very explanatory of his subject'.[100]

Just over ten years ago, the Conway Maritime Press published *The Evolution of the Sailing Ship, 1250–1580*, the first in a proposed series of extracts of some of the best articles from *The Mariner's Mirror*. The fact that the publisher's blurb singles out Robert Morton Nance as one of the 'very fathers of modern maritime research' is proof of the standing that his pioneering work still enjoys in nauti-cal circles.[101]

Conclusion: his true memorial
Included on the slate slab that was erected over Nance's grave in Zennor Churchyard in 1963 is the Cornish sentence 'Oberow y vewnans yu y wyr govath' – His life's works are his true memorial. Although his legacy is huge,

much of it, both his Cornish and non-Cornish output, has remained hidden from view for a long time. How appropriate it was to publish as a memorial volume *A Glossary of Cornish Sea-Words*, surely the perfect synthesis of his Cornish, nautical and – to a much lesser extent – his artistic expertise. Its editor, the late Peter Pool, aptly described the volume as 'the happy combination of *Mordon*'s Cornish and Nautical studies'[102] and one could argue that his articles for *The Mariner's Mirror* were an extension of that work – work that had been largely completed by about 1920. Despite – perhaps also because of – the controversy that still surrounds his Unified project, Nance's Cornish language interests have been subject to no little scrutiny, whereas his artistic achievements have virtually disappeared from view. On a more positive note, I hope that I have shown that his standing as a ship modeller and maritime historian is slowly undergoing something of a revival. Although much remains to be done, thanks to new technology it is now possible to view online an annotated list of the astounding 120 or so items by Nance – many of them consisting of more than one sketch or page – that are held in the Prints and Drawings Collection of the National Maritime Museum: items such as 'Sketches and notes relating to Brittany and Breton small craft', an 1890 watercolour entitled 'Rowing ashore from the *Bride* of Hayle' and numerous original illustrations for articles in *The Mariner's Mirror*.[103] And, of course, the legacy of his talent lived on in the work of his sons Robin and Dicon, and lives on in that of his grandson, the maritime researcher Jonathan Nance.

Notes

1. Geo. W. Nance (1904) *The Nance Memorial: A history of the Nance family in general...* Bloomington, Illinois: J. E. Burke and Co., Printers. Transcription at http://webpages.charter.net/bobnance/memorial, accessed 16 February 2005.
2. Grant Longman (1991) *Robert Morton Nance* [fact sheet to accompany the exhibition 'Three Bushey Artists and a photographer', Bushey Museum and Art Gallery, 6–28 July].
3. Mrs C. Morton Raymont (1962) *The Early Life of Robert Morton Nance* [Leedstown]: New Cornwall.
4. Idid., p. 7.
5. Ibid., pp. 11–12.
6. Ibid., pp. 25 and 8.
7. Items 87.25.1–3, Bushey Museum and Art Gallery, Bushey.
8. Raymont (1962) op. cit., p. 18.
9. Ibid., pp. 10, 30, 37.
10. Ibid., p. 21.
11. Longman (1991) op. cit.

12. Raymont (1962) op. cit., p. 25.
13. *The Studio* (1898) vol. 14.
14. Professor Herkomer, R. A. (1889) 'How we teach at Bushey. A practical Lesson' in *The Universal Review*, Sept–Dec, p. 50.
15. Transcription of the Herkomer School Prospectus for 1890–91, in Grant Longman (1976) The Herkomer Art School, 1883–1900, Bushey: E. G. Longman, p. 12.
16. Lee MacCormick Edwards (1999) *Herkomer: A Victorian Artist*, Aldershot: Ashgate, p. 110. See also Herkomer (1889) op. cit. and Lee MacCormick Edwards (2004) 'Herkomer, Sir Hubert von (1849–1914)' in *Oxford Dictionary of National Biography*, Oxford: O.U P. and http://www.oxforddnb.com/view/article33836, accessed 28 February 2005.
17. Herkomer (1889) op. cit., p. 52.
18. [Anon] (1892) 'Professor Herkomer's School' in *Art Journal*, October, pp. 289–293.
19. Raymont (1962) op. cit., p. 26.
20. Edwards (1999) op. cit.
21. Herkomer (1889) op. cit., p. 51.
22. A. Lys Baldry (1895), 'The Herkomer School' in *The Studio*, vol. 6, pp. 3–17.
23. Longman (1976) op. cit., p. 13.
24. Herkomer (1889) op. cit., p. 52.
25. Ibid.; A. Lys Baldry (1895) op. cit., pp. 15–16.
26. Herkomer (1889) op. cit., p. 52.
27. Longman (1976) op. cit., p. 14.
28. Herkomer (1889) op. cit., p. 54.
29. Ibid; Edwards (2004) op. cit., p. 4.
30. Maxwell Fraser (1963), 'Vestments of true poetry' in *Country Quest*, Summer, p. 41; R. Morton Nance, 'Wales & the Cornish Language & Gorsedd', paper read to the Royal Institution of South Wales, Swansea, 24 February 1938, Nance Collection Box 4, Nance Essay and Lectures, Courtney Library, Truro.
31. Herkomer (1889) op. cit., p.51.
32. [Anon] (1892) op. cit.
33. His address at this time was Bourne Hall Road, Bushey. Email from Elizabeth King, Research Assistant, Royal Academy Library, 1 March 2005.
34. Email from Grant Longman, Collections Curator, Bushey Museum and Art Gallery, 7 April 2005.
35. Ibid. He refers to this information from Mrs Raymont correcting her statement in *The Early Life of Robert Morton Nance* that a rule stipulating that no married people could be students at Bushey resulted in Robert and Beatrice leaving for Penarth as soon as they were married.
36. Raymont (1962), op. cit., pp. 28–29.
37. Ibid; Longman op. cit., 7 April 2005.
38. Raymont (1962), op. cit., p. 29.
39. Email from Katrina Coopey, Cardiff Local Studies Library, 28 February 2005.
40. Longman (1991), op. cit.
41. Item 87.25.6, Bushey Museum and Art Gallery, Bushey. It is probably the painting that Toby Proctor, in conversation with Peter Thomas, remembers as being in the room that he slept in when he stayed with his grandfather. It was reproduced in *The Studio*, 15 November 1915.
42. Bushey Museum Artist Data Sheet: Beatrice Michell.
43. Alan Crawford (2004) 'United Kingdom: Origins and First Flowering' in *The Arts and Crafts Movement in Europe and America: Design for the Modern World*, ed. Wendy Kaplan, London: Thames and Hudson, p. 64.
44. W. L. Courtney (1892) 'The life and work of Hubert Herkomer, R. A.' in *Art Journal*, Christmas number, cited in Edwards (1999).

45. Arthur Quiller-Couch (ed) (1898–1899) *The Cornish Magazine*, Truro: Pollard, vol. 1, pp. 126, 357–359, 438–440; vol. 2, p. 323.
46. Ibid., vol. 1, p. 435.
47. E. E. Speight and R. Morton Nance (eds.) (1905) *Britain's Sea Story BC 55–AD 1805…* London: Hodder and Stoughton, p. v.
48. E. E. Speight (1906) *The Romance of the Merchant Venturers*, London: Hodder and Stoughton, p. ix.
49. Sir Alan Moore (1925) *Last Days of Mast and Sail: An Essay in Nautical Comparative Anatomy*, Oxford: Clarendon Press, p. 7.
50. From one of two letters in Nance's own copy of *Last Days of Mast and Sail* in the Morrab Library, Penzance.
51. Crawford (2004) op. cit., p. 64.
52. Arts and Crafts Exhibition Society (1899) *Catalogue of the sixth exhibition*, London: Chiswick Press, pp. 78, 80, 91, 168. 'The Sea Serpent' was reproduced in the November 1899 issue of the *Architectural Review*.
53. See Virginia Anne Bonito, 'The Cardinal Virtues Screen by Carolyn Brady, Don Eddy and Joseph Raffael: An Essay', http://www.artregister.com/SeavestIntroductiontoCollection/Catalogue/CardinalVirtuesEssay.html, accessed 21 December 2005.
54. Janet Woodbury Adams (1982) *Decorative folding screens in the west from 1600 to the present day*, London: Thames and Hudson, p. 9.
55. Michael Komanecky (1984) 'A Perfect Gem of Art' in Michael Komanecky and Virginia Fabbri Butera, *The Folding Image: screens by Western artists of the nineteenth and twentieth centuries*, New Haven: Yale University Art Gallery, p. 41.
56. Ibid., pp. 42–43.
57. Letter to the present owner of 'The Sea Serpent', 14 May 1999.
58. 'The Arts and Crafts Exhibition. 1st Notice' in *The Studio* (1903), vol. 28, February.
59. Arts and Crafts Exhibition. First Notice' in *The Studio* (1906), vol. 37, pp. 50, 61. A painting by Nance entitled 'Homeward Bound' was exhibited at Wolverhampton Municipal Art Gallery and Museum towards the end of 1907.
60. Arts and Crafts Exhibition Society (1906) *Catalogue of the eighth exhibition…*, London: Chiswick Press, pp. 18, 24, 30, 193.
61. Arts and Crafts Exhibition Society (1910) *Catalogue of the ninth exhibition*, London: Chiswick Press, pp. 138, 142, 194. 'The King: his ships' was reproduced in *The Studio* (1910), vol. 49, p. 39.
62. Arts and Crafts Exhibition Society (1928) *Catalogue (revised edition) of the fourteenth exhibition*, London: W. H. Smith and son, pp. 10, 31, 139.
63. Raymont (1962) op. cit., pp. 29–30.
64. R. Morton Nance (1924, 2nd rev. edn. 1949) *Sailing-ship Models*, London: Halton, p. 25.
65. 'Studio Talk [London]' in *The Studio* (1903), vol. 28, pp. 49–51.
66. Letter to George W. Nance, op. cit.
67. Information from South Wales Art Society catalogues, Cardiff Local Studies Library, 28 February 2005. Nance's membership continued at least until 1909 and 1910, although he did not exhibit with the society in either year.
68. J. Johnson and A. Greutzner (comps.) (1976) *Dictionary of British Artists 1880–1940*, Woodbridge: Antique Collectors Club, p. 371. Information from Alex Kidson, Curator of Art, Walker Art Gallery, Liverpool, 25 February 2005.
69. 'The British Exhibit at St Louis' in *The Times* (1904), 24 February and 26 May.
70. Letter to George W. Nance, op. cit.
71. *The Times* 20 July 1905.
72. 'Studio-Talk' in *The Studio* (1905), vol. 35, p. 337.

73. L. G. Carr Laughton (1925) 'The Study of Ship Models' in *The Mariner's Mirror*, vol. 11, no. 1, January, pp. 4–5.
74. 'Studio Talk' (1905) op. cit., pp. 337–338.
75. Robin Nance (1951), 'My World as a Woodcutter', in *The Cornish Review*, 8, Summer, p. 40.
76. Nance (1924, 1949), op. cit., pp. 2, 6.
77. Derek R. Williams (2004) 'Henry Jenner, F. S. A. : City Scholar and Local Patriot' in *Henry and Katharine Jenner: A Celebration of Cornwall's Culture, Language and Identity*, ed. Derek R. Williams, London: Francis Boutle, p. 71.
78. Raymont (1962) op. cit., p. 31.
79. Amy W. Baker (1963) '[R. Morton Nance 1873–1959 Memoir and Appreciations]: From an old Friend' in R. Morton Nance, *A Glossary of Cornish Sea-Words*, St Ives: Federation of Old Cornwall Societies, p. 15. Information from Dr Jane Harrold, Britannia Royal Naval College, Dartmouth, 16 March 2005.
80. Baker (1963), op. cit.
81. Raymont (1962), op. cit., pp. 35, 37.
82. Ibid., p. 7.
83. Robin Nance (1951), op. cit., p. 37.
84. Letter, dated 19 December 1996, from G. P. Fitzgerald, Collection Assistant (Water Transport), Science Museum, and summary of the contents of file ScM 143, 'Nance, R. W. M.'.
85. Fitzgerald (1996), op. cit., and summary of file ScM 1218, 'Nance, R. M.'.
86. R. Morton Nance (1920), 'Ship-Modelling as a Craft', in *Royal Cornwall Polytechnic Society Transactions*, 87, pp. 228–229.
87. Nance (1924, 1949), op. cit., pp. 5, 9.
88. *The Times* 31 May 1913.
89. Fitzgerald (1996), op. cit.
90. Sir Alan H. Moore (1953), 'The Beginning of the S. N. R.', in *The Mariner's Mirror*, vol. 41, pp. 267–268.
91. Ibid., p. 270.
92. Ibid., pp. 271–272.
93. R. Morton Nance (1944), 'West Cornwall Fishing Luggers before 1850', in *The Mariner's Mirror*, vol. 30, no. 2, April, p. 93.
94. Moore (1953), op. cit., pp. 272–278; *The Times* 15 June 1910.
95. 'Obituaries', in *The Mariner's Mirror*, vol. 45, 1959, pp. 267–268.
96. R. M. N. (1911), 'Queries: Polacca…', in *The Mariner's Mirror*, vol. 1, no. 4, April, p. 125.
97. R. M. N. (1951), 'Notes: captain Richard Keigwin', in *The Mariner's Mirror*, vol. 37, no. 1, January, p. 80.
98. R. Morton Nance (1913), 'Sea-stones and killicks in West Cornwall', in *The Mariner's Mirror*, vol. 3, pp. 295–303; R. Morton Nance (1921), 'Killicks again', in *The Mariner's Mirror*, vol. 7, p. 135f.
99. R. Morton Nance (1912), 'Trows, past and present', in *The Mariner's Mirror*, vol. 2, no. 7, July, p. 201.
100. H. Oliver Hill (1963), '[R. Morton Nance 1873–1959 Memoir and Appreciations]: A Nautical Tribute', in R. Morton Nance, *A Glossary of Cornish Sea-Words*, St Ives: Federation of Old Cornwall Societies, pp. 17–18.
101. *The Evolution of the Sailing Ship, 1250–1580*: From the publisher, Barnes and Noble website, http://search.barnesandnoble, accessed 19 February 2006.
102. P. A. S. Pool (1963), 'Editor's Preface', in R. Morton Nance, *A Glossary of Cornish Sea-Words*, St Ives: Federation of Old Cornwall Societies, p. 7.
103. The National Maritime Museum website, http://www.nmm.ac.uk, accessed 19 February 2006.

Acknowledgements

I am grateful to the following individuals and institutions for their help in writing this chapter: Birmingham Central Library; Britannia Royal Naval College (Dr Jane Harrold); Bushey Museum and Art Gallery (Grant Longman, Collections Curator, and colleagues); Cardiff Local Studies Library (Katrina Coopey and colleagues); Courtney Library, Royal Institution of Cornwall, Truro (Angela Broome, Librarian and Archivist); Graham S. Gadd; Morrab Library, Penzance; National Maritime Museum (Daphne Knott, Roger Quarm, Mike Bevan); Audrey Randle Pool; Royal Academy Library (Elizabeth King, Research Assistant); St Ives Archive Study Centre (Janet Axten and Mary Quick); Science Museum (G. P. Fitzgerald, Collections Assistant, Water Transport); Society for Nautical Research (Liza Verity); South Wales Art Society (Dr Robert Ll. Davies, Archivist); Peter Thomas; Walker Art Gallery, Liverpool (Alex Kidson, Curator of British Art).

Bushey Models

[An article published in *The Studio*, Special Winter Number, 1896–1897]

R. Morton Nance

If he takes his walks abroad at a fairly early hour on a weekday morning, the uninitiated visitor to the village of Bushey will be somewhat surprised, on approaching the celebrated school, to find the gates of that establishment walled in by a heterogeneous crowd of villagers of all ages, sizes, and sexes, and he will instinctively nerve himself for a Punch and Judy show, a dancing bear, or a dog fight. These good people, however, are not here for diversion, but have come with a fierce resolve to be "taken on" for the day at the school, and old folks and children, "boys and girls, the vacant and the busy, maids and youths, and urchins newly breeched," elbow and jostle one another in the hope of being selected to "sit" as models for the students.

On these occasions representatives of the working population of the village are usually conspicuous by their absence, and the adult portion of the picturesque crowd consists for the most part of those who look upon field labour as savouring too much of hard work, and who prefer a life of masterly inactivity to one devoted to the irksome, if more remunerative occupation of tilling the soil.

Under this category, however, must not be included the grandfathers of the hamlet whose mundane task is done, and who have an indisputable right to pass the evening of their days in blissful repose, and to earn a little beer and tobacco money by permitting their fine old rugged features to be transferred to paper or to canvas by young aspirants to a niche in the temple of artistic fame. Certain of our imaginative transatlantic cousins aver that there is a village in the state of Illinois which is so healthy "that people are obliged to go somewhere else to die," and although Bushey cannot perhaps claim to approach such a truly admirable standard of sanitation, the salubriousness of the locality is no doubt responsible for the large number of hoary-headed swains who appear to rival Old Parr or even Methuselah himself in ripeness of years; and these ancients are naturally much sought after as models by Professor Herkomer's pupils.

When the gates of the school are opened and a selection made from the expectant groups, the chosen ones, young and old, are marched through the cloisters to the preliminary class-room, where they ascend the throne and sit as well as the infirmities of old age or extreme youth will permit; while, flushed with enthusiasm and inexperience, the budding artist not yet admitted to the life class, tries to reproduce their charms in sooty charcoal drawings and weird experiments in oil. These charms not infrequently prove on paper to be of a nature calculated to strike dismay into the hearts of their owners – an extensive and blobby nose, a vivid shock of that shade of hair known locally as "carroty tops," and a face that exhibits planes, bones, or features in such a way as to impress their existence forcibly and indelibly upon the mind of the most care-less observer, and to cause those in authority to exclaim with Wordsworth, "Avaunt! this vile abuse of pictured page."

When requisitioned for a sitting it is difficult to persuade a villager that he is not required to be "dressed all in his best," and one is often saddened by the sight of a stiff, starched, cropped and hair-oiled old swell in whom, at first sight, one fails to recognise the weather-worn, unbarbered, and consequently pic-turesque rustic of yesterday, who has got himself up to have his "fortygraft tooked."

In the seclusion of a private studio these old fellows often prove themselves to be decided "characters." Like most sitters, they sit with unlimited patience and heroic endurance when allowed to talk about themselves. This usually means the recitation of a catalogue of nearly all the disorders known to medical science that have occurred in divers regions of the Busheyite's anatomy, and one hears with mixed feelings of the "haricot veins" and "screwmatics" which are a source of trouble to one old gentleman whom all the lady students devoutly adore. In the talk of these old country people one often catches something sug-

Bushey Model, one of Nance's lead-pencil drawings in The Studio, *Special Winter No., 1896–97*

gestive of the primitive life that still lingers on in such old-fashioned places as this, despite the modernisation and "betterment" which are gradually spreading their pall over the majority of rural districts.

Children, as models, are obtainable here by the score, and scarcely one will refuse to sit, although peace has to be made with the Board school, where attendances are sometimes apt to be distressingly small. The children often begin to "sit" before they have made even elementary attempts to walk, and continue to do so until they go out to work for their daily bread. Although they are not encouraged as models for beginners, there is, nevertheless, a good demand for them in connection with work that is not purely educational, and, moreover, the rate of payment for children is only half that demanded by adult models – which is no small consideration for many an embryo academician.

In addition to the native models, tramps will sometimes be graciously pleased to rest on their way and give a sitting or two in return for a trifle. These peripatetics, of any one of whom it may be said that

> Misery and mirth are blended in his face,
> Much innate vileness and some outward grace,

are delightful subjects to work from, but, amongst a few other disadvantages, they possess that of disappearing in the middle of a sitting and turning up again some time next year. Those who favour these parts with their patronage belong chiefly to that tribe whose motto is "We've got no work to do, and we wouldn't do it if we had any" – the tribe which had a typical representative in an applicant to a contractor for a job: "I have no more vacancies," replied the employer of labour, "sufficient hands are already engaged for the work." "Well, *that* needn't stand in the way," urged the unemployed, "'cos the little I'd do wouldn't make no difference."

The artists and their ways are a continual source of wonderment to the villagers. As an explanation of the existence of the Colony, an idea prevails in the mind of one of the native wiseacres that the Bushey school is a kind of picture factory, and that during the summer months Professor Herkomer hawks the works of art produced by his students through the country in a costerbarrow, bearing such devices as "Try our Noted Portraits," "Landscapes are Cheap

Today," and so forth.

This would also satisfactorily explain to the rural mind the severe "slatings" which are popularly supposed to be meted out to the perpetrators of unsalable articles.

Tail piece from The Cornish Magazine *by Robert Morton Nance*

A Bibliography of the writings of Robert Morton Nance

P.A.S. Pool, revised and updated by Derek R. Williams, with Peter W. Thomas

This bibliography has been compiled from that of Peter Pool in *A Glossary of Cornish Sea-Words* and from the COPAC Union Catalogue (http://copac.ac.uk), the Cornwall Library Catalogue (http://library.cornwall.gov.uk/TalisPrism) and the stock of the Cornish Studies Library, Cornwall Centre, Redruth. Where the compilers have been unable to verify Nance's contributions, in the form of notes and additions, to Henderson's parish topographies in Doble's booklets, the entries in the first section are marked with an asterisk. The arrangement in each of the four sections is chronological.

Cornish books, monographs and contributions to the works of other authors

Cornish translation [of A.B. Donaldson's words] for *Eglos Kernow; Hymn for the Church in Cornwall*, [n.p.] [n.d.].

A Glossary of Celtic Words in Cornish Dialect, Falmouth: "Cornish Echo"/Royal Cornwall Polytechnic Society, 1923.

Twentieth-century Traditions of the Cornish Numerals…, Truro: [Journal of the Royal Institution of Cornwall], 1924.

Folk-Lore Recorded in the Cornish Language, Camborne: Royal Cornwall Polytechnic Society/Camborne Printing and Stationery Co., [1925]; as Folklore in the Cornish Language, Penzance: Oakmagic, 2000.

Modern Stone Implements in Cornwall, [Penzance]: [Royal Cornwall Polytechnic

Society], 1926.

Four Cornish Folk-tales, Truro: Royal Institution of Cornwall/Blackford, 1926.

An den ha'y dheu Wreg and some Short Stories in the Cornish Language [with Edith Grenville and Hal Wyn/R. St. V. Allin-Collins], St Ives: James Lanham, [1927/8].

Contributions to Ralph Dunstan's *Cornish Song Book*, London: Reid, 1929, namely: 'Can Kerth Tus Kernow Goth' [words and music], 'Arta ef a-dhe' [words], 'Dynergh dhe Dus a Vreten Vyghan' [words], 'Kernow agan Mam-vro' [words and music],' Yeghes da dhe'n Myghtern!' [words], 'Auld Lang Syne/Sol-a-Brys' [Cornish words], 'Morvah Fair' [words and music], 'A Cornish "Grace"' [words], conjectural restoration of 'The Hal-an-Tow' [English words], restoration of 'The Plough-Boy' [English words].

Cornish for All, St Ives: Federation of Old Cornwall Societies/James Lanham, [1929/30]; rev. ed., 1949; 3rd ed., Penzance: J.W. Saundry, c. 1961.

'Cornish Names of Trees and Shrubs', in E. Thurston's *British and Foreign Trees and Shrubs in Cornwall*, Cambridge: C.U.P. for Royal Institution of Cornwall, 1930.

'Place-names and Field-names of Mabe', in Charles Henderson's *Mabe Church and Parish, Cornwall*, Shipston-on-Stour: 'King's Stone' Press, [1930/1].

Foreword and map, in Sarah L. Enys' *Cornish Drolls compiled from Bottrell*, Plymouth: W. Brendon/Mayflower Press, [1931].

'Tom Bawcock's Eve' [words], in Ralph Dunstan's *Cornish Dialect and Folk Songs*, Truro: Jordan's Bookshop, 1932.

An Balores, St Ives: Federation of Old Cornwall Societies/James Lanham, c. 1932; reprinted c. 1950.

* Notes and additions for Charles Henderson's topography of Redruth, in G.H. Doble's *Saint Euny, Abbot and Confessor*, 2nd ed., Shipston-on-Stour: 'King's Stone' Press, [1933].

An English-Cornish Dictionary [with A.S.D. Smith], St Ives: Federation of Old Cornwall Societies/James Lanham, 1934.

An Awayl herwyth Synt Mark [with A.S.D. Smith], Porth Ia: James Lanham, 1936; rev. ed., as *An Awayl herwyth Sen Mark*, Camborne: An Lef Kernewek, 1960.

* Notes and additions for Charles Henderson's topographies of Mawgan in Pydar and Mawgan and Martin in Meneage, in G.H. Doble's *Saint Mawgan*, 1st ed. and rev. ed., Shipston-on-Stour: 'King's Stone' Press, 1936.

'Place-names and Field-names of Constantine', revised appendix, in C.G. Henderson's *A History of the Parish of Constantine in Cornwall*, Long Compton: 'King's Stone' Press for the Royal Institution of Cornwall, 1937.

* Notes and additions for Charles Henderson's topography of St Budock, in G.H. Doble's *Saint Budock*, 2nd ed., Shipston-on-Stour: 'King's Stone' Press, 1937.

* Notes and additions for Charles Henderson's topography of St Ewe, in G.H. Doble's *A History of the Parish of Saint Ewe*, Shipston-on-Stour: 'King's Stone' Press, 1937.

* Notes and additions for Charles Henderson's topography of Gerrans, in G.H. Doble's *Saint Gerent... with a History of the Parish of Gerens*, Shipston-on-Stour: 'King's Stone' Press, 1938.

Gerlyver Noweth Kernewek ha Sawsnek. A new Cornish-English Dictionary, St Ives: Federation of Old Cornwall Societies/J. Lanham, 1938.

Lyver an pymp Marthus Seleven, Porth Ya: Jamys Lanham, 1939; Penzance: Headland Printers, 1977.

A short topography, in G.H. Doble's *A History of the Parish and Church of Saint Euny-Lelant*, Long Compton/Shipston-on-Stour: 'King's Stone' Press, 1939.

A topography, in G.H. Doble's *St Ives: its Patron Saint and Church*, St Ives: James Lanham, 1939.

Explanations of place-name meanings, in G.H. Doble's *A History of the Parish of Crowan...*, Shipston-on-Stour: 'King's Stone' Press, 1939.

A short topography, in G.H. Doble's *A History of the Parish and Church of St Meubred*, Cardynham, Shipston-on-Stour: 'King's Stone' Press, 1939.

Maps, in G.H. Doble's *Dedications to Celtic Saints in Normandy*, [St Ives]: G.H. Doble/James Lanham, 1940.

* Notes and additions for Charles Henderson's topography of St Winnow, in G.H. Doble's *Saint Winnoc, Abbot and Confessor*, Shipston-on-Stour: 'King's Stone' Press, 1940.

* Notes and additions for Charles Henderson's topography of Paul, in G.H. Doble's *Saint Paul (Paulinus) of Leon, Bishop and Confessor*, Lampeter: Caxton Hall Printing Co., 1941.

Explanations for Charles Henderson's 'Topography of Penzance', in G.H. Doble's *Old Penzance and St Mary's Chapel*, [Shipston-on-Stour]: 'King's Stone' Press, 1943.

'The Topography of Roche', revised chapter from notes by Charles Henderson, in H.M. Creswell Payne's *The Story of the Parish of Roche*, Newquay: H.M. Creswell Payne, [1948].

'Gwennap Place-names', in C.C. James' *A History of the Parish of Gwennap*, Penzance: C.C. James, 1949.

Bewnans Meryasek, lines 759–1096, [with A.S.D. Smith] (Extracts from the Cornish Texts, in unified spelling with amended translation, no. 1), Camborne: Federation of Old Cornwall Societies, 1949; 2nd ed. as *St Meriasek in Cornwall/Bewnans Meryasek*, lines 587–1099, St Ives: F.O.C.S., 1966.

Foreword to Charles Thomas' *Studies in the Folk-Lore of Cornwall No. 1: The Taboo in Cornwall*, Camborne: Charles Thomas, 1951.

'Cornwall and the Drama', in Cornish Summer Festival of Amateur Drama's *Calendar of Productions. Souvenir Programme*, Marazion: County Drama Committee/Worden, 1951.

A Guide to Cornish Place-names, Marazion: Federation of Old Cornwall Societies/Worden, [1951]; [2nd ed.], [1952]; 3rd ed., [1961]; 4th ed., 1963; 5th ed., 1967.

An tyr Marya/R.D., lines 679–834, [with A.S.D. Smith] (Extracts from the Cornish Texts… no. 2), [Camborne/Marazion]: [Federation of Old Cornwall Societies/Worden], [1951].

Sylvester ha'n Dhragon:B.M., lines 3896–4180, [with A.S.D. Smith] (Extracts from the Cornish Texts… no. 3), [Camborne]: [Federation of Old Cornwall Societies], [1951/2]; [St Ives]: F.O.C.S., [197–]; St Neot: Cornish Language Board, 1974.

Introduction to R.J. Noall's *Little Feathers and Stray Fancies*, St Ives: Jacobs, [1952].

An English-Cornish Dictionary, revision of 1934 ed., Marazion: Federation of Old Cornwall Societies/Worden, 1952; London: Haycock Printers, 1965; St Ives: Cornish Language Board, 1973.

'Kernow agan Mamvro', 'Arta ef a dhe', 'Can Kerth Tus Kernow Goth' and other contributions, including translations, in *Cornish in Song and Ceremony, with English translations*, Marazion: Federation of Old Cornwall Societies, [1953]

Abram hag Ysak/O.M., lines 1259–1394, [with A.S.D. Smith] (Extracts from the Cornish Texts… no. 4), [Camborne/Marazion]: [Federation of Old Cornwall Societies/Worden], [1954]; St Neot: Cornish Language Board, 1973.

Vinyl recordings of *Pader Agan Arluth/Lord's Prayer, Dyscansow dyworth Ordenal Gwesperow/Lessons in Cornish Service, Jowan Chy-an-Horth/John of Chyannor* and *Boorde's Colloquies*, Federation of Old Cornwall Societies, c. 1954; reissued as cassette tape with accompanying texts *Lef Mordon: readings in Cornish [Jowan Chy-an-Horth, Kescowsow Kernewek, Dyscansow dyworth Ordenal Gwesperow, Pader Agan Arluth]*, [Redruth]: Agan Tavas, 1992.

A Cornish-English Dictionary, Marazion: Federation of Old Cornwall Societies/Worden, 1955; reprinted London: Pitman Press, for the Cornish Language Board.

The Rood legend, the *Three Marys*, and the *Death of Pilate*: F.E. Halliday's English verse translations in his *The Legend of the Rood*, London: Duckworth, 1955 were based on Nance and Smith's translations of the Cornish miracle-plays.

Adam ha Seth/O.M., lines 684–880, [with A.S.D. Smith] (Extracts from the Cornish Texts… no. 5), [Camborne]: [Federation of Old Cornwall Societies], [c. 1955]; reprinted? Marazion and Penzance: Worden, [1957].

Davyd hag Urry/O.M., lines 2105–2254, [with A.S.D. Smith] (Extracts from the Cornish Texts... no. 6), [Camborne/St Ives]: [Federation of Old Cornwall Societies], [c. 1955]; [St Neot]/Penzance: Cornish Language Board/Headland Printing Co., 1973.

The Cledry Plays: Drolls of Old Cornwall for Village Acting and Home Reading, Marazion/Penzance: Federation of Old Cornwall Societies/Worden, 1956.

The Death of Pilate: A.C. Cawley's literal rendering of Norris' translation for his ed. of *Everyman and Medieval Miracle Plays*, 2nd ed., London: Dent, 1957 was revised in the light of a transcript by Nance and Smith and on Nance's English translation of it.

Gwryans an Bys: The Creation of the World, as written by William Jordan..., [with A.S.D. Smith], St Ives: [Federation of Old Cornwall Societies], 1959; as *Cayn hag Abel, an Episode from Gwryans an Bys*, Padstow: Lodenek Press, 1979; as *Gwryans an Bys...*, Redruth: Dyllansow Truran, 1985.

A Glossary of Cornish Sea-words, ed. P.A.S. Pool, [Truro/Marazion/St Ives]: Federation of Old Cornwall Societies, 1963.

Comments on "Llawlyfr Cernyweg Canol" Henry Lewis (Cornish Studies No. 2) [Handbook of Middle Cornish] [with A.S.D. Smith], Camborne: An Lef Kernewek, 1968.

An Venen ha'y map/Bewnans Meryasek, lines 3156–3244 and 3444–3802, [with A.S.D. Smith] (Extracts from the Cornish Texts... no. 7), [St Ives]: Cornish Language Board, 1969.

John of Chyannor or the Three Points of Wisdom by Nicholas Boson, revised and translated, [St Ives]: Cornish Language Board, 1969.

Passyon agan Arluth/Cornish Poem of the Passion, [with A.S.D. Smith], [St Ives]: Kesvd [sic] an Tavas Kernewek, 1972.

When was Cornish last spoken Traditionally?, [Truro]/Penzance: Royal Institution of Cornwall/Wordens, 1973.

An English-Cornish and Cornish-English Dictionary, [Redruth/Penzance]: Cornish Language Board, 1978, [corrected reprint of *An English-Cornish Dictionary*, 1952 and *Cornish-English Dictionary*, 1955].

The Cornish Ordinalia, second play: Christ's Passion..., [with A.S.D. Smith], [Saltash/Truro/Penzance]: Cornish Language Board, 1982.

The Cornish Ordinalia, third play: Resurrection..., [with A.S.D. Smith], [Saltash/Penzance]: Kesva an Tavas Kernewek/Cornish Language Board, 1984.

The Cornish Ordinalia, first play (Origo Mundi) lines 1–465, [with A.S.D. Smith], [n.p.]: Kesva an Taves Kernewek, 1989.

Gerlyver Noweth Kernewek-Sawsnek ha Sawsnek-Kernewek, Redruth: Dyllansow

Truran, 1990 [facsim. of *Gerlyver Noweth Kernewek...*, 1938, and *An English-Cornish Dictionary*, 1934]; memorial ed. Redruth: Agan Tavas, 1999 [facsim. of *Gerlyver Noweth Kernewek...*, 1938, and *An English-Cornish Dictionary*, 1952].

The Cornish Ordinalia, first play: Origo Mundi..., [with A.S.D. Smith], Redruth: Agan Tavas, 2001.

Maritime and other books

Illustrations in Richard Jobson's *The Golden Trade...*, Teignmouth: E.E. Speight & R.H. Walpole, 1904.

Illustrations and maps in E.E. Speight's *Hakluyt's English Voyages*, London: H. Marshall, 1905.

Illustrations [with W.G. Collingwood] in *Stories from the Northern sagas...*, 2nd ed. revised, London: H. Marshall, 1905.

Co-editor [with E.E. Speight] and illustrator of *Britain's Sea Story, B.C. 55–A.D. 1805*, London: Hodder & Stoughton, 1905; 2nd ed., 1906; 3rd ed., 1909; 5th ed., 1913.

Illustrations in E.E. Speight's *The Romance of the Merchant Venturers*, London: Hodder & Stoughton, 1906.

Appendices of diagrams of ships and their equipment, in Sir G.A.R. Callender's *Sea Kings of Britain*, vols. 2 and 3, 2nd ed., London: Longmans, Green & Co., 1917.

Sailing-ship Models: a Selection from European and American Collections..., London: Halton & Truscott Smith, 1924; 2nd ed., 1949; as *Classic Sailing-ship Models in Photographs*, Mineola, N.Y.: Dover, 2000.

Illustrations in Sir Alan Moore's *Last Days of Mast and Sail: an Essay in Nautical Comparative Anatomy*, Oxford: Clarendon Press, 1925; reprint with new information, Newton Abbot: David & Charles/Camden, Maine: Inter-Marine Pub. Co., 1970.

The Ship of the Renaissance, Cambridge: C.U.P., 1955 [Maritime Miscellany series no. 10, reprinted from *The Mariner's Mirror*).

Contributions to Cornish journals and magazines

Cornish Magazine (1898–1899):

The Merry Ballad of the Cornish Pasty, vol. 1, July 1898, pp. 48–50.

[Nance also contributed numerous illustrations and, possibly, the unsigned verses 'The Press-Gang' and 'Parson Hogg', to this magazine]

Cornish Magazine (1958–1969):

Aims of the Gorsedd, vol. 1, no. 7, November 1958, pp. 244–245.

Cornish Opera Group Newsletter:
Guise Dance Drolls and Cornish Opera, no. 1, 1955, p. 3.
The Name Minack, no. 2, p. 2; no. 3, p. 2.
Pronunciation of the Word Logan, no. 5, p. 4.
The Cornish Review:
Cornish Culture, no. 1, Spring 1949, pp. 11–17; reprinted, new series no. 10, Winter
  1968, pp. 18–24.
The Cornish Gorsedd, no. 7, Spring 1951, pp. 22–27.
Kernow:
Passyon Agan Arluth [original and unified texts of the play, with translation], no. 1,
  April 1934, pp. 6–10; no. 2, May 1934, pp. 9–12; no. 3, June 1934, pp. 10–13; no. 4,
  July 1934, pp. 12–15; no. 5, October 1934, pp. 12–15; no. 6, November 1934, pp.
  12–15; no. 7, December 1934, p. 12–15; no. 8, January 1935, pp. 8–11; no. 9,
  February 1935, pp. 12–15; no. 10, March 1935, pp. 12–15; no. 11, June 1935, pp.
  18–24; no. 12, October 1935, pp. 18–30; no. 13, December 1935, pp. 14–22; no. 14,
  March 1936, pp. 16–24.
An Dasserghyans Kernewek [notes on the Cornish Revival], no. 3, pp. 5–6; no. 4, pp.
  4–5; no. 5, pp. 5–6; no. 6, p. 9; no. 7, p. 3; no. 8, pp. 3–4; no. 9, p. 4; no. 10, p. 9; no.
  11, p. 3; no. 12, p. 7; no. 13, pp. 4–5; no. 14, p. 2.
Parabolen: Temmyk ha Temmyk, no. 2, p. 5.
An Ger "Ketteryn", no. 2, p. 7.
Gramasek, no. 3, p. 7; no. 11, p. 15.
An Vowes Doth, no. 7, p. 1.
Ewnans, no. 7, p. 1; no. 13, p. 5.
Warlergh Can Breten Vyghan, no. 14, p. 1.
The Lizard: A Magazine of Field Studies:
On Cornish, vol. 1, no. 2, 1957, pp. 17–18.
Old Cornwall:
[Those marked with an asterisk are in Cornish]
What we Stand for, no. 1, April 1925, pp. 3–6; vol. 7, no. 7, Autumn 1970, pp.
  293–296.
Cornish Family Mottoes, no. 1, pp. 18–21; no. 3, April 1926, p. 29; no. 4, October
  1926, pp. 26–27; no. 7, April 1928, pp. 27–28.
Note on A Redruth Christmas Play, no. 1, pp. 30–31.
Note on A Guise-Dance Play, St Keverne, no. 1, p. 32.
Word Collecting, no. 1, p. 34.
Some Cornish Shibboleths, no. 1, pp. 35–36.
The Word "Letterpooch", no. 1, p. 36.

The Cornish Language in America, 1710, no. 1, p. 37.

A Hurling-Ball Inscription of 1705 in Cornish, no. 1, pp. 37–38.

Draa' Foo'th and Bread your Baasins!, no. 2, October 1925, p. 32.

Hallan-apples, no. 2, p. 32.

When the Mount was Mainland, no. 2, pp. 33–34.

"French" Nuts and "French" Furze: Why?, no. 2, p. 35.

An Old Charm, no. 2, pp. 35–36.

Saint Golder, no. 2, pp. 36–37.

Parson Drake's Cornish Certificate, no. 2, pp. 38–41.

A Cornish Letter, 1711, no. 3, April 1926, pp. 23–25.

* An Trok Dyges, no. 3, pp. 25–26.

Fooch, no. 3, p. 39.

Two Ancient Invocations in Cornwall, no. 3, pp. 39–40.

Bowling and the Cornish Language, no. 3, pp. 40–42.

* An Edhen a gowsas re, no. 4, October 1926, pp. 22–23.

Floods of Dava, no. 4, pp. 28–29.

Lankyloo, no. 4, pp. 29–30.

A New Year's Wish in Cornish, no. 4, p. 30.

"Spit and Cut" [with W[ilfred] S[arre]], no. 4, pp. 31–32.

Placing of Stones near a Menhir, no. 4, p. 32.

The Names Gwavas, Hendra and Laity, no. 4, pp. 32–34.

The "Snodderwig" Story, no. 4, pp. 34–35.

John Keigwin's Cornish Translation of King Charles the First's Letter of Thanks to the County of Cornwall, no. 4, pp. 35–40; no. 5, April 1927, pp. 26–27; no. 12, Winter 1930, p. 35; vol. 3, no. 8, Winter 1940, p. 321.

The Criss-Cross-row, no. 5, April 1927, pp. 9–13.

Tom Bawcock's Eve, no. 5, pp. 20–22.

* Dyal a-dhe e'n Dhewedhva, (P.N., nebes moghées gans R.M.N. [Phoebe Nance, somewhat expanded by Robert Morton Nance]), no. 5, pp. 28–30.

A Fifteenth-century Legend of St Michael's Mount, no. 5, pp. 34–35.

Counting-out Rhymes at Penzance, no. 5, pp. 41–42.

* Nyns-yu Marow Maghtern Arthur!, no. 6, October 1927, p. 31.

Harvey-Darvey, no. 6, pp. 36–37.

The Reason Why, no. 6, pp. 38–40.

Thomas Tonkin on Piskies, etc., c. 1727, no. 6, pp. 40–41.

The Hammer of the Giants, no. 6, p. 42.

* "Gwell yu Gwytha es Govyn", no. 7, April 1928, pp. 22–24.

A Cornish Letter from John Boson to William Gwavas, 1710, no. 7, pp. 24–27.

* An Gwyns-adro, no. 8, October 1928, pp. 25–26.

Italian Names in Cornwall, no. 8, pp. 42–43.

Shirt-sleever, no. 8, p. 43.

A Cornish Three-men's-song, no. 9, April 1929, pp. 1–4.

* An Venen-fur, no. 9, pp. 27–28.

A Cornish Translation of the Hundredth Psalm [probably by Nance], no. 9, pp. 33–35.

Billy Foss and his Fellow-rhymesters, no. 10, October 1929, pp. 6–15.

A St Ives Mackerel-boat, 1814, no. 10, pp. 20–22.

Two hitherto-unnoticed Cornish Pieces, no. 10, pp. 22–24.

* Res yu Gones rag Les an Re-erel, no. 10, p. 30.

Cornish for All, no. 10, pp. 36–38; no. 11, Summer 1930, p. 19; vol. 2, no. 5, Summer 1933, pp. 27–28.

* An Pyth: Whethel heb Dhyscas, no. 11, Summer 1930, pp. 16–18.

A Cornish Song, to the Tune of "The Modest Maid of Kent", no. 11, pp. 26–29.

Hilla and Stag, no. 11, pp. 37–38.

Devil Rhymes, no. 11, pp. 40–41.

Two New-found Cornish Scraps, no. 12, Winter 1930, pp. 29–30; A Puzzle Solved, vol. 2, no. 1, Summer 1931, pp. 23–24.

* Tulla Tuller nyns-yu Tull, no. 12, pp. 31–34.

Traditional Cornish Numerals, no. 12, p. 35.

Kanna Kernuak, no. 12, pp. 41–42; Can Kernewek, vol. 2, no. 1, Summer 1931, pp. 24–27.

Pillas, an Extinct Grain, no. 12, pp. 43–44.

Editorial Ultimatum, no. 12, p. 44.

Celtic Shibboleths, vol. 2, no. 1, Summer 1931, p. 44.

* Hager-awel, vol. 2, no. 2, Winter 1931, pp. 24–28.

Accroshay, vol. 2, no. 2, p. 32.

* Nyns-yu dhe Ladra nep na-n-jeves Man, vol. 2, no. 3, Summer 1932, pp. 23–26.

The Hour is Come, but not the Man, vol. 2, no. 3, pp. 35–36; vol. 4, no. 7, Summer 1948, pp. 259–260.

[Henry Goodman of St Cleer], vol. 2, no. 3, p. 40.

A Long-ago Visit to Penzance, vol. 2, no. 3, p. 41.

An Unprinted Cornish Scrap, vol. 2, no. 3, p. 43.

Old Cornwall and the Celtic Congress, vol. 2, no. 4, Winter 1932, pp. 21–25.

* An Marghak ha'n Eos, vol. 2, no. 4, pp. 27–30.

* An Margh Coth, vol. 2, no. 4, pp. 31–32.

The Charter Endorsement in Cornish, vol. 2, no. 4, pp. 34–36; New Light on
     Cornish, vol. 4, no. 6, Summer 1947, pp. 214–216.
Some Old Signboards at St Ives, vol. 2, no. 4, p. 44.
[Splitting Granite], vol. 2, no. 5, Summer 1933, pp. 24–25.
* Jowan hag Arluth an Maner, vol. 2, no. 5, pp. 25–27.
The Other Halfstone, vol. 2, no. 5, p. 36; vol. 2, no. 6, Winter 1933, p. 10; vol. 2, no.
     11, Summer 1936, pp. 15–16.
Cornish in 1756, vol. 2, no. 5, p. 44.
The Lizard Lights, vol. 2, no. 6, Winter 1933, p. 18.
* An Creftor na-vynna Fysky, vol. 2, no. 6, pp. 27–31.
A Query, vol. 2, no. 6, p. 44; The Chywoon of John of Chy-an-Horth, vol. 2, no. 10,
     Winter 1935, p. 43.
* An Arlodhes Othys a Stavoren, vol. 2, no. 7, Summer 1934, pp. 26–29.
"Gwas Myghal" and the Cornish Revival, vol. 2, no. 8, Winter 1934, pp. 1–5.
Cornish Names in the Isle of Man, vol. 2, no. 8, p. 5.
The Cornish Inscriptions of Mawnan Church, vol. 2, no. 8, pp. 18–19.
* An Edhen Huder, vol. 2, no. 8, pp. 26–28.
Some Verses by John Boson, vol. 2, no. 8, pp. 30–31.
New Light on Cornish, vol. 2, no. 8, pp. 32–34; vol. 2, no. 9, Summer 1935, pp.
     28–30; vol. 3, no. 10, Winter 1941, p 426; vol. 4, no. 5, summer 1946, pp. 156–157;
     vol. 4, no. 8, Winter 1948, p. 273; vol. 5, no. 2, Summer 1952, pp. 59–60.
* Honna dres Oll a-garaf, vol. 2, no. 9, Summer 1935, pp. 6 and 10.
The Tally-ow, vol. 2, no. 9, p. 12.
Names of Cornish Giants, vol. 2, no. 9, pp. 14–15.
* An Lorgan y'n Dour, vol. 2, no. 9, pp. 25–27.
The Jenner Memorial Fund, vol. 2, no. 9, p. 40.
* An Oy-yar ha'n Velyn-wyns, vol. 2, no. 10, Winter 1935, pp. 19–24.
"Streek! Hold! Winnd up!", vol. 2, no. 10, p. 24.
An Old Charm from Lawhitton, vol. 2, no. 10, p. 29.
The Proposed Landewednack Tablet, vol. 2, no. 10, p. 44.
Further Note on Dolly Pentreath, vol. 2, no. 11, Summer 1936, pp. 9–11.
* An Dheu Bajya, vol. 2, no. 11, pp. 19–22.
The Cornish of Wm. Rowe (Wella Kerew), vol. 2, no. 11, pp. 32–36; vol. 2, no. 12,
     Winter 1936, pp. 25–27; vol. 3, no. 1, Summer 1937, pp. 41–44.
The Pool of Pilate, vol. 2, no. 11, p. 44.
More Cornish from Gwavas, vol. 2, no. 12, Winter 1936, pp. 34–36.
Traditional Cornish at Paul, vol. 2, no. 12, pp. 39–40.
Fly-leaf Literature, vol. 2, no. 12, pp. 41–42.

* An Varf, vol. 3, no. 1, Summer 1937, pp. 22–25.

Hoofprint Legends, vol. 3, no. 2, Winter 1937, p. 65.

* Nyns-us Scapya an pyth a-res Hapya, vol. 3, no. 2, pp. 66–71.

Cornish Names of the Seal, vol. 3, no. 2, pp. 85–88.

* An try Lavar, vol. 3, no. 3, Summer 1938, pp. 111–116.

* An Besont Tarosvanus, vol. 3, no. 4, Winter 1938, pp. 142–147.

Cornish and Breton, vol. 3, no. 4, p. 165.

The Pilchard Rhyme, vol. 3, no. 4, pp. 169–174; vol. 3, no. 5, Summer 1939, p. 220.

The Frog and the Mouse, vol. 3, no. 5, Summer 1939, pp. 195–199.

* Jowan Bras ha Jowan Byghan, vol. 3, no. 5, pp. 200–204.

Note [The "False Foxes" Rhyme], vol. 3, no. 5, pp. 206–208.

Original Spelling of "Jowan Chy-an-Horth" [probably by Nance], vol. 3, no. 5, pp. 219–220.

Some Old Cornish Weirs, vol. 3, no. 6, Winter 1939, pp. 225–228.

* Gorseth Kernow, vol. 3, no. 6, p. 228.

* Skyans us Pernys yu an Gwella Skyans Oll, vol. 3, no. 6, pp. 240–244

"Cornish Simplified", vol. 3, no. 6, p. 256.

Hints for Place-name Study, vol. 3, no. 6, pp. 257–260; vol. 3, no. 9, Summer 1941, pp. 396–398; vol. 3, no. 11, Summer 1942, pp. 482–485.

To Neighbour Nicholas Pentreath, vol. 3, no. 6, p. 264; John Boson's Message, vol. 4, no. 3, Summer 1944, pp. 106–107.

* An Vugh hy Holon Trogh, vol. 3, no. 7, Summer 1940, p. 299.

* Sa! Sa! Gas hy dhe Wandra!, vol. 3, no. 7, pp. 300–301.

William Bodener's Letter, vol. 3, no. 7, pp. 306–308.

* An Dullores, vol. 3, no. 8, Winter 1940, p. 337.

* Hycca ha Davy, vol. 3, no. 8, pp. 343–346.

Dr Borlase and Cornish, vol. 3, no. 8, p. 348.

The Kitareen, vol. 3, no. 8, pp. 349–350; A Comeback for "Kitareen", vol. 5, no. 6, 1955, pp. 276–277.

* Can Kernow Dyvres, vol. 3, no. 9, Summer 1941, pp. 360–361.

* An Marner Du, vol. 3, no. 9, pp. 388–391.

* An Lowarn, vol. 3, no. 10, Winter 1941, p. 421.

* Omdowl Bras Coryn ha Goemagot, vol. 3, no. 10, pp. 422–425.

Tame-Furze, vol. 3, no. 11, Summer 1942, p. 455; vol. 3, no. 12, Winter 1942, p. 508.

* Benen Worth hep Nam, vol. 3, no. 11, pp. 464–465.

Cornish Proverbial Sayings, vol. 3, no. 11, p. 486.

A Primitive Three-legged Stool, vol. 3, no. 12, Winter 1942, pp. 494–495.

The Fox and Goose Story [probably by Nance], vol. 3, no. 12, pp. 510–513.

* Cas ha Caradewder, vol. 3, no. 12, pp. 518–520.

Cornish Comparisons, vol. 3, no. 12, p. 520.

Two Old Christmas Beliefs, vol. 3, no. 12, pp. 529–531.

Celtic Personal Names of Cornwall, vol. 4, no. 1, Summer 1943, pp. 10–17; vol. 4, no. 2, Winter 1943, pp. 61–68.

Newquay and the Sea, vol. 4, no. 1, p. 21.

* Bewnans Sen Florent, vol. 4, no. 1, pp. 25–27.

Flemints, vol. 4, no. 1, p. 35.

Cornish Proverbs and Maxims, vol. 4, no. 1, pp. 36–38.

Capstans and Caunses, vol. 4, no. 1, p. 38.

Thornpelles and Whirlepools, vol. 4, no. 1, p. 44.

* Synt Galdwyn ha'n Trethoryon, vol. 4, no. 2, Winter 1943, pp. 72–74.

* Sugal dhe'n Velyn, vol. 4, no. 3, Summer 1944, pp. 102–103.

"Normans", vol. 4, no. 3, p. 107.

* Melyn-dreth, vol. 4, no. 4, Summer 1945, pp. 119–121.

A Tradition concerning John Wesley, vol. 4, no. 5, Summer 1946, pp. 140–141; vol. 4, no. 6, Summer 1947, pp. 205–208.

* An Pysk Ryal, vol. 4, no. 5, pp. 152–155.

From Adit back to Aqueduct, vol. 4, no. 5, pp. 158–159.

Malotta, vol. 4, no. 5, p. 164.

* An Canjeon, vol. 4, no. 6, Summer 1947, pp. 182–184.

Edward Chirgwin's Cornish Song, vol. 4, no. 6, pp. 210–213.

Pomster and Palmistry, vol. 4, no. 7, Summer 1948, pp. 228–230.

* An Mayl war an Forth, vol. 4, no. 7, pp. 237–239.

Oan, etc., in Field-names, vol. 4, no. 7, p. 251.

The Cornish Rhymes of James Jenkins of Alverton, vol. 4, no. 8, Winter 1948, pp. 268–273.

* An Managh a-synsys dhe'n Gwyryoneth, vol. 4, no. 8, pp. 288–289.

William Allen's Cornish Rhyme, vol. 4, no. 9, Summer 1949, pp. 325–326.

* Sagh Dom Jowan, vol. 4, no. 9, pp. 332–336.

"Morask Russches", vol. 4, no. 9, pp. 346–347.

A Cornish Poem Restored, vol. 4, no. 10, Winter 1949, pp. 368–371.

* An Pader nag-o Dewedhys [probably by Nance], vol. 4, no. 10, pp. 376–377.

A New-Old Appeal, vol. 4, no. 10, p. 387.

"Blind Horse", vol. 4, no. 10, pp. 389–391.

Hawker and the Cornish Language, vol. 4, no. 11, Summer 1950, p. 415.

* Can an Yar, vol. 4, no. 11, p. 423.

The Tregear Manuscript, vol. 4, no. 11, pp. 429–434.

Collins's Cow, vol. 4, no. 11, p. 434.

[Christian-names from Registers of a few W. Cornwall Parishes, 16th to early 19th Centuries], vol. 4, no. 12, Winter 1951, pp. 439–442.

Cornish Prophecies, vol. 4, no. 12, pp. 443–453.

The Harvest Flower, vol. 4, no. 12, p. 453.

* An Stryfores, vol. 4, no. 12, p. 472.

Brockets, vol. 4, no. 12, p. 476.

"Caradar" [obituary of A.S.D. Smith], vol. 4, no. 12, p. 477.

"Only the Moon", vol. 4, no. 12, pp. 478–479.

Landiok, vol. 4, no. 12, p. 480.

More about the Tregear Manuscript, vol. 5, no. 1, Summer 1951, pp. 21–27.

Dillue, vol. 5, no. 1, p. 36.

* An Kenyas ha'n Lugh, vol. 5, no. 1, p. 37.

Killigrew, vol. 5, no. 1, p. 41.

* An Tregher a-dorras y Benys, vol. 5, no. 2, Summer 1952, pp. 65–67.

[Lobcock], vol. 5, no. 2, pp. 68–69.

The Pengersick Panels, vol. 5, no. 3, Summer 1953, pp. 89–93, with an illustration preceding p. 89.

"Creature" and "Quaker", vol. 5, no. 3, p. 100.

* Gwytha'n Gwaneth Gwyn, vol. 5, no. 3, p. 134.

* Skentoleth Prenys, vol. 5, no. 4, Winter 1953, pp. 152–153.

Queer Old Words, vol. 5, no. 4, p. 158.

A Saint Ives Endearment, vol. 5, no. 4, p. 163.

Why Gowna?, vol. 5, no. 4, pp. 164–169.

The Gump [probably by Nance], vol. 5, no. 5, 1954, p. 185.

* An Den y'n Lor, vol. 5, no. 5, pp. 214–215.

Mermaids in Cornwall, vol. 5, no. 5, pp. 218–225.

Painted Windows & Miracle Plays, vol. 5, no. 6, 1955, pp. 244–248.

* Hunros Perys Tollor, vol. 5, no. 6, pp. 250–253.

Note [The Three Advices], vol. 5, no. 6, pp. 257–258.

A Tapnett of Reasons, vol. 5, no. 6, p. 273.

Avon and Dowr, vol. 5, no. 6, pp. 274–275.

Metheklan, vol. 5, no. 7, 1956, p. 294.

Lasking, vol. 5, no. 7, p. 309.

Bulorn and its Congeners; Snail Lore, vol. 5, no. 7, pp. 311–315; Snail Lore, vol. 5, no. 8, 1957, pp. 347–348.

Note on Cornish Spelling, vol. 5, no. 7, p. 315.

* An Aval Ruth, vol. 5, no. 7, pp. 321–324.

Cornish for Cul-de-sac, vol. 5, no. 8, 1957, p. 339.

* Nebes Rymys Coth us Noweth Kernewekhes, vol. 5, no. 8, p. 349.
Scawen on Carols in Cornish, vol. 5, no. 8, p. 352.
Costislost, vol. 5, no. 8, p. 353.
Cornish Beginnings, vol. 5, no. 9, 1958, pp. 368–369.
More New-found Cornish, vol. 5, no. 9, pp. 374–377.
Rose-nobles, vol. 5, no. 9, p. 379.
* Dres an Glaw a-berth y'n Chy, vol. 5, no. 9, p. 380.
Some Cornish Schools of Long Ago, vol. 5, no. 10, 1959, pp. 405–406.
* Gwythyas an Dremenysy, vol. 5, no. 10, pp. 426–429.
Hammer and Apron String, vol. 5, no. 11, 1960, pp. 468–470.
* An Pystryor, vol. 5, no. 11, pp. 488–490.
Lyver Jonah [translation by Nance and E. Chirgwin], vol. 5, no. 12, 1961, pp. 520–522.

The Cornish Language in the Seventeenth Century, vol. 6, no. 1, Autumn 1961, pp. 20–26.
An Old Footnote by Mordon, vol. 6, no. 1, p. 48.
* Hympna Encledhyas Plu Gostentyn yn Keryer, vol. 6, no. 2, Spring 1962, p. 61.
* An Venenvas pan Whys, re Dom 'vyth Oll an Bys, vol. 6, no. 2, p. 72.
* Can An Den Medhow/The Drunkard's Song, vol. 6, no. 4, Spring 1963, p. 157.
Costen, vol. 6, no. 5, Autumn 1963, pp. 215–216.
Reskymer, vol. 6, no. 5, pp. 233–234.
Spanges and Trappe, vol. 6, no. 6, Spring 1964, pp. 269–270.
* An Cruskyn Lun po Na wra Scullya Banna/The Full Pitcher, or Don't Spare a Drop, vol. 6, no. 7, Autumn 1964, p. 310.
Yn-dan Onnen [article in English], vol. 6, no. 7, p. 313.
The Celtic Bird-names of Cornwall, vol. 6, no. 8, Spring 1965, pp. 362–366; vol. 6, no. 9, Autumn, 1965, pp. 410–413.
Drawing [Sketch of Christmas Bush], vol. 6, no. 10, Spring 1966, p. 477.

* Carol Canoryon Nos, vol. 7, no. 1, Autumn 1967, p. 11; vol. 8, no. 3, Autumn 1974, pp. 138–139.

Notes on the Beunans Meriasek Manuscript, vol. 9, no. 1, Autumn, 1979, pp. 34–36.
An Early Exercise in Cornish, vol. 9, no. 5, Autumn 1981, pp. 257–258.
The 'Mordon' Collection of Cornish Dialect Words, vol. 9, no. 9, Autumn 1983, pp. 447–451; vol. 9, no. 10, Spring 1984, pp. 512–520; vol. 9, no. 11, Autumn 1984, pp. 570–572; vol. 9, no. 12, Spring 1985, pp. 610–611; vol. 10, no. 1, Autumn 1985, pp. 18–20; vol. 10, no. 2, Spring 1986, pp. 90–94; vol. 10, no. 3, Autumn 1986, pp.

114–120; vol. 10, no. 4, Spring 1987, pp. 197–203; vol. 10, no. 5, Autumn 1987, p. 237; vol. 10, no. 6, Spring 1988, pp. 290–293; vol. 10, no. 7, Autumn 1988, pp. 320–321; vol. 10, no. 8, Spring 1989, pp. 409–410; vol. 10, no. 9, Autumn 1989, pp. 465–467; vol. 10, no. 10, Spring 1990, pp. 513–515; vol. 10, no. 11, Autumn 1990, pp. 559–563; vol. 10, no. 12, Spring 1991, pp. 618–619; vol. 11, no. 1, Autumn 1991, pp. 48–49; vol. 11, no. 2, Spring 1992, pp. 102–103; vol. 11, no. 3, Autumn 1992, pp. 153–154; vol. 11, no. 4, Spring 1993, p. 208; vol. 11, no. 5, Autumn 1993, pp. 250–251; vol. 11, no. 6, Spring 1994, pp. 311–312; vol. 11, no. 7, Autumn 1994, p. 363; vol. 11, no. 9, Autumn 1995, pp. 466–468; vol. 11, no. 10, Spring 1996, pp. 518–519; vol. 11, no. 11, Autumn 1996, p. 572; vol. 11, no. 12, Spring 1997, pp. 623–624.
[A change of editorship at this point resulted in the publishing of Mordon's Cornish dialect words being abandoned].

* Lost Gwyn, vol. 10, no. 2, Spring 1986, p. 101.

Reports of the Royal Cornwall Polytechnic Society:
Celtic Words in Cornish Dialect, no. 86, (new series, vol. 4, pt. 2), 1919, pp. 143–154; no. 88, (new series, vol. 4, pt. 4), 1921–22, pp. 71–82.
Ship Modelling as a Craft, no. 87, (new series, vol. 4, pt. 3), 1920, pp. 224–231.
Modern Stone Implements in Cornwall, no. 90, (new series, vol. 5, pt.1), 1923, pp. 51–60.
Folk-lore Recorded in the Cornish Language, no. 91, (new series, vol. 5, pt. 2), 1924, pp. 124–145.
Interpretations of place-names in Charles Henderson's 'The Topography of the Parish of St Keverne', no. 98, (new series, vol. 7, pt. 1), 1931, pp. 49–75; no. 99, (new series, vol. 7, pt. 2), 1932, pp. 185–192; no. 101, (new series, vol. 8, pt. 1), 1934, pp. 13–25.
The Topography of the Parish of Paul, compiled from Charles Henderson's Notes on the Topography of Penwith, no. 108, (new series, vol. 9, pt. 5), 1941, pp. 55–67.

Transactions of the Royal Geological Society of Cornwall:
Geological Terms used in S. W. England, [with J. Robson], vol. 19, pt. 1, 1959, pp. 33–41.

Journal of the Royal Institution of Cornwall:
Guise-Dancing and the Christmas Play, no. 69, (vol. 21, pt. 1), 1922, pp. 70–75.
John Davey, of Boswednack, and his Cornish Rhyme, no. 70, (vol. 21, pt. 2), 1923, pp. 146–153.
Troy Town, no. 71, (vol. 21, pt. 3), 1924, pp. 261–279.

Twentieth-century Traditions of the Cornish Numerals, no. 71, (vol. 21, pt. 3), 1924, pp. 300–320.

The Celtic Congress, Quimper, 1924, no. 72, (vol. 21, pt. 4), 1925, pp. 451–454.

Taboo-names in Cornwall, no. 72, pp. 470–477.

Four Cornish Folk-tales, no. 73, (vol. 22, pt. 1), 1926, pp. 62–76.

A New-found Traditional Sentence of Cornish, no. 74, (vol. 22, pt. 2), 1927, pp. 281–287.

Andrew Boorde on Cornwall, no. 75, (vol. 22, pt. 3), 1928, pp. 366–381.

Nicholas Boson's "Nebbaz Gerriau dro tho Carnoack", no. 77, (vol. 23, pt.2), 1930, pp. 327–354.

Some Implements and Objects connected with Cornish Fisheries, nos. 80–81, (vol. 24, pts. 1 and 2), 1933–34, pp. 89–98.

The Plen an Gwary or Cornish Playing-Place, no. 82, (vol. 24, pt. 3), 1935, pp. 190–211.

Cornish Manuscripts in the National Library of Wales [note], nos. 84–85, (vol. 25, pts. 1 and 2), 1937–38, pp. 3–4.

The Gatley Collection of Cornish Manuscripts [note], nos. 84–85, pp. 28–29.

Local Cornish Names of Crustacea, new series, vol. 1, pt. 1, 1946, pp. 34–42.

Something New in Cornish [the Tregear Manuscript], new series, vol. 1, pt. 2, 1952, pp. 119–121.

The Celtic Names of Fish in Cornwall, new series, vol. 2, pt. 2, 1954, pp. 74–87.

Helston Furry Day, new series, vol. 4, pt. 1, 1961, pp. 36–48.

When was Cornish last spoken Traditionally?, new series, vol. 7, p. 1, 1973, pp. 76–82.

Tre Pol and Pen:
Cornwall and the Gorsedd, 1928, pp. 97–99.

Contributions to maritime and other journals and magazines
The Mariner's Mirror:
Hoy [Query], vol. 1, 1911, p. 64.

A Fifteenth-Century Trader, vol. 1, pp. 65–67.

Spritsail topmast [Answer], vol. 1, p. 92.

Flyboat [Answer], vol. 1, p. 92.

Round-sterned ships [with Sir Alan Moore]: the Buss and the Dogger, vol. 1, pp. 105–111; No. 2: the Hooker, pp. 293–297.

Polaccas [Answer], vol. 1, p. 123.

Posaberga [Query], vol. 1, p. 124.

Polacca [Query], vol. 1, p. 125.
Tyminoguy [Query], vol. 1, p. 125.
Argosy [Query], vol. 1, p. 158.
Clue Garnets [Query], vol. 1, p. 158.
Dutch gable-stones, vol. 1, pp. 171–178, plus drawing in Note, p. 283.
Timmynoggy and vargord [Note], vol. 1, p. 247.
Change the Mizzen [Answer], vol. 1, pp. 252–253.
An Italian Ship of 1339, vol. 1, pp. 334–339.
Shifter [Note], vol. 1, p. 349.

A Yacht "en fête" [Query], drawing by Nance, vol. 2, 1912, p. 30.
Hurrel [Query], vol. 2, p. 31.
Lifts [Query], vol. 2, p. 32.
Some additional notes concerning the Le Testu ships [with L.G.C. Laughton], vol. 2, pp. 76–78.
Slate-Room [Answer], vol. 2, p. 91.
Jibber the Kibber [Answer], vol. 2, p. 92.
Kirkeskib [Answer], vol. 2, p. 92.
Weekly Account [Answer], vol. 2, p. 93.
A sixteenth-century sea-monster, vol. 2, pp. 97–104.
A sixteenth-century ship of Lubeck [with R.C. Anderson], vol. 2, pp. 152–153.
A Trader and a man-of-war, late 14th century, vol. 2, pp. 174–176.
Scant Wind [Answer], vol. 2, p. 188.
Trows, Past and Present, vol. 2, pp. 201–205.
The Flying Dutchman [Answer], vol. 2, pp. 218–219.
A doubtful ship-portrait [Answer], vol. 2, p. 219.
The Jolly Roger [Answer], vol. 2, pp. 219–220.
A grotesque block [Answer], vol. 2, p. 221.
Catchop [Query], vol. 2, p. 222.
Banyan [Query], vol. 2, pp. 222–223.
Fly-boats on the Clyde [Query], vol. 2, p. 223.
Some old time ship pictures: The Kraeck of "W.A.", vol. 2, pp. 225–232; A Mediterranean Carrack, pp. 309–315; Two fifteenth-century Fishing Vessels, vol. 3, 1913, pp. 65–70; The Ark Royal, vol. 3, pp. 138–142; A Hanseatic Bergen-trader of 1489, vol. 3, pp. 161–167; A Group of Florentines, vol. 3, pp. 238–245, 276–279; A Batch of Carracks, vol. 4, 1914, pp. 275–282.
A Cromwellian ship-stern [Note], vol. 2, pp. 249–251.
Sea ceremonies [Answer], vol. 2, p. 253.
Phrases [Answer], vol. 2, p. 254.

Snow [Note], vol. 2, p. 283.
Early chain wales [Note], vol. 2, pp. 283–284.
East-Indiamen of 1720 [Answer], vol. 2, p. 319.
Ketches, vol. 2, pp. 362–370.
Knighthead [Answer], vol. 2, pp. 382–383.
Seeker [Answer], vol. 2, p. 383.
Bulljowler [Query], vol. 2, p. 384.

Cubridge Head [Dictionary words], vol. 3, 1913, p. 22.
Sheevo [Dictionary words], vol. 3, p. 22.
An Unnamed type [Answer], vol. 3, p. 29.
Superstitions [Query], vol. 3, p. 31.
Northern ships of c. 1340, vol. 3, pp. 33–39.
Chapel [Words and phrases], vol. 3, p. 53.
Vargord [Words and phrases], vol. 3, p. 121.
Spritsails [Note], vol. 3, pp. 122–123.
A Register of models [Note], vol. 3, p. 124.
Scaith [Words and phrases], vol. 3, pp. 147–148.
The Mediteranean carrack [Note], vol. 3, pp. 150–151.
Seventeenth century rigging [Note], vol. 3, p. 151.
Spritsails [Answer], vol. 3, pp. 155–157.
Ships in a 15th century Froissart ms. [Note], vol. 3, pp. 182–184.
The ships of Maso Finiguerra [Note], vol. 3, pp. 184–185.
Trow [Note], vol. 3, p. 186.
Trows [Note], vol. 3, pp. 219–220.
A difficult passage [Answer], vol. 3, p. 223.
Caravels, vol. 3, pp. 265–271.
Chain-cables [Note], vol. 3, pp. 284–285.
Sea-stones and Killicks in West Cornwall, vol. 3, pp. 295–303.
Skeg [Words and phrases], vol. 3, p. 310.
Quafe [Words and phrases], vol. 3, p. 312.
Boat davits [Note], vol. 3, p. 312.
Unexplained aversions [Answer], vol. 3, pp. 316–317.
Studding sails [Answer], vol. 3, p. 318.
Early three-masted ships [Answer], vol. 3, p. 318.
Brouage graffiti [Note], vol. 3, p. 344.
Seventeeth century bows [Note], vol. 3, pp. 345–346.
The Bergen model [Note], vol. 3, pp. 346–347.

Sea-fire [Answer], vol. 3, p. 378.

Terradas and Talismans, vol. 4, 1914, pp. 3–13.
15th century sails [Note], vol. 4, pp. 51–52.
Saint Louis of Hondius [Note], p. 52 plus plate facing p. 33.
State Room [Answer], vol. 4, p. 56.
An English ship's "side shelf" [Note], vol. 4, p. 55.
The Marsilian, vol. 4, pp. 77–81.
Brandiernwise [Words and phrases], vol. 4, p. 82.
Stem-ropes [Note], vol. 4, p. 83.
Trows [Note], vol. 4, pp. 85–86.
Stone sinkers [Note], vol. 4, p. 87.
Unexplained aversions [Answer], vol. 4, p. 90.
Claw-boards [Answer], vol. 4, p. 92.
Barge on wheels [Answer], vol. 4, p. 92.
Ties and burton [Answer], vol. 4, pp. 93–94.
The Jerusalem flag [Answer], vol. 4, pp. 115–116.
Tile-ship at the Rijks Museum; A sixteenth century ship [Notes], vol. 4, pp. 118–120
    and 120–121.
Unexplained aversions [Answer], vol. 4, p. 123.
Tiller pins and bosses [Note], vol. 4, pp. 152–153.
The "Ark Royal" [Note], vol. 4, pp. 154–155.
Patience [Note], vol. 4, pp. 209–210.
Marsilian [Note], vol. 4, pp. 210–211.
The horns talisman at sea [Note], vol. 4, pp. 211–212.
Wapp [Note], vol. 4, pp. 212–213.
Argosies and bertons [Note], vol. 4, p. 213.
Dog-buoys, danns and sinkers [Note], vol. 4, pp. 214–215.
A "Great Dane" of 1600, vol. 4, pp. 225–232.
Killick [Note], vol. 4, pp. 249–250.
Mizzen braces [Answer], vol. 4, p. 253.
Mizzen and misaine [Answer], vol. 4, p. 253.
Lerynges [Note], vol. 4, p. 285.
Scheltbemes and kelsweyn [Answer], vol. 4, p. 287.
A Primitive Western Type, vol. 4, pp. 304–311.
Side rudders [Note], vol. 4, p. 314.

British Ships through Dutch Spectacles, vol. 5, 1919, pp. 3–9.

Brigantines, vol. 7, 1921, pp. 22–24.
Gwyn's book of ships [Note], vol. 7, pp. 120–121.
Jack Nickel [Answer], vol. 7, p. 127.
Killicks again, vol. 7, pp. 135–141.
Model vessel [Answer], vol. 7, p. 319.
Some Ships of 1541–2, vol. 7, pp. 368–373 plus plates, including facing p. 353.

Rained/Doughcock [Words and phrases], vol. 8, 1922, p. 93.
Dab says Daniel [Words and phrases], vol. 8, p. 93.
Wicker Vessels, vol. 8, pp. 199–205.

Wicker Vessels [Note], vol. 9, 1923, pp. 93–94.
Our Lady of the Good Wind [Note], vol. 9, p. 119.
Some French Carracks, vol. 9, pp. 130–136 and plate facing p. 128.
Brownies at sea [Note], vol. 9, pp. 213–214.
The Manger [Note], vol. 9, p. 214.
A bow view of the *Kraeck* [Note], vol. 9, pp. 341–342.

Ship models in the Louvre [Note], vol. 10, 1924, pp. 88–89.
Quicksilver, carvedwork, and painting of ships, c. 1760 [Note], vol. 10, p. 89.
The *Santa Anna* [Note] vol. 10, pp. 212–214.
The Decks of the *Kraeck* [Note], vol. 10, pp. 304–305.
Two-masted ships 15th century [Answer], vol. 10, pp. 309–310.

Stone-carved ships in Brittany, vol. 11, 1925, pp. 292–300.
Killicks in Brittany [Note], vol. 11, pp. 321–322.
A fifteenth-century windlass [Note], vol. 11, pp. 432–434.
The square tuck in English and Dutch ships [Note], vol. 11, p. 437.

Graffito in Winchelsea Church [Note], vol. 16, 1930, pp. 290–291.

Martnets [Note], vol. 17, 1931, pp. 88–90.
West Country luggers [Answer], vol. 17, p. 91.
Martnets [Note], vol. 17, pp. 288–289 plus plates.
Bideford Polaccas [Note], vol. 17, pp. 396–397.

Roman anchors found at Nemi [Note], vol. 18, 1932, p. 188.
A Spanish caravel of the fifteenth century [Note], vol. 18, pp. 188–189.

Killick from Rosscarbery [Note], pp. 324–325.

The Little Ship of the Ashmolean, vol. 24, 1938, pp. 95–100 plus plates.
Earliest royal [Note], vol. 24, pp. 356–357.
Stone-carved ships in Flanders [Note], vol. 24, pp. 481–482 plus plates.

West Cornwall fishing luggers before 1850, vol. 30, 1944, pp. 93–108.
Steering Gear of the *Royal Louis* model [Answer], vol. 30, p. 166.

The Ashmolean model [Note], vol. 32, 1946, p. 59.
The voyol [Note], vol. 32, pp. 59–61.

The King's College Chapel Window Ship [additional note to article by K.
    Harrison], vol. 34, 1948, pp. 14–15.
A bone model of a small clinker-built vessel [Note], vol. 34, p. 304.

Ketch rig, [Answer], vol. 36, 1950, pp. 368–369; vol. 37, 1951, p. 87 and pp. 329–330.

Captain Richard Keigwin [Note], vol. 37, 1951, p. 80.
The Anchor [Note], vol. 37, p. 238.
Visscher's *Arca Rale* [Note], vol. 37, p. 319.

The *Ark Royal*, vol. 39, 1953, p. 63.

A copper processional ship [Note], vol. 41, 1955, p. 162 plus plates.
'Rybbes' and 'susterys' [Query], vol. 41, p. 76.
The Ship of the Renaissance Pts. 1 and 2, vol. 41, pp. 180–192, 281–298.
The St Winnow ship [Note], vol. 41, p. 329.

Pram [Answer], vol. 42, 1956, p. 87.
Cutter-brig [Answer], vol. 42, p. 166.
Belly and foot [Answer], vol. 42, p. 166.

The anchor [Answer], vol. 43, 1957, pp. 84–85.
Some drawings of old ships (sprit-sails) [Note], vol. 43, pp. 156–157.

Proceedings of the Cambridge Antiquarian Society:
Killicks: a study in the evolution of anchors, vol. 23, 1920/21 (1922), pp. 46–62.

Man:
Killicks, vol. 19 (no. 62) (August 1919), pp. 113–117 plus plate.
The Studio:
Bushey Models, Special Winter Number, 1896–97, pp. 37–38 plus drawings.
Leaves from the Sketch-book of R. Morton Nance, vol. 14, 1898, 6 pages of drawings following p. 257.

Notes on Contributors

Brian Coombes, a native of Falmouth, was a town planner before being ordained in retirement as a non-stipendary Anglican priest. Having served Cornwall as Grand Bard of Gorseth Kernow (1994–97), Examinations Secretary of the Cornish Language Board, President of the Cornwall Amateur Fencing Union and President of the Federation of Old Cornwall Societies (2003–06), he is currently Secretary of the Bishop's Advisory Group for Services in Cornish. He has contributed to *Henry and Katharine Jenner* (2004) and to *Old Cornwall* and *An Baner Kernewek*.

Ann Trevenen Jenkin (*Bryallen*) is a writer, former teacher/librarian, founder member of Mebyon Kernow and publisher. A Cornish speaker who, as a young student, started learning the language with Robert Morton Nance in 1949, she was the first woman Grand Bard of Gorseth Kernow (1997–2000). She has taken part in Gorseth ceremonies in Wales and Brittany, and addressed Cornish Gatherings in many other parts of the world. She organised the first Dehwelans/Cornish Homecoming from overseas in 2002, having earlier helped organise and taken part in the Keskerdh Kernow march to Blackheath with her dog Brengy. She has held many posts in the Cornish Branch of the Celtic Congress and is now Life President. She has lectured or taken part in activities in all the Celtic countries, with close links with Brittany where she has three Breton-speaking grand-children. She was recently Honorary President of and addressed the CAVA 21st Century Celts Conference in Cornwall. Publications include two books about Leedstown, her own Cornish community, two collections of poetry, *Cornwall the Hidden Land* (with Richard Jenkin) (1966 and 2005) and *The Dog who Walked to London* (2003), as well as many articles.

Alan M. Kent M.Phil., M.Ed., was born in St Austell in 1967. He lectures in Literature for the Open University in South West Britain and has been Visiting Lecturer in Celtic Literature at the University of Coruña in Galicia, Spain. As well as being a poet, novelist and dramatist, he has written extensively on Anglo-Cornish and Cornish literatures. Recent articles have been published in *Celtic Englishes*, *Cornish Studies* and *Language and Region*. His latest books include *Stannary Parliament* (2006) and *Nativitas Christi* (2006).

Rod Lyon was born in Newquay and, following formal education, spent his early adult days at sea, followed by life on shore as an engineer, working both in private practice and with the local authority. He has been directly involved with the Cornish language since the early 1970s, writing simplified booklets in and about it, such as *Let's Learn Cornish* (1993) and *Cornish: the struggle for survival* (2001), but above all, promoting the spoken word.

Hugh Miners is Cornish born and bred, but was forced by economic circumstances to work outside his native land for many years as a customs officer in Bristol and London. A former Grand Bard of Gorseth Kernow (1982–1985) and Past President of the Federation of Old Cornwall Societies, he is the author of *The Story of the Bristol Cornish* (1975), *Gorseth Kernow: the first 50 years* (1978) and *Half a League Onwards: the story of the West Cornwall Footpath Preservation Society* (2004).

Brian Murdoch is Professor of German at the University of Stirling in Scotland, and has published books, translations and articles in three areas: the Middle Ages (especially religious writings and heroic poetry); the world wars (especially the works of Erich Maria Remarque); and comparative literature (including the Celtic literatures in particular). He has written extensively on Cornish literature (in journals published in England, Italy, Mexico and Japan) and his book *Cornish Literature* appeared in 1993.

Peter Pool learnt Cornish from Robert Morton Nance, was made a language bard (*Gwas Galva*) in 1955 and devoted much of his life to the continued revival of the language. An historian and a practicing solicitor, firstly in London and then in Cornwall, he was a founder member of the Cornish Language Board, five times President of Penzance Old Cornwall Society, President of the Royal Institution of Cornwall, a Fellow of the Society of Antiquaries and a Freeman of Penzance. His published works included *Cornish for Beginners* (1961), *The Place Names of West Penwith* (1973), *The Death of Cornish* (1975), *William Borlase* (1986) and, as editor, Nance's *A Glossary of Cornish Sea-Words* (1963).

Donald R. Rawe began his writing career in 1950 with a story in the first series of *The Cornish Review*. Since then he has written novels, short stories, folklore studies, plays and poetry in both Cornish and English, being made a bard of Gorseth Kernow in 1970 for his services to Cornish drama. His plays include *Hawker of Morwenstow* and *The Last Voyage of Alfred Wallis*, *Petroc of Cornwall*, *The Trials of St Piran* and a modern acting version of *Gwryans an Bys* (the Creation of the World) have all been produced at Piran Round. His poetry collection *Eglosow Kernow* (Cornish Church Poems) was published in 2005.

Peter W. Thomas was born and brought up in St Agnes, where he has returned to live. He is an academic/rare books librarian by profession, and his publications include the entry for Henry Jenner in the *Oxford Dictionary of National Biography*. He was made a bard in 1980, has worked on the Gorsedd Archives and is a member of the Archives Committee and the Holyer an Gof Committee.

Derek R. Williams was born and brought up near Camborne and has retained very close links with his homeland, despite working trans-Tamar as a librarian for many years. A bard of Gorseth Kernow, he is the author of *Prying Into Every Hole and Corner: Edward Lhuyd in Cornwall in 1700* (1993), editor of *Henry and Katharine Jenner* (2004) and has contributed to *Old Cornwall*, *An Baner Kernewek*, *Cornish Scene* and *Scryfa*. His compilation of quotations about Cornwall and the Cornish, *A Strange and Unquenchable Race*, was published in 2007.

Index